Brian Fleming Research & Learning Lid
Ministry of Education
Ministry of Training, Colleges & Universities
900 Bay St. 13th Floor, Mowat Block
Toronto, ON M7A 1L2

Understanding and Addressing Bullying:

An International Perspective
PREVNet Series, Volume 1

Edited by Debra Pepler & Wendy Craig

AuthorHouse™
1663 Liberty Drive, Suite 200
Bloomington, IN 47403
www.authorhouse.com
Phone: 1-800-839-8640

©2008 Edited by Debra Pepler & Wendy Craig. All rights reserved.

No part of this book may be reproduced, stored in a retrieval system, or transmitted by any means without the written permission of the author.

First published by AuthorHouse 5/22/2008

ISBN: 978-1-4343-8866-7 (sc)

Printed in the United States of America
Bloomington, Indiana

This book is printed on acid-free paper.

Contents

Acknowledgements ix

About the Editors and Contributors xi

Introduction: xix
    Understanding and Addressing Bullying: An International Perspective
    Dr. Wendy M. Craig & Dr. Debra Pepler, PREVNet Scientific Co-Directors

Introduction to Section One: 1
    Understanding Bullying
    Dr. Joanne Cummings, PREVNet Partnership Manager

Chapter 1: 4
    Towards a Relational Perspective of Peer Bullying
    Ana Maria Tomás de Almeida, María Jesus Caurcel & José Cunha Machado

Chapter 2: 26
    New Directions in Research and Practice Addressing Bullying: Focus on Defending Behaviour
    Virpi Pöyhönen and Christina Salmivalli

Chapter 3: 44
    Consequences of Being Bullied at School
    Tanya N. Beran

Chapter 4: 67
    Lord of the E-Flies: School Supervision Challenges in the Virtual Islands of Cyberspace
    Shaheen Shariff and Dianne L. Hoff

Chapter 5: 97
    Matching Interventions to Bullying Subtypes: Ensuring Programs Fit the Multifaceted Needs of Children Involved in Bullying
    Zopito A. Marini and Andrew V. Dane

Introduction to Section Two: **127**

Addressing Bullying

Joanne Cummings, PREVNet Partnership Manager

Chapter 6:   **132**

Promoting a Positive School Climate: Restorative Practices for the Classroom

David Smith

Chapter 7:   **144**

Best Practices in School-Based Bullying Prevention Programs: What Works?

Leslie M. Tutty

Chapter 8:   **166**

Engaging Community Champions in the Prevention of Bullying

Bonnie Leadbeater

Chapter 9:   **184**

The Fourth R: A School-Based Program to Reduce Violence and Risk Behaviours among Youth

David A. Wolfe, Claire V. Crooks, Ray Hughes, Debbie Chiodo and Peter G. Jaffe

Chapter 10:   **198**

Engaging Aboriginal Youth in School-Based Violence Prevention: A Comprehensive Evaluation Perspective

Claire V. Crooks

Chapter 11:   **215**

The Norwegian Manifesto Against Bullying: Opportunities, Challenges And Results On A National And School Level

Unni Vere Midthassel and Erling Roland

Chapter 12:   **230**

Bullying in Kindergarten and Prevention

Françoise D. Alsaker and Christof Nägele

Chapter 13:   **253**

School Bullying in Italy: Nature and Functions from Childhood to Adolescence and Related Interventions

Ersilia Menesini

Chapter 14: 271
Preventing School Bullying: The Irish Experience
Mona O'Moore

Chapter 15: 289
School-based Intervention Research to Reduce Bullying in Australia 1999-2007: What Works, What Doesn't, and What's Promising?
Donna Cross, Therese Shaw, Natasha Pearce, Erin Erceg, Stacey Waters, Yolanda Pintabona, Margaret Hall

Conclusion 311
Moving Forward from Lessons Learned
Dr. Debra Pepler & Dr. Wendy M. Craig, PREVNet Scientific Co-Directors

Index 321

Acknowledgements

This book would not have been possible without the participation of many individuals – too many to name. We would like to thank all of the authors for their contributions and for sharing their wisdom. We are grateful to our PREVNet staff: Peter Aitken, Joanne Cummings, Jennifer Ma, Kelly Petrunka, and Caroline Teske, who work diligently every day to ensure that PREVNet fulfills its mission to stop bullying in Canada. We could not do all that we do without their support. Jennifer Amos stepped in with extraordinary editorial support, working tirelessly to ensure that we met our deadline. We are indebted to Gill German for her creativity in designing the book cover and all of the graphics for PREVNet. We would also like to acknowledge the funding agencies and conference sponsors that have so generously contributed to our work over the years and to creating PREVNet including: Networks of Centres of Excellence, Canadian Institutes of Health Research, National Crime Prevention Strategy, Ontario Mental Health Foundation, The Hospital for Sick Children, Queen's University, York University, and Cadbury Canada.

Both of us would personally like to thank our families for their never ending support and generosity in allowing us to do this work. Thanks to our children, Andrew, Gillian, Matthew, and Sophie who inspire and remind us everyday of why we do this work.

We would like to dedicate this book to all the professionals and volunteers who work everyday with children and youth. Through their moment-to-moment and programmatic efforts, they ensure the safety and healthy development of children and youth. This book is also for all the children who have participated in research over the years, been involved in bullying, or been affected by watching it. We truly hope the insights from this book contribute to making their world safer.

About the Editors and Contributors

EDITORS

Dr. Wendy Craig

Dr. Craig is a Full Professor of Psychology at Queen's University. In 1993, Dr. Craig received her Ph.D. in Clinical-Developmental Psychology from York University. Her seminal research using naturalistic observations of bullying interactions on the school playground has laid the foundation for research to understand and intervene in bullying problems. Together with Dr. Debra Pepler, Dr. Craig is leading a national network, PREVNet (Promoting Relationships and Eliminating Violence Network), a Networks of Centres of Excellence – New Initiative.

In recognition of her seminal research on bullying and victimization, Dr. Craig won an Investigator Award from the Canadian Institutes of Health Research. In 2008, she was awarded the Canadian Psychological Association Award for Distinguished Community and Public Service. She has published widely on topics of bullying and victimization, peer processes, sexual harassment and aggression in girls. She was editor of a volume on childhood social development. As a Canadian representative, Dr. Craig works with the World Health Organization on the Health Behaviours of School-aged Children survey examining issues of bullying, victimization, and promoting healthy relationships. As a leader in the field of bullying and victimization, Dr. Craig is sought for consultations both within Canada and internationally. She developed the background research materials for the Ontario Ministry of Education Safe Schools Action Team. With a long-time commitment to knowledge mobilization, Dr. Craig speaks regularly to the media and to parents, educators, and other professionals on the importance of healthy relationships and concerns about bullying, victimization, and school violence.

Dr. Debra Pepler

Dr. Debra Pepler is a Distinguished Research Professor of Psychology at York University and a Senior Associate Scientist at the Hospital for Sick Children. Her research focuses on aggression and victimization among children and youth with a focus on the individual and relationship processes related to these problems. Dr. Pepler is co-leading a national network, PREVNet (Promoting Relationships and Eliminating Violence Network), with 42 national non-government organizations and 50 Canadian research partners working together to promote safe and healthy relationships for all Canadian children and youth (www.prevnet.ca)

AUTHORS

Dr. Françoise Alasker is a professor in developmental psychology at the University of Berne, Switzerland. Her special interests are: socio-emotional development and developmental psychopathology. In the past years, she has led two large research projects on: 1) victimization and its prevention through kindergarten and primary school and 2) on Swiss adolescents' health (national study).

Dr. Ana Almeida is an Associate Professor at the University of Minho, Braga Protugal. Throughout her research and professional career, the focus of Dr. Almeida's interests have been circumscribed in the area of evaluation of social competence and maladjustment and intervention in school contexts. These studies have been conducted as part of cross-sectional and short-longitudinal research currently ongoing, which have permitted me to compare different age-groups and trace individual adjustment during school years in different countries (Portugal, Spain and Brazil). Recently, she has been involved in an European Research Network aiming at studying peer bullying in schools, and ways to prevent it. As part of project development, she has been involved in designing instruments and methodologies that can be used interchangeably in research and educational settings. Along with her interests on studying peer relationships and examining the role and significance of these particular relations to the child's self and social adjustment, she has been addressing other related issues which re-position the child as a social actor and actively construing his or her social experiences. This approach has called for the integration of more qualitative methodologies to the traditional quantitative and experimental research designs. Combining different research approaches have allowed me to view individuals in relations and social groups. Systemic perspectives have been particularly relevant in studying peer bullying, while making more comprehensive the representation of linkages between individual factors and the social systems. This conceptualization made it possible to target bullying as a social phenomenon and raise the awareness of parents and teachers to the relevance of context and value-based interventions.

About the Editors and Contributors

Dr. Tanya Beran has conducted research in the area of school bullying over the last 10 years, and more recently has begun publishing research on cyber-bullying. She is the Chair of the Action Committee on School Bullying and Family Violence, which is a network of organizations in Calgary that address community violence. Dr. Beran has received awards for her research and frequently speaks to the media on the topic of school bullying.

Dr. Claire Crooks is the Associate Director of the CAMH Centre for Prevention Science in London, Ontario. She is also an Assistant Professor at the Centre for Research and Education on Violence Against Women and Children at the University of Western Ontario. Her main research is the development, implementation, and evaluation of the *Fourth R*, a relationship-based comprehensive school program aimed at preventing violence and other risk behaviours among adolescents. The *Fourth R* has been evaluated in 20 schools (10 demonstration and 10 control) in the Thames Valley District School Board as part of a CIHR-funded Randomized Controlled Trial. She is Co-Director of an Ontario Trillium Foundation funded project to develop materials to assist schools in evaluating their current violence prevention programs and to choose initiatives that match their unique needs. Most recently, Dr. Crooks has launched several projects in partnership with community members and educators to investigate the cultural adaptation of best practices in violence prevention to maximize relevancy for Aboriginal youth. Dr. Crooks is also a co-founder of the Caring Dads program, a parenting intervention for men who have maltreated their children. She has written numerous articles and chapters on topics including children's exposure to domestic violence, child custody and access, adolescent dating violence and risk behaviours, intervening with fathers who maltreat their children, and violence prevention. Along with Drs. David Wolfe and Peter Jaffe she is an author of the book *Adolescent Risk Behaviours: Why teens experiment and strategies to keep the safe* (Yale University Press, 2006).

Understanding and Addressing Bullying: An International Perspective

Dr. Donna Cross is the Professor of Child and Adolescent Health at Edith Cowan University in Western Australia, and Director of the Child Health Promotion Research Centre. She has been involved in children's health promotion research in Australia and the USA since 1988. She conducts applied research involving teachers, children, adolescents and their parents in the areas of bullying prevention, aggression and violence, depression and anxiety, school connectedness and drug use, obesity prevention, smoking cessation and road safety.

Dr. Joanne Cummings received her Ph.D. in Clinical Developmental Psychology from York University and is a member of the College of Psychology of Ontario. Her research is in the areas of the development of aggression, parenting, and parent-child relationship interventions. Since 1995 she has consulted to schools, community agencies, and summer camps with the goal of creating positive social climates and reducing bullying. Joanne was an Ontario Mental Health Foundation Postdoctoral Fellow and Researcher in the Infant Program of the Department of Psychiatry at The Hospital for Sick Children before joining PREVNet. Her research evaluated a parent-child relationship focused treatment for aggressive/noncompliant behaviour problems in preschoolers and an attachment-based group intervention for mothers and infants. As Partnership Manager with PREVNet Joanne's work focuses on translating knowledge and brokering partnerships between university researchers and national nongovernmental organizations to promote healthy social development for Canada's youth.

Dr. Andrew Dane is an Associate Professor in the Department of Psychology of Brock University, St. Catharines, Ontario, Canada. He received his Ph.D. in Child Clinical Psychology from the University of Toronto in 2001, and has held clinical positions at the Hospital for Sick Children in Toronto, Canada, the Centre for Addiction and Mental Health, Clarke Division, and Child and Adolescent Services of Public Health Services of the City of Hamilton. His research interests centre around the study of child and adolescent psychopathology, particularly aggression, victimization, antisocial behaviour, and youth problem gambling. Recent research projects have been focused on the relations of parenting, peer relationships, and temperament to child and adolescent psychopathology, with particular emphasis on delineating differential predictors of direct and indirect forms of aggression, aggression with proactive and reactive functions, as well as dual involvement with aggression and victimization.

About the Editors and Contributors

Dr. Bonnie Leadbeater is a Professor in the department of Psychology at the University of Victoria in Victoria, British Columbia, Canada. Dr. Leadbeater joined the University of Victoria in 1997 after 9 years as faculty at Yale University. She is Director of the Centre for Youth and Society's research and programs that promote youth health and resilience through community-university research partnerships. She is also co-director of the BC Child and Youth Health Network funded by the Michael Smith Foundation for Health Research. This network provides funds to enable community-university research partnerships. Dr. Leadbeater's areas of research expertise include depression in adolescence, resilience among high-risk youth, and the prevention of peer victimization.

Dr. Zopito Marini, Ph.D., a sociocognitive developmental psychologist, is a Full Professor in the Department of Child and Youth Studies at Brock University. Dr. Marini does research, writes and lectures on issues related to family and school conflicts, bullying and victimization, the development of conscience and self-regulation. He is interested in investigating the cognitive mechanisms and social processes underlying the development of a range of sociocognitive abilities in typical and atypical children and youths. Projects currently underway in his lab examine the mediating and moderating impact of biopsychosocial factors, such as temperament, anti-social beliefs, and parenting practices on children's adjustment, with a view of developing effective prevention strategies.

Dr. Ersilia Menesini is an Associate Professor of Developmental Psychology at the University of Florence (Italy) – Department of Psychology. She received her Ph.D from the University of Florence in 1994. From 1996 to 2000 was a senior researcher in the area of Developmental Psychology, at the University of Padua and from 2000 onwards she moved back to Florence. Her main areas of research are: (1) psycho-social risk factors in the school context: peer rejection, isolation, bullying and victimization; (2) risk and protective factors in adolescence; (3) dating aggression in adolescence; (4) development and evaluation of school interventions against bullying; and (5) the development of moral emotions and moral sensibility. She had several international learning experiences with NATO countries and European Science Foundation and spent some periods abroad as a visiting professor. She has been involved in several European projects on bullying, violence and school interventions against violence. In the more recent years, she coordinated several projects funded by national and regional grants: a longitudinal research on "Violence and risk factors in adolescence"; a study on "The development of emotional competence in preadolescents"; a study on dating aggression and a more recent one on cyber-bullying.

Dr. Unni Vere Midthassel is an Associate Professor and head of the Centre for Behavioural Research, University of Stavanger. She has been head of the Zero-programme since its start in 2003. More than 300 schools have completed the programme during these three years. Besides managing the programme from the Centre of Behavioral Research and collecting data she has also been one of the instructors in the programme and thus worked directly with some of the schools each year. From 2004-2006 she have managed a follow up study of 79 of the first cohort of Zero-schools. The last data collecting is going on this spring. Her special interest is school development and factors and processes that enhance teacher learning and change. Dr. Midthassel's research topics include implementation and teacher involvement in school development activities.

Dr. Mona O'Moore, Associate Professor of Education, is a Graduate and Fellow of Trinity College Dublin, having gained an M.A. (Child and Educational Psychology) from University of Nottingham and a Ph.D. (Psychology) from University of Edinburgh. She is the Founder and Academic Director of the Anti-Bullying Research and Resource Centre (www.abc.tcd.ie) in the School of Education in Trinity College Dublin. Publications include: Dealing with Bullying in Schools: A Training Manual for Teachers, Parents and other Professionals (O'Moore & Minton, 2004) and Silent Witnesses, a DVD based resource pack (2006).

Dr. Erling Roland, is a Professor at Centre for Behavioural Research, University of Stavanger. Professor Roland initiated Centre for Behavioural Research (CBR) in 1989 and has since been its' director. The centre has developed steadily and has today a highly qualified staff of about 30, including administration unit. Professor Roland was deeply involved in the complex processes that made Stavanger University College succeed in being a university (UiS), as a key person when the University College was equipped with sufficient PhD programs and as member of the rectors' steering committee for reorganizing the College to fit a university structure. Professor Roland's research topics include, bullying behaviour and school influences of bullying.

About the Editors and Contributors

At national level, professor Roland has been central in many national initiatives to improve the Norwegian school system: Member of the committee that designed the first national program against bullying in Norway (82-83), and responsible for one of the two effect studies. Director of the Management program for all National and Regional Competence Centres of Special Education (95-97), Director of the Ministry's second national program against bullying (96-97). Director of the Ministry's national program, Samtak, for all management at primary, lower and higher secondary school and school-psychological staff concerning pupils with special needs (00-02). Member of the Ministry's' expert group on pupils' behavioural problems (03-). Norwegian national co-ordinator of the present OECD-program on School Bullying and Violence (SBV).

Dr. Christina Salmivalli is a Professor of psychology at the department of psychology, University of Turku, Finland, and a professor-II at the Center for Behavioral Research, University of Stavanger, Norway. Her research interests include bullying and victimization, especially group-level mechanisms contributing to such problems. Currently, the Peer Relations Research Group led by Salmivalli examines factors that increase children's and adolescents' likelihood of taking sides with the victimized peers. Other research topics include children's social cognitions and their variation across situations and in different dyadic contexts. Salmivalli is also a co-leader of the development and evaluation of a national anti-bullying program, KiVa, funded by the Finnish Ministry of Education.

Dr. Shaheen Shariff is an Assistant Professor in the department of Integrated Studies in Education in the faculty of Education at McGill University, Montreal, Quebec, Canada. Dr. Shariff's research and teaching are grounded in the study of legal considerations that impact educational policy and practice. She is currently Principal Investigator on two projects funded by Social Science and Humanities Research Council of Canada: 1) to develop international guidelines for school administrators on cyber-bullying; and 2) to study school policy and legal boundaries on cyber-bullying in Canadian schools. In relation to these projects, she is authoring two books with Routledge and Cambridge University Press. She is also an Associate of the Centre for Human Rights and Legal Pluralism at McGill's Law Faculty.

Understanding and Addressing Bullying: An International Perspective

Dr. J. David Smith, PhD, is an Associate Professor of Educational Counseling at the University of Ottawa. He received his PhD in counseling psychology from McGill University in 1998. His primary research interests centre on school-based bullying prevention programs, with a particular emphasis on understanding how they can be made to be more effective.

Dr. Leslie Tutty is a Full Professor with the Faculty of Social Work at the University of Calgary where she teaches courses in both clinical social work methods and research. Over the past nineteen years, her research has focused on services for family violence including a number of evaluations of shelter and post-shelter programs for abused women, support groups for abused women, treatment for adult and child victims of sexual abuse and groups for men who abuse their partners. Since 1999, Leslie has served as the Academic Research Co-ordinator of RESOLVE Alberta, a tri-provincial research institute on family violence. RESOLVE is one of Canada's Alliance of research centres on violence against women and children. Her body of research on domestic violence spans the perspectives of social services, justice, health and mental health and addresses prevention, intervention and policy. A special interest has been the effectiveness of school-based violence prevention programs, with published evaluations of child sexual abuse, dating violence and bullying programs.

Dr. David Wolfe is a Professor the University of Western Ontario and Director, CAMH Centre for Prevention Science. After completing his PhD in Clinical Psychology at the University of South Florida, David Wolfe pursued an academic career in Canada focusing on child abuse and domestic violence. His interests in prevention have culminated into a comprehensive school-based initiative for reducing adolescent violence and related risk behaviors. He holds the inaugural RBC Chair in Children's Mental Health at the Centre for Addiction and Mental Health (CAMH), where he is Head of the Centre for Prevention Science. He is a Professor of Psychiatry and Psychology at the University of Toronto, and Editor-in-Chief of *Child Abuse & Neglect: The International Journal*.

Introduction:

Understanding and Addressing Bullying: An International Perspective

Dr. Wendy M. Craig & Dr. Debra Pepler
PREVNet Scientific Co-Directors

Bullying and victimization comprise a significant global health problem. Today, an estimated 200 million children and youth around the world are being abused by their peers (Richter & Howard, 2003). The economic costs associated with the use of power and aggression, including direct medical, lost earnings and opportunity cost (time, employment and workers productivity), psychological costs, legal services, and incarceration, have been estimated at 9.1 billion annually (World Health Organization and the Department of Health and Human Services Centers for Disease Control and Prevention, 2008). Canada's youth do not fare well on international comparisons for general well-being and bullying problems. Canada ranks 12th out of 21 developed countries for children's wellbeing, based on education, behaviour, and family and peer relationships (UNICEF, 2007). On the World Health Organization Health Behaviours in School-aged Children survey, Canada ranked a disappointing 26th and 27th of 35 countries on measures of bullying and victimization, respectively (Craig & Yossi 2004). In contrast, Canada's children perform relatively well on academic indicators. On the Organisation for Economic Co-operation and Development report (2006) Canada ranked 3rd on reading, 7th on mathematics, and 11th on science of 41 countries. These reports reveal a striking discrepancy between Canada's rankings on children's relationships, bullying, and emotional well-being and rankings on academic performance, indicating a pressing need for better public policies focused on promoting children's social-emotional development.

Although efforts to address bullying have occurred in many countries with some success, Canada has a significant way to go in addressing this problem. In this book, we highlight research from around the world on bullying in an effort to increase our current understanding of the nature, severity, and development of the problem and the effective strategies and interventions to reduce bullying and victimization problems. Through increased understanding, we can continue to develop and implement programs that will be more successful at decreasing this significant and universal problem. Through international collaboration on promoting positive relationships and eliminating violence, we can truly begin to create a world without bullying.

Canada's Effort to Prevent Bullying: Promoting Relationships and Eliminating Violence Network (PREVNet)

PREVNet is a national network funded to stop bullying in Canada, through the Networks of Centres of Excellence- New Initiatives funding. PREVNet's mandate is to identify university, government and community partners, develop relationships, and create a viable and effective working network for social innovation. PREVNet's vision is to stop the use of power and aggression in bullying and to promote safe and healthy relationships for children and youth. At this point, PREVNet includes 45 researchers from universities across Canada, and 42 national non-governmental organizations (NGOs) that work with children and youth. We contend these partnerships are essential in addressing this public health problem because knowledge about bullying problems and strategies to promote healthy relationships are required in every place where Canadian children and youth live, work, and play.

Before PREVNet, the channels that researchers used for knowledge dissemination were inadequate for such a broad and deep reach. The many and diverse bullying prevention activities implemented at local, provincial, and national levels operated in isolation without an evidence-based national platform for coordination and implementation. As a national network, PREVNet is now bringing together researchers and national organizations to: enhance awareness, build research capacity, assess bullying problems, and promote evidence-based programs and effective policies across Canada. PREVNet is mobilizing knowledge through its four strategy pillars: Education and Training, Assessment and Evaluation, Prevention and Intervention, and Policy and Advocacy.

The PREVNet partnerships serve as the catalyst for social-cultural change through enhanced professional and research practice and informed social policy. Practice within the 42 NGOs is transforming as professionals join researchers with new exposure to scientific knowledge, tools, resources, and collaborations. PREVNet collaborations add value through the development of empirically based tools to: build awareness, change attitudes, assess bullying, implement evidenced-based strategies, and develop policies. PREVNet's NGOs partners have outreach to promote these activities within every community in Canada. Through our partnerships, we have the potential to reach 9,540,098 children and 1,002,600 adults who work with them. According to Statistics Canada (2007), this number exceeds the Canadian population under 19 years of age. This "double counting" indicates the added value of the network: we can reach children in multiple contexts to provide consistent messages and responses to promote healthy relationships across settings where they live, work, and play. By changing the professional practice of those who work with children and their families, PREVNet is enhancing healthy relationships and the social-emotional development of Canada's children. PREVNet also adds value through scientific practices. PREVNet links researchers with NGOs to ask new questions, within new contexts, with new methodologies, and in large, diverse samples. In this way, the PREVNet partnership model provides a new platform for knowledge development, exchange, mobilization, and uptake that will improve professional and research practice in Canada.

Within the PREVNet partnership model, we envision social-cultural change unfolding through improved professional practice in our partner organizations throughout the country. Those professionals who work with children and youth and their families will have: a deeper understanding of the importance of healthy relationships, tools to address problems of power and aggression in relationships, and tools to evaluate how effective they are at reducing these problems. Although we are working from the top through national NGOs, activities under the four strategy pillars will take place on the ground – in homes, classrooms, playgrounds, and recreation settings within every community in the country. Knowledge about promoting children's safe and healthy relationships is required in millions of settings within Canada. With 42 NGOs, PREVNet has channels for disseminating its education, assessment, intervention, and policy tools into every setting. The PREVNet model also provides for sustainable efforts to reduce the use of power and aggression in relationships. By working with NGOs with decades of experience in programming for youth, PREVNet can enhance and change the practices and services of those delivering the programs. The NGOs are experts in program development and sustained delivery; the researchers provide the capacity to ensure that these programs are based on current knowledge and are evaluated. With evaluation data, the NGOs will have evidence to lobby for continued funding and ensure sustainability of empirically-validated effective programs. Improved efforts to promote relationships will enhance children and youths' social-emotional development, social capacity and well being and will contribute to long term social, health, and economic benefits for Canada. The successful implementation of knowledge and technology transfer will build a comprehensive and unified monitoring system and intervention strategies to address bullying problems and create safe, healthy relationships. Through its partnerships PREVNet is creating social innovation that will foster a new society – one in which all Canadians are respected, safe, and healthy.

The PREVNet partnership model is unique in the world, providing opportunities to transfer knowledge about children's healthy relationships through organizations that reach into every community in Canada. We are confident that the PREVNet model is a globally relevant model that is currently being reviewed by at least seven different countries. As we consolidate our national efforts and network to prevent bullying, we need to learn from and engage with other researchers and community organizations around the world to promote healthy relationships for children and youth.

An International Effort to Stop Bullying: The Kandersteg Declaration

At a recent meeting in Switzerland, fifteen countries were represented in developing an international declaration to prevent bullying, given that it is a global, complex, and serious problem. Bullying has many faces, including the use of emerging technologies, and varies by age, gender, and culture. The mental and physical health, social, and academic consequences of bullying have an enormous impact on human and social capital (Wilkins-Shurmer et al., 2003; Glover, Gough, Johnson, & Cartwright, 2000). The costs of bullying burden our education, health care, social services, and criminal justice systems (Heames & Harvey, 2006), as well as work force productivity and innovation (Biggam & Power, 1999). The next steps require that we as a global society recognize that every child and youth has the right to be respected and safe and that bullying affects us all. Bullying is a violation of this basic human right (July 5, 2007, http://prevnet.ca/bullying/bullyingandhumanrights/tabid/120/default.aspx). It is the moral responsibility of adults to ensure these rights are honoured and that healthy development and citizenship are promoted. Many adults want more understanding and strategies to address bullying problems effectively (Whitted & Dupper, 2005).

At this meeting the following actions were supported.

1) Stop bullying now in all the places where children and youth live, work, and play.

2) Start prevention efforts early and continue these through childhood and adolescence, targeting known risk and protective factors and promoting healthy relationships.

3) Educate and empower all adults involved with children and youth to promote healthy relationships and prevent bullying.

4) Use policy and prevention programs, based on scientific research, that are appropriate for age, gender, and culture, and that involve families, peers, schools, and communities.

5) Provide ongoing assessment and monitoring necessary to evaluate the success of policy and programs and to guarantee the rights of children and youth.

Introduction

Bullying:
A Relationship Problem

Over the past twenty years, the dominant perspective of bullying has been as an aggressive behaviour problem that requires a punitive approach with consistent sanctions for those who bully (McGrath & Stanley, 2005; Olweus, 1993). Recent research has highlighted the diversity among those children who bully: some have serious problems with aggression and behavioural regulation; others are socially skilled and central members of the peer group who have learned to acquire power through bullying (Farmer, Estell, Bishop, O'Neal, & Cairns, 2003; Rodkin, Farmer, Pearl, & Van Acker, 2000; Xie, Cairns, & Cairns, 2005). Although bullying is a form of aggression, it appears as if at least some of the children who consistently bully, do not suffer from the disruptive behaviour problems that generally characterize aggressive children. Therefore, the behavioural management and punitive approaches typically used to intervene with aggressive children may not be well suited to shifting the behaviour patterns of socially competent children who understand the social dynamics of their peer group and use power and aggression to augment their status among peers. These approaches may also fall short of meeting the needs of children who bully because they have not acquired the skills, motivation, and understanding that are essential for prosocial behaviour and healthy relationships.

Through our research on bullying, we have come to understand bullying as a relationship problem, suggesting that the problems arise from complex interpersonal dynamics rather than simply from an individual child's problem with aggression or with being unable to defend him or herself. Within the relationship context of bullying, those children who bully are learning how to use power and aggression to control and distress another; those children who are repeatedly victimized become trapped in abusive relationships that are increasingly difficult to escape. Our observational and survey research has led us to recognize bullying as a relationship problem, leading to a basic tenet for interventions: A relationship problem requires relationship solutions. Within this positive perspective of promoting healthy relationships to prevent and intervene in bullying, we avoid labeling children as "victims" or "bullies," but take a broader perspective on children's strengths and challenges.

Children develop the capacity to form healthy relationships from moment-to-moment learning experiences starting at birth. Children need warm and supportive relationships, as well as consistent messages and responses to support their healthy social development across all of the contexts in which they live, learn, work, and play. For the skills necessary to learn, to read, or to do mathematics, there is a step-by-step process that enables most children to acquire these skills. In comparison, the lessons for successful social interactions are much more complex: they require understanding of one's own behaviours and emotions and the behaviours and emotions of other people. The others with whom children interact are highly variable and often unpredictable: even a single person varies from day to day in warmth, responsivity, and emotionality. The complexity of social interactions highlights the need to provide extensive, dynamic, and ongoing support to youth to enable them to learn how to: relate to others positively, be effective in achieving social goals, and use power positively, rather than negatively as in bullying. Therefore, the goal of interventions with children who bully, who are victimized, or who are bystanders to bullying is to enhance their relationship capacity to promote their healthy relationships in the present and to lay the foundation for healthy relationships throughout the lifespan.

From a developmental perspective, we are concerned about involvement in bullying because these problems can start in early childhood and persist through the school years, peaking during school transitions (Pellegrini & Long, 2002; Pepler, Jiang, Craig, & Connolly 2008). When children enter adolescence, new forms of aggression combined with power emerge. As children develop cognitive and social skills, they become more aware of others' vulnerabilities and differences and of their own power relative to others. Bullying becomes diversified into more sophisticated forms of verbal, social, electronic, sexually- and racially-based aggression. All of these forms of bullying are destructive and need to be actively addressed. The lessons of power and aggression learned in playground bullying can transfer to sexual harassment, dating aggression and may extend to workplace harassment, as well as marital, child, and elder abuse (Pepler, Craig, Connolly, & Henderson, 2001). In tailoring our responses to bullying, we must consider children's developmental stages and gender, so that our relationship solutions match the students' developmental needs.

Conclusion

This book reflects the leading-edge thinking of scholars, practionners, and researchers from around the world that gathered at our 1st Annual Conference in Ottawa in May 2006. Each year, we will publish a book from the presentations at our annual conference. This book series will reflect the new understanding, knowledge, and practise that has emerged through PREVNet. The collection in this book, represent the ideas, dedication, and commitment of PREVNet and our international partners to moving the Kandersteg Declaration from an idea to a reality. This book represents the global effort that is mobilizing to stop bullying and create a world without bullying.

References

Biggam F. & Power, K. (1999). *A comparison of the problem-solving abilities and psychological distress of suicidal, bullied, and protected prisoners.* Criminal Justice and Behavior 26, 196-216

Craig, W. M. & Yossi, J. (2004) Bullying and fighting. In C. Currie et al (Eds.) *Young People's Health in Context international report from the HBSC 2001/02 survey.* World Health International Report. WHO Policy Series Health policy for children and adolescents Issue 4, WHO Regional Office for Europe, Copenhagen. World Health Organization.

Farmer, T. W., Estell, D. B., Bishop, J. L., O'Neal, K. K., & Cairns, B. D. (2003). *Rejected bullies or popular leaders? The social relations of aggressive subtypes of rural African American early adolescents.* Developmental Psychology, 39, 992-1004.

Glover D., Gough G., Johnson M., & Cartwright N. (2000). *Bullying in 25 secondary schools: incidence, impact and intervention.* Educational Research, 42(2), 11-156

Heames, J.T., Harvey, M., & Treadway, D. (2006). *Status inconsistency: An antecedent to bullying in groups.* International Journal of Human Resource Management, 17, 348-361.

McGrath, H. & Stanley, M. (2005). *A comparison of two nonpunitive approaches to bullying.* In H. McGrath and T. Noble (Eds.) *Bullying Solutions: Evidence-based approaches to bullying in Australian schools.* (pp. 189-201), Frenchs Forest NSW: Pearson Longman.

Olweus, D. (1993). *Bullying at school: What we know and what we can do.* Oxford: Blackwell.

Pellegrini, A., & Long, J. (2002). *A longitudinal study of bullying, dominance, and victimization during the transition from primary school through secondary school.* British Journal of Developmental Psychology, 20(2), 259-280.

Pepler, D., Craig, W., Connolly, J., & Henderson, K. (2001). *Bullying, sexual harassment, dating violence, and substance use among adolescents. In C. Wekerle & A. M. Wall (Eds.), The violence and addiction equation: Theoretical and clinical issues in substance abuse and relationship violence.* (pp. 153-168). Philadelphia: Brunner/Mazel.

Pepler, D., Jiang, D., Craig, W., & Connolly, J. (in press). *Developmental trajectories in bullying.* Child Development.

Richter, S. & Howard, B. (2003). *Review of bullying behaviour: Current issues, research and intervention.* Journal of Development and Behaviour Pediatrics, 24, 382 – 383.

Rodkin, P. C., Farmer, T. W., Pearl, R., & Van Acker, R. (2000). *Heterogeneity of popular boys: Antisocial and prosocial configurations*. Developmental Psychology, 36, 14-24.

Whitted, K.S. & Dupper, D.R. (2005). *Best Practices for Preventing or Reducing Bullying in Schools*. Children and Schools, 27, (3),167-175.

Wilkins-Shurmer A, O'Callaghan MJ, Najman JM, Bor W, Williams GM, Anderson MJ. *Association of bullying with adolescent health-related quality of life*. J Paediatr Child Health 2003, 39, 436–41.

World Health Organization and the Department of Health and Human Services Centers for Disease Control and Prevention (2008). *Manual for estimating the economic costs of injuries due to interpersonal and self-directed violence*. WHO library Cataloguing in Publication Data.

Xie, H., Cairns, B. D., & Cairns, R. B. (2005). *The development of aggressive behaviors among girls: Measurement issues, social functions, and differential trajectories*. In D. J. Pepler, K. C. Madsen, C. Webster, & K. S. Levene (Eds.). *The development and treatment of girlhood aggression* (pp. 105-136). Mahwah, NJ: Lawrence Erlbaum Associates Publishers.

Introduction to Section One:

Understanding Bullying

Dr. Joanne Cummings, PREVNet Partnership Manager

The first five chapters of this book extend our understanding of the multi-faceted nature of bullying. The breadth and scope of the international research on bullying and victimization described in Section One attest to the complex nature of this problem. Within these chapters you will find bullying examined and explored from multiple perspectives. Varying levels of attention are placed on individual characteristics and correlates, relationships between individuals, group dynamics, prevailing cultural understandings, and institutional and legal policies and frameworks. Several contributors investigate the emotions, social cognitions and beliefs that underlie the many forms of bullying, as well as the experience of being bullied or witnessing the bullying of others. Other contributors document the prevalence, and patterns of stability and change of participant roles with respect to bullying, (e.g., those who bully, those who are "dually involved" in both bullying and victimization, those who are victimized, and those who are bystanders). Despite the multiplicity of perspectives offered in Section One, there is agreement that bullying is multi-determined and reflects the interplay of individual and situational factors.

The first two chapters identify a major challenge for bullying intervention – overcoming children's and youths' ambivalence and motivating them to take ethical and morally-based action. In the first chapter, Almeida, Caurcel, and Machado explore how the experience of victimization by bullying is understood by Portuguese and Spanish adolescents. Almeida, Caurcel, and Machado suggest that viewing bullying through a relational framework directs our attention to the social processes and shared understandings that occur in these relationships. Relationships characterized by bullying affect adolescents' developing self-identities, as well as the social categories into which they place their peers. These identities and categorizations consolidate existing roles and constrain change. Almeida and colleagues found that 80% of the adolescents they surveyed believed that victimized youth are "kind" and "good people" but, consistent with the prevailing international stereotype, are weak and unable to defend themselves. Despite this view, the majority of youth do not act on the ethical imperative to defend their peers who are victimized by bullying.

In the next chapter, Pöyhönen and Salmivalli provide a comprehensive literature review of the roles children and youth play within the group dynamics of bullying interactions, and the individual variables that predict ethical action on the part of bystanders (e.g., younger children versus adolescents, female versus male, popularity and high status in the peer group). The authors report new empirical findings pertaining to social cognitions that expand our understanding. Key to determining whether children or youth who witness bullying will take the role of defender are beliefs about one's own capability to effectively stop bullying, as well as expectations about the likely consequences of taking such action. Their study found that while children and youth typically hold both positive and negative expectations regarding defending behaviour, negative expectations trump positive ones. Pöyhönen and Salmivalli also describe Finland's national school-based bullying prevention program, instituted in 2006, with a clear emphasis on mobilizing bystanders to take ethical action. This goal of engaging bystanders is reiterated in virtually all the other bullying prevention programs you will read about in Section Two.

The third and fourth chapters discuss bullying in the two most significant social contexts for children and youth, the school and the internet. The third chapter by Beran examines the complex linkages between bullying involvement, the ability to deploy attention and engage in learning, and academic achievement. The fourth chapter by Shariff and Hoff likens cyber-space to the unsafe and lawless society created by the children and youth in the novel, "Lord of the Flies", as both environments are characterized by the absence of adult supervision and the violation of the rights of the vulnerable. Shariff and Hoff discuss the destructive consequences of cyber-bullying for involved youth. They provide an extensive review of the legal considerations with respect to defamation, freedom of expression, and student privacy, followed by recommendations for the prevention of cyber-bullying.

Introduction to Section One: Understanding Bullying

The final chapter by Marini and Dane emphasizes the heterogeneous nature of children and youth involved in bullying and victimization problems, and propose a number of subtypes based on the kind of aggressive behaviour (direct or indirect), its function (proactive or reactive), and type of involvement (bullying, victimization, or both). The authors summarize psychosocial correlates of these subtypes, including temperament, associated psychopathology, social cognitions, parenting and peer relationships. In this chapter, you will find a brief literature review of bullying interventions, using four broad categories to describe them: whole school approaches, social skills training, social participant-role approaches, and parent management training. This framework provides a useful roadmap to preview themes more fully discussed in Section Two. Marini and Dane integrate subtype characteristics with the intervention literature, and make many useful recommendations for individualizing and customizing interventions.

In summary, the first section of this book emphasizes that bullying is a relationship problem that requires understanding of the roles of individuals, peers, and adults, and their relationships in order to intervene effectively in the problem. By addressing each of these levels and the relationships among children, youth, peers, and adults, systemic interventions can reduce the significant social problem of bullying.

Chapter 1:

Towards a Relational Perspective of Peer Bullying

Ana Maria Tomás de Almeida, María Jesus Caurcel & José Cunha Machado
Instituto de Estudos da Criança & Instituto de Ciências Sociais - Universidade do Minho
Facultad de Ciencias de la Educación - Universidad de Granada

Introduction

"It is typical of our age", says a fifteen year-old girl when asked to state the motives for bullying other classmates in school. This girl's acknowledgement that peer abuse is related to age and enmeshed in the normality of everyday school life is a warning for parents, teachers, school administrators, psychologists, policy makers, and social scientists. In spite of its seriousness, the ubiquitous phenomenon of bullying is often addressed with condescending ears and incredulous eyes. This form of abuse is, in many circumstances, implicitly interpreted as normal part of growing up. However, no matter how insidious, bullying involves prolonged and intentional aggressive interactions with the asymmetry of size, status, strength and/or the number of youth involved in harassing. Bullying leads to cruel and insensitive maltreatment of more vulnerable, defenceless, and quite often isolated peers.

Children and adolescents often describe common themes when discussing bullying, revealing that they share social and cultural perceptions regarding bullying dynamics within groups, the dysfunction that leads to particular problems, and ways to cope with the phenomenon. To study these more closely, we conducted interviews and questionnaires that explored cognitions, emotions, and attitudes associated with peer bullying. We asked children and adolescents to describe: 1. how bullying evolves; 2. the reasons for bullying; 3. the feelings of all the parties involved – those who bully, are victimized, or are bystanders to bullying; and 4. how to cope with abuse and coercive attitudes such as the ones that are normally associated with peer bullying. In contrast to the majority of survey studies, which begin by presenting a clear definition of bullying, we presented a set of ten figures portraying physical and relational aggression scenes of dyads or group of schoolmates interacting in a school setting. We presented the ten cartoons in a pre-determined order to represent a sequence of incidents that occur in a given time and a closed setting and to ascertain the constrained nature of school bullying. This strategy with scenarios also matched our inductive approach to exploring children and adolescents' definitions and representations of peer bullying.

Undoubtedly, peer relations play an important role in personal and social adjustment, particularly in the childhood and adolescent years (Hartup, 1983; Laursen, 2005; Rubin, Bukowski & Parker, 1998; Sullivan, 1953). Throughout the school years, having friends and rubbing shoulders with peers about the same age gives access to new social worlds and foster children's social selves. Nevertheless, these relationships are not always enjoyable or free of hassles and not all children experience a sense of belonging among their classmates. Moreover the stable nature of peer groups does not always lead to camaraderie or the emergence of friendships; on the contrary, it can perpetuate and even aggravate poor peer relations (Salmivalli, 2001). Difficulties in fitting in with one's peer group and troubled relationships can lay the foundation for unhappiness and a long series of frustrated expectations about self-perceived social competence and group membership.

Poor peer relations have been well-documented in terms of the development of psychopathology (Alsaker & Olweus, 1992; Olweus, 1993; Rubin et al., 1998). A number of studies have emphasized how detrimental poor peer relations can be for group cohesion, affective communication, and interpersonal attitudes among classmates (DeRosier, Cillessen, Coie & Dodge, 1994; Pepler, Craig & O'Connell, 1996; Perry, Willard & Perry, 1990). Peer bullying, whether a cause or a consequence of poor social relationships, entails negative effects for both the individual and the peer group. Given its origin and perpetuation in a social context, it is essential to understand and explain the bullying phenomenon within a relationship perspective (Pepler & Craig, 2006).

A relationship perspective is an integrative framework and puts forward an interesting research agenda. Until now, the bulk of empirical studies have mainly focused on the development of behavioural, cognitive, and emotional patterns of aggressive, victimized or passive-aggressive children, or they have taken a peer group perspective, substantiated in a view of its structural organization and role differentiation of group members (Salmivalli, Lagerspetz, Björkqvist, Österman & Kaukiainen, 1996; Salmivalli, 2001). The peer perspective focuses on exploring how processes and group mechanisms contribute to the development of bullying. While personality and systemic approaches have echoed the principal contrasting conceptualizations about the phenomenon of bullying, more recently, the relationship perspective has directed the focus to how individuals actively participate in the processes of constructing social experiences. This co-construction process is embedded in collective interactions facilitating thoughts, symbolic representations, meaning attribution, communication, organizing behaviour, and setting shared expectations about each other's behaviour.

In the child development domain, these ideas have arisen from theories of the self and symbolic interactionism (Baldwin, 1906; Mead, 1925, 1934), from constructs such as the internal working model (Bretherton & Munholland, 1999), and also from modern interactive models of socioemotional development (Carlson, Sroufe, & Egeland, 2004).

Complementary representations of self and others' experiences have long been investigated in the social psychological tradition. According to Moscovici (1981) knowledge is socially elaborated and collectively shared (common sense). Such knowledge refers not only to a given reality, as it is also involved in the construction of such reality. Such construction shapes what is perceived as common sense knowledge, also designated as implicit theories, or else, ethno-theories. It refers to certain shared ideas, thoughts, and images about particular realities (natural or socio-cultural) which, due to their social fabrication, are embodied with an intense feeling of logical necessity. Social representations guide behaviour and help in anticipating action and outcomes.

There is a need for research to understand the development of these general interactional and relationship dynamics and to understand the specific dynamics in bullying. Many different researchers have highlighted the need to understand the processes in bullying by looking beyond a focus on individual children's behaviour as a way of investigating the processes that maintain victimization status (Kochenderfer-Ladd, 2003; Vaillancourt, McDougall, Hymel & Welch, 2001; Boivin, Hymel & Hodges, 2001). Beyond the individual children involved, there may be social interactions, relationship experiences, and social representational processes of reciprocal roles contributing to the experiences of bullying.

Even though children who are victimized by their peers differ in a number of ways from those who are not victimized it is often misleading to attribute the victimized child's vulnerability to an individual attribute such as physical strength (Olweus, 1978), disability (Naylor, Granizo, Tantam & Deurzen, 2005), race or ethnicity, sex or religious orientation (Mellor, 1999; Rivers, 2001; Siann, Callaghan, Glissov, Lockhart, & Rawson, 1994), mental disabilities (Tattum, 1989), or special education needs (Tattum, 1997). It would also be misleading to expect that the quality of relations or social environments affect every child in the exact same way. As Boivin, Hymel and Hodges (2001) indicate, to be rejected or socially withdrawn at school does not necessarily trap children in a dysfunctional pathway of peer victimization.

Ortega y Gasset (1935/2005) captured this complexity in his statement that "I am myself and my circumstances"[1], acknowledging that any prediction of social adjustment must take into account the mutual, dynamic influence of individual, representational self-experiences and contextual factors. With development, children's self-representations may become more influential in the expression of behaviour, whether this is translated into positive outcomes or not. In transitional periods, specifically, through adolescence, when adaptation becomes a challenging developmental task, a perceived vulnerability can weaken adolescents' expectations about their own behaviours and their peer relationships. Unfortunately, many victimized youths' reports of real life experiences attest to the troubled interactions that can unfold.

---

[1] Paraphrasing the philosophical thought of José Ortega y Gasset (1883-1955): "yo soy yo y mi circunstancia".

Given that vulnerability is an interactional process, it is important to investigate how and why behavioural and nonbehavioural characteristics are associated with the experiences of children involved in bullying and/or victimization. At the same time, it is important to consider that specific negative outcomes for the victims of peer bullying (e.g., social reputations) are affected by the identity of the perceiver and severity of the victimization. Negative social reputations affect both the social status and self-perceptions of children and adolescents. Hymel, Wagner and Butler (1990) demonstrated how the effects of difficult relationships become meaningful and pernicious to one's perceived social competence in the transition from childhood to adolescence. As such, we hypothesized that individual attributes, in order to become risk factors or predispositions to being victimized (or bullying others), acquire social meaning and, consequently, become internalized as social categories that differentiate members in a group. In social psychology terms, these categorization processes, including interpersonal differentiation, are social cognitive operations that lead to the social construction of personal and social identities. Individual differences and, concomitantly, group boundaries represent such social constructions and simultaneously anchor and strengthen self and social identities (Tajfel, 1978).

At this point, combining these two levels of explanation presents a challenge. As children develop, self-representations of interpersonal experience may gain relevance in organizing cognitions, emotions, and behaviours. From a group or societal perspective shared social representations may maintain a range of stereotypes about individuals in and out of the social group. As a result of categorization processes, stereotypes might simultaneously serve the self and the group, but it is doubtful that they will be beneficial to interpersonal relations

In the present study, we had three main goals. The first goal was to examine psychological descriptions of youth victimized by peer bullying. These descriptions were based on peer ratings of different physical, social, and emotional characteristics. The second aim was to determine whether these descriptions corroborate the perceived vulnerability and common stereotypes of victimized youths' social (in)competence. The third aim was to examine how these social representations of victimized youth are associated with characteristics such as country of origin, age, gender and relational status (victimization role assigned by peers) and self-reported experience of involvement in bullying situations.

Method

Participants

A total of 1237 adolescents aged 11 to 16 years old ($\underline{M}$ = 13.3 years) were involved in this study. They were drawn from 35 classrooms in fourteen public and private elementary and secondary schools in Granada (Spain) and Braga (Portugal). The participants were balanced across grades, as well as across urban and suburban schools from the two cities. Both cities are mid-size university towns, known for their rapid socioeconomic and cultural development in the last decade. Besides location, schools were selected based on size and educational levels, with an attempt to achieve even distributions of age, grade and educational levels of students in the two countries. The participants came from low, middle. and upper-middle class families. The overall goals of the study, the questionnaires and the application procedures were described in initial interviews with school staff. Written informed parental consent was obtained, with teachers and students providing verbal consent to voluntary participation.

Participant distribution according to country, sex and age (N=1237)

Variables	Levels	N
Country	Spain	842
	Portugal	395
Sex	Male	631
	Female	606
Age groups	11 - 12	278
	13 - 14	514
	15 - 16	445

Instruments

Victimization Status. A peer assessment procedure developed by Cerezo (2000) was used to identify which students were assigned to the different roles. This questionnaire gathers information on preferred and non-preferred friendship choices, self-perceptions of mutual choices and rejections, plus six items to nominate up to three individuals in the classroom who fit the behavioural description of being aggressive or victimized. These six items comprise: who bosses, who whines and is afraid, who teases and hits others, who gets picked on by others, who is envied by others, and who is the smartest. Five additional items assessed the frequency, type, and location of bullying; the perceived severity of bullying; and safety at school. In the present sample, 7.3% of the participants were identified as victimized students, 8.3% as aggressive students, 82% as bystanders and 0.6% as those involved in both the bullying and victimized role. In total, 5.2% of the participants stated that they were bullied very often or always, 5.3% identified themselves as aggressive, 52% identified themselves as supportive of victimized students and 8% as supportive of the aggressive students.

Procedure

Students completed a self-report assessment – the SCAN-Bullying Quest (Almeida & Caurcel, 2005). This measure comprises a narrative description, as well as ratings of expectations, attitudes and feelings regarding a peer bullying story. This measure explored the experiences of students who were aggressive and/or victimized, as well as students' perceptions of whether they projected themselves onto the story roles of the victimized, aggressive, or bystanding students.

The SCAN-Bullying Quest was designed after the *Scripted-Cartoon Narrative of Peer Bullying* (Almeida et al., 2001; Del Barrio et al., 2003). The original narrative assessment comprises a scripted-cartoon story and a semi-structured, open-ended interview through which participants' representations regarding bullying and the victimized and aggressive students' experiences were elicited.

The questionnaire was created simultaneously in Portuguese and Spanish languages (an English version was presented at the PREVNet conference, May 2006). The questionnaire was administered in each country during the last two months of the school year, between May and June, allowing for better interpersonal knowledge among classmates. Along with the questionnaire, a separate slip was handed to each student depicting the scripted-cartoon story.

Figure 1. Examples of feminine and masculine vignettes taken from the SCAN-Bullying.

Similar to the gender-specific versions of the bullying cartoon-narrative, masculine and feminine versions of the questionnaires were presented, each portraying a group of students (i.e., predominantly male or female) involved in different bullying interactions: physical and relational, direct, and indirect. At the beginning, to get the students acquainted with length, scale format and questioning, the researchers read through some examples calling attention to the sections of the questionnaire, specifically clarifying wording and encouraging students to ask any questions. The assessment started with a storytelling task, followed by questions to examine attitudes, emotions, and expectations concerning the victimized student, the aggressive student, and the bystanders. The 36 items were classified into a series of scales tapping different themes.

In the current study, the adolescents' descriptions of victimized students' attributes were based on a list of 14 bipolar adjectives (e.g. friendly/unfriendly; funny/boring; cool/nerd). A *semantic differential scale* (Osgood, Suci & Tannenbaum, 1957) was used to assess the subjective meaning of a concept to the respondent; thus providing an attitude scale associated with the underlying dimensions (Robson, 1993). Each adjective pair was scored on a five-point scale, with 1 corresponding to the negative pole and 5 to the positive pole, providing a rating from a less sociable to a more sociable orientation.

Results

The means of the 14 adjective pair ratings are presented in Figure 2 and indicate that respondents had differentiated perspectives, with the exception of a neutral mean score for three adjective pairs: "Boring/Funny"; "Nerd/Cool" and "Weak/Brave".

Figure 2. **Mean and standard deviation scores for the victim categorization**

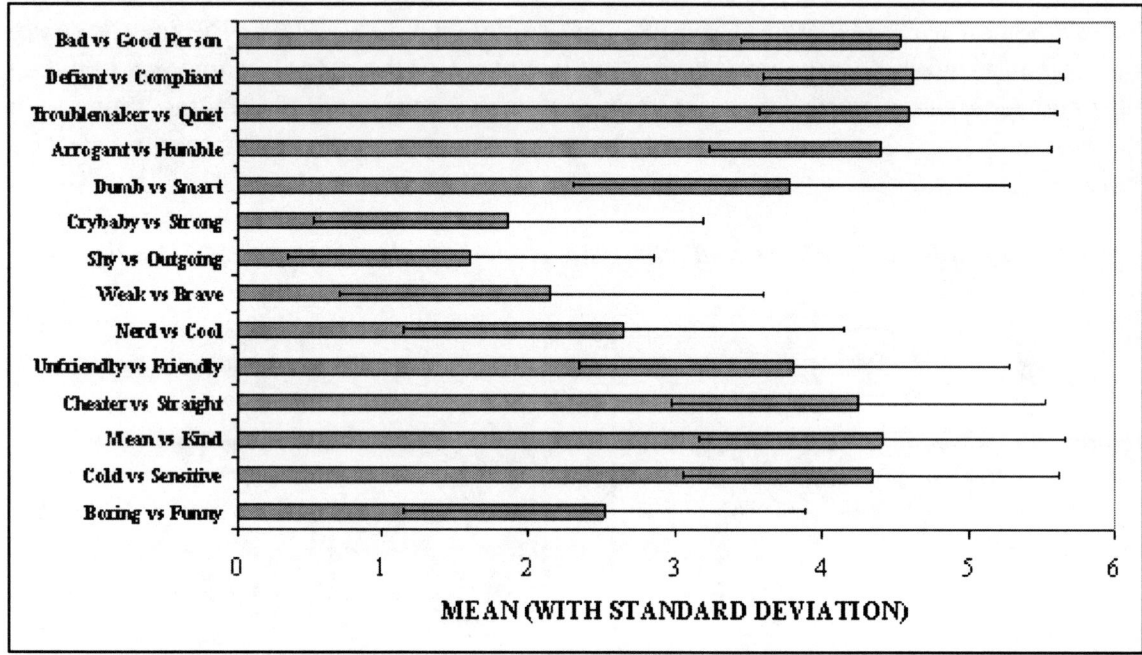

A complementary analysis of percentage distributions for each pair of adjectives showed that the participants describe victimized students with a wide range of sociable attributes, describing them as 'Compliant' (86.4%), 'Quiet' (86.3%), a 'Good person' (82.3 %), 'Kind' (79.2%), 'Sensitive' (75.6%), 'Humble' (75.5%) and 'Sincere' (71.1%). These perceptions suggest an empathic characterization of victimized students. There also was consensus on a perception of vulnerability regarding shyness (79.6%) and weakness (67.2%) of victimized students. In contrast to these stereotyped descriptions, fewer participants ascribed to attributes like 'Crybaby' (56.7%), 'Boring' (38.6%) and 'Nerd' (38.2%), pointing to either a lack of consensus or a midpoint opinion of the attribute classification.

Overall, participants' rating reflected descriptions of victimized students found in the literature and, undoubtedly, the evaluative process is somewhat revealing of adolescents' common justifications for peer bullying.

Figure 3. Percentage distribution according to the bipolar adjectives in the victim profile (N = 1230)

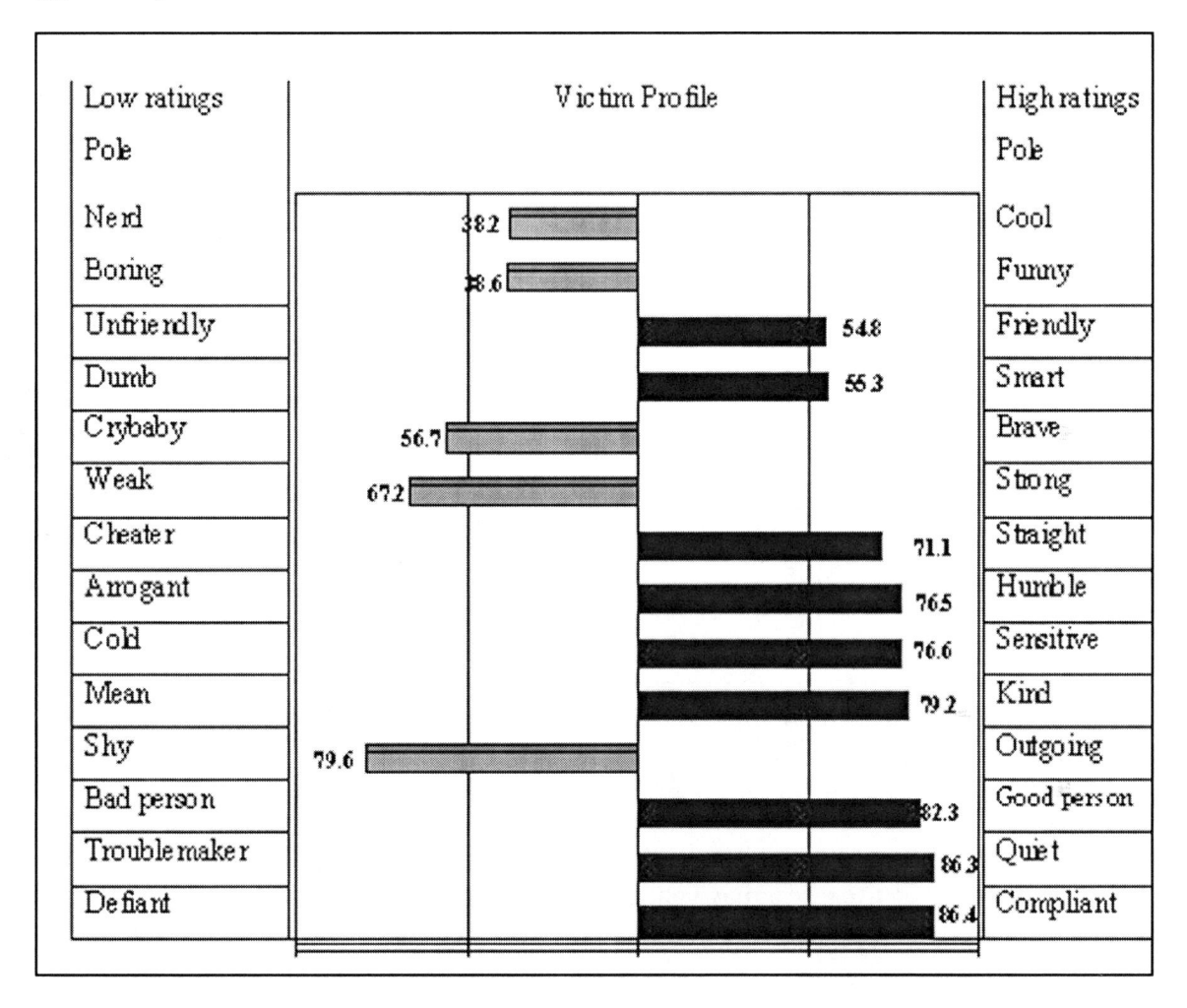

Low ratings Pole	Victim Profile	High ratings Pole
Nerd	38.2	Cool
Boring	38.6	Funny
Unfriendly	54.8	Friendly
Dumb	55.3	Smart
Crybaby	56.7	Brave
Weak	67.2	Strong
Cheater	71.1	Straight
Arrogant	76.5	Humble
Cold	76.6	Sensitive
Mean	79.2	Kind
Shy	79.6	Outgoing
Bad person	82.3	Good person
Troublemaker	86.3	Quiet
Defiant	86.4	Compliant

Following the descriptive analysis, a factor analysis was carried out to examine associations among the adjective pairs and links to underlying dimensions. The five-point scale was transformed into a three-point scale (the values 2 and 4 of the original scale were collapsed into 1 and 5, respectively) to reduce score dispersion.

A principal component analysis was conducted to determine the number of major dimensions characterizing the data. A rotated varimax transformation and the slope of eigenvalues suggested that two main factors were present, with the first two principal components (KMO=0.865), explaining 49% of the total variance.

The first factor aggregated 9 components and corresponded to the adjectives on the positive pole with high ratings, forming a dimension that is in favour of a sociable and more positive characterization of victimized students. The remaining five components corresponded to the adjectives with lower scores, reflecting a less socially competent, more vulnerable and somewhat negative stereotyped perception of victimized students. Internal consistency, as measured by Cronbach alpha, was 0.83 for the first factor and 0.71 for the second factor. The correlations are presented in Figure 4.

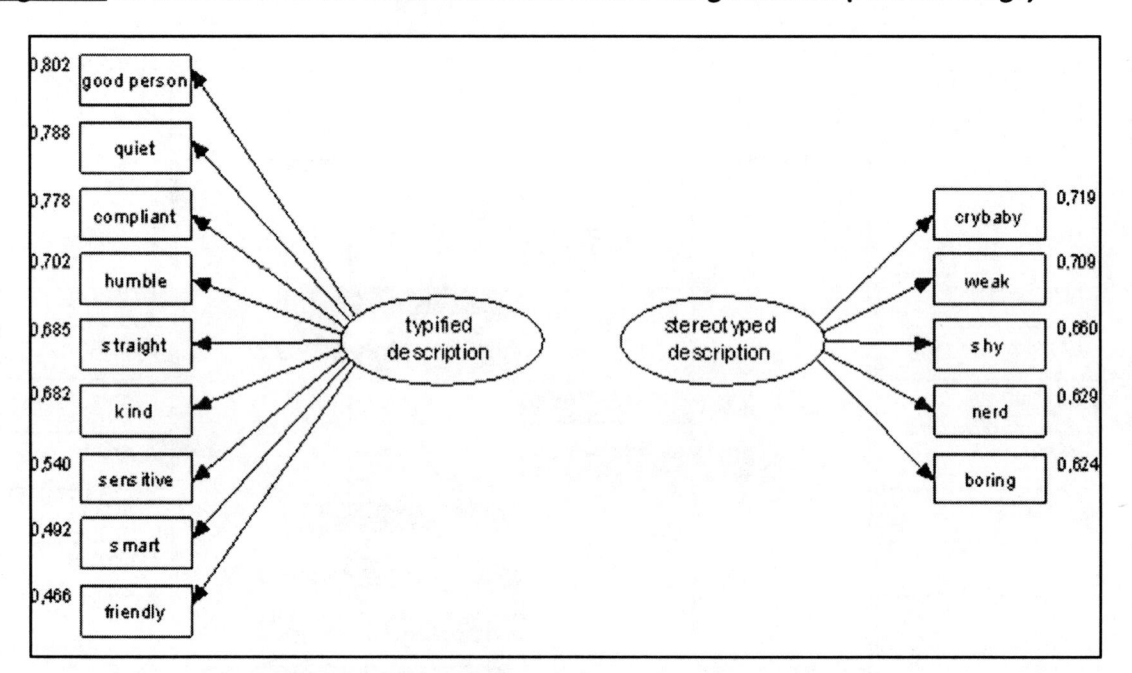

Figure 4. Rotated two-factor structure of the victim categorization (with loadings)

Typified description loadings:
- good person: 0,802
- quiet: 0,788
- compliant: 0,778
- humble: 0,702
- straight: 0,685
- kind: 0,682
- sensitive: 0,540
- smart: 0,492
- friendly: 0,466

Stereotyped description loadings:
- crybaby: 0,719
- weak: 0,709
- shy: 0,660
- nerd: 0,629
- boring: 0,624

We also explored differences according to the participants' country, gender, age, and role in bullying situations, as reported by peers. We had no *a priori* expectations about differences related to cultural or geographical location. As indicated in Table 2, however, the Spanish adolescents tended to display a more sociable profile of the victimized students. Conversely, the Portuguese participants perceived the victimized students more negatively and accentuated their vulnerability.

Descriptives of victim characterization according to Country

Factors	Independent variable Country	N	Mean	t	Sig.
1. Typified description of the victim	Portugal	391	38.0793	-2.497	.013
	Spain	839	39.1907		
	Total	1230	38.8374		
2. Stereotyped description of the victim	Portugal	391	11.6974	4.736	.000
	Spain	839	10.3381		
	Total	1230	10.7691		

In examining gender differences, we found two patterns, which are consistent with traditional gender stereotypes. Adolescent girls showed a more prosocial and empathic attitude towards victimized students, being more positive and less negative in their characterization compared to boys. In contrast, boys' ratings reflected a more negative and stereotyped perception of victimized students.

Descriptives of victim characterization according to gender

Factors	Independent variable Sex	N	Mean	t	Sig.
1. Typified description of the victim	Boys	628	38.6545	-3.887	.000
	Girls	602	39.6545		
	Total	1230	39.1545		
2. Stereotyped description of the victim	Boys	628	9.9219	-6.520	.000
	Girls	602	11.6501		
	Total	1230	10,7895		

In comparing the three age groups, we found a significant age effect only for the second dimension corresponding to a stereotyped image of victimized students. The pattern suggests that as adolescents grow older, particularly from age 13, there is an accentuation of the stereotype of victimized youth.

Descriptives of victim characterization according to age

Factors	Independent variable Age	N	Mean	SD	F	Sig.
1. Typified description of the victim	11 to 12	276	38.95	7.15	2.177	.114
	13 to 14	511	39.26	7.04		
	15 to 16	443	38.28	7.62		
	Total	1230	38.84	7.28		
2. Stereotyped description of the victim	11 to 12	276	11.84	5.14	12.053	.000
	13 to 14	511	10.79	4.66		
	15 to 16	443	10.08	4.46		
	Total	1230	10.77	4.73		

In the current study, we were particularly interested in whether perceptions of victimized students are related to adolescents' own experiences within bullying situations, as identified through peer ratings. Eighty-nine students were identified as victimized, one-hundred and nine were identified as aggressive and the remaining, who were not classified in these two roles, were grouped under the category of observers. Analyses of variance were performed to identify whether there were differences in perceptions of victimized students, depending on a participant's role in bullying situations. We expected that aggressive youth would subscribe to a stereotyped and vulnerable perception of victimized students. In addition, in line with social appropriateness often reported in the literature (Smith, 2004), we expected to find a generally favourable image of the victimized students among observers. It was also plausible that adolescents identified as victimized would describe victimized students in a more empathic and sociable mode, as a reflection of activated identification with the experience of the story's protagonist. This was not a strong prediction because if stereotypes reflect a social representation of the vulnerability of those who are victimized, students identified in this role by their peers may perceive themselves as vulnerable and less socially valued, reflecting the burden of this interpersonal negative categorization.

As seen in Table 5, these hypotheses were partially confirmed. Role assignment was related to the above predictions, with one exception. A participant's status as victimized did not relate positively to the stereotyped description. For their own sake, victimized students do not share a negative belief about those in this role. As predicted, ratings of adolescents in the aggressive group reflected a less positive image of victimized students and an amplified perception of their negative attributes, as shown in the low ratings assigned to the second factor. This finding may be a reflection of these students' nonemotional involvement or a justification to reinforce anticipated aggressive behaviours toward the group of victimized students. Finally, observers' descriptions were similar to the victimized group's perceptions, but were more neutral, as expected.

Descriptives of victim characterization according to victimization status

Factors	Independent variable Status	N	Mean	SD	F	Sig.
1. Typified description of the victim	Victim	89	39.72	6.61	5.767	.000
	Aggressor	103	36.55	8.42		
	Observer	1009	39.11	7.07		
	Total	1201	38.46	7.37		
2. Stereotyped description of the victim	Victim	89	11.43	5.41	4.769	.001
	Aggressor	103	9.09	4.45		
	Observer	1009	10.93	4.67		
	Total	1201	10.48	4.85		

Given our interest in exploring the contributions of representational and behavioural experiences to the perceptions of victimized students, we conducted additional analyses to investigate how self-reported experiences as a victimized, aggressive, pro-victimized student, or a pro-aggressive student were related to positive and negative dimensions of perceptions of victimized students.

We assessed the association between participants' self-reported experiences of victimization and found that participants with no or few experiences of victimization held a more stigmatized perception of victimized students (see Table 6). In contrast, those students who reported having been victimized had less stereotyped views and, indeed, revealed a self-serving social image and a positive orientation towards their own group. Those students who were aggressive had perceptions reflecting a marked negative view of victimized students' vulnerabilities as well as a less positive view of their sociability (see Table 7).

Descriptives of victim characterization according to self-reported experience as victim

Factors	Independent variable Self-reported experience	N	Mean	SD	F	Sig.
1. Typified description of the victim	Never	722	38.58	7.53	.993	.395
	A few times	327	39.40	6.27		
	Sometimes	115	38.72	7.76		
	Very often/Always	64	39.12	8.22		
	Total	1228	38.84	7.28		
2. Stereotyped description of the victim	Never	722	10.57	4.69	5.509	.001
	A few times	327	10.55	4.54		
	Sometimes	115	11.54	4.55		
	Very often/Always	64	12.75	5.87		
	Total	1228	10.77	4.73		

Descriptives of victim characterization according to self-reported experience as aggressor

Factors	Independent variable Self-reported experience	N	Mean	SD	F	Sig.
1. Typified description of the victim	Never	655	39.44	7.08	14.055	.000
	A few times	351	39.13	6.76		
	Sometimes	152	37.91	7.51		
	Very often/Always	65	33.61	9.15		
	Total	1223	38.84	7.28		
2. Stereotyped description of the victim	Never	655	11.59	4.72	15.719	.000
	A few times	351	10.01	4.35		
	Sometimes	152	9.26	4.58		
	Very often/Always	65	10.16	5.54		
	Total	1223	10.77	4.73		

The final analysis examined perceptions associated with self-reported experiences as a bystander who is supportive of either victimized students or aggressive students or is uninvolved (see Table 8 and 9). Again, the results indicated that experience was directly related to the characterization of the victimized students. Congruent with the tendencies described above, a more systematic helping attitude was associated with positive characterization of the victimized youth while the opposite association was observed for non-involvement and a more negative description of victims' vulnerabilities. In addition, less involved pro-aggressor bystanders held a more favourable perception of the victimized students, as compared to students who were supportive reinforcers of youth who bullied, who sustain the typical stereotyped image of the victim.

Descriptives of victim characterization according to self-reported experience as provictim bystander

Factors	Independent variable Self-reported experience	N	Mean	SD	F	Sig.
1. Typified description of the victim	Never	97	36.46	7.91	5.640	.001
	A few times	163	38.08	7.85		
	Sometimes	326	38.75	6.82		
	Very often/Always	638	39.45	7.18		
	Total	1224	38.85	7.28		
2. Stereotyped description of the victim	Never	98	9.43	4.78	11.693	.000
	A few times	163	9.71	4.63		
	Sometimes	326	10.31	4.36		
	Very often/Always	637	11.49	4.80		
	Total	1224	10.78	4.73		

Descriptives of victim characterization according to self-reported experience proaggressor bystander

Factors	Independent variable Self-reported experience	N	Mean	SD	F	Sig.
1. Typified description of the victim	Never	705	39.91	6.62	18.689	.000
	A few times	255	38.33	7.09		
	Sometimes	165	37.65	7.03		
	Very often/Always	99	34.63	10.22		
	Total	1224	38.85	7.28		
2. Stereotyped description of the victim	Never	705	11.45	4.69	11.989	.000
	A few times	255	9.93	4.38		
	Sometimes	165	9.56	4.48		
	Very often/Always	99	10.17	5.41		
	Total	1224	10.78	4.73		

Discussion

This study investigated perceived characteristics of youth victimized by peer bullying in a sample of adolescents from two southern European countries. Following several international reports claiming that bullying is a worldwide phenomenon, it continues to be important to provide data from different societies and cultural backgrounds. Moreover, the present study provides a critical reflection of explanations of peer bullying and reinforces the importance of examining it from a relationship perspective. Focusing upon the perceived characteristics of victimized peers, the main goal was to inspect how descriptions of victimized students varied according to participants' own roles in bullying (whether aggressive, victimized, or a bystander) in bullying interactions. This chapter is the first report of part of a larger project investigating attitudes of youth involved in a range of participant roles. In this paper, we articulate our theoretical framework and describe the first findings regarding perceived characteristics of victimized youth according to their nonvictimized and victimized peers.

There has been substantial interest in research on bullying in adolescence. A strong argument for the attention devoted to this age period derives from developmental studies on peer relationships. In particular, it has been assumed that peer bullying can be especially damaging to adolescents, when failure to fit into the peer group may symbolize a failure to master a critical developmental task (Lease, McFall & Viken, 2003). Wondering about their similarities and dissimilarities with others in and out of the peer group typically consumes a good deal of adolescents' daily experiences (Rubin et al., 1998). Furthermore, to perceive oneself as possessing characteristics that others find awkward induces concerns about peer acceptance and self-adequacy which, in the case of victimized adolescents, can reinforce the behaviour of aggressive youth (Perry, Kusel & Perry, 1988; Perry et al., 1990). A concern for the consequences of victimized students' behaviour has led many researchers to investigate the individual characteristics of children who are targets of their peers' aggressive acts (for a review, see Almeida, 2006). In the present research, we broaden the lens to examine how peer perceptions of victimized youth may contribute to bullying problems.

Another reason to study youth who are victimized by their peers lies in the controversial opinion that victimized children can become aggressive by identifying with the children who bullied them (unconscious defence mechanism) or by transferring aggressive feelings or retaliating against the more vulnerable. The potential for transformation from victimized to victimizer calls for a broader focus of study extending the individual perspective to include an interpersonal and a relational point of view – a more integrative psychological paradigm. Despite the claim that victimization cannot be accounted for by victimized students' behavioural or nonbehavioural characteristics, the fact is that too often the victims are sanctioned (Sweeting & West, 2001). This issue is particularly relevant during adolescence. Both self-definitional concerns of typical adolescents, as well as the increased preoccupation regarding their social image ("how others see me") introduce extra risk factors for those who have earlier experiences of rejection or other difficulties in their peer relations. Even in the presence of different coping strategies and envisioning their adaptive outcomes, individual differences do not explain victimization histories. Victimization, whether experienced, observed, or enacted is an experience that is socially shared. In this line of reasoning, perceptions of bullying and peer reputations are mutually informing and constitutive elements of experiences and representations. Exploring different perspectives associated with different roles will contribute to understanding the co-construction of the interpersonal experiences and meaning within bullying interactions.

The present study highlights the importance of understanding bullying from multiple perspectives. Although the majority of boys and girls in our sample were assigned to a bystander role and, consequently, reported that they had not experienced bullying on a regular basis, a smaller number did report having experience being victimized or being aggressive, with equal distribution in each role. Thus, the set of descriptions of characteristics of victimized students reflect the social perceptions of adolescents in these three subgroups. Our findings revealed the social image of a passive victimized youth, whose perceived vulnerability consists mainly of a shy, fearful, fragile nature, coupled with a sensitive, compliant, quiet and humble personality. Although this characterization is somewhat consistent with the public stereotype of the passive victimized youth, it is far from being highly discriminative or negative. Whereas shyness and fearful might denote that these perceptions focus on an insecure and anxious socioemotional pattern, other attributes such as "boring" and "nerd", or even "dumb" associated with incompetence and deviance were not strongly endorsed. Besides, about 80% of the adolescents perceived the victim as "kind" and a "good person", indicating that their underlying attitude is favourable and reflects empathy towards the victimized peer. In other words, this attitude aligns with an appropriate social orientation that, unless challenged, peers will continue to verbalize. This commentary should not be interpreted as a criticism, but as a widely observed trend.

Sympathy and friendly attitudes towards victimized peers apparently gather high consensus among adolescents, but at the same time, their ethical concerns are not coupled with action. It is undoubtedly less attractive to act in support of victimized students. According to Salmivalli (2001), 60 to 70% of students do nothing to stop bullying. Regardless of the emphasis within prevention programs to encourage enlistment of defenders of victimized peers, it is important to be aware of these numbers and to be conscious about the relative ease of considering bullying an ethical and moral issue. Particularly in adolescence, challenging and promoting anti-bullying attitudes have to go beyond enrolling defenders.

Within the present study, reported differences with age and gender showed that the perceived vulnerability of victimized students is accentuated as adolescents grow older and that boys have a more critical attitude towards victimized peers compared to girls. These findings are not surprising in themselves, but again evoke self-definitional issues which reflect a concept of "manliness". In addition, there are salient implications for boys whenever bullying takes more overt expressions. Other findings allow us to extend our reflections about the transactional relations of interpersonal perceptions. The reported data are extremely consistent across the two conditions. Peer nominations and self-reported experience point in the same direction: Peer ratings and experience as an aggressive adolescent are linked to less favourable and increased vulnerability in perceptions of victimized students, whereas bystanders and other adolescents having experienced or being peer-rated as victimized youth held less stereotyped perceptions.

In conclusion, finding explanations for bullying are an ongoing challenge to research, but the research is essential to provide direction for prevention and intervention strategies. The findings of the present study raise a number of controversial issues about human nature, and the function and manifestations of aggression in development, and they collide with a complex puzzle of educational approaches. Responses to bullying have not always been grounded in a research evidence basis. In bullying and victimization research, for instance, the different disciplines offer a vast array of descriptions about "what is bullying", "which children are perpetrators and targets of bullying behaviour", "what are its psychological and health consequences", "how can it be prevented", etc. This information generates debates which have influenced the ideas of teachers, parents, experts, and others, in turn influencing intervention programs and attitudes towards the involved children and youth.

However, information is not enough to dismantle beliefs and attitudes which are sometimes opposed to action and resistant to change. Myths and misconceptions can have insidious effects in dealing with peer victimization issues. Sullivan (2000) examined a number of these 'long-standing truths' to discuss their underlying justifications. A rather common and particularly dangerous myth stresses that bullying is character-building, suggesting that it is victimized youths' fault if they are bullied because they should stand up for themselves. While this and other similar beliefs accentuate the vulnerability of victimized youths, objectivity in science is far from socially innocuous.

Chapter 1: Towards a Relational Perspective of Peer Bullying

Key Messages

1. Concerns about fitting in, belonging and social image ("how others see me") are normal concerns of adolescence that easily become problematic for vulnerable adolescents due to earlier difficulties in their peer relationships. It is helpful to understand that vulnerability arises from social interpersonal mechanisms and group processes, rather than from individual characteristics. Therefore, these interpersonal mechanisms and group processes should be the target of bullying prevention efforts.

2. Sympathetic and friendly attitudes towards victimized peers are apparently held by adolescents, but at the same time, these attitudes are not coupled with action. From the adolescent bystander's perspective, it is clearly not attractive to act in support of victimized peers. Different beliefs, shared group-norms, friendship ties, and affective bonds with victimized peers can either promote moral engagement or moral disengagement. In particular, the beliefs that bullying is character-building and that it is "none of my business" mixed with the emotion of fear explain why bullying remains unchallenged.

3. Victimization, whether experienced, observed, or enacted is an experience that is socially shared. Exploring different perspectives associated with different roles in natural peer groups can be pursued if adolescents feel comfortable to talk and reflect out loud about their own or others' experiences. Challenging opinions and bridging perspective in a collective conversation can provide tools to dismantle stereotypes about the different participant roles in bullying relationships.

References

Almeida, A. (2006). *Para além das tendências normativas: o que aprendemos com o estudo dos maus tratos entre pares. [Beyond normative tendencies: what we learn from the study of bullying.]* Psychologica, 43, 79-104.

Almeida, A. & Caurcel, M. (2005). *Questionário Scan-Bullying. Versão Portuguesa e Castelhana. [Scan-Bullying Questionnaire. Portuguese and Spanish versions.]* Registo de obra na Inspecção-Geral das Actividades Culturais, Ministério da Cultura.

Almeida, A., del Barrio, C., Marques, M., Fernández, I., Gutiérrez, H. & Cruz, J. (2001). *A script-cartoon narrative of peer-bullying in children and adolescents.* In M. Martínez (Ed.), *Prevention and control of aggression and its impact on its victims* (pp. 161-168). New York: Kluwer Academic/ Plenum Publishers.

Alsaker, F. D. & Olweus, D. (1992). *Stability of self-esteem in early adolescence: A cohort longitudinal study.* Journal of Research on Adolescence, 2,123-145.

Baldwin, J. M. (1897). *Social and ethical interpretations in mental development.* New York: Macmillan.

Baldwin, J. M. (1906). *Mental development in the child and the race* (3rd ed.). New York: Kelley.

Boivin, M., Hymel, S. & Hodges, E. V. E. (2001). *Toward a process view of peer rejection and harassment.* In J. Juvonen & S. Graham (Eds.), *Peer Harrassment in School: The Plight of the Vulnerable and Victimized* (pp. 265 - 309). New York: The Guilford Press.

Bretherton, I., & Munholland, K. A. (1999). *Internal working models in attachment relationships: A construct revisited.* In J. Cassidy & P. R. Shaver (Eds.), *Handbook of attachment: Theory, research, and clinical applications* (pp. 89 – 111). New York: Guilford.

Carlson, E., A. Sroufe, L. A. & Egeland, B. (2004). *The Construction of Experience: A Longitudinal Study of Representation and Behavior.* Child Development, 75, 1, 66 – 83.

Cerezo, F. (2000). Bull-S. *Test de evaluación de la agresividad entre escolares. [Bull-S. Test for evaluating aggressiveness among schoolchildren.]* Madrid: Albor-Cohs.

Del Barrio, C., Almeida, A., van der Meulen, K., Barrios, A. & Gutiérrez, H. (2003). *Representaciones acerca del maltrato entre iguales, atribuciones emocionales y percepción de estrategias de cambio a partir de un instrumento narrativo: SCAN-Bullying. [Representations about bullying, emotional attributions and change strategies, based on a narrative instrument: SCAN- Bullying.]* Infancia y Aprendizaje, 26, 63-78.

DeRosier, M. E., Cillessen, A. H. N., Coie, J. D., & Dodge, K. A. (1994). *Group context and children's aggressive behavior*. Child Development, 65, 1068-1079.

Hartup, W. W. (1983). *Peer relations*. In E. M. Hetherington (Ed.) & P. H. Mussen (Series Ed.), *Handbook of child psychology: Vol. 4. Socialization, personality, and social development* (pp. 103-196). New York: Wiley.

Hartup, W.W. (1996). *The company they keep: friendships and their developmental significance*. Child Development, 67, 1-13.

Hymel, S., Wagner, E. & Butler, L. J. (1990). *Reputational bias: View from the peer group*. In S. R. Asher & J. D. Coie (Eds.), *Peer rejection in childhood* (pp. 156-186).New York: Cambridge University Press.

Hymel, S., Woody, E., Bowker, A. (1993). *Social withdrawal in childhood: considering the child's perspective*. In K. H .Rubin & J. B. Asendorpf (Eds.), *Social withdrawal, inhibition, and shyness in childhood* (pp.237-264). Hillsdale, NJ.: Lawrence Erlbaum.

Kochenderfer-Ladd, B. (2003). *Identification of Aggressive and Asocial Victims and the Stability of Their Peer Victimization*. Merrill-Palmer Quarterly, 49, 4, 401

Laursen, B. (2005). *Dyadic and group perspectives on close relationships*. International Journal of Behavioral Development, 29, 2, 97-100.

Lease, A. M., McFall, R.M. & Viken, R.J. (2003). *Distance From Peers in the Group's Perceived Organizational Structure: Relation to Individual Characteristics*. Journal of Early Adolescence, 23, 2, 194-217

Mead, G. H. (1925). *The genesis of the self and social control*. International Journal of Ethics, 35, 251-277.

Mead, G. H. (1934). *Mind, self, and society from the standpoint of a social behaviorist*. Chicago: University of Chicago Press.

Mellor, A. (1999). Scotland . In Smith, P., Morita, Y., Junger-Tas, J. Olweus, D. Catalano, R. & Slee, P. (Eds) *The Nature of School Bullying: A cross national perspective* (pp.91-111). London: Routledge.

Moscovici, S. (1981). *On social representation*. In J. P. Forgas (Ed.), *Social Cognition*. London: Academic Press.

Naylor, P. Granizo, L., Tantam, D. & Deurzen, E. (2005). *Bullying of secondary school pupils with Asperger syndrome/high functioning autism (AS/HFA): a pilot study.* Poster presented at the XII European Conference on Developmental Psychology, Tenerife, August, 24-28.

Olweus, D. (1978). *Aggression in the Schools: Bullies and whipping boys.* Washington DC: Hemisphere.

Olweus, D. (1993). *Victimization by peers: antecedents and long-term outcomes*. In K. Rubin & J. Asendorpf (Eds.), Social withdrawal, inhibition, and shyness in childhood (pp. 315-342). Hilldsdale, NJ: Erlbaum.

Ortega y Gasset, J. (1983). *Obras Completas, Vol. 1-12. [Complete Works, Vol. 1-12]*. Madrid: Alianza Editorial.

Osgood, C. E., Suci, C. J. & Tannenbaum, P. H. (1957). *The measurement of meaning*. Urbana, Ill.: University of Illinois Press.

Pepler, D. J. & Craig, W.(2006). *Introduction to Prevnet Pillars*. Keynote oral presentation at PREVNet First International Conference, Ottawa, Ontario, May, 25 – 26.

Pepler, D. J., Craig, W. & O'Connell, P. (1996). *Understanding bullying and victimization from a dynamic systems perspective*. In A. Slater & d. Muir (Eds.), Developmental Psychology: An advanced reader (pp. 441-451). London: Blackwell.

Perry, D., Williard, J. & Perry, L. (1990). *Peers' perceptions of the consequences that victimized children provide aggressors*. Child Development, 61, 1310-25.

Perry, D.G., Kusel, S. J. & Perry, L.C. (1988). *Victims of peer aggression*, Developmental Psychology, 24, 807-814.

Rivers, I. (2001). *The bullying of sexual minorities at school: Its nature and long-term correlates*. Educational and Child Psychology, 18, 32–46.

Robinson, W. P. (1996). *Social groups & identities. Developing the legacy of Henry Tafel*. Oxford: Butterworth-Heinemann.

Robson, C (1993). *Real World Research: A resource for social scientists and practitioner researchers*. Blackwell. Oxford.

Rubin, K. D., Bukowski, W. M. & Parker, J. G. (1998). *Peer interactions, relationships and groups*. In W. Damon & N. Eisenberg (Eds.), Handbook of child psychology: Vol.3, Social and emotional development (pp. 619-700). Wiley, New York,.

Salmivalli, C. (1998). *Not only bullies and victims. Participation in harassment in school classes: some social and personality factors*. Humaniora, Annales Universitatis Turkuensis, 7-37.

Salmivalli, C. (2001). *Group view on victimization. Empirical findings and their implications*. In J. Juvonen & S. Graham (Eds.), Peer harassment in school. The plight of the vulnerable and victimized (398-420). Guilford: New York.

Salmivalli, C., Lagerspetz, K., Björkqvist, K., Österman, K. & Kaukiainen, A. (1996). *Bullying as a group process: Participant roles and their relations to social status within the group*. Aggressive Behavior, 22, 1-15.

Siann, G., Callaghan, M., Glissov, P., Lockhart, R. And Rawson, L. (1994). *Who gets bullied? The effect of school, gender and ethnic group*, Educational Research, 36, 123 - 34.

Smith, P. (2004). *Bullying: Recent Developments. Child and Adolescent Mental Health*, 9, 3, 98–103.

Sullivan, H. S. (1953). *The interpersonal theory of psychiatry*. New York: Norton.

Sullivan, K., (2000). *The anti-bullying handbook*. Oxford University Press.

Sweeting, H. & West, P. (2001). *Being different: correlates of the experience of teasing and bullying at age 11*, Research Papers in Education 16, 3, 225 – 246.

Tajfel, H. (1978). *European Monographs in Social Psychology: Differentiation between social groups. Vol. 14*. London: Academic Press.

Tattum, D. (1989). *Violence and aggression in schools*. In Tattum, D. & Lane, D. (Eds) Bullying in Schools. Stoke on Trent: Trentham.

Tattum, D. (1997). *A whole-school response: from crisis management to prevention*, Irish Journal of Psychology, 18, 221 - 32.

Vaillancourt, T., McDougall, P., Hymel, S. & Welch, E. (2001). *A comprehensive profile of peer victimized adolescent and their oppressors*. Poster presented at the X European conference on Developmental Psychology, August, 22-26.

Chapter 2:
___

New Directions in Research and Practice Addressing Bullying: Focus on Defending Behaviour

Virpi Pöyhönen[1] and Christina Salmivalli[1,2]
[1] Department of Psychology, University of Turku, Finland
[2] Centre for Behavioural Research, University of Stavanger, Norway

Background: Bullying in Finland

In Finland, approximately 5-15% of students are repeatedly victimized by their peers at school. Self-reported victimization is more frequent in primary than in secondary schools. The School Health Promotion Study is conducted each year in Finnish secondary schools by the National Research and Development Centre for Welfare and Health (www.stakes.fi). There are more than 75,000 respondents yearly. The results of the survey show that during the past ten years, there has been no change in the frequency of victimized students, at least at the secondary school level. Figures 1a-1c show the frequencies of students who report being victimized once a week or more, students who bully others once a week or more , and students who are never involved in bullying others. Although the frequencies of victimized students (1a) and those who bully others (1b) are very stable, we can see a slight increase in the frequency of students (especially boys) who report not being involved in bullying others at all (1c).

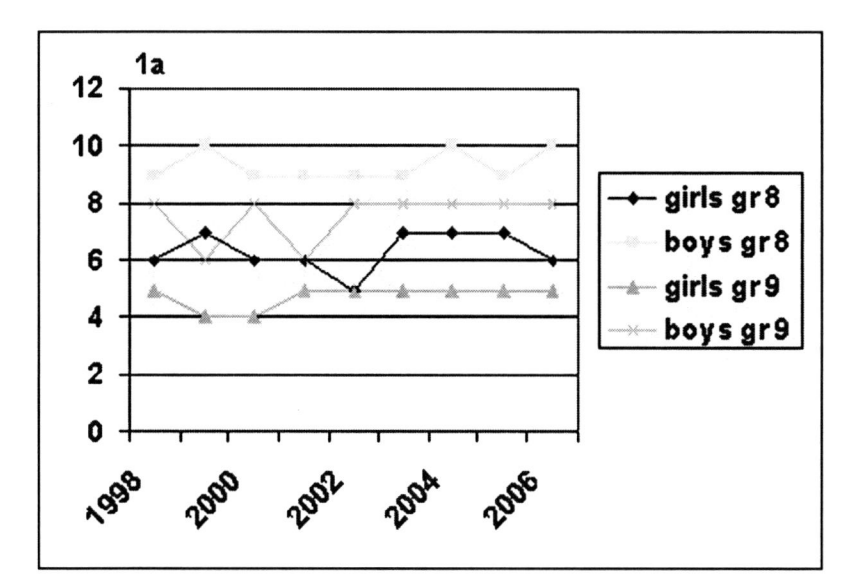

Chapter 2: New Directions in Research and Practice Addressing Bullying

Percentages of Finnish eighth- and ninth-graders who reported being bullied once a week or more often (1a), bullying others once a week or more often (1b), and of those "never" bullying others (1c) during 1998-2006.

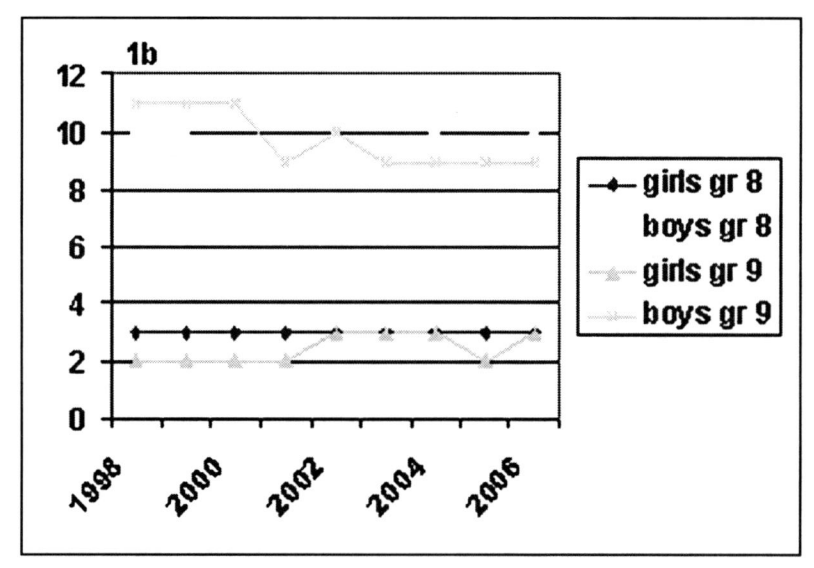

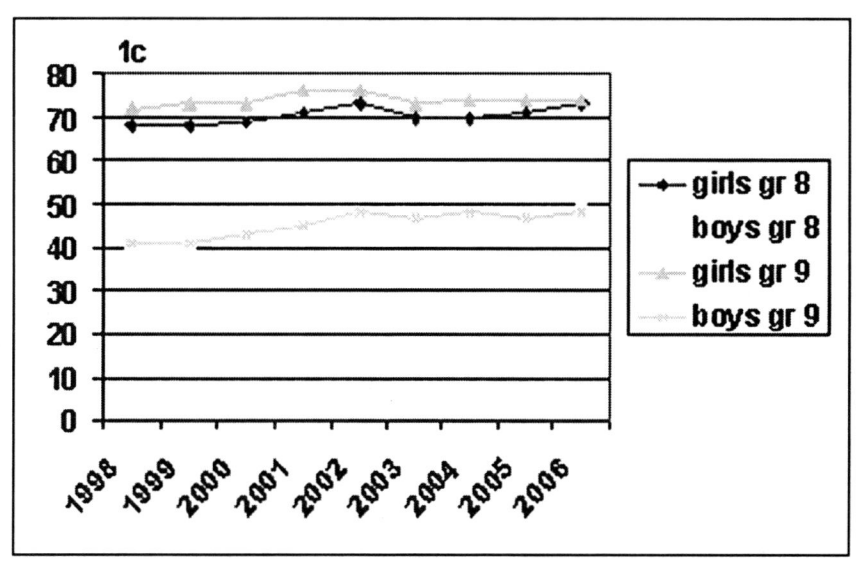

Since the beginning of the 1990's, there has been a lot of public attention to bullying and victimization in Finland. There have been changes in legislation concerning school safety and the development of bullying prevention policies at schools. For instance, the Finnish Basic Education Act (since 1999) states that every student has the right to a safe school environment. Education providers have the responsibility of making sure that students do not experience acts of violence or bullying while at school. The legislation concerns all educational levels. It was further amended in 2003, stating that "the education provider shall draw up a plan, in connection with curriculum design, for safeguarding pupils against violence, bullying and harassment, execute the plan and supervise adherence to it and its implementation". Finally, the amendments of the Comprehensive School Act (453/2001) and the Senior School Education Act (454/2001) introduced health education as an independent subject in schools. One goal of health education is to "foster physical, mental and social health and well-being and the students' acquisition of good manners. The students shall be educated in responsibility and co-operation and activities that pursue tolerance and trust among ethnic groups, peoples and cultures. The education also shall promote growing up as responsible members of society and provide capabilities to function in a democratic and equal society as well as uphold sustainable growth."

In addition to public attention and legislative changes, several local initiatives to address bullying have been carried out during the past ten years - only few of these interventions have been evaluated, however (for examples, see Koivisto, 2004; Salmivalli, Kaukiainen, & Voeten, 2005). What has been missing so far is a national strategy, or a large-scale intervention program, widely implemented in Finnish schools. In the fall of 2006 the Finnish Ministry of Education made a contract with the University of Turku concerning a development of such a program for national use. Prior to describing this program, we will introduce some of the recent research findings that are – among other relevant literature – guiding the development of the program.

The Group View on Bullying

Bullying research in Finland has very much been concerned with a group view on the phenomenon. Already in the 1980s, Lagerspetz and colleagues (Lagerspetz, Björkqvist, Berts, & King, 1982) defined bullying as group aggression, based on the social relationships between the members of the school class. In the next decade, Salmivalli, Lagerspetz, Björkqvist, Österman and Kaukiainen (1996) focused on the question: "What do the other students do, when the bully is harassing the victim?" They started a series of studies with the focus on so-called participant roles in bullying. Utilizing a peer-report questionnaire, they identified six different participant roles children may have in the bullying process (victims, bullies, assistants of bullies, reinforcers of bullies, outsiders, and defenders of the victim)[2]. Since then, a bulk of studies from various countries (Andreou & Metallidou, 2004; Camodeca & Goossens, 2005; Goossens, Olthof & Dekker, 2006; Menesini,

---

[2] The latest version of the questionnaire consist of 15 + 3 (for victimization) items, which are available from the authors.

Codecasa, Benelli & Cowie, 2003; Salmivalli, Kaukiainen, Kaistaniemi & Lagerspetz, 1999; Salmivalli et al., 1996; Salmivalli, Lappalainen & Lagerspetz, 1998; Salmivalli & Voeten, 2004; Schäfer & Korn, 2004; Sutton & Smith, 1999) have indicated that many students act in ways that maintain bullying problems. Even if not actually bullying others, they may, for instance, assist the child who is bullying, or reinforce the bullying behaviour by laughing along or cheering. Some students tend to silently witness what is happening or stay outside the situation. Fortunately a reasonable number of students also defend and support their victimized peers. In addition to direct intervening in bullying situations, defending behaviour involves comforting the victimized child and telling the teacher about bullying. According to the Finnish studies utilizing peer-reports of each child's behaviour, the frequency of students in the defender role is around 17-20% among sixth to eighth graders.

Observational studies have also shown that many peers are present in bullying situations, and yet they seldom intervene. Hawkins, Pepler and Craig (2001), for instance, discovered in their observational study that peers were present in 88% of all bullying episodes but tried to intervene in only 19% of cases. Similarly, the study by O'Connell, Pepler, and Craig (1999) showed that peers actively reinforced the child who was bullying 53.7% of the time in each bullying segment and supported the victimized child only 25.4% of the time. It seems that the presence of classmates is more likely to maintain the bullying interaction instead of ending it.

What would happen if peers intervened more frequently? Hawkins and colleagues (2001) discovered that when peers intervened, 57% of their efforts were actually successful in stopping the bullying episode. In addition, it should be considered that even if the peer intervention was not successful in ending the bullying, the support received from classmates is very likely to make the victimized child feel better. Thus, if peers are part of the problem, they can also be an important part of the solution. We therefore consider the mobilization of the peer group as a key element in bullying interventions.

Who are the defenders?

The roles of children involved in bullying and/or being victimized have been extensively studied for decades, beginning with the pioneering work of Olweus (1973; 1978). However, we know almost nothing about factors explaining involvement in the other participant roles. Recently, in our research group, there has been a growing attention to the defender role. If we want to engage more children in supporting victimized children and taking sides with them, we must know more about factors associated with such behaviours.

It should be noted that most children hold attitudes that are against bullying (i.e., they think it is not right) and that are supportive of victimized children (i.e., they know it is right to support the victimized child or to tell the teacher if someone is being bullied) (Boulton, Trueman & Flemington, 2002; Rigby & Johnson, 2006; Rigby & Slee, 1991; Whitney & Smith, 1993). Likewise, after watching bullying episodes on a video, 48% of the students reported that they would defend the victimized student if they were in that situation (Rigby & Johnson, 2006). There seems to be a disconnect – something prevents children from defending their bullied peers even if they think that it would be the right thing to do and have intentions of doing so.

There are sex differences in attitudes towards victimized children: Girls tend to feel even more sympathy towards those who are victimized than boys (Rigby & Slee, 1991). Similarly, the study by Rigby and Johnson (2006) showed that in primary school, girls tended to be more ready to support the victimized children than boys. The gender differences found in attitudes seem to hold for actual behaviours as well. Several studies have found that girls tend to engage in defending behaviour more than boys (Goossens et al., 2006; Menesini et al., 2003; Salmivalli, Kaukiainen, Kaistaniemi & Lagerspetz, 1999; Salmivalli et al., 1996; Salmivalli, Lappalainen & Lagerspetz, 1998; Salmivalli & Voeten, 2004, Sutton & Smith, 1999). For instance, in the study by Salmivalli and colleagues (1996), only 4.5% of the sixth-grade boys were identified as defenders of victimized students, while 30.1% of the girls were assigned this role. These findings are not surprising in the light of studies showing that girls are generally more empathic and engage in prosocial behaviours more often than boys (for a recent review, see Rose & Rudolph, 2006).

Age is another relevant factor. When students grow older their anti-bullying attitudes decrease. Rigby and Slee (1991) found in their study that along with age, students' attitudes towards victimized youth became less supportive, at least up to age 16. Also, as compared to early secondary school pupils, primary school students appear to be more ready to defend children who are bullied (Rigby & Johnson, 2006). Salmivalli and Voeten (2004) provided similar evidence in their study of fourth, fifth, and sixth-graders. Both anti-bullying attitudes and anti-bullying norms decreased when children entered preadolescence. Similarly, actual defending behaviour decreases as a function of age (Salmivalli & Voeten, 2004).

Personality traits also have been associated with defending victimized children; defenders tend to be more friendly, and have higher levels of emotional stability than pro-bullies (bullies, assistants, and reinforcers) (Tani, Greenman, Schneider, & Fregoso, 2003). Defending also has been associated with high scores in affective empathy, but it is not related to cognitive empathy (Caravita, DiBlasio, & Salmivalli, in press).

Andreou and Metallidou (2004) studied the association between different academic and social cognitions and self-reported behaviour in bullying situations in a sample of preadolescents. Both academic cognitions (self-efficacy for learning and performance) and social cognitions (self-efficacy for assertion) failed to predict defending behaviours. Along with these findings, Rigby and Johnson (2006) found that perceived self-efficacy did not predict intentions to intervene in bullying situations. There were other attributes related to defending, however: Children who had rarely or never bullied others, had previously intervened, had positive attitude towards victimized peers, or believed that their parents and friends expected them to support victimized children were more willing to intervene in bullying situations.

Overall, the participant roles have proved to be quite stable, but the role of defender does not seem to show as strong consistency as other participant roles (Salmivalli et al., 1998), suggesting that it might be determined by contextual factors as well. Actually, the strongest predictor for defending behaviour in the eighth grade was the friends' tendency to defend victimized peers, i.e. students whose current friends defended the victim also tended to do so themselves.

Classrooms differed from each other in how much the students in each class tend to side with the victimized student(s). Whereas students' attitudes towards bullying predict behaviour at the individual level, classroom norms predict variation in defending behaviour at the classroom level (Salmivalli & Voeten, 2004). Class context seems to predict girls' engagement even more strongly than that of boys.

Also students' social status within the peer group is associated with defending victimized peers. The defenders are usually well liked among their classmates (Goossens et al., 2006; Schäfer, 2004; Salmivalli et al., 1996). In an Italian sample of both primary and secondary school students (Caravita et al., in press), it was found that defending behaviour was related to social preference in both age groups. In addition, it was associated with perceived popularity among the primary school children.

In a sample of almost 500 fourth- and eighth-graders, we have just conducted preliminary analyses regarding the individual and group-level factors associated with assisting and reinforcing children who bully, withdrawing from bullying situations, and defending the bullied student(s). When controlling for the other behaviours, each way of participating in bullying has its unique correlates. When it comes to defending behaviour, we have found it to be associated with being well-liked, being admired, being perceived as popular, having many friends, not being alone, doing well at school, being well-known, co-operating, having communal (prosocial) goals, and with getting what one wants. Furthermore, defending is even related to looking good and being good at sports! In other words, students who defend their bullied peers are described in very positive terms by their classmates – this in itself might be an important message to children and adolescents.

A Study on Social Cognitive Factors Behind Defending Victimized Peers

Although there are some hints about the factors associated with defending behaviours, a great deal remains unknown. We have recently started to examine some social cognitive associates of defending, namely, self-efficacy beliefs and outcome expectations. *Self-efficacy beliefs* are defined as "beliefs in one's capability to organize and execute the courses of action required to manage prospective situations" (Bandura, 1997). These beliefs are context-specific in their nature: self-efficacy thus refers to one's self-perceived ability to perform a specific act in a specific situation (i.e., perceived ability to support and defend the victim of bullying). They influence, for instance, the choices people make, the amount of effort spent on an activity, and the maintenance of the action when facing obstacles. Self-efficacy beliefs also affect the amount of stress and anxiety individuals experience when performing certain tasks.

Research indicates that self-efficacy beliefs are associated with behaviour. For instance, children's self-efficacy for aggression is related to aggressive behaviour (Perry, Perry & Rasmussen, 1986) and bullying (Andreou, Vlachou & Didaskalou, 2005), whilst self-efficacy for assertiveness is associated with lower scores in physical victimization (Andreou et al., 2005). In adult samples interpersonal self-efficacy (i.e., individuals' perception of how well they are able to handle their relationships effectively) has been found to be related to prosocial behaviour (Caprara & Steca, 2005) and self-efficacy for helping is associated with higher scores in helping behaviour (George, Carroll, Kersnick, & Calderon, 1998). Quite surprisingly, the latter study also indicated that although women were more engaged in helping behaviours, they did not feel more efficacious than men in relation to such behaviours.

Outcome expectations *are* "judgments of the likely consequences that behaviour will produce" (Bandura 1986). They are considered to be independent from self-efficacy beliefs and therefore should make an independent contribution to the prediction of behaviour. Studies have provided evidence that outcome expectations are associated with behaviour: For instance, positive outcome expectations for aggression are associated with higher levels of aggressive behaviour (Perry et al., 1986).

In our study, we were interested specifically in self-efficacy beliefs for defending and supporting those victimized by bullying and the outcome expectations students had concerning these behaviours. In addition we were interested whether these cognitions predicted actual behaviour in bullying situations. More specifically, we examined:

1. Sex and age differences in efficacy beliefs and outcome expectations regarding defending behaviour in bullying situations.

2. Whether self-efficacy beliefs and outcome expectations are related to behaviour in bullying situations (defending and supporting victimized peers, staying outside bullying situations, or reinforcing the bullying).

Participants

The target sample consisted of all fourth and eight graders (N=563) from a small sized town (approximately 20,000 inhabitants) in south-west Finland. Originally 517 students filled in the questionnaires, but 6 were excluded from the analysis due to excessive missing data. Thus, the final sample included 511 students (271 girls and 240 boys) from the fourth (M=10.6 years, n=293) and eight grades (M=14.6 years, n=218) from 25 school classes. Subsequently we excluded students who were evaluated by less than five classmates from all analyses involving peer reports. Consequently, the sample size in these analyses was 481.

Measures

Behaviour in bullying situations (defending victimized peers, staying outside of bullying situations, or reinforcing the bullying) was assessed by nine peer report items from the 15-item version of the Participant Role Questionnaire (PRQ) (Salmivalli & Voeten, 2004). These nine items constitute the defender, outsider, and reinforcer scales. The participants read the items and marked (with an "X") in a class roster, which ones of their same-sex classmates engaged in each behaviour in situations of bullying. They were allowed to mark an unlimited number of same-sex classmates for each item.

Defender scale (álpha = .89) consists of three items describing behaviours indicative of defending and supporting the child who is victimized in bullying situations: "Tries to make the others stop bullying"; "Comforts the victim or encourages him/her to tell the teacher about the bullying"; "Tells the others to stop bullying or says that bullying is stupid". Outsider scale (álpha = .85) consists of three items describing behaviours indicative of staying outside or withdrawing from bullying situations: "Stays outside the situation;" "Is usually not present;" "Doesn't take sides with anyone". Reinforcer scale (álpha = .75) consists of three items describing behaviours indicative of reinforcing the child who is bullying: "Comes around to see the situation;" "Laughs;" "Incites the student who is bullying by shouting or by saying: Show him/her!" For each scale, the total number of nominations received by each student was summed up and divided by the number of peers doing the evaluation. Scale scores were created by averaging across the three items on each scale.

Efficacy beliefs and outcome expectations with respect to defending were assessed by self reports. To assess self-efficacy beliefs for defending behaviour students were asked to evaluate on a three-item scale how easy or difficult it would be for them to defend the victim of bullying (e.g., Trying to make the others stop the bullying would be (0 = very easy… 3 = very difficult) for me.) The items were drawn from the PRQ items describing the defending behaviour. Answers were reverse coded, so that higher self-efficacy scores indicated higher self-efficacy for defending. Scores were averaged across three items, with three being the highest possible score. Internal consistency (Chronbach alpha) for the scale was .65.

Two scales were formed to measure outcome expectations: Positive outcome expectations (álpha = .82) were assessed by means of nine items measuring positive outcome expectations regarding the defending behaviours (e.g., If I would try to make the others stop the bullying, the bullying would end or decrease). The students evaluated how likely it would be for the consequence mentioned in each item to happen (0 = not likely at all… 3 = very likely). Similarly, the Negative Outcome Expectations scale (álpha = .84) consisted of means of nine items measuring negative outcome expectations regarding the defending behaviours (e.g., If I would try to make others stop bullying, the bullying would increase). The behaviours were again identical to the ones in the PRQ defender scale. The items for both positive and negative outcome expectations included expected outcomes for the victim (e.g., the victim would feel better / the victim would feel worse), for the self (e.g., I would be respected by others / I would be disliked and harassed, too), and for the occurrence of bullying (e.g., bullying would end or decrease / bullying would increase).

Results

Means and standard deviations of all study variables are displayed in Table 1. Overall the students reported feeling most efficacious to comfort victimized peers and to encourage them to tell the teacher about bullying. Altogether 73.6% of the students reported that it would be easy or very easy for them to comfort a victimized child, whereas only 4.3% reported it would be very difficult. The most difficult course of action was trying to make the others stop bullying, although 42.8 % of the students felt it would be easy or very easy. Concerning outcome expectations, students generally believed that defending would have more positive than negative consequences in all three outcome areas, for the victimized student, for the self, as well as for the occurrence of bullying. Similarly, the results of paired samples t-test in which all positive and all negative outcome expectations were treated as two separate scales indicated that overall, students expected more positive than negative consequences for defending behaviour (t(511)=28.87, p<.001. However, examination of the subscales reveals that most negative outcomes (being disliked and harassed) and least positive outcomes (being respected) were expected for the self (see Figure 2.). Interestingly, negative and positive outcome expectations concerning self were not correlated, which indicates that it was possible for a student to expect *both* positive and negative outcomes for themselves if they defended the victim. In contrast, negative and positive outcome expectations concerning occurrence of bullying, as well as the victims' feelings were negatively related to each other.

Means for positive and negative expectations regarding defending behaviour in three outcome areas.

Means and standard deviations for all study variables grouped by grade level and sex

	Fourth Grade		Eighth Grade	
Scale	M	SD	M	SD
Self-efficacy for defending				
Male	1.56	.57	1.58	.59
Female	1.73	.67	1.79	.63
Positive outcomes for defending				
Male	1.62	.61	1.50	.47
Female	1.76	.47	1.62	.45
Negative outcomes for defending				
Male	.70	.54	.71	.53
Female	.61	.46	.59	.48
Defending				
Male	.19	.18	.10	.11
Female	.25	.16	.22	.17
Staying outside				
Male	.24	.18	.32	.21
Female	.24	.14	.40	.19
Reinforcing				
Male	.18	.13	.28	.15
Female	.12	.09	.10	.12

Sex and grade differences for all study variables were evaluated by running a series of 2 (sex) x 2 (grade) ANOVAs. We found a significant sex difference for self-efficacy beliefs, $F(1,507) = 11.50$, $p < .01$, indicating that girls felt more efficacious to defend the victimized student(s) than boys. With respect to outcome expectations, girls expected more positive outcomes for defending than boys, $F(1,507) = 7.48$, $p < .01$. In contrast, boys were more likely to believe that defending would result in negative consequences than girls, F (1,507) = 5.08, p < .05. In addition, younger students anticipated more positive outcomes for defending behaviour than older students, F (1,507) = 8.20, p < .01. There were no significant sex by grade interactions for either self-efficacy beliefs or outcome expectations, indicating that the sex differences were similar in both age groups.

Associations Between Cognitions and Behaviour

The associations between social cognitions (self-efficacy for defending behaviour, positive and negative outcome expectations) and three types of behaviours in bullying situations (defending, staying outside, reinforcing the bully) were investigated by three separate hierarchical regression models. Sex and grade (step1), self-efficacy beliefs, and both negative and positive outcome expectations (step 2) were included as predictors in the model. For each model, one of the behaviours in bullying situations (defending, staying outside, reinforcing the bully) was entered as the dependent variable.

Grade and sex (step 1) explained 9 % of the variance in defending behaviour, ΔR^2 = .09, ΔF = 23.01, p < .001. Girls and younger students tended to defend the victimized peers more than boys and older students. At step 2, positive and negative outcome expectations did not have any significant effect on defending behaviour and those variables were removed from the model. However, after taking into account sex and grade effects reported above, self-efficacy added significantly to defending behaviour, ΔR^2 = .02, ΔF = 8.03, p < .01. The more efficacious the child felt regarding defending, the more likely he/she was to defend the victimized student(s), Beta = .12, p < .001.

Staying outside bullying situations was more typical for girls and older students than for boys and younger students, R^2 = .12, ΔF = 31.34, p <.001. At step 2, positive outcome expectations were removed from the model since they did not have any significant effect on tendency to stay out of bullying situations. However, self-efficacy and negative outcome expectations explained additional variance in staying outside the bullying situations ΔR^2 = .04, ΔF =11.42, p <.001. The effects of both efficacy beliefs (Beta = -.18, p < .001), and negative outcome expectations (Beta = -.14, p<.01) were negative. Thus, students who stayed outside lacked self-efficacy to defend the victimized peer(s), but they did not anticipate negative outcomes for defending.

Boys and older students tended to reinforce the student who is bullying more than girls and younger students, ΔR^2 = .16, ΔF = 45.46, p <.001. Again, positive outcome expectations did not have any significant effect on reinforcing behaviour and were removed from the model. However, efficacy beliefs (Beta = .13, p < .01) and negative outcome expectations (Beta = .18, p<.001) were both significant positive predictors of reinforcing behaviour, ΔR^2 = .04, ΔF =11.42, p<.001. Thus, students who felt efficacious to defend victimized peers, but expected negative consequences from defending were likely to reinforce the bullying.

Conclusions

Our results indicated that girls felt more efficacious to defend their bullied peers and also expected more positive outcomes from such behaviours than boys did. Boys expected more negative consequences for defending behaviour than girls. Eighth graders felt as efficacious to defend the victimized student(s) as fourth graders, but they expected less positive outcomes from defending behaviour than younger students. Overall, the participants had more positive than negative outcome expectations for defending victimized peer(s). Most negative outcomes were expected for self, however. It seems that students know that defending the victimized student would make a difference (positive outcome expectations), but many of them just don't have the courage to do it or don't know how to do it.

Overall, our findings regarding the sex difference in self-efficacy to defend differ from some previous studies (e.g., Andreou et al., 2005; Caprara & Steca, 2005) who did not find such a difference. Furthermore, some studies have failed to find an association between self-efficacy and defending (Andreou & Metallidou, 2004). One explanation might be the different context of self-efficacy studied. We focused specifically on *self-efficacy related to defending the victimized student*, whereas previous studies examined self-efficacy for assertion, or interpersonal self-efficacy.

In accordance with previous studies (Goossens et al., 2006; Menesini et al., 2003; Salmivalli et al., 1999; Salmivalli & Voeten, 2004), sex and age also predicted actual behaviours in bullying situations. Girls tended to defend the victim of bullying or stay outside bullying situations more than boys, while boys reinforced the bully more than girls. Younger students were more likely to defend the victimized peer(s) whilst older students tended to engage to behaviours which maintained the bullying (staying outside, reinforce the bullying child). All these findings suggest that bullying prevention programs might be more effective if initiated from a young age – this is the experience gained from several intervention studies as well (Smith, Pepler, & Rigby, 2004).

Both self-efficacy beliefs and negative outcome expectations predicted behaviours in bullying situations over and above the effects of age and gender. Students who tended to defend and support the victimized students(s) also felt more efficacious to do so. On the basis of our results, students who tend to stay outside bullying situations or reinforce bullying – the two groups that we might like to target in our peer group interventions – might have different obstacles for defending. Reinforcing the bullying was related to expecting negative outcomes for defending, whereas staying outside bullying situations was associated with low efficacy for defending.

Based on our findings we suggest that interventions should aim especially at providing students with skills and courage to intervene in bullying situations and to support victimized students. Our results indicate that while self-efficacy for defending and supporting the victimized peer(s) is an important individual factor that predicts behaviour in bullying situations, the outcomes students expect from such behaviour also contribute to their behaviour. Interestingly, negative outcome expectations predict behaviour more strongly than positive ones. In other words, students generally seem to believe that defending would have positive effects, but their behaviour is not guided by this belief, but rather by their expectations concerning possible negative outcomes. This discrepancy should also be taken into account in bullying prevention and interventions. There is still a pressing need for knowledge about other factors predicting defending behaviours. Furthermore, if girls' behaviour is more affected by group level factors those should also be taken into account in future research. Given the role of context, the effects of cognitions may vary from one school class to another, i.e., the context might moderate the influence of cognitions on behaviour. Finally, follow-up data are needed in order to distinguish the precursors of defending from the consequences of such behaviours.

The KiVa program

In the Finnish language, KiVa stands for "Kiusaamista Vastaan" or ``Against Bullying``, and it is the name of the new national bullying prevention program in Finland[3]. The development of the program, as well as the teacher education component and the program evaluation component, are financed by the Finnish Ministry of Education. The KiVa team works in the University of Turku and involves people from the Department of Psychology as well as from the Centre for Learning Research. The program is based on the latest research on bullying and victimization and it involves several unique features: 1. An exceptionally large variety of materials for students, teachers, and parents; 2. Utilizing the web and virtual learning environments, such as a computer game designed to discourage bullying; and 3. Emphasis on the bystanders, in order to encourage bystanders to show that they are against bullying and supportive of victimized students and to discourage bystanders from joining in the bullying.

Ten student lessons (one lesson each month, starting at the beginning of the school year in August) involve discussion, group work, short video clips, and role-play exercises. The themes go from inter-individual respect to bullying and its mechanisms and consequences. Several lessons concern the role of the group in either maintaining bullying or putting an end to it. The teacher education and materials provide the teachers with knowledge about best practices in handling acute bullying cases that come to their attention. We encourage the teachers in each school to form a team that deals with the acute cases as they arise, intervening in the behaviour of children who bully and also involving prosocial classmates who are encouraged to support the victimized child. Parents are provided with information about bullying and victimization and advice concerning strategies they can use to prevent these problems. The KiVa program utilizes

---

[3] Kiva also means something which is nice, jolly good, great, or cute

the virtual learning environment in several ways. Many of the core components of the program such as teacher materials, student lessons and exercises, and the anti-bullying computer game can be found in the web.

The role of bystanders is emphasized in the KiVa program. The ideology behind the program is thus very similar to a previous Finnish intervention study (Salmivalli, Kaukiainen, Voeten, & Sinisammal , 2004; Salmivalli, Kaukiainen, & Voeten, 2005), which has been one of the most effective ones studied to date (Smith, Schneider, Smith, & Ananiadou, 2004). This time, however, the program offers more concrete tools and a clearer schedule to be followed in the participating schools, as well as more systematic guidance for the teachers during the implementation. The teacher education has begun and the program was launched in the first 39 pilot schools in the fall of 2007. We believe it will have positive effects – among other things - on efficacy beliefs, outcome expectations, and group norms, all of which are ultimately expected to encourage students to take action against bullying. This way, the aims of the legislation we already have in Finland will actually become realized in our children's lives.

Key Messages

1. Bullying prevention is likely to be most effective when initiated when children are young.

2. Bullying is a group phenomenon. Mobilization of the peer group to support and defend victimized peers is crucial for successful bullying prevention and intervention.

3. Compared to students who do not, students who do defend victimized peers tend to feel more efficacious about their own defending behaviour. Therefore interventions should provide students with skills and strategies to increase feelings of competence about providing support to peers in need.

4. Students generally believe that defending would have positive effects. Their behaviour, however, is not guided by this belief, but rather by their beliefs about possible negative outcomes. This discrepancy should be taken into account in bullying prevention and interventions.

References

Andreou, E. & Metallidou, P. (2004). *The relationship of academic and social cognition to behaviour in bullying situations among greek primary school children.* Educational Psychology, 24, 27-41.

Andreou, E., Vlachou, A., & Didaskalou, E. (2005). *The roles of self-efficacy, peer interactions and attitudes in bully-victim incidents: Implications for intervention policy-practices.* School Psychology International, 26, 545-562.

Bandura, A. (1986). *Social foundations of thought and action: A social cognitive theory.* Englewood Cliffs, NJ: Prentice Hall.

Bandura, A. (1997). *Self-efficacy: The exercise of control.* New York: Freeman.

Boulton, M. J., Trueman, M., & Flemington, I. (2002). *Educational Associations between secondary school pupils' definitions of bullying, attitudes towards bullying, and tendencies to engage in bullying: Age and sex differences.* Educational Studies, 28, 353-370.

Camodeca, M. & Goossens, F.A. (2005). *Children's opinions on effective strategies to cope with bullying: The importance of bullying role and perspective.* Educational Research, 47, 93-105.

Caprara, G. V. & Steca, P. (2005). *Self-efficacy beliefs as determinants of prosocial behavior conducive to life satisfaction across ages.* Journal of Social & Clinical Psychology, 24, 191-217.

Caravita, S., DiBlasio, P., & Salmivalli, C. (In press). *Unique and interactive effects of empathy and social status on bullying, victimization, and defending the victim: are middle childhood and adolescence different?* Social Development.

George, D. M., Carroll, P., Kersnick, R. & Calderton, K. (1998). *Gender-related patterns of helping among friends.* Psychology of Women Quarterly, 22, 685-704.

Goossens, F.A., Olthof, T., & Dekker, P. H. (2006). *New participant role scales: comparison between various criteria for assigning roles and indications for their validity.* Aggressive Behavior, 32, 343-357.

Hawkins, D. L., Pepler, D. J., & Craig, W. M. (2001). *Naturalistic observations of peer interventions in bullying.* Social Development, 10, 512-527.

Koivisto, M. (2004). *A follow-up survey of anti-bullying interventions in the comprehensive schools of Kempele in 1990-98.* In P.Smith, D. Pepler, & K. Rigby (eds.), Bullying in schools: How successful can interventions be? NY: Cambridge UP, 235-249.

Lagerspetz, K., Björkqvist, K., Berts, M., & King, E. (1982). *Group aggression among school children in three schools.* Scandinavian Journal of Psychology, 23, 45-52.

Menesini, E., Codecasa, E., Benelli, B. & Cowie, H. (2003). *Enhancing children's responsibility to take action against bullying: Evaluation of a befriending intervention in Italian middle schools.* Aggressive Behavior, 29, 10-14.

National Research and Development Centre for Welfare and Health. (2007). www.stakes.fi

O'Connell, P., Pepler, D., & Craig, W., (1999). *Peer involvement in bullying: Insights and challenges for intervention.* Journal of Adolescence, 22, 437-452.

Olweus, D. (1973). *Hackkycklingar och översittare.* Stockhol: Almqvist & Wiksell.

Olweus, D. (1978). *Aggression in the schools: Bullies and whipping boys.* Washington, DC: Hemisphere (Wiley).

Perry, D. G., Perry, L. C., & Rasmussen, P. (1986). *Cognitive social learning mediators of aggression.* Child Development, 57, 700-711.

Rose, A. J. & Rudolph, K.D. (2006). *A review of sex differences in peer relationship processes: Potential trade-offs for the emotional and behavioral development of girls and boys.* Psychological Bulletin, 132, 98-131.

Rigby, K. & Johnson, B. (2006). *Expressed readiness of Australian schoolchildren to act as bystanders in support of children who are being bullied.* Educational Psychology, 26, 425-440.

Rigby, K., & Slee, P. T., (1991). *Bullying among Australian school children: Reported behavior and attitudes toward victims.* Journal of Social Psychology, 131, 615-627.

Salmivalli, C., Kaukiainen, A., Kaistaniemi, L. & Lagerspetz, K. (1999). *Self-evaluated self-esteem, peer-evaluated self-esteem, and defensive egotism as predictors of adolescents' participation in bullying situations.* Personality and Social Psychology Bulletin, 25, 1268-1278.

Salmivalli, C., Kaukiainen, A., & Voeten, M. (2005). *Anti-bullying intervention: implementation and outcome.* British Journal of Educational Psychology, 75, 465-487.

Salmivalli, C., Kaukiainen, A., Voeten, M., & Sinisammal, M. (2004). *Targeting the group as a whole: The Finnish anti-bullying intervention.* In P.K.Smith, D.Pepler, & K. Rigby (eds.) *Bullying in schools: How successful can interventions be?* NY: Cambridge UP, pp. 251-273.

Salmivalli, C., Lagerspetz, K., Björkqvist, K., Österman, K. & Kaukiainen, A. (1996). *Bullying as a group process: Participant roles and their relations to social status within the group.* Aggressive Behavior, 22, 1-15.

Salmivalli, C., Lappalainen, M., & Lagerspetz, K. (1998). *Stability and change of behavior in connection with bullying in schools: A two-year follow-up.* Aggressive Behavior, 24, 205-218.

Salmivalli, C., & Voeten, M. (2004). *Connections between attitudes, group norms, and behaviors associated with bullying in schools.* International Journal of Behavioral Development, 28, 246-258.

Schäfer, M. & Korn, S. (2004). *Zeitschrift Bullying als Gruppenphänomen: Eine Adaptation des 'Participant Role'-Ansatzes.* Entwicklungspsychologie und Pädagogische Psychologie, 36, 19-29.

Smith, P., Pepler, D., & Rigby, K. (2004), *Bullying in schools: How successful can interventions be?* NY: Cambridge UP.

Smith, D., Schneider, B., Smith, P., & Ananiadou, K. (2004). *The effectiveness of whole-school antibullying programs: A synthesis of evaluation research.* School Psychology Review, 33, 547-560.

Sutton, J., & Smith, P. K. (1999). *Bullying as a group process: An adaptation of the participant role approach.* Aggressive Behavior, 25, 97-111.

Tani, F., Greenman, P. S., Schneider, B. H., &Fregoso, M. (2003). *Bullying and the Big Five: A study of childhood personality and participant roles in bullying incidents.* School Psychology International, 24, 131-146.

Whitney, I., & Smith, P.K. (1993). *A survey of the nature and extent of bullying in junior/ middle and secondary schools.* Educational Research, 35, 3-25.

Author Notes

Writing of the present chapter has been supported by the Academy of Finland grants to the second author (grant numbers 202554/68884 and 121091).

Chapter 3:

Consequences of Being Bullied at School

Tanya N. Beran
Division of Applied Psychology
Faculty of Education
University of Calgary

School Achievement Consequences of School Bullying

Friendships have been long recognized as critical to development (Sullivan, 1953). Problematic peer relations contribute to victimization whereby children who are victimized are typically described as having few friends (Hugh-Jones & Smith, 1999). Children are expected to develop friendships as they grow and mature, which provides a sense of acceptance and belonging that buffers children from adjustment difficulties including low self-esteem, loneliness, depression, and anxiety (Asher, Parkhurst, Hymel, & Williams, 1990). Indeed, researchers suggest that children's emotional needs can be met through friendship (Erdley, Nangle, Newman, & Carpenter, 2001). Although many children develop healthy reciprocal relationships with their peers, some children feel intimidated and unsafe with peers who are aggressive. This lack of peer support and fear through intimidation results in serious adjustment difficulties such as depression and anxiety (Hawker & Boulton, 2000), and for some children even suicide (Morita, Soeda, Soeda, & Taki, 1998; Olweus, 1993; Rigby, 2000).

These serious adjustment problems may be partly due to the chronicity of school bullying. Considering that children selectively target their peers (Perry, Kusel, & Perry, 1988), some peers may be victimized year after year (Hodges & Perry, 1999). Indeed, preliminary findings from our analyses of bullying from children across Canada indicate that about 60% of children bullied in grades 5 to 8, continue to experience bullying two years later. Given the impact and consistency of school bullying, it is crucial to examine how it may impact student learning. The focus of this chapter is to review the impact of school bullying on school achievement, and present other functioning difficulties that explain why children who are bullied may experience poor school achievement

Consequences of Being Bullied at School

Researchers have documented numerous physical and psychological difficulties of children who have been bullied. Descriptions of children's functioning are consistent across studies conducted over the last 15 years. In 1978, Dan Olweus published the first English account of the experiences of victimized children, or so-called "whipping boys" (Olweus, 1978).

In terms of the physical impact, children who are bullied may report symptoms such as sleeplessness, headaches, stomachaches, bed wetting, and a variety of health problems (Balding, Regis, Wise, Bish, & Muirden, 1996; Sharp, 1995; Williams, Chambers, Logan, & Robinson, 1996). Moreover, Williams et al., (1996) showed that the number of symptoms is high among children who experience frequent bullying. These health symptoms may also be associated with insecurity and irritability, possibly as a result of high levels of stress (Olweus, 1989; Sharp, Thompson, & Arora, 2000).

Additional psychological difficulties have been identified. Researchers have shown that children who are bullied are likely to report anxiety and low self-esteem, which may be partly attributed to self-blame (Boulton & Underwood, 1992; Graham & Juvonen, 1998; Olweus, 1989). They may describe themselves as detached, critical, serious, shy, and timid (Bryne, 1989), and indicate that they are afraid of going to school (Olweus, 1992). Children who are often victimized may also experience loneliness, particularly when they receive little social support (Skinner & Kochenderfer-Ladd, 2000). In a meta-analysis of peer victimization and psychosocial adjustment, Hawker and Boulton (2000) reported mean effect sizes ranging from .29 to .45, indicating that victims are particularly at risk for depression.

The behaviours of children who are bullied also have been well-researched. Children who submit to their more aggressive peers provide mostly passive alternatives to interpersonal dilemmas, and evaluate these responses more favorably than non-passive responses (Deluty, 1981; 1985; Frost, 1991). In addition, these children may select more cooperative strategies in situations thereby appearing submissive to their peers, whereas children who are not victimized are likely to choose competitive strategies (Schuster, 2001). Children who are bullied are described as often reacting to their peers by crying, and as lacking the skills and confidence in seeking support for their victimization (Olweus, 1978; 1989; Rigby, 1996; Whitney & Smith, 1993). Schwartz et al., (1993) observed that children who exhibit a meek, subservient and inflexible style of play are at risk for victimization in a play group of unfamiliar peers. Besag (1989) described victimized children as unpopular and passive, and Graham and Juvonen (1998) reported that victimized children are likely to experience rejection by their peers

The above descriptions suggest that children who are bullied are isolated from their peer group. This status, if undesirable to the child, may create a sense of disengagement from school in general (Osborne, 2004). Given that school learning occurs in a social context, with students and teachers, difficulties interacting with peers on the school grounds may result in awkward and distressing interactions in the classroom. These latter interactions can be observed when students are asked to self-select partners and working groups. Peers may not invite these students to join a group and be reluctant to accept them when requested by a teacher. These awkward incidents may increase stress and prevent victimized students from focusing on their school work. Indeed, research has shown that these children are likely to experience impaired concentration (Sharp et al., 2000). As a result, their achievement at school may be negatively affected.

School Achievement

Various attempts have been made to define school achievement; however, definitions vary considerably. For example, Spence and Helmreich (1983) described achievement as any performance in which evaluation of the performance routinely occurs. Stetson, Stetson, and Sattler (2001) defined achievement more generally as, "the skills children learn through direct intervention or instruction (p.577)." More recent definitions have included, "the accuracy with which children could solve progressively advanced reading, mathematics, and spelling problems on an individualized achievement test (Buhs, Ladd, & Herald, 2006, p. 5)." For the present study, Ebel and Frisbie's (1986) definition was used, namely that school achievement is a student's comprehension of particular information and proficiency with specific skills.

Ecological models provide the most comprehensive and contemporary understanding of the development of achievement (Broussard & Garrison, 2004). Accordingly, children's achievement is influenced by their social contexts including their interactions with parents, teachers, friends, and others. The Expectancy-Value theory (Eccles et al., 1983) emphasizes the importance of an environmental "fit" whereby achievement is enhanced when these socialization experiences meet children's learning needs. At school, students progress into wider social contexts from their homes, which influence their cognition, behaviour, and socio-emotional development (Eccles, Roeser, Wigfield, & Freedman-Doan, 1999). Schools provide new life experiences that encourage and challenge children in their intellectual development. However, some students may experience these environments as discordant with their needs and develop academic and social difficulties as a result of low expectancy for success (Eccles et al., 1999). In fact, Kulka, Klingel, and Mann (1980) suggested that poor person-environment fit can lead to frustration, rejection, and even violence towards others. Alternatively, poor fit can lead to rejection and victimization whereby students become passively isolated from their peers. It is possible, therefore, that social experiences such as being bullied may reduce a student's sense of competence for social and, perhaps, academic situations.

Bullying and School Achievement

Perhaps as a result of these functioning difficulties and for fear of being repeatedly attendance targeted, children who are bullied indicate that they are afraid of going to school and seek out ways to try to avoid attending school (Kochenderfer & Ladd, 1996;

Olweus, 1992; Reid, 1985). Indeed, Fried and Fried (1996) noted that students who were victimized dropped out of school at a higher rate than those students who were not victimized. When at school, these children report difficulty concentrating on their schoolwork (Mellor, 1990), and their positive attitudes at the beginning of the school year may become negative due to fear and vulnerability (Kochenderfer & Ladd; 1996). Moreover, these feelings may persist even after the bullying ends (Kochenderfer & Ladd, 1996). Thus, it seems plausible that involvement in bullying interferes with learning when children avoid school due to negative perceptions about attending. Indeed, researchers have shown that children who are bullied are at risk of developing academic difficulties (Juvonen, Nishina, & Graham, 2000; Olweus, 1978; Schwartz, 2000).

Other studies, however, show contrary results. Hanish and Guerra (2002) examined the effects of peer victimization on levels of academic achievement and determined that "[P]eer victimization was correlated with concurrent and subsequent aggressive behaviour, inattention in the classroom, delinquency, symptoms of anxiety and depression, rejection, and low popularity among classmates. It was not, however, correlated with academic maladjustment or withdrawal" (p. 85). As such, being bullied did affect some aspects of academic life (such as inattention in the classroom and low popularity among classmates); however, peer victimization did not predict low achievement (Hanish & Guerra, 2002). In addition, Woods and Wolke (2004) reported achievement levels to be similar between children who are victimized and those who are not. Perhaps children who are bullied actually increase their academic abilities by focusing more on schoolwork as a method of escaping the victimization (Woods & Wolke, 2004). Thus, some victimized children may experience poor achievement whereas others may not.

To further determine whether targeted children experience academic difficulties and reasons for this outcome, it is important to examine various factors related to achievement. Osborne (2004) argued that children may obtain low levels of achievement when they disengage from their learning. This disengagement may be exhibited in the form of detachment or disinterest in school work. Indeed, low student conscientiousness, such as individual effort and involvement in school work, has been linked to low student performance (Amenkhienan & Kogan, 2004). Also, students who do not enjoy academic activities are likely to obtain low scores on achievement measures (Flowers, 2003; Otten, Stigler, Woodward, & Staley, 2004).

In addition to disengagement, parent support of children's education has been associated with school achievement. Englund, Luckner, Whaley, and Egeland (2004) found that parental involvement in education significantly predicts children's achievement in school. Parental involvement may occur at home or at school, with each moderately but significantly increasing the child's academic success (Christenson, Rounds, & Gorney, 1992; Englund, et al., 2004; Fehrmann, Keith, & Reimers, 1987; Izzo, Weissberg, Kasprow, & Fendrich, 1999; Keith, Keith, Quirk, Cohen-Rosenthal, & Franzese, 1996). Other studies contradict these findings (Bobbett, French, Achilles, & Bobbett, 1995; Okpala, Okpala, & Smith, 2001). Some studies have only explored parental involvement on junior or senior high student achievement (Bobbett, et al., 1995; Deslandes, Royer, Turcotte, & Bertrand,

1997), so further studies investigating parental support and involvement at the elementary level in comparison to the junior high level are needed. Moreover, the interrelationships among parental involvement and other achievement-related factors such as student academic disengagement and experience of bullying have yet to be examined.

Adding to the complexity of the relationship between bullying and achievement are other factors shown in previous research to be associated with achievement. Bullied children who are themselves aggressive may antagonize and annoy their peers, perhaps provoking an attack. Children who exhibit these behaviours are identified as "aggressive victims" or "provocative victims" and may also display hyperactivity, which may negatively impact learning (Haynie et al., 2001; Kumpulainen et al., 1998). These characteristics call attention to the possibility that children who are bullied and exhibit behaviour problems such as aggression and hyperactivity are likely to also experience academic difficulties.

Researchers report that these disruptive behaviour problems are often related to children's social skill development (Gresham, 2001; Gresham & Elliott, 1990; Merrell, 1993; Walker & McConnell, 1995). Nangle and Erdley (2001) stated, "The idea that children's peer relations play a critical role in their overall psychological adjustment is now assumed" (p.1). Adjustment difficulties such as loneliness and depression are less likely to occur among students who are liked by their peers and who have friends in comparison to those children who are isolated and alone (Erdley et al., 2001). Thus, peer acceptance and reciprocal friendships may prevent social-emotional maladjustment. In the context of school bullying, students who are bullied may not gain a sense of protection from affiliation with a group (Beran & Violato, 2004; Boulton et al., 1999; Schwartz et al., 1993). They are also likely to lack pro-social skills (Larke & Beran, 2006; Rigby, 1996; Whitney & Smith, 1993). These limited social skills and access to friends increase the likelihood of bullying. Furthermore, this lack of peer support may inhibit children from seeking academic support from teachers. If children do not trust their teachers to stop the bullying, they may not seek their assistance with academic difficulties.

In sum, to obtain a broad understanding of how bullied children function at school, a comprehensive model of achievement-related factors was explored in the present study. It is likely that children who are bullied disengage from their learning, experiencing little enjoyment and low consciousness for academic work. In addition, children, whose parents provide little support for their education, are likely to experience academic difficulties. When these students also exhibit behaviour problems in the form of hyperactivity, aggression, and poor social skills, they may experience learning difficulties. The focus of our study was to simultaneously examine all these characteristics to develop a comprehensive view of being bullied in relation to achievement.

Method

Participants

Participants in the present study were drawn from the National Longitudinal Survey of Children and Youth (NLSCY). This database contains national stratified random data and it is funded by Statistics Canada and the Applied Research Branch of Human Resources Development Canada. This national database contains information on the characteristics and experiences of children as they grow from infancy to adulthood (Willms, 2002). The primary objective of the NLSCY is to establish the prevalence of various biological, social, and economic characteristics and risk factors of Canadian children and youth (Statistics Canada, 1997). The most complete data are found in cycle 3, with a sample size of 22,831 children, and were collected in 1998 and 1999. Two age groups of children were selected for the present study to determine age differences in factors related to bullying and achievement: 10 to11 year-olds (n = 2,084), and 12 to15 year-olds (n = 4,111). Data from teachers and parents of these children also were included.

Measures

To derive the measures of bullying, harassment, achievement, conscientiousness, school enjoyment, and parental support, questions that appeared to measure these constructs and that had been used in previous research were selected. A principal component analysis followed by oblique rotation was used to determine whether these questions formed clusters that measure common characteristics. Items were retained if they were correlated with other items comprising the factor. Finally, inter-item reliability analyses of the cluster items within each factor identified in the component analysis were calculated. In this way, it was possible to select the best indicators of each factor from among the hundreds of variables in the data file. For the measures of disruptive behaviours and peer interactions, scales developed by Statistics Canada were used. Data for all variables were evenly distributed according to dispersion analyses. Analyses using both weighted and unweighted data showed very similar results, so only unweighted results are presented.

Bullying (10 to 11 year olds). The 10- to 11-year-old children were asked questions about bullying. Self-reports are considered to be reliable and accurate (Ahmed & Braithwaite, 2004; Hanish & Guerra, 2004), and so the following statements were used: I am bullied in school and I am bullied on my way to and from school (Statistics Canada, 1999). Reponses are based on a 5-point scale from Never to All the time. The Statistics Canada codes were reversed so that a high score indicated high rates of being bullied. Cronbach's alpha was .74 indicating good reliability.

Harassment (12 to 15 year olds). Adolescents responded to questions about harassment: I am attacked at school, I am threatened at school, and I feel uncomfortable at school (Statistics Canada, 1999). Responses are based on a 4-point response scale from Never to 5 times or more. The Statistics Canada codes were reversed so that a high score indicated high rates of harassment. Reliability analyses using Cronbach's alpha of .60 shows reasonable reliability.

Achievement (10 to 11 year olds). Teacher reports of achievement are often used in research and are considered accurate measures of children's achievement (Englund, et al., 2004; Hecht & Greenfield, 2002; Nansel et al., 2001; Schwartz, 2000; Woods & Wolke, 2004). For the 10 to 11 year olds, student achievement was determined from responses to three questions from the student's homeroom teacher: How would you rate this student's current academic achievement in reading, written work (e.g., spelling and composition), and mathematics/arithmetic? (Statistics Canada, 1999). These three questions were asked separately and are based on a 5-point scale from Near the top of the class to Near the bottom of the class. Codes were reversed so that high scores indicated a high level of achievement. Cronbach's alpha was .93 indicating good internal consistency.

Achievement (12 to 15 year olds). Youths' parents, as well as their language and math teachers were asked: How good is the individual's overall ability in school? Also, adolescents were asked, How well are you doing in school? (Statistics Canada, 1999). The language and math teachers responded to a 5-point scale with responses ranging from Near the top of the class to Near the bottom of the class. The parents and adolescents responded to a 5-point scale with responses ranging from Very well to Very poorly. Codes were reversed so that high scores indicated a high level of achievement. Cronbach's alpha was .80 indicating good internal consistency

Students' conscientiousness (10 to 11 year olds). Students' conscientiousness was asked to only the elementary homeroom teachers: How often does this student listen attentively? and How often does this student follow directions? (Statistics Canada, 1999). Responses to the questions were based on a 5-point scale from Never to Always. High scores indicated high rates of listening and following directions. Internal consistency was high indicated by a Cronbach's alpha of .92.

School enjoyment (10 to 11 year olds). School enjoyment was categorized by the students' elementary homeroom teachers' responses to the questions: This student seems to enjoy most classes; and This student seems bored in most classes (Statistics Canada, 1999). A 5-point scale from Always to Never was used to judge the responses to both of the aforementioned statements. To compare the enjoyment and boredom items, the high scores on the boredom question were reversed. Thus, high scores indicated high levels of enjoyment and low levels of boredom. Cronbach's alpha was .80, showing good reliability.

Parental support (10-15 year-olds). To measure the degree of support parents provided for their children's education, the teachers were asked two questions: In your opinion, how involved is (are) the parent(s)/guardian(s) in this student's education? and In your opinion, how strongly does (do) this student's parent(s)/guardian(s) support your teaching efforts? (Statistics Canada, 1999). Responses to the first question were based on a three-point scale from Not involved to Very involved. Responses to the second question were also made on a three-point scale from Does (do) not support to Strongly supports. About 3% of the teachers did not know the parent(s)/guardian(s) well enough to respond to these questions. These responses were coded as missing values. High scores indicated high levels of support. Internal consistency is high as shown by Cronbach's alpha of .72.

Disruptive behaviours (12 to 15 year olds). Only the older children were administered scales about disruptive behaviours. On the Conduct Problems scale adolescents responded to six questions such as: I kick, bite, or hit others my age, and I am cruel, bully or am mean to others. Responses were recorded on a 3-point response scale, Never or not true to Often or very true. Scores ranged from 0-12 with higher scores indicating more conduct problems. Cronbach's alpha for this scale was .74, indicating good internal consistency (Statistics Canada, 1997).

The second disruptive behaviours scale is the Hyperactivity scale. Adolescents responded to eight questions such as: I am nervous, high-strung or tense, and I cannot settle to anything for more than a few moments. Responses on a 5-point scale ranged from Never or not true to Often or very true. Its internal consistency according to Cronbach's alpha was .75 (Statistics Canada, 1997).

Peer interactions (12 to 15 year olds). Peer interactions among older children were measured by two scales. The Friends scale consists of four items measuring adolescents' perceptions of peer acceptance. Exemplar items include, Others my age want me to be their friend, and Most others my age like me. There are four response categories on this scale along varying degrees from False to True. The internal consistency as measured by Cronbach's alpha was .78, and higher scores indicate more friendships (Statistics Canada, 1997).

The Pro-social scale measured adolescents' perceptions of their social skills according to 10 questions such as, I comfort another young person (friend, brother, or sister) who is crying or upset, and I help to pick up things which another young person has dropped. Responses are recorded according to three categories: Never or not true to Often or very true. Scores on this scale range from 0-20 with higher scores indicating more pro-social skills. Its internal consistency according to Cronbach's alpha is .77 (Statistics Canada, 1997).

Procedure

Model development

The bivariate correlations (Pearson's r) between all of the variables were calculated. They ranged from .02 to .84. To view the tables, please contact the author. These correlations guided the specifications of the structural equation model tests to understand the pattern of relationship among these variables. Two latent variable path models were created for the two age groups because different variables were measured and the results were different for each age group. Using EQS: A Structural Equation Program software package (Version 6.1; Bentler, 2004), the models were fit to the covariance matrix with Maximum Likelihood (ML) estimation. As this step was intended to explore the relationships among numerous variables simultaneously, and since these patterns of relationships have not been explored in previous research, the models were re-specified to develop the best fit. Due to many missing values in the 12-15 year-old sample, listwise deletion of missing cases was used to obtain the most conservative sample, resulting in a lower sample size for the model of 613.

Results

The demographic characteristics of the children and their families represent the Canadian population as indicated by Statistics Canada, with the exception of the native population (not sampled). An approximately even number of boys and girls were included in this sample, and the majority of adult respondents had attended post-secondary school. The majority also reported that their household income was greater than $40 000. Consistent with the population of Canadian provinces, the majority of the respondents resided in Ontario, followed by Quebec (Statistics Canada, 1997). Mean scores on all of the variables were similar across provinces, and no sex differences emerged for any of the variables.

The model for the 10 to 11 year olds converged in 6 iterations providing a good fit for the data ($\chi2(32) = 300.00$, $p < .001$; SRMR= .05; CFI = .98). See Figure 1. Thus, the model accounted for 98% of the variance in the data, and all variables in the model are significant. For the 12 to 15 year olds, the model converged in 6 iterations providing a good fit for the data ($\chi2(37) = 224.49$, $p < .001$; SRMR= .05; CFI = .91). See Figure 2. Thus, this model accounted for 91% of the variance.

Figure 1 depicts bullying to the right of achievement at the top of the model. The latent variable achievement is measured by the homeroom teacher's report of achievement in reading, writing, and math. Achievement was negatively correlated with students' reports of being bullied at or when going to and from school; $r = -.17$. The small correlation indicates that being bullied and low achievement are modestly associated.

Continuing down the model, the relationship between achievement and school engagement is depicted. That is, the homeroom teacher's perception of the students' enjoyment of school and conscientiousness were also correlated with achievement. Enjoyment and conscientiousness are also highly correlated. Thus, when students enjoy school and are conscientious in their work, they are likely to obtain high levels of achievement.

The final factor in the model is parent support, as measured by the homeroom teacher. Parent support was correlated with enjoyment and conscientiousness, indicating that when parents support their children's education, these children are likely to enjoy school and work conscientiously. Parental support is correlated with achievement, indicating that incremental parental support is directly related to student achievement. Overall, it appears that children who obtain high levels of achievement are conscientious, enjoy school, receive parental support, and to some extent, are not bullied.

Latent variable path model of bullying and achievement employing Maximum Likelihood estimation (n = 2084)

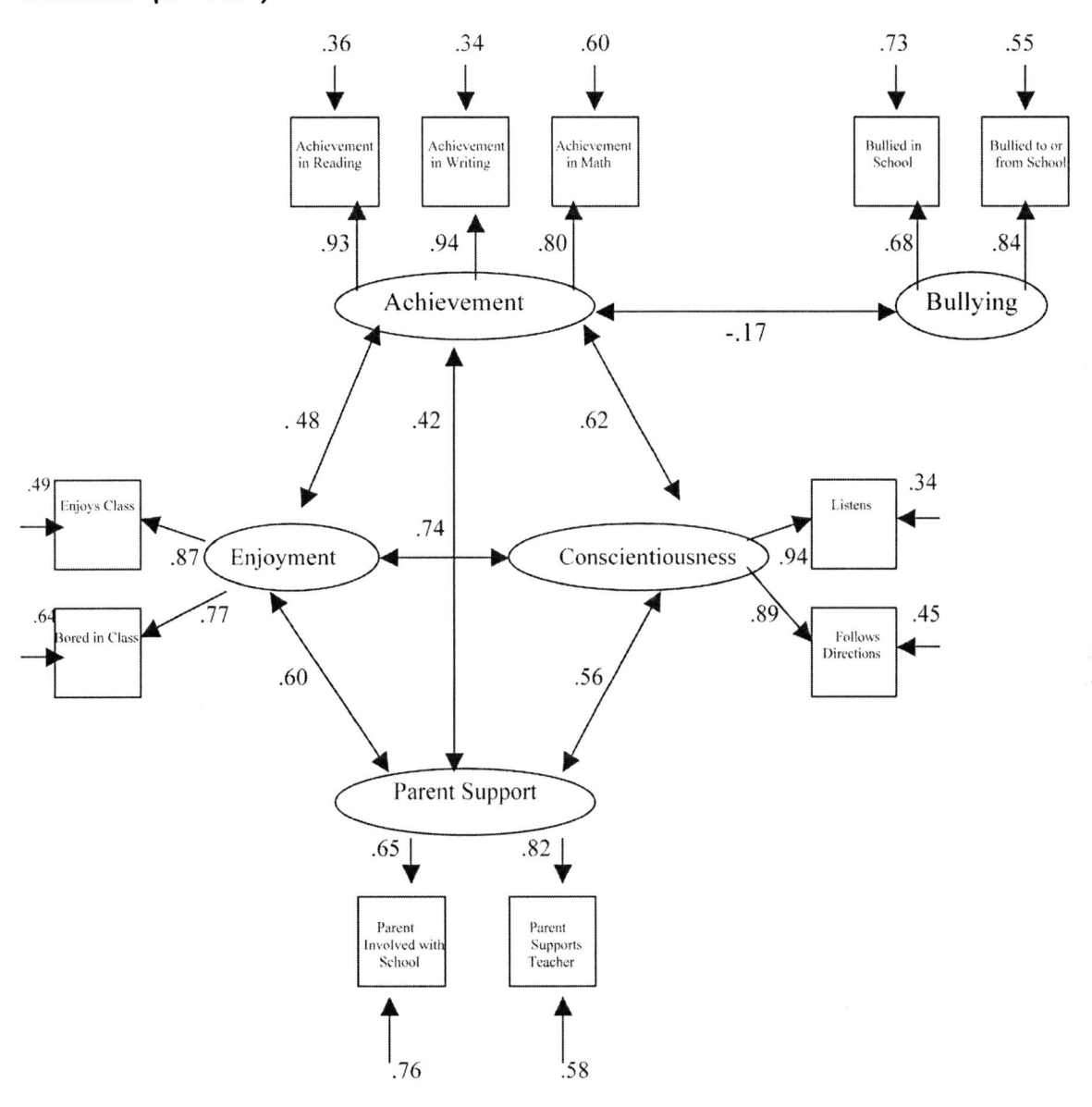

53

Latent variable path model of harassment and achievement employing Maximum Likelihood estimation (n = 613)

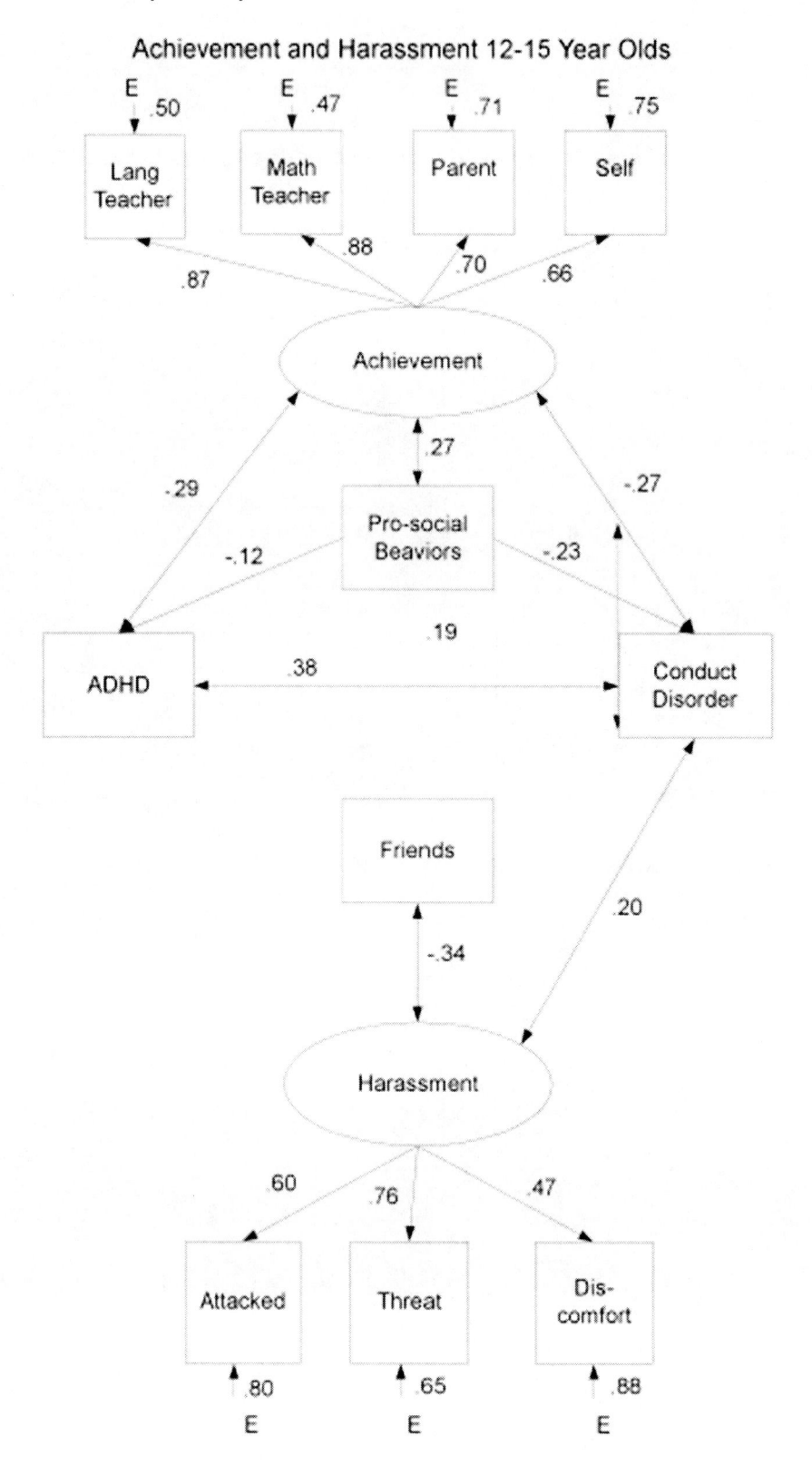

Achievement and Harassment 12-15 Year Olds

Indicators of Achievement (with error terms E):
- Lang Teacher: loading .87, E = .50
- Math Teacher: loading .88, E = .47
- Parent: loading .70, E = .71
- Self: loading .66, E = .75

Paths from/to Achievement:
- Achievement → ADHD: −.29
- Achievement ↔ Pro-social Behaviors: .27
- Achievement → Conduct Disorder: −.27

Pro-social Behaviors:
- Pro-social Behaviors → ADHD: −.12
- Pro-social Behaviors → Conduct Disorder: −.23
- Pro-social Behaviors → Harassment: .19

ADHD ↔ Conduct Disorder: .38

Conduct Disorder → Harassment: .20
Friends → Harassment: −.34

Indicators of Harassment (with error terms E):
- Attacked: loading .60, E = .80
- Threat: loading .76, E = .65
- Discomfort: loading .47, E = .88

Chapter 3: Consequences of Being Bullied at School

In the second model (Figure 2), the pathway for adolescents from harassment at the bottom to achievement at the top of the model is depicted. Achievement was reported by the language and math teachers, parents, and students, themselves. Harassment was measured by the adolescents' own reports of being attacked and threatened, and feeling uncomfortable at school. The correlation between harassment and achievement were very low and not significant in this model. Further specification of the model indicated that disruptive behaviours and peer interactions mediate harassment and achievement. That is, high achievement was related to few conduct and hyperactivity problems. It is also related to high levels of pro-social behaviours. In other words, adolescents who obtain poor achievement, exhibit conduct problems, hyperactivity, and few pro-social skills, are also likely to be harassed at school.

These factors were also inter-related in our model. That is, adolescents' perceptions of their conduct problems, and of how liked they are by their peers as measured by the Friends scale, are related to harassment. Accordingly, adolescents with few friends and higher disruptive behaviour problems are likely to experience peer harassment. Also shown in the model is the inter-relationship between behaviour problems and peer interactions. Adolescents with few pro-social behaviours are likely to have difficulty with hyperactivity, as well as with conduct problems. The perception of having few friends was also linked to disruptive behaviours, but was mediated by pro-social skills.

In sum, this model indicates that adolescents who are harassed do not necessarily obtain low marks at school. However, if they are harassed their achievement may be negatively impacted if they have few friends, exhibit few pro-social skills, and experience behaviour problems such as hyperactivity and misconduct. It is interesting to note that parent support was not significantly related to any of the factors in this second model.

Discussion

The models developed in this study provide a comprehensive understanding of how bullied children may obtain low levels of achievement. These explanations involve several factors and differ between younger and older children. Children who are 10-11 years old are likely to experience academic difficulties, particularly when they are disengaged from their learning experiences in school and receive little parental support. Adolescents, aged 12-15 years, are likely to experience low achievement only if they exhibit behaviour and social skills problems. The link between bullying and achievement is related to several family and individual characteristics. Thus, it is not surprising that previous research has shown mixed results of the link between bullying and achievement (e.g., Kochenderfer & Ladd, 1996; Olweus, 1978; Schwartz, 2000; Woods & Wolke; 2004 Consistent with Eccles' Expectancy-Value theory (Eccles et al., 1983) numerous factors impact and are influenced by achievement. Thus, research that examines one or a few factors in isolation may provide misleading conclusions about the complex relationship between achievement and bullying. Moreover, this relationship is more complex in older than in younger children.

10- to 11-year-old children

For this age group, public humiliation in the form of bullying may erode a child's sense of competence for positive social interactions and functioning at school, which may generalize to their competence for success in academic achievement. It also is possible that children in these elementary school years become ridiculed because of their achievement difficulties. Regardless of the source of stress children first experience, competence in the social domain is related to competence in the academic domain. This stress may decrease the child's ability to concentrate on academics and manage attacks from peers.

In addition to examining the relationship between bullying and achievement from the child's individual experiences, the present model suggests the importance of examining the functioning of children in the family and peer context. Parents play a key role in their children's achievement both directly and indirectly (Ketsetzis, Ryan & Adams, 1998; Zhan, 2006). When parents support their children's academic pursuits through support to the teacher and the school, they can become aware of their children's academic activities, and, hence, better assist them in their learning. For example, parents who are supportive of the school, are likely supportive of the school's workload demands (e.g., homework), and will support their children in meeting those demands at home. With parental guidance and supervision of assignments at home, children may be more likely to complete homework on time with higher effort than if they were unsupervised. Increased completion of homework and work completed with a high amount of effort may result in increased grades and achievement levels. In regards to the role of peers, since academic work takes place in a social context, it follows that problematic peer relationships may undermine participation in academic activities (Parker & Asher, 1987). Given the low correlation between achievement and bullying in the model, it is also important to consider that some children who are bullied may actually work hard at school and obtain high marks. By immersing themselves in their studies, negative feelings about their peer experiences may subside. Thus, 10- to 11-year-old children are at low risk for experiencing achievement problems if they are bullied, but are at high risk if they are also disengaged from their learning and receive little parent support.

12- to 15-year-old children

Among 12 to 15 year olds, the relationship between achievement and bullying is complex and mediated by several factors. These factors include both the characteristics of the bullied adolescent as well as their peers. When the adolescents experience problems with hyperactivity and misconduct, achievement is low. Indeed, research has shown that these difficulties interfere with learning (Abikoff et al., 2002; Mattison, Hooper, & Glassberg, 2002). Moreover, peer difficulties such as few or no friendships, and limited pro-social interactions increase the likelihood of bullied adolescents obtaining low levels of achievement.

Harassment and learning both occur in the social context of the peer group. When adolescents are harassed, their sense of competence for social and academic situations may be impaired only when they experience behaviour and peer problems. Since many students report being bullied (Bosworth et al., 1999), they may consider the incident itself as "normal", or a common school experience. For these students, their sense of competence may not be impacted. Other students are more vulnerable to bullying because of a range of difficulties in psychosocial functioning. These adolescents may experience impaired competence for academic work if they also have few or no friends, limited pro-social skills, conduct problems, and hyperactivity.

Another explanation for the indirect relation between harassment and achievement is the experience of fear. Although freedom from fear is not sufficient to ensure academic success, it is a necessary component (Galloway, 1994). Indeed, researchers have found that victimized students may not report the harassment due to fear of retaliation (Slee, 1994; Whitney & Smith, 1993). This fear may prevent them from talking to or trusting teachers. This avoidance of teachers may also create reluctance to approach them about academic problems. It is likely that the relationship between students, who have functioning difficulties such as hyperactivity and few pro-social skills, and their teachers is strained, particularly for this age group (Midgley, Feldlaufer, & Eccles, 1989). The role of teachers in supporting harassed students requires further research, but preliminary evidence suggests that young children who are bullied at school report feeling safe when they feel supported by their teachers (Beran & Tutty, 2002). The role of fear for adolescents involved in harassment has received little research attention and in light of the present findings, requires further exploration.

In summary, results from both models suggest that when children are bullied by their peers, they may become disengaged from academic activities. Since learning occurs in the context of the peer group in the form of small group projects, field trips, and classroom activities, students who feel afraid and threatened by their peers may be disinclined to participate in such group learning activities, which can result in poor school achievement and behavioural misconduct (Ekstrom, Goertz, Pollack, & Rock, 1986; Finn & Rock, 1997; Fredricks, Blumenfeld, & Paris, 2004). Thus, bullying is one of several risk factors that may increase the likelihood of poor achievement. On a more positive note, the models indicate that children who are bullied do not necessarily experience impaired academic performance.

The strength of this study is the simultaneous examination of multiple factors implicated in the relation between bullying and achievement for children of various ages across Canada. By using several latent variables, measurement error was reduced to create two comprehensive models. There are also some limitations to consider, however. That harassment occurs over time and in some cases over several years, makes determining the precipitating cause for the harassment problematic. Our model is an exploratory examination of various factors related to bullying and achievement. Since studies show that other aspects of school functioning such as depression are characteristic of children who are bullied (Hanish & Guerra, 2002), these factors must be included in future models. Thus, the models, although complex, may not represent the multitude of interacting risk factors implicated in bullying and achievement. Also, there are also some difficulties with the measures used in our study. The definition of bullying was not clearly specified during survey administration, and children may not have been consistent in their reports of types of aggressive behaviours that constitute bullying. Nevertheless, these findings point to the importance of addressing bullying through partnerships between schools and families. The purpose of education is to prepare people to function effectively in society. Since academic success "rests on a foundation of social-emotional competencies...," (Elias, Zins, Graczyk, & Weissberg, 2003, p. 304) those children who are bullied by their peers at school are in particular need of attention from educators and parents.

Chapter 3: Consequences of Being Bullied at School

Key Messages

1. The link between experiencing bullying and academic achievement is complex and influenced by numerous factors. Research that examines only one or a few factors in isolation may provide misleading or contradictory conclusions.

2. Children who are 10-11 years old are likely to experience academic difficulties, particularly when they are disengaged from their learning experiences in school and receive little parental support. Although being bullied is only modestly related to low achievement, the stress from being bullied is likely to decrease some children's ability to concentrate on academics and increase school disengagement.

3. Among 12 to 15 year olds, the relationship between achievement and being bullied is mediated by hyperactivity and misconduct. Moreover, peer difficulties such as few or no friendships, and limited pro-social interactions increase the likelihood of bullied adolescents obtaining low levels of achievement.

4. Bullying is one of several risk factors that lead to poor academic achievement. On a more positive note, the present research indicates that children who are bullied do not necessarily experience impaired academic achievement.

References

Abikoff, H. B., Jensen, P. S., Arnold, L. L. E., Hoza, B., Hechtman, L., Pollack, S., et al. (2002). *Observed classroom behavior of children with ADHD: Relationship to gender and comorbidity.* Journal of Abnormal Child Psychology, 30(4), 349-359.

Ahmed, E., & Braithwaite, V. (2004). *Bullying and victimization: Cause for concern for both families and schools.* Social Psychology of Education, 7, 35-54.

Amenkhienan, C. A., & Kogan, L. R. (2004). *Engineering students' perceptions of academic activities and support services: Factors that influence their academic performance.* College Student Journal, 38(4), 523-540.

Asher, S. R., Parkhurst, J. T, Hymel, S., & Williams, G. A. (1990). *Peer rejection and loneliness in childhood.* In S. R. Asher & J. D. Coie (Eds.), Peer rejection in childhood (pp. 253-273). New York, NY: Cambridge University Press.

Balding, J., Regis, D., Wise, A., Bish, D., & Muirden, J. (1996). *Bully off: Young people that fear going to school.* Exeter: School Health Education Unit, University of Exeter.

Bentler, P. M. (2004). *EQS: A structural equation program (Version 6.1)* [Computer Software]. Encino, CA: Multivariate Software.

Beran, T., & Tutty, L. (2002). *Children's reports of bullying and safety at school.* Canadian Journal of School Psychology, 17(2), 1-14.

Beran, T., & Violato, C. (2004). *A model of childhood perceived peer harassment: Analyses of the Canadian National Longitudinal Survey of Children and Youth data.* Journal of Psychology, 138(2), 129-147.

Besag, V. E. (1989). *Bullies and victims in schools.* Milton Keknes: Open University Press.

Bobbett, G. C., French, R. L., Achilles, C. M., & Bobbett, N. C. (1995, November). *An analysis of Nevada's report cards on high school.* Paper presented at the annual meeting of the Mid-South Educational Research Association Annual General Meeting, Biloxi, MI.

Bosworth, K., Espelage, D. L., & Simon, T. R. (1999). *Factors associated with bullying behavior in middle school students.* Journal of Early Adolescence, 19, 341-362.

Boulton, M. J., Trueman, M., Chau, C., Whitehand, C., & Amatya, K. (1999). *Concurrent and longitudinal links between friendship and peer victimization: Implications for befriending interventions.* Journal of Adolescence, 22, 461-466.

Boulton, M. J., & Underwood, K. (1992). *Bully/victim problems among middle school children.* British Journal of Educational Psychology, 62, 73-87.

Broussard, S. C., & Garrison, M. E. B. (2004). *Motivation and academic achievement in elementary-school-aged children.* Family and Consumer Sciences Research Journal, 33(2), 106-120.

Buhs, E. S, Ladd, G. W., & Herald, S. L. (2006). *Peer exclusion and victimization: Processes that mediate the relation between peer group rejection and children's classroom engagement and achievement?* Journal of Educational Psychology, 98(1), 1-13.

Bryne, B. (1989). *A study of the incidence and nature of bullies and whipping boys (victims) in Dublin city post primary for boys.* Unpublished master's thesis, Trinity College, Dublin.

Christenson, S. L., Rounds, T., & Gorney, D. (1992). *Family factors and student achievement: An avenue to increase students' success.* School Psychology Quarterly, 7, 178-193.

Deluty, R. H. (1981). *Alternative-thinking ability of aggressive, assertive and submissive children.* Cognitive Therapy and Research, 5, 309-312.

Deluty, R. H. (1985). *Cognitive mediation of aggressive, assertive, and submissive behavior in children.* International Journal of Behavioral Development, 8, 355-369.

Deslandes, R., Royer, E., Turcotte, D., & Bertrand, R. (1997). *School achievement at the secondary level: Influence of parenting style and parent involvement in schooling.* McGill Journal of Education, 32, 191-207.

Ebel, R. L., & Frisbie, D. A. (1986). *Essentials of educational measurement (4th ed.).* Englewood Cliffs, NJ: Prentice-Hall.

Eccles, J. S. (1994). *Understanding women's educational and occupational choices: Applying the Eccles et al. model of achievement-related choices.* Psychology of Women Quarterly, 18, 585-609.

Eccles, J. S., Adler, T. F., Futterman, R., Goff, S. B., Kaczala, C. M., Meece, J. L., & Midgley, C. (1983). *Expectancies, values, and academic behaviors. In J. T. Spence (Ed.), Achievement and achievement motivation (pp. 75–146).* San Francisco, CA: W. H. Freeman.

Eccles, J. S., Roeser, R., Wigfield, A., & Freedman-Doan, C. (1999). *Academic and motivational pathways through middle childhood.* In L. Balter & C. S. Tamler-LeMonda (Eds.), *Child psychology: A handbook of contemporary issues* (pp. 287-317). Philadelphia: Psychology Press.

Ekstrom, R. B., Goertz, M. E., Pollack, J. M., & Rock, D. A. (1986). *Who drops out of high school and why? Findings from a national study.* Teachers College Record, 87, 356-373.

Elias, M. J., Zins, J. E., Graczyk, P. A., & Weissberg, R. P. (2003). *Implementation, sustainability, and scaling up of social-emotional and academic innovations in public schools.* School Psychology Review, 32(3), 303-319.

Englund, M. M., Luckner, A. E., Whaley, G. J., & Egeland, B. (2004). *Children's achievement in early elementary school: Longitudinal effects of parental involvement, expectations, and quality of assistance.* Journal of Educational Psychology, 96(4), 723-730.

Erdley, C. A., Nangle, D. W., Newman, J. E., & Carpenter, E. M. (2001). *Children's friendship experiences and psychological adjustment: Theory and research.* In D. W. Nangle, & C. A. Erdley (Eds.), *The role of friendship in psychological adjustment* (pp. 5-24). San Francisco, CA: Jossey-Bass.

Fehrmann, P. G., Keith, T. Z., & Reimers, T. M. (1987). *Home influences on school learning: Direct and indirect effects of parental involvement on high school grades.* Journal of Educational Psychology, 80, 330-337.

Finn, J. D., & Rock, D. A. (1997). *Academic success among students at risk for school failure.* Journal of Applied Psychology, 82, 221-234.

Flowers, T. A. (2003). *Exploring the influence of reading for pleasure on African American high school students' reading achievement.* High School Journal, 87(1), 58-62.

Fredericks, J. A., Blumenfeld, P. C., & Paris, A. H. (2004). *School engagement: Potential of the concept, state of the evidence.* Review of Educational Research, 74, 59-109.

Fried, S., & Fried, P. (1996). *Bullies and victims: Helping your child through the schoolyard battlefield.* New York: M. Evans and Company.

Frost, L. (1991). *A primary school approach: What can be done about the bully?* In M. Elliott (Ed.), *Bullying: A practical guide to coping for schools.* Harlow: Longman.

Galloway, D. (1994). *Bullying: The importance of a whole school approach* Therapeutic Care & Education, 3, 19-26.

Graham, S., & Juvonen, J. (1998). *Self-blame and peer victimization in middle schools: An attributional analysis.* Developmental Psychology, 34(3), 587-599.

Gresham, F. M. (2001). *Assessment of social skills in children and adolescents.* In J. J. Andrews, D. H. Saklofske, & H. L. Janzen (Eds.), *Handbook of psychoeducational assessment: Ability, achievement, and behavior in children* (pp. 325-355). San Diego, CA: Academic Press.

Gresham, F.M., & Elliott, S. N. (1990). *Social skills rating system.* Circle Pines, MN: American Guidance Service.

Hanish, L. D., & Guerra, N. G. (2002). *A longitudinal analysis of patterns of adjustment following peer victimization.* Development and Psychopathology, 14, 69-89.

Hanish, L. D., & Guerra, N. G. (2004). *Aggressive victims, passive victims, and bullies: Developmental continuity or developmental change?* Merrill-Palmer Quarterly, 50, 17-38.

Hawker, D. S. J., & Boulton, M. J. (2000). *Twenty years' research on peer victimization and psychosocial maladjustment: A meta-analytic review of cross-sectional studies.* Journal of Child Psychology and Psychiatry, 41(4), 441-455.

Haynie, D. L., Nansel, T., Eitel, P., Crump, A. D., Saylor, K., Yu, K. Simons-Morton, B. (2001). *Bullies, victims, and bully/victims: Distinct groups of at-risk youth.* Journal of Early Adolescence, 21(1), 29-49.

Hecht, S. A., & Greenfield, D. B. (2002). *Explaining the predictive accuracy of teacher judgments of their students' reading achievement: The role of gender, classroom behavior, and emergent literacy skills in a longitudinal sample of children exposed to poverty.* Reading and Writing: An Interdisciplinary Journal, 15, 789-809.

Hodges, E. V., & Perry, D. G. (1999). *Personal and interpersonal antecedents and consequences of victimization by peers.* Journal of Personality and Social Psychology, 76, 677-685.

Hugh-Jones, S. & Smith, P. K. (1999). *Self-reports of short- and long-term effects of bullying on children who stammer.* British Journal of Educational Psychology, 69, 141-158.

Izzo, C. V., Weissberg, R. P., Kasprow, W. J., & Fendrich, M. (1999). *A longitudinal assessment of teacher perceptions and parent involvement in children's education and school performance.* American Journal of Community Psychology, 27, 817-839.

Juvonen, J., Nishina, A., & Graham, S. (2000). *Peer harassment, psychological adjustment, and school functioning in early adolescence.* Journal of Educational Psychology, 92(2), 349-359.

Keith, T. Z., Keith, P. B., Quirk, K. J., Cohen-Rosenthal, E., & Franzese, B. (1996). *Effects of parental involvement on achievement for students who attend school in rural America.* Journal of Research in Rural Education, 12, 55-67.

Ketsetzis, M., Ryan, B. A., & Adams, G. R. (1998). *Family processes, parent-child interactions, and child characteristics influencing school-based social adjustment.* Journal of Marriage & Family, 60(2), 374-387.

Kochenderfer, B. J., & Ladd, G. W. (1996). *Peer victimization: Cause or consequence of school maladjustment?* Child Development, 67, 1305-1317.

Kulka, R. A., Klingel, D., & Mann, D. W. (1980). *School crime and disruption as a function of student-school fit: An empirical assessment.* Journal of Youth and Adolescence, 9(4), 353-370.

Kumpulainen, K., Räsänen, E., Henttonen, I., Almqvist, F., Kresanov, K., Linna, S., Moilanen, I., Piha, J., Puura, K., & Tamminen, T. (1998). *Bullying and psychiatric symptoms among elementary school-age children.* Child Abuse & Neglect, 22, 705-717.

Larke, I., & Beran, T. (2006). *The relationship between bullying and social skills in elementary school students*. Issues in Educational Research, 16(1), 38-51.

Mattison, R.E., Hooper, S. R., & Glassberg, L. A. (2002). *Three-year course of learning disorders in special education students classified as behavioral disorder*. Journal of the American Academy of Child & Adolescent Psychiatry, 41(12), 1454-1461.

Miedel, W. T, & Reynolds, A. J. (1999). *Parent involvement in early intervention for disadvantaged children: Does it matter?* Journal of School Psychology, 37, 379-402.

Mellor, A. (1990). *Bullying in Scottish secondary schools*. Edinburgh: Scottish Council for Research in Education.

Merrell, K. W., (1993). *School social behavior scales*. Austin: Pro-Ed.

Midgley, C., Feldlaufer, H., & Eccles, J. S. (1989). *Student teacher relations and attitudes toward mathematics before and after the transition to junior high school*. Child Development, 60, 981-992.

Morita, Y., Soeda, H., Soeda, K., & Taki, M. (1998). Japan. In P. K. Smith, Y. Morita, J. Junger-Tas, D., Olweus, R. Catalano, & P. T. Slee (Eds.), *The nature of school bullying: A cross-national perspective* (pp. 309-323). London: Routledge.

Nangle, D. W., & Erdley, C. A. (2001). *The role of friendship in psychological adjustment*. San Francisco, CA: Jossey-Bass.

Nansel, T. R., Overpeck, M., Pilla, R. S., Ruan, W. J., Simons-Morton, B., & Scheidt, P. (2001). *Bullying behaviors among US youth: Prevalence and association with psychosocial adjustment*. Journal of the American Medical Association, 285, 2094-2100.

Okpala, C. O., Okpala, A. O., & Smith, F. E. (2001). *Parental involvement, instructional expenditures, family socioeconomic attributes, and student achievement*. Journal of Educational Research, 95(2), 110-115.

Olweus, D. (1978). *Aggression in the schools: Bullies and whipping boys*. Washington, D.C.: Hemisphere.

Olweus, D. (1989). *Prevalence and incidence in the study of antisocial behavior: Definitions and measurement*. In M. Klein (Ed.), *Cross-national research in self-reported crime and delinquency* (pp. 187-201). Dodrecht, Netherlands: Kluwer.

Olweus, D. (1992). *Bullying among schoolchildren: Intervention and prevention*. In R. D. Peters, R. J. McMahon, & V. L. Quincy (Eds.), *Aggression and violence throughout the life span* (pp. 100-125). Newbury Park, CA: Sage.

Olweus, D. (1993). Bullying at school: What we know and what we can do. Oxford, United Kingdom: Blackwell.

Osborne, J. W. (2004). *Identification with academics and violence in schools.* Review of General Psychology, 8(3), 147-162.

Otten, M., Stigler, J. W., Woodward, J. A., & Staley, L. (2004). *Performing history: The effects of a dramatic art-based history program on student achievement and enjoyment.* Theory & Research in Social Education, 32(2), 187-212.

Parker, J. G., & Asher, S. A. (1987). *Peer relations and later personal adjustment: Are low-accepted children at risk?* Psychological Bulletin, 102(3), 357-389.

Perry, D. G., Kusel, S. J., & Perry, L. C. (1988). *Victims of peer aggression.* Developmental Psychology, 24, 807-814.

Reid, W. H. (1985). *The antisocial personality: A review.* Hospital and Community Psychiatry, 36, 831-837.

Rigby, K. (1996). *Bullying in schools and what to do about it.* Melbourne: ACER.

Rigby, K. (2000). *Effects of peer victimization in schools and perceived social support on adolescent well-being.* Journal of Adolescence, 23, 57-68.

Schuster, B. (2001). *Rejections and victimization by peers: Social perception and social behavior mechanisms.* In J. Juvonen, & S. Graham (Eds.), *Peer harassment in school: The plight of the vulnerable and victimized* (pp. 290-309). New York, NY: Guilford Press.

Schwartz, D. (2000). *Subtypes of victims and aggressors in children's peer groups.* Journal of Abnormal Child Psychology, 28(2), 181-192.

Schwartz, D., Dodge, K. A., & Coie, J. D. (1993). *The emergence of chronic peer victimization in boys' play groups.* Child Development, 64, 1755-1772.

Sharp, S. (1995). *How much does bullying hurt? The effects of bullying on the personal wellbeing and educational progress of secondary aged students.* Educational and Child Psychology, 12, 81-88.

Sharp, S., Thompson, D., & Arora, T. (2000). *How long before it hurts?* School Psychology International, 21, 37-46.

Skinner, K., & Kochenderfer-Ladd, B. (2000, March). *Coping strategies of victimized children.* In A. Nishina & J. Juvonen (Chairs), *Harassment across diverse contexts.* Symposium conducted at the biennial meetings of the Society for Research on Adolescence, Chicago.

Slee, P. T. (1994). *Situational and interpersonal correlates of anxiety associated with peer victimization.* Child Psychiatry & Human Development, 25, 97-107.

Spence, J. T., & Helmreich, R. L. (1983). *Achievement-related motives and behaviors.* In J. T. Spence (Eds.), *Achievement and achievement motives* (pp. 7-68). San Francisco, CA: Freeman and Company.

Stetson, R., Stetson, E. G., & Sattler, J. M. (2001). *Assessment of academic achievement.* In J. M. Sattler (Ed.), *Assessment of children: Cognitive applications* (4th ed., pp.576-608). San Diego, CA: Jerome M. Sattler, Publisher.

Statistics Canada. (1997). *National longitudinal survey of children and youth: User's handbook and microdata guide.* Human Resources Development Canada.

Statistics Canada. (1999). *National longitudinal survey of children and youth: Cycle three survey instruments.* Human Resources Development Canada.

Sullivan, H. S. (1953). *The interpersonal theory of psychiatry.* New York: Norton.

Walker, H. M., & McConnell, S. R. (1995). *Walker-McConnell scale of social competence and school adjustment: Adolescent version.* San Diego: Singular Publishing.

Whitney, I., & Smith, P. K. (1993). *A survey of the nature and extent of bullying in junior/middle and secondary schools.* Educational Research, 35, 3-25.

Williams, K., Chambers, M., Logan, S., & Robinson, D. (1996). *Association of common health symptoms with bullying in primary school children.* British Medical Journal, 313, 17-19.

Willms, J. D. (Ed.). (2002). *Vulnerable children: Findings from Canada's national longitudinal survey of children and youth.* Edmonton, Alberta: The University of Alberta Press.

Woods, S., & Wolke, D. (2004). *Direct and relational bullying among primary school children and academic achievement.* Journal of School Psychology, 42, 135-155.

Zhan, M. (2006). *Assets, parental expectations and involvement, and children's educational performance.* Children and Youth Services Review, 28(8), 961-975.

Author Notes

This research was supported by the Initiatives on the New Economy grant #539-2003-0013 from the Social Sciences and Humanities Research Council.

Chapter 4:

Lord of the E-Flies: School Supervision Challenges in the Virtual Islands of Cyberspace

Shaheen Shariff and Dianne L. Hoff

Introduction

On a seemingly normal Tuesday afternoon, an eighth grade girl walks out of school and steps into her mother's car, ashen and visibly shaken. Unsure of how to proceed, her mother waits – she doesn't ask, she doesn't move the car. Finally her daughter speaks, saying she received the following cyber-message during class: *"Bitch, i know where you live. you'd better sleep each night with one eye open, on your knees. if you don't . . . I'll be there to be sure you do!!!."* The Avenger.

Scenes like this are playing out in schools around the world. Students, especially adolescent girls, are increasingly being victimized (and sometimes perpetrators) of degrading, threatening, and/or sexually explicit messages and images conveyed electronically via cell phones, email, chat rooms, and personal online profiles (Barak, 2005; Herring, 2002; Ybarra & Mitchell, 2004; Blair, 2003; Campbell, 2005; Jackson, Cassidy & Brown, 2006). As Harmon (2004) observes, the internet has provided young people with an arsenal of weapons for social cruelty. This form of social cruelty (cyber-bullying) has its roots in forms of bullying that take place in the physical school setting; however, the medium of cyber-space allows it to flourish in distinct ways creating numerous challenges.

Cyber-bullying is especially insidious because of its anonymous nature. Moreover, it allows participation by an infinite audience. From an educator's perspective, it is dangerous because it most often takes place outside school hours on home computers, making it difficult, if not impossible, to supervise. In that regard, cyber-bullying is a modern day version of Golding's (1954) *Lord of the Flies*. In this classic tale, Golding places a small group of schoolboys on a deserted island, where the rule-makers are removed, compelling the boys to deal with the resulting vacuum. Their first thoughts are to look for adult authority figures:

"Where's the man with the megaphone?' ... "Aren't there any grownups at all?"

"I don't think so." The fair boy said this solemnly; but then the delight of a realized ambition overcame him (p. 7).

The parallels between what happens on that island and what is happening today in schools are astounding. Left alone with no supervision, for example, Golding's boys harass, then terrorize, and ultimately kill one another. Cyber-bullying similarly puts students on a virtual island with no supervision and very few rules, which allows bullying to escalate to dangerous, even life-threatening levels. Further, the boys on the island realize that being evil is easier when they assume a different persona, and so they paint their faces for anonymity before they attack. Youth engaging in cyber-bullying are no different; they hide behind pseudonyms (*The Avenger*) and well-disguised IP addresses, making it difficult, if not impossible, for victimized youth to determine the source of the threat. This anonymous nature of cyber-bullying is perhaps the most troubling of all, for it leaves victimized youth wondering which of their classmates might be the "Avenger." Indeed, the entire class might be involved. For youth victimized by cyber-bullying, attending school, confronting unknown perpetrators is like being on an island -- there is no escape.

Unlike in Golding's time, today's young people do not have to go to a remote island to find such a world. It is as close as the cell phone or the family computer. Cyberspace has become a real locale without rules and without civilization. On the internet, no one has yet found an acceptable and workable way to create and enforce the modicum of culture that allows people to get along with each other. Nowhere on the internet is this more true than in the virtual space frequented by children, who often have the technological capacity and skill to run electronic circles around their elders; but, who lack the internal psychological and sociological controls to moderate their behaviour.

Maintaining civilization and civil behaviour is difficult enough in organized society, even where the rule of law is supposed to prevail, and where order and authority exists to protect innocent citizens. But what happens—as in dystopian fiction—when the rules and the authority are removed? This is the dilemma that schools confront as they attempt to navigate the legal and moral challenges around responding to cyber-bullying, and ultimately, develop in students appropriate moral compasses for an electronic age.

Our paper focuses on the legal responsibilities for schools in dealing with cyber-bullying, although we recognize that adults in society (through internet networks, media and technology corporations) have provided the technological tools; condoned, and modeled many of the negative behaviours that evolve in the virtual islands of unsupervised cyber-space. American legislation, in fact, protects technology corporations at the expense of those victimized by cyber-targeting, defamation and harassment (Myers, 2006; Servance, 2003; Wallace, 1999). By reviewing established and emerging law relating to school obligations to prevent cyber-bullying, we draw attention to a need for guidelines that would help schools adopt educational means to prevent and reduce cyber-bullying. We appreciate that legislative initiatives and judicial efforts are often designed to avoid the floodgates of litigation on cyber-bullying and cyber-targeting. Our paper explains how, regrettably, initial judicial and school responses tacitly condone cyber-bullying and perpetuate the problem. We suggest a policy approach that will move the dialogue toward educational and protective measures that might better enable children to learn in physical and virtual school environments without fear of cyber-bullying, as unprecedented problems related to new technologies surface. Ultimately, this policy approach holds greater promise to avoid the floodgates to litigation than criminal liability and laws that protect ISP providers.

In addition, we explore the challenges for schools in monitoring students' online discourses because cyber-bullying typically occurs outside supervision boundaries. This dilemma raises important legal questions about the extent to which schools can be expected to intervene when their students cyber-bully off campus, outside school hours, from home computers. The policy vacuum must be addressed because parents are often too busy with their own lives and careers to be aware of what their children are doing online. As Wallis (2006) observes, most family homes are wired with computers in each room, cell phones for each member of the family, i-pods, CD players, and televisions, many of which are in use at the same time. Young people are far more adept at multi-tasking than their parents, and as they grow up, they become immersed in technology, making the lines between their virtual and "real" or physical lives increasingly blurred.

We review and analyze relevant case law to identify applicable legal standards for schools, both in Canada and the United States. The international focus is intentional, since cyber-bullying quickly crosses jurisdictional boundaries rarely encountered in other school challenges. We close with recommendations for the development of an ontology of the legal boundaries in cyber-space as they relate to schools. We encourage the development of informed guidelines for the implementation of inclusive, educational, and legally defensible policy approaches to cyber-bullying.

Although cyber-bullying begins anonymously in the virtual environment, it affects learning in the physical school environment. The consequences can be psychologically devastating for victimized youth, and socially detrimental for all students (Gáti, Tényi, Túry, & Wildmann, 2002). Just as the immaturity of Golding's boys on that deserted island drove them to commit acts they might never have endorsed under the watchful eye of adults; so too in cyber-space, young people who might otherwise be inclusive and respectful in face-to-face interactions, are increasingly tempted to engage in negative online discourse without realizing the impact of their actions (Willard, 2005; Parks & Floyd, 1996). Ybarra and Mitchell (2004) explain that adolescents are able to withhold their identity in cyber-space, providing them with a unique method by which to assert their dominance. Moreover, the computer keyboard provides the control and sense of power that some students cannot achieve in face-to-face relationships (Jackson, et al., 2006).

Young people in cyber-space lose their inhibitions in the absence of no central power, clear institutional or familial boundaries, or hierarchical structures (Milson & Chu, 2002).

As Bandura (1991) explained over a decade ago, physical distance provides a context in which students can ignore or trivialize their misbehaviour, as easily as Golding's boys did on their distant island. In cyber-space this form of moral disengagement is amplified. Parks and Floyd (1996) for example, observe that cyber-space is "another life-world, a parallel universe" (p.93). Consequently, students who may not fit into the "cool" crowd for reasons of appearance, disability, ethnicity, accent, or in some cases, giftedness, are often singled out for online harassment because institutional and family contexts do not exist in cyber-space and sensitivity to hurting others' feelings is reduced. This was illustrated in *Lord of the Flies*, when young Piggy (nearsighted and overweight) is excluded, isolated, harassed and hunted down. His perpetrators take advantage of his disabilities leading to his eventual death. The fear and isolation that Piggy experiences on that island is not far removed from that regularly experienced by those victimized by cyber-bullying. Fear of unknown cyber-perpetrators among classmates and bullying that continues at school distracts all students (those who bully, are bullied, and bystanders) from schoolwork. It creates a hostile school environment where students feel unwelcome and unsafe. In such an atmosphere, equal opportunities to learn are greatly reduced (Devlin, 1997; Shariff & Strong-Wilson, 2005).

It is interesting to note that although Golding's *Lord of the Flies* was written in 1954, the author had tremendous foresight into what can happen when authority figures, caregivers, and parents are absent for long periods of time from any setting, including a virtual one. He might well have been predicting young people's social relations on the Internet. Society would have been wise to heed the strong message in his book before inundating the market with the range of technologies available to young people today. As we noted earlier, the Internet has provided young people with the tools without making allowances for supervision of their use. Not only is this similar to Golding's analysis of what might occur if adolescents were placed on a deserted island completely unsupervised, it is also akin to providing them with ways in which they can harm each other.

The characteristics and conditions relating to the power shifts, and the behavioural and ethical breakdowns in cyber-space, suggest an obligation on adults and public institutions that influence young people's lives (parents, teachers, school administrators, network providers, community stakeholders and the courts), to work toward improved supervision, attention to adolescent online discourse, and increased accountability on the part of Internet providers.

While school administrators and teachers argue that they cannot possibly be expected to supervise students on home computers, parents are increasingly beginning to sue schools and technology companies, for failing to protect their children. One such example is David Knight, a boy from Ontario, Canada, who was bullied persistently in the physical school setting from elementary through high school (by the same classmates). In high school, the bullying was magnified as cyber-bullying took over. His classmates set up a website where they described him as homosexual (which he wasn't), a drug trafficker and pedophile (which were also untrue). The website received millions of hits where participants contributed insults and derogatory comments.

Unsupervised by school or parents (with the web-provider refusing to close down the website for fear of being challenged as breaching free expression rights), David's nightmare continued for six months until he sued the school board and Internet provider. Scholars of cyber-bullying internationally, await the Canadian judicial decision in David's case, which continues to be postponed. Some of the issues raised in his case are nonetheless important and we address them as part of our analysis of the legal considerations.

Although research suggests that bullying is reduced by 50% when young people are allowed to contribute to rule-making (Olweus, 1997), a complete lack of supervision can result in enormous power differentials between dominant and weaker peers resulting in anarchy and a total breakdown of social and ethical norms and structures. This is especially true when adolescents are involved, because their social development is influenced by hormonal changes and social influences (Boyd, 2000; Tolman, Spencer, Rosen-Reynoso & Porches 2001).

Importantly, research on bullying finds that typically 30% of onlookers and bystanders support those who bully rather than those who are victimized (Salmivalli Lagerspetz, Björkqvist, Österman & Kaukianen, 1996; Boulton, 1993). The longer it persists, the more bystanders join in the abuse, creating a power imbalance between the victimized and bullying children. Isolation renders victimized children vulnerable to continued abuse, and the cycle repeats itself. What might begin as friendly banter among classmates at school, can quickly turn into verbal bullying that continues in cyber-space as covert psychological bullying. The difference in cyber-space is that hundreds of perpetrators can get involved in the abuse, and, as in *Lord of the Flies*, peers who may not engage in the bullying at school, can hide behind technology (masks, face paint and screen-names), to inflict the most serious abuse (see examples in Shariff, 2004; Shariff & Strong-Wilson, 2005). With this public forum, there can be many more times the number of bystanders, as well.

Consider another internationally known case of the "Star Wars Kid." Young Ghyzlain Reza (a slightly overweight boy from Quebec, Canada) had filmed himself playing out a Star Wars character. He left the video in his school's film room. Two class-mates found the tape and posted it on the Internet (see www. jedimaster.net). This website attracted 15 million hits. 106 clones of the video were made and redistributed. Wherever Ghyzlain went, his school-mates would jump on desks and tables and imitate him. He finally withdrew from school and is now home-schooled. The case was to be heard on April 10, 2006, but was settled out of court.

These examples illustrate that even when frustrated parents turn to the courts for guidance, their claims are often delayed or settled out of court because of the lack of clear legal boundaries regarding freedom of expression; student privacy and protection in cyber-space (Wallace, 2001; Shariff & Johnny, in press). In cases where cyber-perpetrators are known (as they were in the Star Wars case), classmates are also being charged with criminal harassment. While David and Reza have supportive parents to turn to, our concern is with victims of cyber-bullying, who, like Piggy in *Lord of the Flies*, cannot turn to parents or caregivers for support. This lack of concern by caregivers about cyber-bullying is confirmed in the findings of a survey conducted by the British children's charitable organization, National Children's Home, NCH, making it a significant issue (NCHTM, 2002).

Research also suggests that children who are victimized are reluctant to report cyber-bullying for fear that their own computer and cell-phone privileges will be removed (iSafeAmerica, 2006). Lost computer privileges would ostracize them to an even greater extent from their peer groups whose virtual relationships have become an integral aspect of their social relationships. In some cases, the isolation and ridicule becomes too much, resulting in suicide (see Shariff, 2004; 2005, for case examples). Prior to moving on to a discussion of stakeholder roles and responsibilities, it is important to note that sexual and homophobic harassment have been found to be highly prevalent in cyber-bullying.

Prevalence of Sexual and Homophobic Harassment

Preliminary research suggests that although both genders engage in cyber-bullying, there are differences (Chu, 2005; Li, 2005). Studies (Dibbell,1993; Evard, 1996) have shown that teenage girls are more often at the receiving end of cyber violence.

A review of the scholarly literature (Shariff & Gouin, 2005) finds that according to Herring (2002), 25% of Internet users aged 10-17 were exposed to unwanted pornographic images in the past year; 8% of the images involved violence, in addition to sex and nudity. Mitchell *et al* (2001, cited in Barak, 2005), who conducted a survey of American teenagers, found that 19% of these youths (mostly older girls) had experienced at least one sexual solicitation online in the preceding year. Research on dating and harassment practices at the middle school level (Tolman, 2001) shows that peer pressure causes males to engage in increased homophobic bullying of male peers and increased sexual harassment of female peers to establish their manhood. During this confusing stage of adolescent life, the conditions are ripe for bullying to take place. The Internet provides a perfect medium for adolescent anxieties to play themselves out

Roles and Responsibilities: Schools or Parents?

While its nebulous nature and ability to spread like wildfire are indeed challenging, cyber-bullying does not elicit school responses that differ significantly from reported reactions to general forms of bullying (Shariff, 2004; Harmon, 2004). A review of emerging litigation on bullying (Shariff, 2003) disclosed common patterns in school responses to victimized students' complaints. For example, plaintiffs explained that when approached for support, school administrators and teachers put up a "wall of defense." According to some parents surveyed during that research, school administrators allegedly: a) assumed that the victim-plaintiffs invited the abuse; b) believed parents exaggerated the problem; and c) assumed that written bullying prevention policies absolved them from doing more to protect victims. Despite well-meaning and seemingly sensible bullying prevention programs, this approach means that some educators tacitly condone negative and non-inclusive attitudes, thus sustaining the power structures that exist in a discriminatory school environment. For example, some scholars argue that the tendency in schools to implement blanket zero-tolerance policies (Skiba & Petersen, 1999; DiGiulio, 2001; Giroux, 2003) overlooks the various forms of oppression that marginalize some students in schools.

Not surprisingly, these responses have produced minimally effective results, other than to criminalize young people and add a burden to the criminal justice system (Giroux, 2003, DiGiulio, 2001; Shariff & Strong-Wilson, 2005). To make matters worse, most Internet providers refuse to close websites or block emails to avoid breaching free expression rights because they are protected from liability by legislation, at least in the United States (Myers, 2006). This increases the danger to victimized students. Children's "behaviour" cannot be the sole focus of policy – multi-disciplinary attention to institutional context is crucial. This is where schools can, and in our opinion ought to implement their mandate as educational leaders. While parents undeniably have an obligation to monitor their children's activities on the Internet, teachers, school counselors, administrators, judges and policy makers have no less a responsibility to adapt to a rapidly evolving technological society, address emerging challenges, and guide children to become civic-minded individuals.

It is reasonable to suggest that since schools use technology to deliver curriculum and assign homework (and increasingly provide laptops for students' use at home), it is also imperative they pay attention to how their students use it. They need to recognize and establish standards and codes of conduct with respect to Internet and cell phone use, and define acceptable boundaries for their students' social relationships in cyber-space. Educators, in their valuable role of fostering inclusive and positive school environments, would benefit from scholarship and legally defensible policy guidelines. The study of bullying and especially cyber-bullying must be re-conceptualized from a multi-disciplinary, institutional, educational, and legal perspective.

Legal Obligations

Before we move onto a discussion of the legal obligations for schools, it is worth noting the legal standards currently applied to technology companies. It is these corporations that create and provide the nexus for cyber-bullying, cyber-harassment, cyber-targeting and other forms of online abuse. While a comprehensive survey of the legislation covering technology companies is underway but not completed (Shariff, in progress), David A. Myers (2006) has undertaken an in-depth evaluation of one relevant piece of legislation in the U.S., the *Communications Decency Act* (CDA) of 1996. Under this federal legislation, Congress granted broad immunity to Internet service providers (ISPs). This legislation leaves no one legally accountable for cyber-targeting (which includes cyber-bullying, harassment, stalking, defamation, threats and so on).

Myers (2006) explains that one landmark case, *Zeran v. America Online, Inc.* (1997) is the general precedent used by American courts to rule on Internet abuse. The case involved a series of anonymous postings on America Online's (AOL) message board following the

Oklahoma City bombings in April, 1995. The messages claimed to advertise "naughty Oklahoma t-shirts." The captions on the t-shirts included "Visit Oklahoma . . . It's a Blast!!! And "Finally a Day Care Center That Keeps Kids Quiet – Oklahoma 1995." (*Zeran v. AOL*, 958 F. Supp. 1124, 1127, nn. 3 & 5 (E.D. Va. 1997). The individual who posted the messages identified himself as Ken Z and provided Zeran's phone number as the person to call to order the offensive t-shirts. Zeran received abusive telephone calls and even death threats as a result and notified AOL, which in turn terminated the contract from which the messages originated. However, the perpetrator continued to set up new accounts with false names and credit cards. Zeran finally sued AOL claiming negligence. The court ruled that Section 230 of the CDA provided absolute immunity to AOL regardless of its awareness of the defamatory material.

The Zeran ruling, Myers notes, maintains the status of Internet providers as "distributors" rather than "publishers." Publishers (e.g., book publishers) are liable for defamation by third parties using their services, especially if they are made aware of them and fail to act to prevent the behaviour. By taking on an editorial role, publishers open themselves up to greater liability than computer networks that do not edit content. Thus service providers argued that if they agree to monitor and edit online content, they in fact subject themselves to greater liability. This is why most Internet providers ignore reports of abuse. Most are confident that they will not be held liable subsequent to Zeran. The irony of this, as Myers (2006) points out, is that the title of S.230 reads "Protection for 'Good Samaritan' blocking and screening of offensive material." The objective of the CDA was to protect pro-active online service providers and preserve competition between ISPs on the Internet.

Myers does makes the point that "the winds of change are stirring" (p. 5) for S.230 immunity. In *John Doe v. GTE Corp.* (2003), involving the secret filming of athletes showering in a change room that was posted and sold on a website, the Seventh Circuit Court of Appeals upheld S.230 immunity relying on Zeran, in favor of GTE corporation. However, Judge Easterbrook questioned the reasoning in Zeran, noting that S.230 is supposed to be the "Good Samaritan," blocking and screening offensive material, but in fact, by eliminating liability for ISP's, it ends up defending abusers and defeating legitimate claims by victims of tortuous abuse on the Internet.

The law is slow to change, especially when judges are well aware of the floodgate of litigation that might be unleashed if Internet providers are held liable. In the meantime, schools need guidelines that provide reasonable boundaries and direction as to the extent of their responsibility. This would alleviate their reluctance to breach freedom of expression guarantees or student privacy rights. Educators need to know the extent to which they have the authority to protect victims from abuse by their classmates – and their ultimate responsibility to foster inclusive school environments that encourage socially responsible discourse – on or off school grounds, in the physical school setting and in virtual space.

The Educational Policy Vacuum

Traditional responses to bullying are largely ineffective because of the anonymous nature of cyber-bullying, its capacity for an infinite audience, and participation by large numbers of young people. In this regard, it is important to consider the emerging legal stance adopted by the courts towards cyber-harassment. In the following section we review legal principles of Canada and the United States as they relate to cyber-bullying: freedom of speech/expression, privacy, torts, and human rights/anti-discrimination Law

Freedom of Speech and Expression Rights

Canadian school officials and Internet providers worry that if they intervene with student discourses in cyber-space, they might face challenges under Section 2(b) of the *Charter of Rights and Freedoms* (the "Charter") for infringement of student free expression rights. Freedom of expression, thought, and opinion is guaranteed to all Canadians, including students, under Section 2(b) of the *Charter*. These freedoms are only limited by Section 1 of the *Charter*, which helps the courts weigh and balance individual rights with the collective rights of the greater good in a democracy. Section 1 of the *Charter* states that the rights set out in it are subject "only to such reasonable limits prescribed by law as can be demonstrably justified in a free and democratic society." Any school policy that infringes individual rights must therefore, be justified by the policy-maker as having a pressing and substantial objective to protect the greater good. The onus also rests with policy-makers to establish that the rights in question will be infringed as minimally as possible (*R. v. Oakes*, 1986).

As MacKay and Burt-Gerrans (2005) point out, expression is constitutionally protected as long as it is not violent. This means that any expression that intends to convey non-violent meaning is normally safeguarded by Canadian courts. This interpretation has been extended to the school setting. For instance, one of the best known cases of protected freedom of expression in schools involved a rap song that contained a message to students to reduce promiscuity. In a well-known Canadian freedom of expression case (*Lutes v. Board of Education of Prairie View School Division No. 74* (1992)), Chris Lutes sang a song by Queen Latifah, entitled "Let's Talk About Sex" even though a school district administrator objected to the song. He was suspended and sought judicial review. The court found that his freedom of expression rights under Section 2(b) had been violated and that the administrator's objection to the song did not reasonably justify the infringement of those rights. In fact, the court stated that this was an overreaction to an educational song about sexual abstinence.

This raises important legal questions as they relate to cyber-bullying. Is online harassment considered to be a violent expression? Even though physical force cannot take place online, victimized youth can and do perceive online threats as very real. The impact on the victim is no different from the telephone threat that caused Canadian teenager Dawn Marie Wesley to commit suicide. The words "You're f....g dead!" by a classmate caused her to perceive that real harm would come to her. Her perpetrator was convicted of criminal harassment because the court observed that perceived harm by the victimized individual amounts to the same thing as actual harm (Shariff, 2004). Herring (2002) explains that online harassment which negatively affects the physical, psychological, or emotional well-being of a victimized individual constitutes a form of actual violence. Barak (2005) notes that in the case of sexual harassment, sexual coercion can be obtained through several means – directly offensive sexual remarks that humiliate; passive sexual harassment by using nicknames and online identities such as "wetpussy" or "xlargetool"; or graphic gendered harassment which includes sending unwanted pornographic content, sexual jokes, and other graphic sexual context. These forms of online sexual harassment make recipients feel powerless, demeaned, and threatened.

Some United States judges, however, have refused to acknowledge that online harassment contains a violent message, as illustrated in several cases cited by Wallace (1999); two of which are illustrated here. In *United States of America, Plaintiff v. Jake Baker* (June 21, 1995, as cited in Wallace, 1999), Jake Baker posted a story to the newsgroup alt.sex.stories which graphically described the rape and torture of a university classmate. He also communicated (via email to a friend), his plan to actually carry out the rape. Students who read the story were outraged and charged him with criminal harassment. The district court threw out the claim, holding that because there was no possibility of physical rape on the Internet there could be no claim for harassment. In another case, *Emmett v. Kent School District No. 415* (2000), a boy placed mock obituaries on a website called "The Unofficial Kentlake High Home Page," which allowed visitors to vote on who should be "the next to die." The school, upon learning of the website, expelled the student (and then later reduced this to a five-day suspension). The family brought suit, and the court ruled in favor of the student, stating that the school had not proven the website "intended to threaten anyone."

This reluctance by the courts to avoid involvement in the quagmire of cyber-space is not surprising and not much different from their stance regarding Internet companies. The courts have typically adopted a hands-off approach in matters of educational policy. In the realm of physical violence in schools, for example, American courts have set a very high threshold for plaintiffs to bring claims for negligence against schools, in some cases even when students have been shot or stabbed (Shariff, 2003, 2004; Shariff & Strong-Wilson, 2005). Servance (2003) observes that when addressing cases of cyber-bullying in the school context, American courts continue to apply a standard for protecting student free expression that goes back to the 1960's when students protested against the Vietnam War.

These standards were established in three landmark cases (the "Triumvirate"): *Tinker* (1969), *Fraser* (1986), and *Hazelwood* (1988). *Tinker v. Des Moines Independent Community School District* involved students' rights to wear black armbands as a form of silent protest against the Vietnam War. Despite warnings ahead of time not to engage in this activity, many students participated and were suspended. The students sued the school administration, and the court held in favor of the students – establishing the famous quotation that "students do not leave their free expression rights at the school house gate" (Servance, 2003). The court asserted that unless the speech materially and substantially disrupts learning, schools may not restrict it. This point is illustrated in *Beidler v. North Thurston School District Number 3* (2000). The student in this case denounced the high school assistant principal as an alcoholic and Nazi. Teachers complained about being uncomfortable having Karl Beidler in their classes. He was given emergency suspension and transferred for the remainder of his junior year to an alternative setting within the district. Beidler brought suit saying his website had caused "no substantial disruption," and the court agreed, ruling that the district had not met the Tinker standard regarding disruptive speech.

So far, cases such as Beidler and others (*e.g., Flaherty v. Keystone Oaks School District, 2001*) have usually involved students posting questionable material regarding the *adults* in the school. In the absence of school disruption or direct threats, courts have basically sent the message that schools may not limit student speech (posted online on personally owned computers) that is critical, even offensive about adults. Still emerging are cases involving student-to-student cyber-bullying, which, according to research (Devlin, 1997; Gáti et al. 2002) has an impact on the emotional well-being of the victimized students in the school setting. Based on the research, a strong case could be advanced that cyber-bullying materially and substantially disrupts learning for the victimized students and potentially other students, as well.

A new standard was set in the second case in the Triumvirate in 1986. The Supreme Court held in *Bethel School District #403 v. Fraser* (1986) that schools may prohibit speech that undermines their basic educational mission. In this case a student Matthew Fraser's campaign speech included "obscene, profane language" that contained insinuations to sexual and political prowess. The school suspended Fraser, and the courts upheld the school's action, noting that schools are not the arena for the type of vulgar expression in *Fraser's* speech. Importantly, the judge noted that schools should not have to tolerate speech that is inconsistent with school values. While he acknowledged that it is crucial to allow unpopular speech, he emphasized that schools have a vital role in preparing students to participate in democratic society by teaching appropriate forms of civil discourse that are fundamental to democratic society.

Of significant relevance to cyber-bullying today, this ruling also stated that schools must teach students the boundaries of socially acceptable behaviour. The court stated that threatening or offensive speech has little value in a school setting and cannot be ignored by schools. Moreover, the court noted that the speech infringed the rights of others (although it did not specifically state it, the rights of females in the audience). The sexual insinuations to rape were clearly offensive and threatening to students. The *Fraser* decision extends *Tinker* and is also, in our view, applicable to student freedom of expression in the cyber-bullying context. As explained in the profile of cyber-bullying, a substantial amount of the emerging research on Internet communications reveals the prevalence of sexual harassment, sexual solicitation, homophobia, and threats against women or female students. Not only does this form of cyber-bullying materially disrupt learning and impede educational objectives, it creates power imbalances within the school environment and distracts female and gay or lesbian students from equal opportunities to learn. Consistent with the *Fraser* ruling, expression of this nature infringes their constitutional rights in an educational context and creates a hostile and negative school environment (physical and virtual).

The third American court decision, *Hazelwood vs. Kuhlmeier* (1988), involved the principal's decision to censor portions of the school newspaper. The principal was worried that two articles, one on teen pregnancy and the other on divorce, were too transparent to protect student identities. The students who worked on the articles sued, citing infringement of their First Amendment rights to free speech. The court in *Hazelwood* reasoned that since schools are entitled to exercise control over school sponsored speech, they are not bound by the First Amendment to accept or tolerate speech that goes against the values held by the school system. It is plausible that the reasoning in *Hazelwood* might be extended to cyber-bullying that originates on school computers. First, it is important to note that unlike the Tinker (1969) case, which questioned whether a school should tolerate particular student speech, in *Hazelwood* the courts questioned whether the First Amendment requires a school to promote student speech. They noted that "the standard articulated in *Tinker* for determining when a school may punish student expression need not also be the standard for determining when a school may refuse to lend its name and resources to the dissemination of student expression" (p.509). Certainly, when a school allows students to use its computers for both classroom-related and extra-curricular activities it is providing students with resources and thereby becoming a tacit sponsor of such activities. Therefore, it would seem that educators do not violate First Amendment rights when they exercise control over inappropriate forms of communication disseminated using school computers.

If we apply this logic to the cyber-bullying context, it seems reasonable for schools to place limitations on any form of student expression (including digital forms) that either infringes upon the rights of others or is inconsistent with school values. Similarly, it could be argued that school computers are school property; therefore, any emails or correspondence between students, including websites created using those computers, could be censored. Schools may also impose disciplinary consequences for bullying behaviour generated on school-owned equipment if schools have a policy regulating the type of content that may be sent or received from school computers.

The legal boundaries of supervision are murkier for schools, however, when students are engaged in bullying behaviour from home on their personal computers. For example, in *Emmett v. Kent School District No. 415* (2000), which was mentioned earlier, the courts did not give schools the same authority to act as they have for websites that are created on school computers. A key factor here was that the schools could not show that the off campus-created website would cause a "material and substantial disruption" in school.

Chapter 4: Lord of the E-Flies

Similarly, in *Killion v. Franklin Regional School District*, (2001), the court drew from *Fraser*, *Tinker*, and *Hazelwood* to determine that schools must be able to show substantial disruption in order to limit off-campus speech. In this case a student used his website to denounce the high school athletic director and make attacks on his sex life and his obesity. The court noted that the school could provide no evidence that disruption to classes had occurred. In contrast, if a website is clearly derogatory, profane, threatening, or disruptive, the school may be supported in taking action, even when the website was created on a home computer. In *J.S., a Minor v. Bethlehem Area School District* (2000), a student created a website "Teacher Sux," in which graphic pictures of severed heads, along with a statement to "send $20.00 to help pay for a hit man" was enough for a judge to uphold the expulsion of the student. The court relied on other cases (e.g., *Beussink v. Woodlands R-IV School District*, 1998) holding that websites that are accessed at school, with an intended audience within the school community, can be dealt with as on-campus speech. The court further ruled that disciplining the student for off-school behaviour was appropriate in this case because the action "caused actual and substantial disruption of the work of the school."

More recently, in *Layshock v. Hermitage School District* (2006), senior Justin Layshock created a parody of the principal on Myspace.com, which depicted him as, among other things, too drunk to remember his own birthday. School administrators placed Justin in an alternative school and banned him from participating in any Hermitage High School events, including graduation. The parents went to court, requesting a temporary restraining order to allow Justin to participate at school until the case could come to trial. In deciding about whether or not to lift the restraining order, the court noted that the school was able to show substantial disruption to the work of school. In this case, so many students accessed the website that the school had to shut down its computer system, causing lost of instructional time and access for other students. Indeed, the school was "abuzz about the profiles, who created them, and how they could be accessed." Judge McVerry, therefore, refused to lift the restraining order, upholding the school's discipline. By the time the case can reach a full trial, the student will have long graduated.

In regard to off campus behaviour and Canadian courts, the high court has established in *Ross v. New Brunswick School District No. 15* (1996), that schools must maintain conditions that are conducive to leaning. Although the Ross case involved the free speech of a teacher who distributed anti-Semitic publications outside of school, the following statement from the ruling has been quoted in almost every Charter argument for a positive school environment:

> (S)chools are an arena for the exchange of ideas and must, therefore, be premised upon principles of tolerance and impartiality so that all persons within the school environment feel equally free to participate. As the board of inquiry stated, a school board has a duty to maintain a positive school environment for all persons served by it. (para 42)

Even though Ross's anti-Semitic publications were distributed outside the school context, the court noted that he poisoned the school and classroom environment for his Jewish students within the classroom. They knew about his publications and felt threatened, fearful, and uncomfortable. This is highly applicable to the cyber-bullying context. For example, schools often maintain that cyber-bullying falls outside their realm of responsibility because it occurs after regular schools hours. However, if we are to draw upon the rationale used in the preceding cases from both Canada and the U.S., it would seem that the on-campus/off-campus (physical vs. virtual space) distinction is moot if the actions cause disruption to the learning environment. It is the *effect* of the harassment, bullying, and threats (despite the fact that they are made outside of the physical school setting) that is important. The key for schools is to determine a clear nexus between the cyber-bullying act and the school. This can be established if the cyber-bullying was accessed or displayed at school, if it causes substantial disruption to the learning environment, or if the act created a poisoned or hostile environment for any student. Once the nexus is determined, school officials are justified, even obligated, to address it.

In sum, while U.S. courts lean toward supporting student free expression, they stress certain limits in the school context. Expressions that substantially or materially disrupt learning, interfere with the educational mission, utilize school-owned technology to harass, or threaten other students are not protected by the First Amendment and allow school intervention. The reasoning in these decisions does not substantially differ from a Supreme Court of Canada decision in *R. v. M.R.M* (1998) relating to the right of schools to restrict constitutional rights when school property and student privacy rights are involved.

Student Privacy and Cyber-bullying

Another legal issue that could arise in cyber-bullying situations is the need for schools to search a computer. In Canada, under Section 8 of the Charter, everyone has the right to be free from unreasonable search and seizure. Hence protection of privacy is guaranteed within reasonable limits in a free and democratic society. Furthermore, Section 7 of the Charter states that "everyone has the right to life, liberty, and security of the person." In the cyber-bullying context, both these sections are relevant. The boundaries with respect to the obligations on schools to over-ride search and seizure rights to protect others must be balanced with the right to life, liberty, and security of the person. Furthermore, victims might argue that their rights to life, liberty, and security of the person are infringed under Section 7 when schools fail to intervene and protect them from cyber-bullying.

Based on Section 1 considerations, the courts generally give priority to the safety of the greater number of stakeholders as justification for overriding privacy rights. In *R. v. M.R.M.* (1998) for example, the Supreme Court of Canada ruled that as long as a school principal is not acting as an agent of the police, he or she can search student lockers if there is a suspicion of hidden weapons or drugs. The high court held that school lockers are the property of schools. When there is a danger to safety and learning of the students,

Chapter 4: Lord of the E-Flies

the infringement on student privacy rights can be reasonably justified under Section 1 of the Charter. Given the devastating psychological consequences of cyber-bullying on victimized students and the entire school environment, it is quite possible that a Charter interpretation that requires a balancing of the victimized student's right to safety under S. 7 and the perpetrator's right to computer privacy under S. 8 and free expression under S. 2(b), the court might rule in favor of the victimized student.

The rationale used by the Supreme Court of Canada in *R. v. M.R.M.* (1998) was that students should already have a lowered expectation of privacy because they know that their school principals or administrators may need to conduct searches in schools, and that safety ought to be the overriding concern to protect students. The high court explained its interpretation of a safe and ordered school environment:

> Teachers and principals are placed in a position of trust that carries with it onerous responsibilities. When children attend school or school functions, it is they who must care for the children's safety and well-being. It is they who must carry out the fundamentally important task of teaching children so that they can function in our society and fulfill their potential. In order to teach, school officials must provide an atmosphere that encourages learning. During the school day, they must protect and teach our children. (p. 394)

Similarly in the United States, the Fourth Amendment of the U.S. Constitution guarantees protection from unreasonable searches and seizures. The legal cases involving schools have generally involved searches of lockers and backpacks, but recently the principles of those cases are being applied to searches of computers. Courts have held that schools need only "reasonable suspicion" to search, but caution, "A student's freedom from unreasonable search and seizure must be balanced against the school official's need to maintain order and discipline and to protect the health and welfare of all the students" (Alexander & Alexander, 2005). Schools may search school-owned property, such as lockers for routine maintenance or when they have reasonable suspicion that a student is harboring something illegal. In *People v. Overton* (1967), the courts noted that schools can issue policies regarding what may be stored in school lockers. Correspondingly, educators are entitled to conduct spot checks or involuntary searches of lockers to ensure that students comply with these regulations. In fact, the courts regard the inspection of student lockers not only as a right but also as a duty of schools when it is believed that a student is using school property to harbor illegal materials.

This point might be further justified by cases such as *Garrity v. John Hancock Mut. Life Ins. Co.* (D. Mass. May 7, 2002), where it was found that employers have a right to inspect employee email accounts in cases where employees have been warned their messages are accessible to the organization. With regard to school searches, we can also consider cases such as *New Jersey v. T.L.O.* (1985). In this ruling, it was found that although students have a legitimate expectation of privacy within the school setting, schools also have a right to search student property if there are reasonable grounds for suspecting that the student is violating either the law or the regulations of a school. Since the landmark T.L.O. case, courts have given schools even more latitude in conducting searches.

It would seem reasonable for schools to apply this rationale to technology, since students often use school-owned computers for purposes beyond the academic curriculum. If students are informed in advance that school equipment may be routinely searched (thus reducing their expectation of privacy), schools are likely to be upheld in random searches of their computer networks and school-owned equipment for purposes such as routine maintenance or when they have genuine concern for students' safety.

Tort Law and Negligence

Constitutional claims are expensive and time consuming. When suing schools, parents often turn first to the law of torts and negligence because it is remedial and plaintiffs can seek compensation for torts or "wrongs" by the institution. Negligence in supervision of children at school is one form of a tort. When a claim in negligence is brought against a school, the plaintiff must establish that there was a duty of care and tangible harm, that the tangible harm was foreseeable, and that the school official's actions or omissions either proximately or remotely caused the injury. Even though physical injuries are tangible and (in Canada) easier to establish (MacKay & Dickinson, 1998), the threshold for claimants in the U.S. is very high.

School law cases involving psychological harm are less common, but there are precedents. In *Spears v. Jefferson Parish School Board* (1994), for example, a kindergarten teacher scared one of his students by joking that he had killed another student. He even went so far as to put a rope around the child's neck and have him pretend to be dead. All of this caused considerable psychological damage to the student who was the brunt of joke, causing the court to find the school liable for the actions of the teacher that resulted in emotional harm to the child.

Courts have also supported claimants in cases involving suicide or psychological harm that could potentially result in suicide (Shariff, 2003). Bullying research and numerous media reports confirm that "bullycide" (suicide by victims of bullying) is on the rise (Harmon, 2004; DiGiulio, 2001). Similarly, courts in Britain have ruled that bullying is not only an educational problem -- it is also a health problem, acknowledging the severe consequences on the emotional and sometimes physical health of victims (Shariff, 2003). Gradually, the courts are beginning to recognize emotional and psychological harm as "tangible," including mental shock and suffering (Linden & Klar, 1994). Therefore, claims for negligence against schools under tort law may be more successful than charges of criminal harassment against perpetrators.

Canadian Human Rights and United States Sexual Harassment and Discrimination Law

Another area of law that relates to cyber-bullying (particularly with respect to sexual harassment in institutional settings), is Canadian human rights law which has established an institutional obligation to protect sexual harassment victims. Two cases illustrate this point.

The first involved a Canadian case of sexual harassment by a co-worker, both inside and outside the workplace (*Robichaud v. Canada*, Treasury Board, 1987). The Supreme Court of Canada ruled that institutions are responsible for providing safe environments for their employees even if the sexual harassment by a co-worker occurs outside of the workplace. The fact that the victimized individuals must face their tormentors in the workplace imposes an obligation on employers to address the problem effectively. This case is highly relevant to cyber-bullying because school officials often maintain they are not responsible for harassment by school-mates that occurs outside of school grounds, or outside school hours. As the Supreme Court of Canada confirmed in Robichaud, if the victimized individual has to face the perpetrator within the institution, the institution is responsible for correcting the problem no matter where the harassment actually took place.

A second example involves the homophobic harassment of a male high school student of Iranian heritage in British Columbia, Canada (*Jubran v. North Vancouver School District* 2002). Even though Azmi Jubran was not gay, his appearance caused the majority of students in his class to tease him as being gay for the duration of his four years at Handsworth Secondary School in North Vancouver. The British Columbia Human Rights Tribunal ruled that the school had created a negative school environment in failing to protect Jubran, or disciplining the perpetrators. The tribunal ruled that they did an inadequate job of educating the students to be inclusive and socially responsible. Upon appeal by the school board and the high school, the British Columbia Supreme Court adopted a narrow construction of the case. The judge ruled that, because the claim was brought under S. 8 of the Human Rights Code (which protects homosexuals from harassment), and because Jubran claimed that he was not homosexual – he had no claim! The British Columbia Court of Appeal rendered a more thoughtful and practical ruling, overturning the Supreme Court decision and re-instating the tribunal decision. The court reiterated that Jubran had every right to a claim against the school and school board because they fostered and sustained a negative school environment in which he was prevented from equal opportunities to an education free of discrimination and harassment (see Shariff & Strong-Wilson, 2005).

United States' protection from sexual harassment and gender discrimination is provided under Title IX of the Education Amendments of 1972. Additional protection for all forms of discrimination is provided under the Equal Protection Clause of the 14th Amendment of the U.S. Constitution, along with specific federal laws (e.g. Titles VI and VII of the Civil Rights Act of 1964) and states' Human Rights Laws.

Title IX states that "No person in the United States shall, on basis of sex, be excluded from participation in, be denied the benefits of, or be subjected to the discrimination under any education program or activity receiving federal financial assistance." Schools are clearly included in this group, and courts have held that schools must take reasonable steps to intervene in sexual harassment issues. Title IX guidelines suggest that it is the responsibility of schools to take action when they know or should have known about harassment.

The standard of "actual knowledge" versus "should have known" was tested in a landmark case on sexual harassment in schools. In *Gebser v. Lago Vista Independent School District* (1998), the Supreme Court of the United States, in a 5-4 decision, supported the "actual knowledge" standard. In this case a student was suffering abuse from her teacher, some of which occurred at school during an Advanced Placement class in which she was the only student. The plaintiffs argued that the school should have known about the abuse through proper supervision of the teacher. The court ruled that since the student had told no one about the abuse, the school could not be held liable. Although this seems to relieve schools of some responsibility, the Gebser ruling made it clear that if the school had received any information about this misconduct and had failed to take immediate action, the court would have considered that "deliberate indifference."

This premise was tested in the controversial landmark decision also in 1998. The case of *Davis v. Munroe* (1988) involved the persistent sexual harassment of a grade 5 female student, Lashonda Davis, whose parents informed the teachers and the school principal numerous times to no avail. Lashonda's grades dropped and her health was negatively affected. In a majority 5:4 decision, the Supreme Court ruled that in failing to act to protect Lashonda, the school had created a "deliberately dangerous environment" which prevented "equal opportunities for learning." In *Nabozny v. Podlesny* (1996), the court relied on the protections guaranteed in the 14th Amendment of the U.S. Constitution in finding for the plaintiff when the school failed to protect him against relentless harassment he had faced for being gay. The federal judge pointed out that it was the school's responsibility to protect gay students just as much as they would any other student.

The above cases illustrate that schools will be held liable if they fail to act when students are being harassed at school. The logical next assumption is that schools must likewise protect students from cyber-bullying, which creates a similarly dangerous environment for victimized students: Engendering fear and distraction and preventing those who are victimized from experiencing equal opportunities to learn.

Recommendations

1) Policy Development

As several scholars observe (MacKay & Burt-Gerrans 2005), zero-tolerance policies, suspension and criminal harassment charges against adolescents rarely solve school problems (Giroux, 2003; DiGiulio, 2001). In this regard, it is important that schools acknowledge their important role as educators, and work with parents and relevant stakeholders to develop non-arbitrary policies that can be implemented through positive educational programs and critical thinking tools that provide students with beneficial Internet experiences. In Canada, the Media Awareness Network website provides excellent programming options for students at all grade levels. In the United States, i-SAFE America, a nonprofit internet safety foundation endorsed by the U.S. Congress, also provides valuable resources to schools, students, parents, and law enforcement officials in protecting the online experiences of K-12 students. Schools cannot address this problem alone. They must inform their policies through collaboration with other stakeholders.

2) Research, Teacher Education and Professional Development

University faculties of education and social sciences can assist the efforts of policy makers by conducting research, improving teacher education and providing professional development on this emerging and complex form of harassment. They should also collaborate with the legal community to develop guidelines for schools and incorporate this knowledge into teacher education, leadership preparation, and professional development programs. Educators need tools to develop and implement inclusive, educational, and legally defensible policies and practices in a rapidly evolving age of new technologies

3) Interactive Online Educational Programs .

We also need to increase the development of interactive online educational programs that help students arrive at their own moral and ethical judgments about social relationships, issues of discrimination, and take leadership and responsibility in fostering positive and inclusive virtual environments. A number of positive initiatives and recommendations have been advanced by Media Awareness Network (Steeves & Wing, 2005); as well as Willard (2005) and Balfour (2005) where adult programming provides the support and guidance on Internet and technology use and relationships. Media Awareness Network, for example, found in their recent study (Steeves & Wing, 2005) that children as young as nine were interested in knowing how to authenticate information on the internet to avoid predators and harassment. Many of the students interviewed expressed an interest in finding educational resources and expressed a desire to engage in responsible use of the resources available to them.

4) Student Empowerment and Critical Thinking

Finally, empowerment and student participation in learning, critical thinking and rule-making are essential so that we do not abandon young people on the island of virtual reality. It is crucial that we engage young people in the rule-making aspects relating to responsible-use of new technologies, and work with them (on a consistent and supportive basis) to help them think critically about the consequences of their actions for victimized students, their own education, and their families. In this regard, the international work of TC2 (The Critical Thinking Consortium) directed by Professor Roland Case (in press, 2005) would be highly applicable. The consortium works with schools and teachers to infuse critical thinking into the curriculum, whereby students are presented with problematic scenarios and taught the tools to help them to make reasoned judgments about their actions, attitudes and responses in specific situations. As Willard (2005) suggests, in the cyber-bullying context, it is crucial to provide the supports to help young people reconnect with their sense of ethics, so that they can think critically about the impact of their online actions and attitudes.

Conclusion

In sum, now that the complexities and negative potential of new technologies have emerged, it is time to work collaboratively with students, parents, technology corporations, universities, law enforcement providers, and governments to establish codes of conduct and guidelines. While technology corporations are reluctant to monitor and edit online abuse because of the reverse effect of protective laws that might hold them liable in the U.S., courts need to revisit their approach to liability and develop a more balanced approach that resembles the decision adopted by a British court in *Godfrey v. Demon Internet Ltd.* (1999). The court in that case held that once the ISP knows about the cyber-bullying and fails to act, it is liable under *the Defamation Act of* 1996, 31 (Eng.).

When it comes to supporting and protecting children and youth, we cannot rely solely on Internet providers or the courts. We must monitor virtual discourse on a regular basis, and act quickly to address complaints of cyber-bullying before adolescent relationships deteriorate to the level that they did on that remote island in *Lord of the Flies*. If we can prevent even one child or teenager, like Piggy, from falling through the cracks and down the cliff of virtual reality, then we are well on our way to protecting and educating students, and keeping schools out of court. It will require considerable effort and a unified approach in order to delineate clearly the parameters of civil behaviour and to establish consequences for misbehaviour. But only with such guidelines can we hope to rescue students from the virtual *Lord of the Flies* island where they now find themselves.

Chapter 4: Lord of the E-Flies

Key Messages

1) Cyber-bullying is complex, insidious, and anonymous in nature. It is conveyed primarily on home computers (via email, chat rooms and personal online profiles) and by personal cell-phones. It is largely unsupervised by adults. We have provided the analogy to *Lord of the Flies*, which highlighted the social deterioration that occurs when adolescents are unsupervised by adults. Cyber-bullying contains a significant amount of gender-based harassment and homophobia.

2) Our review of the legal considerations that arise with respect to defamation, freedom of expression, student safety, and privacy in the school context highlights that although online harassment occurs in virtual space, it nonetheless constitutes a form of "real" violence that threatens safety, disrupts learning and impedes the educational mission of the school. It ought to be understood and interpreted this way by schools as directed by the courts.

3) The right of schools to intervene to reduce cyber-bullying is also related to their obligations to provide students with a safe school environment that provides equal opportunities to learn. Canadian constitutional decisions in Ross (1996) and Robichaud (1987) support the need for schools to provide positive school environments, which we have argued extend to virtual space. Furthermore, human rights jurisprudence on sexual harassment in Canada and the U.S. has supported the institutional obligation to address harassment regardless of whether it takes place on or off school property.

4) It is important for schools to foster inclusive school environments and attend to every complaint of cyber-bullying through educational and communicative means. To do so, we propose a four pronged approach, which involves: 1) developing non-arbitrary and non-reactive policies; 2) encouraging university research, teacher education and professional development grounded in substantive law; 3) endorsing interactive online educational programming; and 4) empowering young people to engage in critical thinking to promote positive online interaction.

References

Adam, A. (2001). *Cyberstalking: Gender and computer ethics.* In E. Green & A. Adam (Eds.), *Virtual gender: Technology, consumption and identity* (pp. 209-224). New York: Routledge.

Aftab, P. (2004). *Understanding the cyber-harassment problem.* Information Week. Retrieved July 12, 2005, from http://www.informationweek.com/story/showarticle.jhtml?article ID=29116706.

Alexander, K., & Alexander, M. D. (2005). *American public school law* (6th edition). Belmont, CA: Thomson West.

Anand, S. S. (1999). *Preventing youth crime: What works, what doesn't and what it all means for Canadian juvenile justice.* Queens Law Journal. 25(1), 179-249.

Artz, S., Riecken, E., MacIntyre, B., Lam, E., & Maczewski, M.(2000). *Theorizing gender differences in receptivity to violence prevention programming in schools.* The BC Counsellor, Journal of the B.C. School Counsellors Association. 22(1), 7-35.

Balfour, C. (2005). *A Journey of Social Change: Turning Government Digital Strategy Into CyberSafe Local School Practices.* Paper presented at Oxford Internet Institute, Oxford University, U.K. International Conference on Cyber-Safety. Paper archived at www.oii.ox.ac.uk/cybersafety.

Bandura, A. (1991). *Social cognitive theory of moral thought and action.* In W. M. Kurtines & J. L. Gewirtz (Eds.), *Handbook of moral behaviour and development* (Vol. 1, pp. 45-103). Hillsdale, NJ: Lawrence Erlbaum..

Barak, A. (2005). *Sexual harassment on the internet.* Social Science Computer Review, 23(1), 77-92.

Belsey, B. (2005). *Internet usage: facts and news.* Retrieved July 8, 2005, from http://www.cyber-bullying.ca/fact.html.

Blair, J. (2003). *New breed of bullies torment their peers on the internet.* Education Week. 22 (21). 6.

Boulton, M. J. (1993). *A comparison of adults' and children's abilities to distinguish between aggressive and playful fighting in middle school pupils. Implications for playground supervision and behaviour management.* Educational Studies. 19, 193-203.

Boyd, N. (2000). *The beast within: Why men are violent.* Vancouver, BC: Greystone Books.

Campbell, M. (2005). *Cyber-bullying: An older problem in a new guise?* Australian Journal of Guidance and Counselling. 15(1). 68-76.

Case, R. (in press). *Teaching and assessing the "tools" for thinking.* In J. Sobocan and L. Groarke (Eds), *Critical Thinking, Education and Assessment.* London, ON: Althouse Press.

Case, R. (2005). *Bringing critical thinking to the main stage,* Education Canada, 45(2), 45-49.

Cassidy, W. and Jackson, M. (2005). *The Need for Equality in Education: An Intersectionality Examination of Labeling and Zero Tolerance Practices.* McGill Journal of Education. 40 (3) Fall, 2005. 445-466.

Chu, J. (8 August, 2005). *You wanna take this online? Cyberspace is the 21st century bully's playground where girls play rougher than boys.* Time, 42-43. Toronto.

Curtis, P. (1997). *Mudding: Social phenomena in text-based virtual realities.* In S. Kiesler (Ed.), *Culture of the internet* (pp. 121-142). Mahwah, NJ: Lawrence Erlbaum Associates. Cyber-Libel Website. Retrieved May 2, 2004, from http://www.cyberlibel.com/bibl.html.

Devlin, A. (1997). *Offenders at school: links between school failure and aggressive behaviour.* In D. Tattum, & H. Graham, (Eds.), *Bullying: Home, school and community.* London: David Fulton. 149-158.

Dei, G. S. (1997). *Race and the production of identity in the schooling experiences of African-Canadian youth.* Discourse Studies in the Cultural Politics of Education, 18(2), 241-257.

Dickie, M., Merchant, K., Nakamoto, M., Nuttall, C., Terazono, E., and Yeager, H. (2004, April 13). *Digital Media.* Financial Times. Section: Creative Business. Pg. 8. Retrieved LEXIS NEXIS January 21, 2006.

Dibbell, J. (1993, December 21). *A rape in cyberspace.* Village Voice, 38.

DiGiulio, R. C. (2001). *Educate, medicate, or litigate? What teachers, parents, and administrators must do about student behaviour.* Thousand Oaks, CA: Corwin Press.

Evard, M. (1996). *"So please stop, thank you": Girls online.* In L. Cherny & E. R. Weise (Eds.), *Wired_women: Gender and new realities in cyberspace* (pp. 188-204). Toronto: Seal Press.

Finn, J. (2004). *A survey of online harassment at a university campus.* Journal of Interpersonal Violence, 19(4), 468-483.

Finn, J., & Banach, M. (2000). *Victimization online: The downside of seeking human services for women on the Internet.* Cyberpsychology & Behavior, 3(5), 785-796.

Garbarino, J. (1999). *Lost boys. Why our sons turn violent and how we can save them*. New York: The Free Press.

Gáti, Á., Tényi, T., Túry, F., & Wildmann, M. (2002). *Anorexia nervosa following sexual harassment on the Internet: A case report*. The International Journal of Eating Disorders, 31(4), 474-477.

Giroux, H. (2003). *The Abandoned Generation: Democracy beyond the culture of fear*. New York: Palgrave MacMillan.

Godwin, M. (2003). *Cyber Rights. Defending Free Speech in the Digital Age*. Cambridge, MA: The MIT Press.

Glover, D., Cartwright, N., & Gleeson, D. (1998). *Towards bully-free schools*. Buckingham and Philadelphia: Open University Press.

Golding, W. (1954). *Lord of the Flies*. New York: Penguin Putnam, Inc.

Harmon, A. (26, August, 2004). *Internet Gives Teenage Bullies Weapons…from afar*. New York Times. http://www.nytimes.com./2004/08/26/education. Accessed August 26, 2004.

Herring, S. C. (1999). *The rhetorical dynamic of gender harassment online*. The Information Society, 15, 151-167.

Herring, S. C. (2002). *Cyber violence: Recognizing and resisting abuse in online environments*. Asian Women, 14, 187-212.

Internet Bullying Website. Retrieved May 21, 2004, from http://www.slais.ubc.ca/courses/libr500/02-03-wtl/www/L_Serviss/index

iSafeAmerica, Retrieved May 5, 2006, at www.isafe.org/.

Jackson, M., Cassidy, W., and Brown, K. (unpublished report 2006). *The Need for Policy Development in Response to Cyber-bullying: Where is the balance to be established?* Overview of research conducted as part of a three year research project on cyber-bullying, funded by Social Science and Humanities Research Council of Canada (SSHRC). Shaheen Shariff, McGill University, Principal Investigator, Margaret Jackson and Wanda Cassidy, Simon Fraser University Co-Investigators, Colleen Sheppard, McGill University, Collaborator.

Johnson, G. J., Cohen, P., Smailes, E. M., Kasen, S., & Brook, J. (2002, March). *Television viewing and aggressive behavior during adolescence and adulthood*. Science, 295, 2468-2470.

Katch, J. (2001). *Under deadman's skin: Discovering the meaning of children's violent play*. Boston: Beacon Press.

LaRocque, L. & Shariff, S. (2001). *An analysis of anti-violence policies and programs in British Columbia schools*. Report prepared for British Columbia Ministry of Education.

Larson, C .L. (1997). *Is the Land of Oz an alien nation? A sociopolitical study of school community conflict*. Educational Administration Quarterly. 33(3), 312-350.

Leishman, J. (10, October, 2002). *Cyber-bullying: The Internet is the latest weapon in a bully's arsenal*. CBC News, The National. Retrieved January 27, 2003, from http://cbc.ca/news/national/news/cyber-bullying/index.html.

Li, Q. (2005). *Cyber-bullying in schools: The nature extent of adolescents' experience*. Paper presented at the American Education Research Association (AERA) Conference in Montreal, Quebec, Canada, April, 2005.

Linden, A. M., & Klar, L. N. (Eds.) (1994) (10th) and (1999) (11th). *Canadian tort law: Cases, notes & materials*. Markham, ON and Vancouver, BC: Butterworths Canada Ltd.

MacKay, A.W. & Burt-Gerrans, J. (2005). *Student Freedom of Expression: Violent content and the safe school balance*. McGill Journal of Education. 40 (3). Fall, 2005. 423-443.

MacKay, A.W. & Dickinson, G. M. (1998). *Beyond the "Careful Parent": Tort Liability in Education. Education in Law in Canada Series*. Toronto, Ontario: Emond Montgomery Publications.

MacKinnon, R. (2001). *Virtual rape*. Journal of Computer Mediated Communication, 2(4), np.

McCormick, N., & Leonard, J. (1996). *Gender and sexuality in the cyberspace frontier*. Women & Therapy, 19(4), 109-119.

Milson, A. & Chu, B.W. (2002). *Character Education for Cyberspace: Developing Good Netizens*. The Social Studies (Washington, D.C.) 93 (3). 117-119.

Mitchell, A. (Saturday, January 24, 2004). *Bullied by the click of a mouse*. The Globe and Mail. Retrieved May 21, 2004, from http://www.cyber-bullying.ca/globe-mail_January 24.html.

Myers, .D.A. (2006). *Defamation and the Quiescent Anarchy of the Internet: A Case Study of Cyber-Targeting*. Penn State Law Review. 110 (3). 667-686. Winter, 2006.

National Children's Home and Tesco Mobile (2002). http://www.nch.org.uk/information/index.php?i=237. Retrieved by Karen Brown under SSHRC Cyber-Bullying Project December, 2005.

Olweus, D. (2001). *Peer harassment: A critical analysis and some important issues*. Introduction in J. Juvonen & S. Graham (Eds), *Peer harassment in school: The plight of the vulnerable and victimized* (pp. 3-20). New York, NY: Guildford Press.

Parks, M. and Floyd, K. (1996). *Making friends in cyber-space*. Journal of Communication. 46 (1). 80-97.

Pepler, D. (1997). *Bullying: Research and interventions. Youth Update*. Institute for the Study of Anti-Social Youth. Reported in National Crime Prevention Centre website: www.crime-prevention.org. Retrieved September 8, 2001.

Pollack, W. (1998). *Real Boys*. Markham, ON: Fitzhenry & Whiteside Ltd.

Rice, R.E. (1987). *Computer-mediated communication and organizational innovation*. Journal of Communication. 37. 65-94

Rice, R.E. & Love, G. (1987). *Electonric emotion: Socioemotinoal content in a computer Mediated communication network*. Communication Research. 14. 85-108.

Riley, D. M. (1996). *Sex, fear and condescension on campus: Cybercensorship at Carnegie Mellon*. In L. Cherny & E. R. Weise (Eds.), *Wired women: Gender and new realities in cyberspace*, (pp. 158-168). Toronto: Seal Press.

Razack, S. (1999). *Looking white people in the eye: Gender, race and culture in courtrooms and classrooms*. Toronto: University of Toronto Press.

Ross-Epp, J. (1996). *Schools, Complicity, and Sources of Violence*. In J. Ross-Epp & A. M. Watkinson (Eds.), *Systemic violence: How schools hurt children* (pp. 1-25). London: Falmer Press.

Salmivalli, C., Lagerspetz, K., Björkqvist, K., Österman, K., & Kaukianen, A. (1996). *Bullying as a group process: Participant roles and their relations to social status within the group*. Aggressive Behavior. 25, 81-89.

Servance, R. L. (2003). *Cyber-bullying, cyber-harassment, and the conflict between schools and the First Amendment*. Wisconsin Law Review. 1213 at 1215.

Shariff, S. (2003). *A System on Trial: Identifying Legal Standards for Educational, Ethical and Legally Defensible Approaches to Bullying in Schools*. Doctoral Dissertation. Simon Fraser University, Burnaby, B.C.

Shariff, S. (2004). *Keeping schools out of court: Legally defensible models of leadership to reduce cyber-bullying*. Educational Forum, Delta Kappa Pi. 68(3) 222 – 233.

Shariff, S. (2005) *Cyber-Dilemmas in the New Millennium: Balancing Free Expression and Student Safety in Cyber-Space*. Special Issue: *Schools and Courts: Competing Rights in the New Millennium*. McGill Journal of Education. 40(3) 467-487.

Shariff, S. (2006). *Cyber-dilemmas: Balancing free expression and learning in a virtual school environment*. International Journal of Learning. Common Ground,Volume 12. ISSN. 1447-9494 (print), 1447-9540 (online).

Shariff, S. (in press). *Cyber-Hierarchies: A new arsenal of weapons for gendered violence in schools*. (Claudia Mitchell and Fiona Leech, Eds. 2006). *Combatting Gender Violence in and around Schools*. London, Eng: Trentham Books (chapter and page numbers to be determined).

Shariff, S., & Gouin, R. (2005). *CYBER-DILEMMAS: Gendered Hierarchies, Free Expression and Cyber-Safety in Schools*. Paper presented at Oxford Internet Institute, Oxford University, U.K. International Conference on Cyber-Safety. Paper archived at www.oii.ox.ac.uk/cybersafety.

Shariff, S., & Johnny, L. (in press). *The Role of the Charter in Balancing Freedom of Expression, Safety and Equality in a Virtual School Environment*. (Michael Manley-Casimir, Ed., 2005). *Courts, Charter and the Schools: The Impact of Judicial Decisions on Educational Policy and Practice*. Toronto, ONT: University of Toronto Press. (Chapter and page numbers to be determined).

Shariff, S., & Strong-Wilson, T. (2005). *Bullying and New Technologies* (Kincheloe, J. Ed. 2005). *Classroom Teaching: An Introduction*. New York: David Lang Publishers. Ch.14, 219-240.

Short, J., Williams, E., & Christie, B. (1976). *The social psychology of telecommunication*. London, England: John Wiley.

Skiba, R., & Peterson, R. (1999, January). *The dark side of zero tolerance: Can punishment lead to safe schools?* Phi Delta Kappan. 80 (5): 372-6, 381-3.

Sproull, L. & Kiesler, S. (1991). *Connections: New ways of working in the networked organization*. Cambridge, MA: MIT Press.

Steeves, V. & Wing, C. (2005). *Young Canadians in a Wired World*. Media Awareness Network. www.media-awareness.ca.

Tolman, D. L., Spencer, R., Rosen-Reynoso, M., & Porches, M. (2001, April 13). *"He's the man!" Gender ideologies and early adolescents' experiences with sexual harassment*. Paper presented at the American Educational Researchers Association (AERA), Seattle, Washington.

Wallace, P. (1999). *The Psychology of the Internet*. Cambridge, UK: Cambridge University Press.

Wallis, C. (2006). *The Multitasking Generation*. TIME. Canadian Edition. March 27, 2006. 34–39.

Willard, N. (2005). *Educator's Guide to Cyber-Bullying: addressing the harm caused by online social cruelty*. Retrieved July 19, 2005, from http://cyberbully.org.

Wolak, J., Mitchell, K. J., & Finkelhor, D. (2003). *Escaping or connecting? Characteristics of youth who form close online relationships*. Journal of Adolescence, 26. 105-119.

Ybarra M. & Mitchell, K. (2004b). *Youth engaging in online harassment: Association with caregiver-child relationships, Internet use, and personal characteristics*. Journal of Adolescence. 27 (3). 319-336.

List of Cases

Beidler v. North Thurston School District Number 3, 99--2-00236-6 (Wash. Supr. Ct. 2000).

Bethel School District No. 403 et al. v. Fraser, a minor, et al., 478 U.S. 675 (1986).

Beussink v. Woodland R-IV School District, 30 F. Supp. 2d 1175 (E.D. Mo. 1988).

Board of Education of Independent School District No. 92 of Pottawatomie County v. Earls, 536 U.S. 822, 122 S. Ct. 2559 (2002).

Bryson v. News America Publ'ns, Inc. 627 N.E. 2d. 1207 (Ill. 1996).

Davis v. Monroe County Board of Education, 1107 91 F.3d 1418 (1996).

Emmet v. Kent School District No 413, 92F. Supp. 2d 1088 (WD Wash. 2000).

Flaherty v. Keystone Oaks School District, 247F Supp. 2d 446 (W. D. PA 2001).

Garrity v. John Hancock Mut. Life Ins. Co., 18 IER Cases 981 (D. Mass. May 7, 2002).

Gebser v. Lago Vista Independent School District, 524 U.S. 274 (1998).

Grace v. E-bay Inc. 16 Cal. Rptr. 3d 192, 196 (Cal. Ct. App. 2004), review granted, 99 P. 3d 2 (Cal. 2004), review dismissed and remanded, 101 P. 3d 509 (Cal. 2004).

Godfrey v. Demon Internet Ltd. (1999). [2001] Q.B. 201.

Hazelwood School District v. Kuhlmeier, 484 U.S. 260 (1988).

Irwin Toy Ltd. v. Québec (A.G.), (1989) 1 S.C.R. 927).

J.S., a Minor, v. Bethlehem Area School District, 757 A.2d 412 (Pa.Commw. 2000).

John Doe v. GTE Corp. 347. F. 3d. 655. (7th Cir. 2003).

Jubran v. North Vancouver School District, (2002) BCHRT 10.

Killion v. Franklin Regional School District, 136 F. Supp. 2d 446 (2001).

Layshock v. Hermitage School District, 2:06-cv-00116 TFM (2006).

Lutes v. Board of Education of Prairie View School Division No. 74, (1992).

Nabozny v. Podlesny, 92 F.3d 446 (1996).

New Jersey v. T.L.O., 469 U.S. 325 (1985).

People v. B.F. Jones, 62 Mich. 304, 28 NW 839 (1886).

People v. Overton, 20 N.Y. 360 (1967).

R. v. D.W. and K.P.D., (2002) BCPC 0096.

R. v. M.R.M, (1998) 3 S.C.R. 393.

R. v. Oakes, (1986) 1 S.C.R. 103, 26 D.L.R. 94th) 200, 24 C.C.C. (3d) 321.

Robichaud v. Canada, (Treasury Board), (1987)2 S.C.R.

Ross v. New Brunswick School District No. 15, (1996) 1 S.C.R. 826.

Spears v. Jefferson Parish School Board, 646 So. 2d. 1104 (1994).

Stratton Oakmont v. Prodigy Services Co. (1995). N.Y. Misc. LEXIS 229 (N.Y. App. Div. 1995)

Tinker v. Des Moines Independent Community School District, **393 U.S. 503 (1969).**

Veronia School District 47J v. Acton, 515 U.S. 646, 115 S.Ct. 2386 (1995).

Zeran v. America Online, Inc. 129 F. 3d. 327 (4th Cir. 1997).

Chapter 5:

Matching Interventions to Bullying Subtypes: Ensuring Programs Fit the Multifaceted Needs of Children Involved in Bullying

Zopito A. Marini and Andrew V. Dane
Brock University

Introduction

Bullying Prevalence and Its Psychosocial Consequences

Bullying, a type of peer aggression characterized by repeated and systematic coercive use of power, is a major concern for educators and health practitioners because of its prevalence and its considerable impact on those who bully, are victimized, or are bystanders (Marini, Dane, Bosacki, & YLC-CURA, 2006a; Olweus, 2001; **Smith,** Pepler, & Rigby, 2004). Research has shown that involvement in bullying is pervasive, with estimates ranging from as low as 10% to as high as 30% of the student population (Marini, McWhinnie, & Lacharite, 2004; Nansel, Overpeck, Pilla, Ruan, Simons, & Scheidt, 2001). Although the prevalence statistics are dependent on the way bullying is measured, there is considerable agreement that about 10 to 15% of students are likely to report being bullied, with 5 to 10% reporting having bullied others (Nansel et al., 2001; Rigby, 2001). In addition, there is an emerging group, ranging from 10 to 15%, who are dually involved in both bullying others and being victimized (Craig, 1998; Marini et al., 2006a; Olweus, 2001; Schwartz, Proctor, & Chein, 2001).

Engagement in bullying is associated with a range of psychosocial problems including peer rejection, psychiatric difficulties such as conduct and anxiety disorder, and poor academic performance (Coie, Dodge, & Kupersmidt, 1990; Haynie, Nansel, Eitel, Crump, Saylor, Yu et al., 2001; Loeber, Green, Lahey, & Kalb, 2000; Nansel et al., 2001; Olweus, 2001). Furthermore, several aspects of maladjustment in adulthood have been linked to childhood and adolescent aggression or bullying, including criminal convictions, unemployment, smoking and substance use, partner abuse, depression and anxiety, lower level of education, high school drop out, and lower status occupation (Farrington, 1993;

Moffitt, Caspi, Harrington, & Milne, 2002; Rigby, 2001). Students who are victimized often report an array of internalizing difficulties related to anxiety, depression and self-esteem, as well as a heightened risk of suicide (Craig, 1998; Grills & Ollendick, 2002; Rigby, 2001). In addition to the large spectrum of psychosocial problems associated with bullying and victimization, these aggressive incidents in the school may disrupt classroom activities by diverting teachers' time from other students, affecting the overall school climate, and contributing to a classroom atmosphere that is not conducive to learning (Nucci, 2006).

One obstacle to understanding and preventing bullying and victimization is that bullying is a more complex and heterogenous concept than was originally believed to be the case (Little, Brauner, Jones, Nock, & Hawley, 2003; Toblin, Schwartz, Hopmeyer-Gorman, & Abou-ezzeddine, 2005). For instance, there appear to be several subtypes or variations of bullying, characterized by differences in the manifestation of the bullying behaviour. One distinction is whether the form of bullying is direct, hitting and name calling for example, or indirect, which involves circuitous attacks such as social exclusion or rumour spreading (e.g., Little et al., 2003; Vaillancourt, Brendgen, Boivin, & Tremblay, 2003a). An additional consideration is whether its function is reactive, entailing provoked, emotional, defensive aggression, or proactive, involving planned, reward-driven, instrumental aggression (Little et al., 2003). In addition, recent research has shown that a substantial proportion of students who report involvement in either bullying or victimization indicate that they have experienced both (about 33%) (Marini et al., 2006a).

One caveat worth mentioning before proceeding is that the subtypes are not mutually exclusive categories, but rather are moderately to highly correlated. Published correlations between proactive and reactive aggression range from .09 to .87, with the majority being above .70 (Camodeca, Goossens, Meerum, Terwogt, & Schuengel, 2002; Dodge, Price, Bachorowski, & Newman, 1990; Kupersmidt, Willoughby, & Bryant, 1998; Price & Dodge, 1989). The low correlation of .09 involved direct observations rather than the questionnaire ratings that are more typically used. Furthermore, pure reactive aggression is more common than pure proactive aggression and it is not unusual for children to show both subtypes of aggressive behaviour (Merk et al., 2005). In a similar vein, indirect and direct aggression are moderately correlated, with correlations of .44 and .45 reported in two recent studies (Marini et al., 2006a; Vaillancourt et al., 2003a). However, despite being correlated, the literature suggests that each subtype is uniquely associated with different potential causal factors and consequences, providing evidence for conceptual distinctions among varieties of bullying (see below). Whereas children who bully may well use multiple methods of aggression in perpetrating their attacks, it appears that some children use one type of bullying predominantly (Crick & Dodge, 1996; Crick & Grotpeter, 1995; Vaillancourt et al., 2003a). Thus, one goal of the present paper is to delineate the heterogeneity of bullying in order to raise awareness among those who work with children and youth as to the different forms it may take. A second objective is to explore possibilities for individualizing interventions to meet the specific needs of students who manifest difficulties mainly with a particular type of bullying, or to ensure that interventions are sufficiently comprehensive to address the features of each subtype.

Chapter 5: Matching Interventions to Bullying Subtypes

Table 1 Studies Comparing the Psychosocial Adjustment of Bullying Subtypes

Subtype	Subtype Characteristics					
Form	Temperament	Social Cognition / Social Skills	Co-morbid Psychopathology	Parenting	Peer Relations	
Direct	Shyness -r 25	Hostile attribution bias > NA for instrumental provocations 29		Maternal coercion +r 31	Peer rejection	
				Paternal responsiveness -r 31	Perceived popularity -r 27	
		Positive evaluation of overtly aggressive strategies > NA 30		Maternal physical punishment +r boys OA; paternal physical punishment -r boys' and girls OA		
		Social intelligence -r 28				
		Social skills -r 27				
		Empathy -r 28				

Subtype			Subtype Characteristics		
	Temperament	Social Cognition/ Social Skills	Parenting		
	Co-morbid Psychopathology			Peer Relations	
Form					
Indirect	Shyness -r 25	Hostile attribution bias > NA		Loneliness > NA 34	Paternal responsiveness -r 31	Peer rejection 33
	Sociability +r 26	for relational provocations 29		Depression > NA 34	Maternal coercion +r 31	Perceived popularity +r 27
						Perceived popularity +r later IA; > girls 37
		Evaluation of IA responses			Paternal psychological control +r for girls' RA 32	IA +r later perceived popularity; > girls 36
						Social preference, social impact +r later
		not different than NA 30				IA for boys only 35
					Maternal physical punishment +r	Social preference -r 37; > girls
		Social intelligence +r 27, 28			to boys' RA; paternal physical	Network centrality +r 38
					punishment -r to boys' RA 32	RA +r later social impact, girls only 35
		Empathy -r 28				Dating popularity, number of romantic partners 39, 40

Chapter 5: Matching Interventions to Bullying Subtypes

Subtype Characteristics

Subtype	Temperament / Co-morbid Psychopathology	Social Cognition/ Social Skills		Parenting	Peer Relations
Function					
Proactive	Reduced responsiveness to distressing stimuli 22	Positive outcome evaluation and self-efficacy for aggression > NA 17,19	Delinquency +r 1,14	Monitoring < NA, RA 4	Perceived as leaders 21
		20	Conduct Disorder +r 1, 14	Household rule < NA, RA 4	
			Adult criminality +r 15		Reciprocated friendships > RA 9
			Low remorse or empathy 51		Friends' proactive aggression +r 8
	Withdrawal > NA 1	Anticipated positive intrapersonal consequences in SIP > RA, NA 3	Drug use +r 16		Friends' proactive aggression +r
			Internalizing > NA 3		increase in PA over 1 year 8
			Narcissistic exploitativeness 52		
		Positive relational outcome expect-			Popularity +r 6
		ancies +r 24			

101

Subtype Characteristics

Subtype	Temperament	Social Cognition/ Social Skills	Peer Relations			
	Co-morbid Psychopathology	Parenting				
Function						
Reactive	Inattention > NA 1	Hostile attributions > NA 3,12, 17,18, 20	ADHD +r in DBD boys 12	Controlling > NA, PA 2	Popularity, social preference -r	
	Reactivity > NA 1		Classroom disruption +r 10	Punitiveness > NA, PA 2	with overt RA; +r with relational RA 6	
	Withdrawal > NA 1	Suppressed attention to rejection, ridicule, failure 18	Social skills < NA 11		Peer victimization +r 6	
	Activity > NA 1		Anxiety > NA 1	Physical abuse > NA, PA 3	Peer rejection +r 7	
			Depression > NA 1	Harsh discipline > NA 3	Social preference < NA, PA 3, 5	
	Impulsivity +r 23	Aggressive responses generated in SIP > NA, PA 3, 21	Dating violence			
			Internalizing > NA 3			
			Academic performance -r 11			
		Endorsement, self-efficacy of aggression in SIP > NA 3	Inattention > NA 1, 3			
			Frustration/ hostility > NA 13			
		Instrumental outcome expectations -r 12				

Chapter 5: Matching Interventions to Bullying Subtypes

Subtype Characteristics

Subtype	Temperament	Social Cognition/ Social Skills	Peer Relations	Parenting	
	Co-morbid Psychopathology				
Involvement					
Bully-Victim	Emotionality +r 41	Problem-solving control < B, V, UG 44	Depression > UG 45	Restricive discipline > B,V, UG 50	Social preference < B, V, UG 45
	Irritability +r 42	Emotion Dysregulation > B, V, UG 45	Loneliness > B, UG 45	Marital conflict > V, UG 50	Friends' aggression +r 46
	Frustration tolerance -r 42	Assertiveness < B, UG 45	Anxiety > B, V 48	Maternal hostility > B, V, UG 50	
	Positive mood < UG 43	Submissiveness > B, V 45	Academic competence < V,	Marital aggression > B, V, UG 50	
	Activity level > UG 43	Blame, anger, retaliation in SIP > UG 47	UG 48	Parental aggression > B, V, UG 50	
	Approach -r 42		School refusal > B, V 49		
			Hyperactivity 49		
			Disruptiveness 49		

103

Studies

1 Vitaro, Brendgen & Tremblay (2002); 2 Bowen & Vitaro (1998); 3 Dodge et al (1997); 4 Poulin & Dishion, 2000; 5 Poulin & Boivin (2000a); 6 Prinstein & Cillesen (2003)

7 Dodge et al. (2003); 8 Poulin & Boivin (2000b); 9 Vitaro & Brendgen (2005); 10 Waschbusch, Willoughby & Pelham (1998;) 11 Day, Bream & Paul (1992)

12 Kempes et al (2006); 13 Little et al (2003); 14 Vitaro, Gendreau, Tremblay & Oligny (1998); 15 Pulkkinen (1996);16 Connor, Steingard, Anderson, Melloni (2003)

17 Hubbard et al (2001); 18 Scheppal et al (2003); 19 Crick & Dodge (1996); 20 Orbito de Castro et al (2005); 21 Dodge & Coie (1987); 22 Kimonis et al. (2006)

23 Raine et al (2006); 24 Smithmyer, Hubbard & Simons (2000); 25 Russell et al (2003); 26 Park et al (2005); 27 Andreou (2006); 28 Kaukiainen et al (1999)

29 Crick, Grotpeter & Bigbee (2002); 30 Crick & Werner (1998); 31 Hart et al (1998); 32 Nelson & Crick (2002); 33 Crick et al. (1997); 34 Crick and Grotpeter (1995)

35 Zimmer-Gembeck, Geiger & Crick (2005); 36 Rose, Swenson & Waller (2004); 37 Cillesen & Mayeux (2004); 38 Xie et al (2002); 39Pellegrini & Long (2003)

40 Vaillancourt (2005); 41Pellegrini &Bartini (2000); 42 Hess & Atkins (1998); 43 Marini, Dane, Bosacki & YLC-CURA (2006); 44 Cassidy & Taylor (2005)

45 Toblin, Schwartz, Gorman & Abou-ezzeddine (2005); 46 Mouttapa, Valente, Gallaher, Rohrbach, & Unger (2004); 47 Camodeca, Goossens, Schuengel, & Meerum Terwogt (2003)

48 Schwartz (2000); 49 Kumpulainen et al (1998); 50 Shwartz, Dodge, Pettit & Bates (1997); 51 Cornell et al. (1996); 52 Washburn, McMahon, King, Reinecke & Silver (2004)

Brief Review of Interventions for Bullying and Victimization

Four core strategies are incorporated, either alone or in combination, into established bullying intervention programs, including: (1) Whole-school approaches; (2) Participant-role approaches; (3); Social Competence Training; and (4) Parent Management Training.

Whole-School Approach

The whole-school approach engages multiple levels of the school community in the bullying prevention initiative. At the school level, meetings and discussion groups are held with teachers and administrators to raise awareness and to coordinate school-wide strategies for reducing bullying, such as effectively monitoring students during break times. Within classrooms, teachers establish clear rules against bullying, hold meetings with students to discuss bullying issues, and organize meetings with parents. Finally, when incidents of bullying arise, school staff talk with those who bullied and were bullied, as well as with their respective parents, to address strategies for managing the problem. When appropriate, the students involved are directed to appropriate services (Olweus, 2004).

Participant-Role Approach

This method of intervention involves three steps, the first of which entails raising students' awareness of bullying through class discussions. Participant roles in bullying incidents are emphasized, with special attention given to the role that bystanders can play in de-escalating bullying conflicts, and the challenge of translating anti-bullying attitudes into action. The second step is to encourage students to reflect on their usual roles in bullying incidents, and thirdly, students rehearse different roles through dramas and role play, to increase confidence in their ability to try different prosocial roles in real-life encounters, such as actively protecting a victimized student rather than being a passive bystander (Salmivalli, Kaukiainen, & Voeten, 2005).

Social Competence Training

Social competence training programs are used to teach skills in problem solving, social skills, and self-control. For example, problem solving skills training is used to teach children to identify the problem, generate multiple possible solutions, and evaluate the positive and negative consequences of these potential actions (Kazdin, 2003). Specific social skills that might improve children's peer relations are incorporated into these interventions, such as learning how to join a group, how to start a conversation, and how to handle teasing, (Conduct Problems Prevention Research Group, 1999). To reduce impulsive, explosive outbursts of aggression, children are also taught to consider multiple perspectives on a problem rather than assuming hostile intentions on the part of a peer. They are taught to use self-talk and relaxation techniques to calm down when angry (Lochman & Wells, 2004). Social competence training programs can be used on a class-wide basis for primary prevention or as part of secondary prevention or treatment initiatives, to target specific students with behavioural difficulties.

Parent-Management Training

The primary purpose of parent management training is to improve parents' effectiveness by teaching them to establish clear rules, consistently reward appropriate behaviour, and effectively discipline inappropriate behaviour using procedures such as time out or privilege removal rather than harsh punishment (Kazdin, 2005). Parents are also taught to give effective instructions and establish clear age-appropriate rules. Role play, discussion, and homework exercises are used to teach these skills. Parent-management training programs have been integrated into comprehensive school-based violence prevention programs (Conduct Problems Prevention Research Group, 1999) and also have been used with children referred to clinical settings (Kazdin, 2005).

Effectiveness and Limitations in Bullying Interventions

Researchers involved in evaluating whole-school approaches to bullying prevention have reported varying degrees of effectiveness (see Smith, Ananiadou, & Cowie, 2003; Rigby, 2004). It is worth pointing out that although there is an overabundance of programs aimed at reducing bullying, the number of studies which have employed a systematic evaluation methodology are surprisingly scarce. Overall, those studies that have used some degree of reliable evaluation reveal "mixed results." Numerous studies have shown whole-school bullying prevention programs to be effective, particularly in the short-term, in reducing bullying behaviour and improving peer relations (Olweus, 1991; Ortega & Lera, 2000; Smith et al., 2004). Other studies, however, have reported more modest success and in some cases no effect at all (see Galloway & Roland, 2004; Rigby, 2004; Roland & Munthe, 1997; Smith, Stewart, & Cousins, 2004).

Two large scale studies of bullying programs based largely on a whole-school approach have reported a high reduction in rates of bullying and victimization. One of the first of its kind was carried out in Bergen, Norway by Olweus (1991) and reported a 50% reduction in bullying and victimization, and the other was carried out in Seville, Spain by Ortega and Lera (2000), who reported 57% reduction in bullied students. Other studies such as the Sheffield project have reported lower rates of reduction in the victimization rate, ranging from 14% to 30% (Whitney, Rivers, Smith, & Sharp, 1994). Reflecting the difficulties in carrying out solid evaluations of bullying prevention programs, most of the studies mentioned above had some methodological limitations, ranging from lack of true comparison between the experimental and control schools, to the failure of a large number of schools to participate in post-intervention data collection.

In an evaluation of an intervention program based on the participant-role approach to school bullying, Salmivalli and her colleagues (2005) reported that the intervention had a positive impact on several outcome variables, including increases in perceived efficacy in handling bullying, and reports of decreases in observed and experienced bullying. While the pattern of results is complex, the range of reduction was considered moderate (i.e., reduction from 15% to 29%) in schools with a low level of implementation and considerably higher (i.e., reduction from 46% to 57%) in schools where a high degree of the program was implemented.

Social competence training programs have been shown in numerous studies to be effective, particularly in the short-term, in enabling students to learn the program skills, reducing student behavioural difficulties and improving peer relations (Schneider, 1992). However, one key limitation is that effect sizes pertaining to the learning of program skills are moderate to large in magnitude, whereas effect sizes for behavioural change are small albeit significant (BeelmannPfingsten, & Lösel, 1994; Schneider, 1992). These results suggest that children may learn the skills taught in the program, but may have difficulty applying these skills to everyday situations that involve heightened emotions and greater complexity than scenarios practiced in role plays. Furthermore, evidence of long-term behavioural changes is weaker than that for shorter-term improvements (Schneider, 1992).

Meta-analyses of parent-management-training programs have reported large effect sizes for the reduction of aggression in children up to the age of 10 (Serketich & Dumas, 1996), whereas effect sizes for conduct problems and delinquency in adolescent populations were in the small to moderate range (Woolfenden, Williams, & Peat, 2002; Farrington & Welsh, 2003).

In general, it appears that many programs have demonstrated some degree of success but also have been found to have important limitations. Thus, to make improvements in these programs, it may be essential to individualize interventions to address the specific needs of students, tailoring the intervention to the various subtypes of bullying.

Matching Interventions to Bullying Subtypes

Customizing Interventions to fit Direct and Indirect Forms of Bullying

As shown in Table 1, individuals involved in indirect bullying show a different pattern of psychosocial adjustment than children who engage in direct bullying. Several facets of the table are particularly worth noting. First, directly aggressive students have a more pervasive or consistent pattern of deficits in regard to social information processing or to social skills in general compared to indirectly aggressive students, who evidence a mixture of strengths and weaknesses. Specifically, direct bullying is associated with biases in several steps of the social information processing sequence, including a greater likelihood of making hostile attributions to explain ambiguous provocations (Crick, Grotpeter, & Bigbee, 2002), and of positively evaluating overtly aggressive responses (Crick & Werner, 1998), as well as with a lack of social awareness and the ability to interpret social cues (Andreou, 2006). In contrast, there is a less pervasive pattern of social information processing deficits related to indirect bullying with the main problem being a tendency toward making hostile attributions in the face of relational provocations (Crick et al., 2002).

Furthermore, in the case of indirect bullying there is a positive association with social intelligence, suggesting heightened ability to read people's intentions and emotions, and to be persuasive (Andreou, 2006; Kaukiainen et al, 1999). On the other hand, direct and indirect bullying are both associated with low empathy (Kaukiainen et al., 1999).

Related to the above findings, it appears that some degree of social competence or social status may facilitate involvement in indirect bullying. Evidence to this effect comes from research demonstrating that popular children with prominent social standing (e.g., perceived popularity, high social impact, high social preference) are more likely to engage in indirect aggression in follow-up assessments one to three years later (Cillessen & Mayeux, 2004; Rose, Swenson & Waller, 2004). Although the causal direction is less clear, additional findings from cross-sectional research are consistent with this pattern, demonstrating that sociability, social intelligence and involvement in highly visible peer groups (i.e., high network centrality) are associated with greater risk of engagement in indirect bullying (Kaukianen et al., 1999; Park et al., 2005; Xie et al., 2002). Looking at this issue from another direction, it also seems that indirect bullying may yield social rewards for some students. Specifically, girls who engaged in a high level of indirect bullying were subsequently perceived by their peers as more popular, and as being part of more prominent social groups (Rose et al., 2004; Zimmer-Gembeck et al., 2005).

There are fewer differences between indirect and direct bullying with regard to parenting. Physical punishment, parental responsiveness, and maternal coercion have similar relations to both direct and indirect bullying. Only fathers' psychological control (i.e., guilt trips, love withdrawal) was differentially associated with the two forms of bullying, being significantly related to indirect aggression but only marginally associated with direct forms of bullying (Hart et al., 1998; Nelson & Crick, 2002).

Although Table 1 reveals important differences in the correlates of direct and indirect bullying, there are very few studies that describe interventions tailored to address the specific needs and deficits of indirectly aggressive children, and also very few evaluations to assess whether prevention programs are effective in reducing indirect aggression and victimization. We were only able to identify two studies with data that speak to the impact of prevention programs on relational bullying and victimization. Leadbeater, Hoglund and Woods (2003; this volume) evaluated the WITS program, which was used to teach Grades 1 and 2 students to walk away, ignore, or to talk or seek help when being bullied. Parent-school and school-police liaisons were also established, and children were "deputized" to encourage them to help other children during bullying incidents. The program evaluation indicated that involvement in the intervention did not reduce the level of relational victimization in the schools, whereas the degree of physical victimization was attenuated in schools of high and medium levels of poverty. The description of the program does not explicitly mention whether components were modified to address issues that specifically pertain to indirect bullying, which may partly explain the program's lesser impact on this form of aggression. Van Schoiack-Edstrom, Frey and Beland (2002) evaluated the Second Step prevention program for students in Grades 6 to 8, which consisted of social problem solving, social skills training, anger management, empathy lessons and a participant-role approach, to determine whether it reduced physical, verbal and social aggression. Following the second year of the curriculum, there was a reduction in the program students' endorsement of all three types of aggression from pre-test to post-test, whereas comparison students showed an increase in their endorsement of social exclusion. It is important to note that the Van Schoiack-Edstrom et al. (2002) study differed from the Leadbeater et al. (2003) evaluation in examining changes in attitudes regarding bullying rather than bullying behaviour itself. Furthermore, consistent with the program described by Leadbeater et al. (2003), it is not clear whether program components were modified to differentially target direct and indirect bullying.

In contrast, Pepler, Walsh and Levene (2004) discuss how the Earlscourt Girls Connection intervention was developed to specifically address the unique aspects of girls' aggression, including relational forms of aggression. For example, based on research showing that mother-daughter relationships may be particularly salient to the development of girls' behavioural difficulties (Fagot & Kavanagh, 1990; Pakaslahti, Spoof, Asplund-Peltola, & Keltikangas-jarvinen, 1998), the program gives particular emphasis to building a positive attachment relationship between mothers and daughters. The program also includes parent-management training and social competence training components. The latter includes a focus on social information processing, and Pepler and colleagues suggest that it may be useful during this component of the program to discuss the subtle social signals that may be used in episodes of social and relational aggression. Whereas the authors reported a reduction in frequently reported behavioural problems for girls, including temper tantrums, crankiness, being angry and resentful, defiant and argumentative, as well as improved relations with adults and peers, they do not report program outcomes concerning indirect bullying.

Additional modifications of prevention programs may be useful to address some of the unique features of indirect bullying outlined in Table 1. Given that indirect aggression is positively associated with indexes of social competence such as social intelligence, perceived popularity, and high peer network centrality, social competence training components typically used in programs for direct aggression may need to be altered. For example, social problem solving units are designed to reduce biases in social information processing, and since indirectly aggressive children have difficulties with making hostile attributions but fewer problems with evaluating the consequences of aggressive strategies, it may be helpful to focus greater attention on the former issue through exercises designed to promote perspective taking and anger management (e.g., Lochman & Wells, 2004). Furthermore, social problem solving components may be enhanced by exercises designed to build empathy, which is lacking in relationally aggressive children (Kaukiainen et al., 1999), by teaching children to think of how others are hurt by social exclusion, rumour spreading and so on. This latter augmentation may be especially important considering evidence that indirect bullying may yield attractive benefits to the perpetrator, insofar as it has been linked to increased perceived popularity, social impact, and dating popularity in girls (Rose et al., 2004; Vaillancourt, Balshine, & Clark, 2003b; Zimmer-Gembeck et al., 2005). Therefore, children may need to be persuaded that it is wrong to hurt others in the pursuit of social advantages for the self and shown more prosocial means to attain status and leadership.

In addition, making reference to participant roles in bullying situations, teachers might emphasize that supporters and bystanders make indirect bullying possible. For a child to be excluded and ostracized, or be the victim of a rumour, supporters must cooperate with the student who indirectly bullies in forming a coalition against an unliked peer, and bystanders must let it happen without comment. A major goal of this program segment might be to encourage supporters and bystanders to become defenders of the victimized child, by refusing to exclude him or her from social activities and by actively seeking to include isolated and rejected children in games and group activities that might occur on the playground.

As mentioned earlier, Pepler and colleagues (2004) discussed the potential benefits of emphasizing the mother-daughter relationship in parent or family-focused interventions for girls' aggression. It is interesting to note in Table 1 that children's relationship with the father (i.e., paternal responsiveness, psychological control) also seems to have an important bearing on indirect bullying for both boys and girls. Thus, where possible, it may be beneficial to incorporate the father in parent-focused interventions.

Modifying Interventions to address the Function of Reactive and Proactive Bullying

As illustrated in Table 1, there are several key differences between reactive and proactive bullying. Children who bully reactively have associated temperamental characteristics of impulsivity, emotional reactivity, and a proneness to frustration and hostility, as well as the tendency to make hostile attributions; all of which predispose them to emotional or explosive aggressive reactions to perceived provocation (e.g., Dodge et al., 1997; Vitaro et al., 2002; Raine et al., 2006; Little et al., 2003). It is possible that this emotional volatility is connected to exposure to aversive parenting, as reactively aggressive children have been shown to experience more controlling, punitive and physically abusive parenting than both nonaggressive and proactively aggressive peers (Bown & Vitaro, 1998; Dodge et al., 1997). Another notable issue that distinguishes reactive from proactive bullying is poor peer relations, as indicated by greater levels of rejection and victimization and lower degrees of popularity (Prinstein & Cillessen, 2003; Dodge et al., 2003).

In contrast, the central thread in the deficits demonstrated by proactively aggressive children are factors that contribute to the positive evaluation of aggressive actions. With regard to social information processing, several studies have shown that proactively aggressive children anticipate positive instrumental, intrapersonal and relational outcomes for aggressive behaviour (Hubbard et al., 2001; Crick & Dodge, 1996; Orobio de Castro et al., 2005; Smithmyer, Hubbard, & Simons, 2000). Additional research suggests that children who bully proactively have relationships with parents and peers wherein proactive aggression may be modeled and reinforced, such that they might learn of its potential advantages. Specifically, the parents of proactively aggressive individuals establish fewer household rules and monitor their whereabouts and activities and to a lesser extent than the parents of nonaggressive and reactively aggressive children, making it less likely that the child will be given appropriate consequences for misbehaviour, including aggression (Poulin & Dishion, 2000). In addition, whereas their peer relations are generally better than those of reactively aggressive individuals, proactively aggressive youngsters tend to associate with proactively aggressive friends, and moreover, these friendships have been linked to increases in proactive bullying over a one-year period (Poulin & Boivin, 2000b).

There is a paucity of published research on interventions including components explicitly designed to address the biases and difficulties uniquely associated with reactive and proactive aggression, or that have evaluated differential program effects for reactive and proactive bullying (Merk et al., 2005). Lochman (2004; cited in Merk et al., 2005) reported unpublished data indicating that the Coping Power program was more effective for proactive than reactive aggression, but this is the only such evaluation that we were able to locate. The Coping Power program comprises a child component addressing anger management through emotional awareness, coping self-statements, distraction techniques and relaxation exercises, as well as instruction in social problem solving, study skills, and peer refusal skills. A parent-focused parent-management training component is also included in this program. It is not clear which components were beneficial in reducing reactive and proactive aggression because program children participated in all aspects of the program (Merk et al., 2005).

A number of cogent suggestions have been made in the literature regarding program components that could be used to target the differential impairments exhibited in reactive and proactive bullying (Larson, 1994; Merk et al., 2005). To address reactive aggression, some investigators have indicated that programs should include anger management modules (see Coping Power program described above) to decrease hostile attribution biases in social information processing (see also Hudley & Graham, 1993), training in social skills to improve peer relations and instill confidence in the use of non-aggressive solutions to social problems, and parent-focused interventions to increase warmth in the parent-child relationship (Merk et al., 2005). In contrast, interventions for proactive bullying should emphasize outcome evaluation biases in social information processing, enabling children to better appreciate the negative consequences of aggressive behaviour, while simultaneously illustrating that non-aggressive strategies can yield positive outcomes. In addition, in light of the lack of household rules and poor monitoring shown by parents of proactively aggressive children, parent-management training should be helpful in facilitating more consistent discipline (Merk et al., 2005).

We believe that a few additional modifications may improve program effectiveness for children who bully proactively. To reduce biases concerning expectations of positive outcomes for aggression, it may be useful to include exercises for building empathy and for changing school attitudes regarding bullying. Proactive aggression may yield benefits for the perpetrator, and in light of findings linking proactive aggression to popularity and perceptions of leadership skills (Dodge & Coie, 1987; Prinstein & Cillessen, 2003), it may be difficult for program leaders to convincingly link proactive aggression to negative relational consequences. A further challenge is that proactive aggression has been linked to low remorse and empathy in adult violent offenders (Cornell et al., 1996) and to narcissistic exploitativeness in early adolescents (Washburn et al., 2004), such that proactively aggressive children may focus mainly on consequences for themselves rather than harm befalling others as a result of their aggression.

To increase attention to the damage that proactive aggression does to others, leaders of intervention programs should give particular emphasis to consequences for others when guiding proactively aggressive children through social problems solving components geared to getting children to think about the negative consequences of aggression. Proactively aggressive students may be biased toward thinking only of the consequences for themselves (e.g., getting into trouble, losing friends), which they may easily dismiss as less important than the potential instrumental and social benefits that they may achieve through aggression, and thus it may be essential for program leaders to consistently prompt these individuals to think of their actions from the perspective of others if they hope to persuade them that non-aggressive strategies will produce better outcomes than aggressive ones. School-wide components and participant-role approaches may be also be used to tackle this issue, insofar as they may facilitate less tolerant attitudes toward bullying amongst the students. For example, if bystanders can be encouraged to assist victimized students, and to refrain from implicitly or explicitly approving of bullying (e.g., laughing, praising), then it may be easier to convince students who bully proactively that the negative consequences of aggression outweigh the benefits.

We also suggest that parent-focused components designed to increase parental monitoring might be improved by adding a module to enhance the parent-child relationship. Previous research has shown that parental knowledge of children's whereabouts and activities is best obtained through the child's self-disclosure (Stattin & Kerr, 2000), and self-disclosure is more likely when children have a positive relationship with parents characterized by a secure attachment (Kerns et al, 2001). Elements from attachment-based interventions (Van IJzendoorn, Juffer, & Duyvesteyn, 1995) could be used to supplement parent-management training components, to help parents develop a relationship with their child wherein open communication is encouraged, which in turn may enable parents to monitor child behaviour more effectively. An added advantage of improving parental monitoring is that well-monitored children are less likely to form friendships with other aggressive children (e.g., Granic & Patterson, 2006; Marini et al., 2006a), which in turn would reduce exposure to modeling and social reinforcement processes within these friendships that have been shown to increase proactive aggression (Poulin & Boivin, 2000b).

Modifying Interventions for Children Who are Dually Involved (i.e., Bully-Victims)

A glance at Table 1 suggests that children involved in both bullying and being victimized have much in common with reactively aggressive children. For example, they have a number of temperamental characteristics that may predispose them to reactively aggressive behaviour, including irritability, low frustration tolerance and emotionality

(Hess & Atkins, 1998; Marini et al., 2006a; Pellegrini & Bartini, 2000), social information processing biases for blame, anger and retaliation (Camodeca et al., 2003), and difficulties with emotion regulation (Toblin et al., 2005). An additional similarity is that their peer relations are poor (Mouttapa et al., 2004; Toblin et al., 2005). The findings summarized in Table 1 suggest three unique features of children involved in both bullying and victimization. First, internalizing problems seem to be a major challenge for these youth, given that they are lonelier than students who bully and students who are uninvolved. The dually involved students are more anxious than both students who bully and those who are victimized (Toblin et al., 2005; Schwartz, 2000). They also are less assertive than those who bully and nonaggressive students and they are more submissive than those who bully and those who are victimized (Toblin et al., 2005). These internalizing problems and unassertive behaviour may lead other students to view them as easy targets for victimization. With regard to the family context, children involved in both bullying and victimization are similar to children displaying other subtypes of aggression in being exposed to restrictive discipline and maternal hostility, but a key difference is that they experience more marital aggression and parental aggression than children who only bully, children who are victimized, and uninvolved children (Schwartz et al., 1997).

We were unable to find any studies that discussed specific program modifications to address the needs of children dually involved in bullying and victimization, nor any outcome studies that evaluated program effectiveness for these individuals. However, given the similarities noted between these dually involved and reactively aggressive children, we believe that these children would benefit from program components used to target reactive aggression, including anger-management modules, social skills training and parent-focused components designed to enhance the parent-child relationship and the effectiveness of discipline (Lochman & Wells, 2004; Merk et al., 2005).

As discussed above, children involved in both bullying and victimization differ from those who bully only in having particular difficulties with internalizing problems such as anxiety, depression and loneliness. Cognitive-behavioural programs for anxiety and depression in children and adolescents have similar components to those for aggressive children, and it would therefore seem feasible to incorporate elements of these programs into cognitive-behavioural approaches used to address bullying per se. For example, Kendall and colleagues (Kendall, Aschenbrand, & Hudson2003) have developed a program in which anxious children are taught to recognize thoughts that contribute to anxiety, to challenge them, and ultimately to replace them with more adaptive and more realistic thoughts that reduce anxiety levels. To give a concrete example, a student may learn to recognize that his anxiety levels rise when he assumes that all of his classmates would "think he is stupid" if he were to give an incorrect answer in class. Instead, he may be encouraged to take a more realistic view, recognizing that everyone makes mistakes, and that when other people make mistakes, he does not usually think badly of them. To reinforce this perspective, the student might use some encouraging self-talk, such as "It's OK to make mistakes; it's how we learn." For programs targeting dually involved children, this cognitive restructuring exercise might be a useful supplement to those typically used to address cognitive distortions relating to hostile attribution biases (e.g., Lochman & Wells, 2004).

Children who bully and are victimized are also more likely than those who only bully or those not involved in bullying to face problems with depression (Craig, 1998). Consequently, it may be necessary to combine cognitive-behavioural components that target depression with those typically used in the treatment of aggression. There are a number of effective cognitive-behavioural programs for the treatment of depression in children and adolescents (Weisz et al., 2003; Clarke, DeBar, & Lewinsohn, 2003). Consistent with the approaches that target aggression, these programs include problem-solving components used to identify adaptive strategies for dealing with stress and cognitive restructuring exercises designed to identify, challenge and replace negative thoughts that exacerbate depression (as described above in regard to anxiety). Decreasing levels of depression and anxiety around peer victimization would be beneficial in itself for dually involved children, but it may have the added benefit of reducing factors that create situations in which aggressive confrontations are likely to arise. For one thing, to the extent that it improves peer relations, it may reduce the potential for conflicts leading to aggression. In addition, aggression is more likely to take place when an individual is in a negative mood (Berkowitz, 1993), so a reduction of anxiety and depression may reduce the tendency for dually involved children to engage in explosive, emotional and reactive aggression (Salmivalli et al., 2004).

Two additional modifications may be useful. Social skills training components could be employed to improve assertiveness and reduce submissiveness in dually involved children, because improvements in this area may decrease perceptions on the part of their peers that they are easy targets for victimization. Finally, couples therapy may be a beneficial adjunct to parent-focused interventions that are typically used for parents of children who bully, given the high level of martial and parental aggression to which these children are reportedly exposed.

Caveat

We must qualify our suggestions about modifying interventions to address subtype differences by acknowledging that the modality (i.e., individual or group) or setting (clinic or school) of the program will likely constrain the extent and nature of tailoring that is feasible. Consequently, the program modifications suggested above may need to take one of two forms. A targeted or customized program may be attempted with individuals presenting problems with predominantly one subtype of aggression, such that clinical time and resources are devoted to the most salient issues for this subtype. This approach may be most feasible in the context of individual therapy in a clinical setting. In the context of group therapy or classroom-based primary prevention programs, a comprehensive approach may be needed to ensure that psychosocial factors relating to each subtype are addressed. For example, participant-role approaches could be broadened to highlight the fact that bystanders can play a role in supporting those vulnerable to victimization and preventing bullying incidents in either direct or indirect domains. Similarly, parent-focused components that typically focus primarily on fostering consistent discipline may be expanded to include modules designed to improve parent-child relationships, so that parenting factors applicable to both reactive and proactive aggression are addressed.

Conclusion

As previously discussed, existing bullying interventions and related programs for the prevention and treatment of aggressive behaviour have produced mixed results (Smith et al., 2004; Rigby, 2001; Schneider, 1992). Since bullying remains a major social and educational issue in schools and in society more generally, it behooves us to seek means to improve these programs. One reason for the limited success in preventing bullying may be that it is a more multifaceted construct than was originally believed. As shown in Table 1, subtypes of bullying differing in form (direct versus indirect), function (proactive versus reactive) and type of involvement (in bullying, victimization, or both) have distinct relations with psychosocial factors such as temperament, social cognition, co-morbid psychopathology, parenting, and peer relations. The purpose of this chapter was to provide some suggestions that practitioners may use to modify bullying interventions to better address the unique features of the various subtypes of aggression. Currently, there is a paucity of research concerning the modification of programs or the evaluation of program effectiveness in the reduction of different subtypes of bullying, and we hope that this discussion will serve as a basis for future efforts in this regard by researchers and practitioners alike.

Key Messages

1. Bullying involves a multi-faceted range of behaviours that has both direct (e.g., hitting, insulting) and indirect (e.g., social exclusion, rumour spreading) forms, reactive (e.g., defensive, emotional response to provocation) and proactive (planned, reward-oriented aggression) functions, as well as the possibility of dual involvement in both bullying and victimization.

2. Educators and other professionals working with children and youth with an awareness of the various subtypes of bullying may be better able to monitor incidents of bullying in school and other community settings and to ensure the safety and well-being of children who may be victimized by bullying, insofar as they may recognize peer maltreatment in all of its guises (e.g., indirect as well as direct bullying).

3. Because different subtypes of bullying appear to be associated with distinct risk factors and consequences, bullying interventions may be tailored to emphasize the particular needs of children and youth involved with different subtypes of bullying, in order to improve the overall effectiveness of these programs.

4. Given the lack of research on this topic, it is important for researchers and practitioners working with children who bully and/or who are bullied to develop, implement, and systematically evaluate interventions tailored to address differences in bullying subtypes.

Chapter 5: Matching Interventions to Bullying Subtypes

References

Andreou, E. (2006). *Social preference, perceived popularity and social intelligence: Relations to overt and 4relational aggression.* School Psychology International, 27, 339-351. [27]

Beelmann, A., Pfingsten, U., & Lösel, F. (1994). *Effects of training social competence in children: A meta-analysis of recent evaluation studies.* Journal of Clinical Child Psychology, 23, 260-271.

Berkowitz, L. (1993). *Towards a general theory of anger and emotional aggression: Implications of the cognitive-neoassociationistic perspective for the analysis of anger and other emotions.* In R. S. Wyer Jr. & T. K. Srull (Eds.), *Perspectives on anger and emotion: Advances in social cognition* (Vol. 6, pp. 1-46). Hillsdale, NJ: Erlbaum.

Bowen, F., & Vitaro, F. (1998, July). *Reactively and proactively aggressive children: Antecedent and subsequent characteristics.* Paper presented at the International Society for the Study of Behavioral Development, Berne, Switzerland. [2]

BrendgenVitaroTremblay, & Lavoie, F. (2001). *Reactive and proactive aggression: Predictions to physical violence in different contexts and moderating effects of parental monitoring and caregiving behavior.* Journal of Abnormal Child Psychology, 29, 293-304. [53]

Camodeca, M., Goossens, F. A., Schuengel, C., & Meerum Terwogt, M. (2003). *Links between social information processing in middle childhood and involvement in bullying.* Aggressive Behavior, 29, 116-127. [47]

Camodeca, M., Goossens, F. A., Meerum Terwogt, M., & Schuengel, C. (2002). *Bullying and victimization among school-age children: Stability and links to proactive and reactive aggression.* Social Development, 11, 332-345.

Cassidy, T., & Taylor, L. (2005). *Coping and psychological distress as a function of the bully victim dichotomy in older children.* Social Psychology of Education, 8, 249-262. [45]

Cillessen, A. H. N., & Mayeux, L. (2004). *Sociometric status and peer group behavior: Previous findings and current directions.* In J. Kupersmidt & K. Dodge (Eds.), *Children's peer relations: From development to intervention* (3-20). Washington DC: American Psychological Association. [37]

Clarke, G. N., DeBar, L. L., & Lewinsohn, P. M. (2003). *Cognitive-behavioral group treatment for adolescent depression.* In A. E. Kazdin & J. R. Weisz (Eds.), *Evidence-based psychotherapies for children and adolescents* (pp. 120-134). NY: Guilford Press.

---

4 Numbers in square brackets [x] at the end of each reference correspond to the citation in Table 1

Coie., Dodge., & Kupersmidt. (1990). *Peer group behavior and social status*. In S. R. Asher & J. D. Coie (Eds.), *Peer rejection in childhood: Cambridge studies in social and emotional development* (pp. 17-59). New York: Cambridge University Press.

Conduct Problems Prevention Research Group. (1999). *Initial impact of the Fast Track prevention trial for conduct problems: I. The high-risk sample.* Journal of Consulting and Clinical Psychology, 67(5), 631–647.

Connor, D. F., Steingard, R. J., Anderson, J. J., & Melloni Jr., R. H. (2003). *Gender differences in reactive and proactive aggression.* Child Psychiatry and Human Development, 33, 279-294. [16]

Cornell, D. G., Warren, J., Hawk, G., Stafford, E., Oram, G., & Pine, D. (1996). *Psychopathy in instrumental and reactive offenders.* Journal of Consulting and Clinical Psychology, 64, 783-790. [51]

Craig, W. (1998). *The relationship among bullying, victimization, depression, anxiety and aggression in elementary school children.* Personality and Individual Differences, 24, 123-130.

Crick, N. R., Casas, J. F., & Mosher, M. (1997). *Relational and overt aggression in preschool.* Developmental Psychology, 33, 579-588. [33]

Crick, N. R., & Dodge, K. A. (1996). *Social information-processing mechanisms in reactive and proactive aggression.* Child Development, 67, 993-1002. [19]

Crick, N. R., & Grotpeter, J. K. (1995). *Relational aggression, gender, and social-psychological adjustment.* Child Development, 66, 710-722. [34]

Crick, N. R., Grotpeter, J. K., & Bigbee, M. A. (2002). *Relationally and physically aggressive children's intent attributions and feelings of distress for relational and instrumental peer conflicts.* Child Development, 73, 1134-1142. [29]

Crick, N. R., & Werner, N. E. (1998). *Response decision processes in relational and overt aggression.* Child Development, 69, 1630-1639. [30]

Day, D. M., Bream, L. A., & Paul, A. (1992). *Proactive and reactive aggression: An analysis of subtypes based on teacher perceptions.* Journal of Clinical Child Psychology, 21, 210-217. [11]

Dodge, K. A., & Coie, J. D. (1987). *Social information processing factors in reactive and proactive aggression in children's peer groups.* Journal of Personality and Social Psychology, 53, 1146-1158. [21]

Dodge, K. A., Lansford, J. E., Salzer Burks, V., Bates, J. E., Pettit, G. S., Fontaine, R., & Price, J. M. (2003). *Peer rejection and social information-processing factors in the development of aggressive behavior problems in children.* Child Development, 74, 374-393. [7]

Dodge, K. A., Lochman,J. E., Harnish, J. D., Bates, J. E., & Pettit, G. S. (1997). *Reactive and proactive aggression in school children and psychiatrically impaired chronically assaultive youth*. Journal of Abnormal Psychology, 106, 37-51. [3]

Dodge, K. A., Price, J., M., Bachorowski, J., & Newman, J. P. (1990). *Hostile attributional biases in severely aggressive adolescents*. Journal of Abnormal Psychology, 99, 385-392.

Fagot, B. I., & Kavanagh, K. (1990). *The prediction of antisocial behavior from avoidant attachment classifications*. Child Development, 61, 864-873.

Farrington, D. P. (1993). *Understanding and preventing bullying*. In M. Tonry (Ed.), *Crime and justice* (Vol. 17, pp. 381-458). Chicago: University of Chicago.

Farrington, D. P., & Welsh, B. C. (2003). *Family-based prevention of offending: A meta-analysis*. Australian and New Zealand Journal of Criminology, 36, 127-151.

Galloway, D. M., & E. Roland, E. (2004). *Is the direct approach to bullying always best?* In P. K. Smith, D. Pepler, & K. Rigby, (Eds.), *Bullying in schools: How successful can interventions be?* (pp. 37-53). Cambridge: Cambridge University Press.

Granic, I., & Patterson, G. R. (2006). *Toward a comprehensive model of antisocial development: A dynamic systems approach*. Psychological Review, 113, 101-131.

Grills., & Ollendick. (2002). *Peer victimization, global self-worth, and anxiety in middle school children*. Journal of Clinical Child and Adolescent Psychology, 31, 59-68.

Hart, C. H., Nelson, D. A., Robinson, C. C., Olsen, S. F., & McNeilly-Choque, M. K. (1998). *Overt and relational aggression in Russian nursery-school-age children: Parenting style and marital linkages*. Developmental Psychology, 34, 687–697. [31]

Haynie., Nansel, Eitel Crump Saylor Yu & Simons (2001). *Bullies, victims, and bully/victims: Distinct groups of at-risk youth*. Journal of Early Adolescence, 21, 29-49.

Hess, L., & Atkins, M. (1998). *Victims and aggressors at school: Teacher, self, and peer perceptions of psychosocial functioning*. Applied Developmental Science, 2, 75-89. [42]

Hubbard, J. A., Dodge, K. A., Cillessen, A. H., Coie, J. D., & Schwartz, D. (2001). *The dyadic nature of social information processing in boys' reactiveand proactive aggression*. Journal of Personality and Social Psychology, 80, 268-280. [17]

Hudley, C., & Graham, S. (1993). *An attributional intervention to reduce peer-directed aggression among African-American boys*. Child Development, 64, 124-138.

Kaukiainen, A., Björkqvist, K., Lagerspetz, K., Österman, K., Salmivalli, C., Rothberg, S., & Ahlbo, A. (1999). *The relationship between social intelligence, empathy, three types of aggression*. Aggressive Behavior, 25, 81-89. [28]

Kazdin, A. E. (2005). *Parent management training: Treatment for oppositional, aggressive, and antisocial behavior in children and adolescents.* NY: Oxford University Press.

Kazdin, A. E. (2003). *Psychotherapy for children and adolescents.* Annual Review of Psychology, 54, 253-276.

Kempes, M., Matthys, W., Maassen, G., van Goozen, S., & van Engeland, H. (2006). *A parent questionnaire for distinguishing between reactive and proactive aggression in children.* European Child & Adolescent Psychiatry, 15, 38-45. [12]

Kendall, P. C., Aschenbrand, S. G., & Hudson, J. L. (2003). *Child-focused treatment of anxiety.* In A. E. Kazdin & J. R. Weisz (Eds.), *Evidence-based psychotherapies for children and adolescents* (pp. 81-100). NY: Guilford Press.

Kimonis., Frick., Fazekas & Loney. (2006). *Psychopathy, aggression, and the processing of emotional stimuli in non-referred girls and boys.* Behavioral Sciences & the Law, 24, 21-37. [22]

Kumpulainen, K., Räsänen, E., Henttonen, I., Almqvist, F., Kresanov, K., Linna, S-L., Moilanen, I., Piha, J., Puura, K., & Tamminen, T. (1998). *Bullying and psychiatric symptoms among elementary school-age children.* Child Abuse & Neglect, 22, 705-717. [49]

Kupersmidt, J. B., Willoughby, M., & Bryant, D. (July, 1998). *Distinguishing between proactive and reactive aggression among preschool children.* Paper presented at the International Society for the Study of Behavioral Development, Berne, Switzerland.

Larson, J. (1994). *Violence prevention in the schools: A review of selected programs and procedures.* School Psychology Review, 23, 151-164.

Leadbeater, B., Hoglund, W., & Woods, T. (2003). *Changing contents? The effects of a primary prevention program on classroom levels of peer relational and physical victimization.* Journal of Community Psychology, 31, 397-418.

Little, T. D., Braumer, J., Jones, S. M., Nock, M. K., & Hawley, P. H. (2003). *Rethinking aggression: A typological examination of the functions of aggression.* Merrill-Palmer Quarterly, 49, 343-369. [13]

Lochman, J. E. (2004). *A prevention science perspective on intervention with aggressive children: The Coping Power Program.* Unpublished paper, Utrecht University, The Netherlands.

Lochman, J. E., & Wells, K.C. (2004). *The Coping Power Program for preadolescent aggressive boys and their parents: Outcome effects at the 1-year follow-up.* Journal of Consulting and Clinical Psychology, 72(4), 571-578.

Loeber, R., Green, S.M., Lahey, B.B., & Kalb, L. (2000). *Physical fighting in childhood as a risk factor for later mental health problems*. Journal of the American Academy of Child and Adolescent Psychiatry, 39, 421-428.

Marini, Z.A, Dane, A., Bosacki, S., & YLC-CURA. (2006a). *Direct and indirect bully-victims: Differential psychosocial risk factors associated with adolescents involved in bullying and victimization*. Aggressive Behaviour, 32, 551-569. [43]

Marini, Z.A., Koruna, B., & Dane, A. (2006b). *Individualized interventions for ESL students involved in bullying and victimization*. Contact (Spring Issue), 1-15.

Marini, Z.A., McWhinnie, M., & Lacharite, M. (2004). *Preventing school bullying: Identification and intervention involving bystanders*. Teaching and Learning, 1, 17-21.

Merk, W., Orobio de Castro, B. Koops, W. & Matthys, W. (2005). *The distinction between reactive and proactive aggression: Utility for theory, diagnosis and treatment?* European Journal of Developmental Psychology, 2, 197-220.

Moffitt., Caspi Harrington & Milne. (2002). *Males on the life-course-persistent and adolescence-limited antisocial pathways: Follow-up at age 26 years*. Development and Psychopathology, 14, 179-207.

Mouttapa, M., Valente, T., Gallaher, P., Rohrbach, L. A., & Unger, J. B. (2004). *Social network predictors of bullying and victimization*. Adolescence, 39, 315-335. [46]

Nelson, D. A, & Crick, N. R. (2002). *Parental psychological control: Implications for childhood physical and relational aggression*. In B.K. Barber (Ed.), Intrusive parenting: How psychological control affects children and adolescents (pp. 161-189). Washington, DC: American Psychological Association. [32]

Nansel, T., Overpeck, M., Pilla, R., Ruan, W., Simons-Morton, S., & Scheidt, S. (2001). *Bully behaviors among US youth: Prevalence and association with psychosocial adjustment*. Journal of the American Medical Association, 285, 2094-2100.

Nucci, L. (2006). *Education for moral development*. In M. Killen & J. Smetana (Eds.), Handbook of moral development (pp. 657-681). Mahwah, NJ: Lawrence Erlbaum.

Olweus, D. (1991). *Bully/victim problems among schoolchildren: Basic facts and effects of a school based intervention program*. In D. Pepler & K. H. Rubin (Eds.), The development and treatment of childhood aggression. (pp. 411-448). Hillsdale, NJ: Erlbaum.

Olweus, D. (2001). *Peer harassment: A critical analysis and some important issues*. In J. Juvonen & S. Graham (Eds.), Peer harassment in school: The plight of the vulnerable and victimized (pp. 3-20). NY: Guilford Press.

Olweus, D. (2004). *The Olweus bullying prevention programme: Design and implementation issues and a nes national initiative in Norway.* In P. K. Smith, D. Pepler, & K. Rigby, (Eds.), Bullying in schools: How successful can interventions be? (pp. 13-36) Cambridge: Cambridge University Press.

Orobio de Castro, B., Merk, W., Koops, W., Veerman, J. W., & Bosch, J. D. (2005). *Emotions in social information processing and their relations with reactive and proactive aggression in referred aggressive boys.* Journal of Clinical Child and Adolescent Psychology, 34, 105-16. [20]

OrtegaLera. (2000). *The Seville Anti-Bullying in School Project.* Aggressive Behavior, Special Issue: *Bullying in the schools*, 26, 113-123.

Park, J-H., Essex, M. J, Zahn-Waxler, C., Armstrong, J. M., Klein, M. H., & Goldsmith, H. H. (2005). *Relational and overt aggression in middle childhood: early child and family risk factors.* Early Education and Development. Special Issue: *Relational Aggression During Early Childhood*, 16, 233-256. [26]

Pakaslahti, L., Spoof, I., Asplund-Peltola, R. L., & Keltikangas-jarvinen, L. (1998). *Parents' social problem-solving strategies in families with aggressive and non-aggressive girls.* Aggressive Behavior, 24, 37-51.

Pellegrini, A., & Bartini, M. (2000). *A longitudinal study of bullying, victimization, and peer affiliation during the transition from primary school to middle school.* American Educational Research Journal, 37 (3), 699-725. [41]

Pellegrini, A. D., & Long, J. D. (2003). *A sexual selection theory longitudinal analysis of sexual segregation and integration in early adolescence.* Journal of Experimental Child Psychology, 85, 257-278. [39]

Pepler, D. J., Walsh, M. M., & Levene, K. S. (2004). *Interventions for aggressive girls: Tailoring and measuring the fit.* In M. Moretti, C. Odgers, & M. Jackson (Eds.), *Girls and aggression: Contributing factors and intervention principles* (pp. 131–145). New York, NY: Kluwer Academic Press.

Poulin, F., & Boivin, M. (2000a). *Reactive and proactive aggression: Evidence of a two-factor model.* Psychological Assessment, 12, 115-122. [5]

Poulin, F., & Boivin, M. (2000b). *The role of proactive and reactive aggression in the formation and development of boys' friendships.* Developmental Psychology, 36, 233-240. [8]

Poulin, F., & Dishion, T. J. (2000). *The peer and family experiences of proactively and reactively aggressive pre-adolescents.* Paper presented at the biennial meeting of the Society for Research on Adolescence, Chicago, IL. [4]

Price, J. M., & Dodge, K. A. (1989). *Reactive and proactive aggression in childhood: Relations to peer status and social context dimensions.* Journal of Abnormal Child Psychology, 17, 455-471.

Prinstein, M. J., & Cillessen, A. H. N. (2003). *Forms and functions of adolescent peer aggression associated with high levels of peer status.* Merrill-Palmer Quarterly, 49, 310-342. [6]

Pulkkinen, L. (1996). *Proactive and reactive aggression in early adolescence as precursors to anti- and prosocial behaviors in young adults.* Aggressive Behavior, 22, 241- 257. [15]

Raine Dodge Loeber Gatzke-Kopp Lynam Reynolds Stouthamer-Loeber & Liu (2006). *The reactive-proactive aggression questionnaire: Differential correlates of reactiveand proactive aggression in adolescent boys.* Aggressive Behavior, 32, 159-171. [23]

Rigby (2001). *Health consequences of bullying and its prevention in schools.* In J. Juvonen & S. Graham (Eds.), *Peer harassment in school: The plight of the vulnerable and victimized* (pp. 310-331). New York: Guilford.

Rigby (2004). *Addressing bullying in schools: Theoretical perspectives and their implications.* School Psychology International, 25, 287-300.

Roland, E. & Munthe, E. (1997). *The 1996 Norwegian program for preventing and managing bullying in schools.* Irish Journal of Psychology, 18, 233-247.

Rose, A. J., Swenson, L. P., & Waller, E. M. (2004). *Overt and relational aggression and perceived popularity: Developmental differences in concurrent and prospective relations.* Developmental Psychology, 40, 378-387. [36]

Russell, A., Hart, C. H., Robinson, C. C., & Olsen, S. F. (2003). *Children's sociable and aggressive behavior with peers: A comparison of the US and Australian, and contributions of temperament and parenting styles.* International Journal of Behavioral Development, 27, 74-86. [25]

Salmivalli, C., Kaukiainen, A., & Voeten, M., (2005). *Anti-bullying intervention: implementation and outcome.* British Journal of Educational Psychology, 75, 465-487.

Salmivalli, C., Kaukiainen, A., Voeten, M., & Sinisammal, M. (2004). *Targeting the group as a whole: the Finnish anti-bullying intervention.* In P. K. Smith, D. Pepler & K. Rigby (Eds.), *Bullying in schools: How successful can interventions be?* (pp. 251-273). NY: Cambridge University Press.

Schippel, P. L., Vasey, M. W., Cravens-Brown, L. M., & Bretveld, R. A. (2003). *Suppressed attention to rejection, ridicule, and failure cues: A unique correlate of reactive but not proactive aggression in youth.* Journal of Clinical Child and Adolescent Psychology, 32, 40-55. [18]

Schneider, B. H. (1992). *Didactic methods for enhancing children's peer relations: A quantitative review.* Clinical Psychology Review, 12, 363-382.

Schwartz, D. (2000). *Subtypes of victims and aggressors in children's peer groups.* Journal of Abnormal Child Psychology, 28, 181-192. [48]

Schwartz, D., Dodge, K. A., Pettit, G. S., & Bates, J. E. (1997). *The early socialization of aggressive victims of bullying.* Child Development, 68, 665-675. [50]

Schwartz, Proctor., & Chien. (2001). *The aggressive victim of bullying: Emotional and behavioral dysregulation as a pathway to victimization by peers.* In J. Juvonen and S. Graham (Eds.), Peer harassment in school: The plight of the vulnerable and victimized (pp. 147-174). New York: Guilford Press.

Serketich, W. J., & Dumas, J. E. (1996). *The effectiveness of behavioral parent training to modify antisocial behavior in children: A meta analysis.* Behavior Therapy, 27, 171-186.

Smith, J. D., Stewart, R., & Cousins, B. (2004). *Anti-bullying interventions: A survey of Ontario schools.* Canadian Association of Principals Journal, 12, 9-11.

Smith, P. K., *Ananiadou, K. & Cowie, H. (2003). Interventions to reduce school bullying.* Canadian Journal of Psychiatry, 48, 591-599.

Smith, P. K., Pepler, D. K., & Rigby, K. (Eds.), (2004). *Bullying in schools: How successful can interventions be?* Cambridge: Cambridge University Press.

Smithmyer, C. M., Hubbard, J. A., & Simons, R. F. (2000). *Proactive and reactive aggression in delinquent adolescents: Relations to aggression outcome expectancies.* Journal of Clinical Child Psychology, 29, 86-93. [24]

Stattin, H., & Kerr, M. (2000). *Parent monitoring: A reinterpretation.* Child Development, 71, 1072–1085.

Toblin, R. L., Schwartz, D., Hopmeyer Gorman, A., & Abou-ezzeddine, T. (2005). *Social-cognitive and behavioral attributes of aggressive victims of bullying.* Journal of Applied Developmental Psychology, 26, 329-346. [45]

Vaillancourt, T. (2005). *Indirect aggression among humans: Social construct or evolutionary adaptation?* In R.E. Tremblay, W.H. Hartup, and J. Archer (Eds.), Developmental origins of aggression (pp. 158-177). NY: Guilford Press. [40]

Vaillancourt, T., Balshine, S., & Clark, A. (2003b). *Puberty, dating and the use of indirect aggression: Evolution or social construct?* Paper presented at the Biennial Meeting of the Canadian Psychological Association, Hamilton, ON, Canada

Vaillancourt, T., Brendgen, M., Boivin, M., & Tremblay, R. (2003a). *A longitudinal confirmatory factor analysis of indirect and physical aggression: Evidence of two factors over time?* Child Development, 74, 1628-1638.

Van IJzendoorn, M. H., Juffer, F., & Duyvesteyn, M. G. C. (1995). *Breaking the intergenerational cycle of insecure attachment - A review of the effects of attachment-based interventions on maternal sensitivity and infant security.* Journal of Child Psychology and Psychiatry and Allied Disciplines, 36, 225-248.

Van Schoiack-Edstrom, L., Frey, K. S., & Beland, K. (2002). *Changing adolescents' attitudes about relational and physical aggression.* School Psychology Review, 31, 201-216.

Vitaro, F., Brendgen, M., (2005). *Proactive and reactive aggression: A developmental perspective.* In R. E. Tremblay, W. H. Hartup, and J. Archer (Eds.), *Developmental origins of aggression* (pp. 178-201). NY: Guilford Press. [9]

Vitaro, F., Brendgen, M. & Tremblay, R.. (2002). *Reactively and proactively aggressive children: Antecedent and subsequent characteristics.* Journal of Child Psychology and Psychiatry, 43, 495-506. [1]

Vitaro, F., Gendreau, P. L., Tremblay, R. E., & Oligny, P. (1998). *Reactive and proactive aggression differentially predict later conduct problems.* Journal of Child Psychology and Psychiatry and Allied Disciplines, 39, 377-385. [14]

Waschbusch, D. A.., Willoughby, M. T., & Pelham, W. E. (1998). *Criterion validity and the utility of reactive and proactive aggression: Comparisons to attention deficit hyperactivity disorder, oppositional defiant disorder, conduct disorder, and other measures of functioning.* Journal of Clinical Child Psychology, 27, 396-405. [10]

Washburn, J. J., McMahon, S. D., King, C. A., Reinecke, M. A., & Silver, C. (2004). *Narcissistic features in young adolescents: Relations to aggression and internalizing symptoms.* Journal of Youth and Adolescence, 33, 247-260. [52]

Weisz, J. R., Southam-Gerow, M. A., Gordis, E. B., & Connor-Smith, J. (2003). *Primary and secondary control enhancement training for youth depression: Applying the deployment-focused model of treatment development and testing.* In A. E. Kazdin & J. R. Weisz (Eds.), *Evidence-based psychotherapies for children and adolescents* (pp. 165-182). NY: Guilford Press.

Whitney, I., Rivers, I., Smith, R. K., & Sharp, S. (1994). *The Sheffield Project: Methodology and findings.* In P. K. Smith & S. Sharp (Eds.). *School bullying: Insights and perspectives.* London: Routledge.

Woolfenden, S., Williams, K., & Peat, J. (2002). *Family and parenting interventions for conduct disorder and delinquency: a meta-analysis of randomised controlled trials.* Archives of Disease in Childhood, 86, 251-256.

Xie, H., Swift, D. J., Cairns, B. D., & Cairns, R. B. (2002). *Aggressive behaviors in social interaction and developmental adaptation: A narrative analysis of interpersonal conflicts during early adolescence.* Social Development, 11, 205-224. [38]

Zimmer-Gembeck, M. J., Geiger, T. A., & Crick, N. R. (2005). *Relational and physical aggression, prosocial behavior, and peer relations: Gender moderation and bidirectional associations.* Journal of Early Adolescence, 25, 421-452. [35]

Author Notes

Part of the research reported in this book chapter was supported by a grant from the Social Sciences and Humanities Research Council of Canada to The Youth Lifestyle Choices Community-University Research Alliance (YLC-CURA). We gratefully acknowledge the support we received from Teena Willoughby and Heather Chalmers, co-directors of the YLC-CURA.

Introduction to Section Two:

Addressing Bullying

Joanne Cummings, PREVNet Partnership Manager

The ten chapters that comprise the second part of this book describe bullying prevention or intervention programs. The first five chapters, written by Canadian PREVNet researchers, provide a critical review of bullying and violence prevention programs, highlight the challenges of program implementation and evaluation, and provide details on two Canadian programs. In the final five chapters, our international collaborators provide a rich international perspective on what is happening today in Norway, Switzerland, Italy, Ireland and Australia – in addition to Finland, which was described by Pöyhönen and Salmivalli in Section One.

This section opens with a chapter by Smith, who sets the stage for school based bullying prevention by describing the Whole School Approach - based on the pioneering bullying prevention program implemented in Norway in the early 1980s. There is further information on the development, evaluation and evolution of this program in Norway in the chapter written by Midthassel and Roland in this volume. This systemic approach has been adopted and adapted throughout the world; however, three large international reviews of its effectiveness, summarized in Smith's chapter, have demonstrated only modest or mixed results, with some schools achieving significant reductions in student-reported bullying, whereas others have indicated small reductions or even increases in bullying.

Several authors in Section Two offer ideas to explain and overcome the limited success of Whole School Approach based programs. Smith argues that a critical factor is school climate, a concept that encompasses the prevailing quality of relationships and style of social regulation in the school community. Smith proposes that the Whole School Approach is more likely to be effective in a school climate founded on the principles of restorative justice than in a school climate founded on punitive policies. Smith points out that in a positive social climate, misbehaviour is understood as a violation of relationships, not rules; thus repair of relationships and support (rather than isolation) of the wrongdoer is likely to reduce bullying.

The chapter by Tutty places bullying prevention in the larger context of school-based violence prevention programs. Tutty helps the reader understand the challenge and complexity of the science of program evaluation, describes different types of prevention programs, and provides a comprehensive review of existing evidence-based school violence and bullying prevention programs. Several themes emerge from her review and are echoed in subsequent chapters: 1) Effective prevention programs start early in a child's school career and are sustained throughout; 2) the content and delivery style are adapted to the child's developmental level; and 3) programs for adolescent expand the understanding of bullying to encompass sexual harassment, homophobia and racism, and stress active student participation and peer-to-peer messaging. As well, Tutty discusses the pressing need to better prepare teachers in pre-service training and professional development to enhance their comfort in their challenging role of teaching and modeling positive relationship values and skills, a role for which many teachers feel unprepared.

Leadbeater argues that exposure to family, school, classroom or neighbourhood contexts that support bullying need to be addressed in order to achieve greater success in reducing bullying. We are introduced to the Canadian WITS and WITS LEADS prevention programs developed, implemented, and evaluated through a partnership of university researchers, a local school board, and local police and firefighters. Leadbeater critiques the traditional top-down model of prevention program development and ad hoc dissemination, in which programs are initially developed and evaluated and then "pushed" into schools, with varied success depending on the school's willingness to "pull" the program in and deliver it with enthusiasm and sustain it over time. Several other contributors to this volume also grapple with the difficulty of balancing this push and pull, and like Leadbeater, advocate for strong partnerships between university researchers, education administrators, teachers, and community stakeholders to address this challenge. In addition, strong support in terms of prioritizing the prevention program in light of competing initiatives, the provision of sufficient funding, resources, and ample teacher time for both training and classroom

Introduction to Section Two: Addressing Bullying

implementation are critical, as exemplified by many of the programs reviewed in this volume.

The chapter by Wolfe, Crooks, Hughes, and Chiodo advocates the use of integrated prevention models to address bullying within the "triad of adolescent risk behaviours": violence, substance abuse, and sex. The authors describe their Fourth R program which utilizes an "Information, motivation, behaviour (IMB) model" for students as well as teachers, that is, providing information, developing motivation, and building behaviour skills. Promoting feelings of self-efficacy is achieved through active student participation in program activities. Self-efficacy is of particular relevance for motivating bystanders of bullying to take action, because taking action requires bystanders to believe that coming to the defence of their peers will be effective and will not result in their own endangerment or humiliation. The development of self-efficacy also has particular relevance for teachers who receive extensive and ongoing training. The authors note the importance of researcher-teacher training teams, as researchers are seen as credible for reviewing and summarizing research literature, however teachers themselves are more credible for teaching teachers how to teach.

In the subsequent chapter, Crooks describes an adaptation of the Fourth R program for aboriginal communities. The Aboriginal program was developed through extensive attention to building trusting, collaborative partnerships with community stakeholders in order to increase cultural relevancy. Like Leadbeater, Crooks suggests that meaningful project development and evaluation is achieved through working with stakeholders from an initial local needs assessment through implementation, evaluation, refinement, and finally, efforts to secure sustainability. Crooks recommends that researchers develop increased openness to local input and the resultant variability in program implementation that these adaptations entail, as well as openness to creating new evaluation strategies, methodologies and instruments. Crooks shares many valuable lessons about the development and nurturance of collaborative partnerships and the need to recognize and reconcile the different priorities of researchers and service deliverers.

Turning to the international arena, we start with Norway, the country where the first school-based bullying prevention programs were implemented. The authors provide an interesting historical overview and describe the newly launched current initiative. The Norwegian experience, as described by Midthassel and Roland illustrates that the sustainability of bullying prevention programs is a universal challenge, because program success tends to diminish over time, and sustained efforts must be ongoing despite changes in school personnel, priorities and policies. In a telling comparison of two schools` recent experience in implementing Norway`s bullying prevention program, the authors paint a compelling picture of the critical role of the school administrator and a team of committed staff working together in prioritizing and championing the issue.

The chapter by Alsaker demonstrates that that bullying and victimization problems exist among kindergarten children. Using creative, age-appropriate methodology, Alsaker and her colleagues found the prevalence of the different subtypes of children involved in bullying problems is very similar to prevalences found in school age children. Alsaker describes her highly innovative, systemic program for bullying prevention among very young children that is designed to be flexible and adaptable to different contexts. The prevention program stresses education and support for teachers, with professional development for teachers provided through teacher-mental health multidisciplinary teams.

In the following chapter, Menesini outlines the broad range of basic research and intervention programs that have taken place in Italy over the last fifteen years. Highlights of her program of research include an examination of the construct of bullying as it is translated in different languages; how ecological contexts influence rates of bullying; and, at the individual level, the effects of moral disengagement on bullying behaviour. Menesini describes research that examines bullying among adolescents and the links between bullying and other coercive relationship problems in this developmental stage. To date, the most common form of bullying prevention and intervention programs in Italy have involved curricular interventions at the class group level and peer support models for children, with fewer applications of systemic Whole School Approach based programs. Menesini suggests that despite the substantial strides that have occurred in Italy, there is a strong need to develop a coordinated national policy with regards to bullying prevention.

In the subsequent chapter by O'Moore, we learn about Ireland's national, centralized school program based on the Whole School Approach. Again, the central role of teachers in effective bullying prevention is highlighted. O'Moore advocates for teachers' pre-service education to include learning about the development of aggression, in order to increase teacher's confidence in addressing bullying in their classrooms. As well, innovative and culturally relevant program resources are described.

The final chapter by Cross describes the Australian experience in launching a national prevention program from 1999-2007. Cross describes the deliberately staged process that has culminated in a multi-level whole-school, classroom, and family intervention model. The process commenced with a review of international bullying prevention strategies, followed by an efficacy trial, and finally a national effectiveness trial. In the first stage, the literature review, Cross notes that challenges were presented by the variability in definitions of bullying, theoretical models, goals of interventions, research methodologies, and age groups evaluated. Given the multi-determined, multifaceted nature of bullying, as evidenced in the literature reviewed in this volume, this challenge is readily appreciated. In designing the Australian intervention programs, Cross and her colleagues also paid attention to balancing the push and the pull of program implementation, ensuring, for example, that staff time devoted to the program was acknowledged by the school. Currently, the program has achieved wide dissemination, with 1500 schools using the program.

Introduction to Section Two: Addressing Bullying

In summary, this section illustrates that there is a growing consensus across countries and programs regarding the critical ingredients of successful bullying prevention and intervention programs. These include: 1) Bullying prevention is conceived and enacted upon as a priority by school administrators. 2) The implemented program has been developed and evaluated by a strong partnership between researchers and stakeholders. 3) The bullying prevention and intervention programs are adapted to local contexts. 4) Attention is paid to supporting school uptake and sustainability of the program. 5) Teachers are supported with training and resources. If these conditions are met, we can be optimistic that the overarching goal of these programs, to promote positive relationships, can be achieved.

Chapter 6:

Promoting a Positive School Climate: Restorative Practices for the Classroom

David Smith
University of Ottawa

Introduction

School bullying is an all too common social problem that defies simple solutions. Bullying is a subtype of aggressive behaviour that is repeated over time and in which the perpetrator exerts power over a weaker individual through various means, including physical strength, age, or psychological advantages (Vaillancourt, Hymel, & McDougall, 2003). A recent large-scale international study indicated that bullying and victimization in Canadian schools are commonplace (Craig & Harel, 2004). It also indicated that the prevalence of bullying and victimization among school children in Canada is higher than in the majority of the 35 countries represented in the study.

Increased attention to problems of bullying and victimization in recent years has corresponded to an attitude change in Canada and other Western countries from viewing bullying as a vicissitude of normal child development to viewing it as an experience that is needless, harmful, and consequential for development in the long-term. Research evidence substantiates this latter view, having clearly demonstrated that bullying and victimization are associated with pronounced social, psychological, and academic problems in children (Rigby, 2003). Many victimized children suffer anxiety, depression, diminished self-esteem, and social withdrawal (Nansel et al., 2001). Children who bully are at high risk of future antisocial behaviour and delinquency, such as dating violence (Connolly, Pepler, Craig, & Taradash, 2000). A subgroup of victimized youth who react aggressively to abuse ("aggressive victims") displays both the antisocial behaviour of bullying as well as the social and emotional difficulties of victimized youth (Glover, Gough, Johnson, & Cartwright, 2000; Nansel et al., 2001). Children in this group are at high risk for severe, violent, even deadly, reactions to chronic bullying (Anderson et al., 2001). Clearly, educators need effective solutions to assist all children involved in bullying problems and ultimately to reduce bullying and victimization in their schools.

Chapter 6: Promoting a Positive School Climate

Although earlier conceptualizations of bullying focused on the differentiating characteristics of children involved in bullying or being victimized, scholars now view bullying in systemic terms and describe it as primarily a relationship problem that requires relationship solutions (Craig & Pepler, 2007). An upshot of this way of conceptualizing bullying is that, like other important relationships in people's lives, it exists not only in the discrete moments when it is occurring, but also between bullying episodes inside the minds of the different people involved. This may explain, at least in part, some of the noxious effects of bullying on children, even when it occurs infrequently, and why these effects can endure into adulthood. Working within this relational perspective, I will explore in this chapter how the "school climate" can impact bullying problems, focusing particularly on its constructive potential to create a positive social environment that fosters the academic and personal growth of students and thereby reduce bullying and victimization. For the purposes of this discussion, school climate (also called school ethos) refers to the normative beliefs, values, and ideals that characterize a particular school community. The climate is manifested primarily in the relationships among people in the community, including what and how they communicate among themselves.

Bullying and Relationships

The systemic view of the problem is illustrated by the "bullying circle" developed by pioneering Norwegian researcher, Dan Olweus (1993). At the centre of this circle is the victimized student and arrayed around the perimeter are different people who, whether they realize it or not, all play roles in bullying. They range from the children who attack and disempower the victimized student; the children who actively aid the children who are bullying or encourage them in their attacks; the onlookers who quietly watch bullying occur or leave quickly so they won't be implicated; and the defenders who act in ways to stop the bullying, for example, by telling a teacher or stepping in to protect the victimized student. To the misfortune of victimized children, it appears that the role of defender is rarely adopted. In fact, research indicates that the actions of peers in the vicinity of bullying incidents typically support the bullying behaviour rather than curb it (Salmivalli, 1999; Sutton & Smith, 1999). Additionally, the roles that different individuals play within bullying relationships consolidate over time such that the children who bully have increasing power while victimized children have less and less. Peers' encouragement of bullying, and even their passive attention, reinforces children who perpetrate the aggression, adding to the probability that it will occur in the future (Craig, Pepler, & Atlas, 2000).

Recent research on the relational system within classrooms and schools provides a glimpse of some of the social factors that may influence the incidence of bullying problems. For instance, it appears that children who bully others tend to be disliked by children not involved in bullying and the use of aggression is primarily responsible for the peer rejection they experience (Hanish, Kochenderfer-Ladd, Fabes, Martin, & Denning, 2004). Therefore, it is not surprising that those children who bully who find themselves disliked by many other children and consequently search for and find friends in the ranks of others who bully. This situation in which children who bully befriend others like themselves creates a dynamic in which aggressive behaviour is mutually reinforced, leading to increasing levels of aggression in these children over time. Chronically victimized children, like the children who bully them, tend also to be disliked by their peers. However, whereas children who bully can be popular within some segments of the peer group (cf. Vaillancourt & Hymel, 2003), victimized children tend to have very few or no friends at all. This is a particularly significant consideration for intervention, as social isolation increases the risk of victimization in school age children and, conversely, having close friends, especially popular friends, is a protective factor against involvement in bullying and victimization (Hanish et al., 2004).

There are good reasons to believe that student-teacher relationships can also have a significant influence on bullying and that teachers can be instrumental in solving and preventing serious bullying problems. For example, research indicates that children involved in bullying often have poor relationships with their teachers, including little or no mutual warmth, caring, or generally positive feelings (Hanish et al., 2004). On the other hand, strong, positive attachments between children and teachers constitute a protective factor that can reduce the risk of serious aggression problems in children. At the same time, warm, secure attachments between teachers and students can foster social and academic success.

Prevention Programs

Schools have implemented a variety of measures in recent years to deal with bullying, and in some jurisdictions bullying prevention measures are mandated by law (e.g., bullying prevention became mandatory in Ontario schools in September 2006). One common approach to dealing with bullying problems is what is called a "whole-school" approach, which refers to a class of programs sharing the core features of the Olweus Bullying Prevention Program (Olweus, 1993). This was the first comprehensive whole-school intervention implemented on a large scale and systematically evaluated. In its essential form a whole-school intervention includes the following key components: a clear, consistent policy involving non-physical consequences for bullying; information on bullying and victimization for all members of the school community; curricular activities designed to instil attitudes to counter bullying in all children and assist them in developing prosocial conflict resolution skills; and, finally, interventions for individuals directly involved in or affected by bullying. Whole-school programs are widely implemented in schools in North America and in Europe, but relatively little is known about how effective they are across the wide variety of school contexts. There certainly are reasons to believe that the whole-school approach represents a viable solution to bullying problems, particularly considering that the approach is based on a systemic understanding of the problem and involves the entire school community.

Smith, Schneider, Smith, and Ananiadou (2004) quantitatively synthesized the outcomes of 14 whole-school program evaluations, focusing on changes in victimization and bullying rates reported in these evaluations. All percents and scale scores from the original studies were transformed to effect sizes expressed as *r*-values (calculated as $r = Z/\sqrt{N}$). The evaluations were of two types: uncontrolled studies (seven in total) and controlled studies (also seven in total). In uncontrolled studies, outcomes are measured only for groups that received the intervention. Controlled studies, considered more rigourous than uncontrolled studies, include a comparison condition in which students do not received the bullying prevention program and their outcomes are compared to those students who received the intervention. Smith et al. classified the outcomes from each study into one of the following categories: large, medium, small, negligible, and negative (cf. Cohen, 1988). Results revealed that 93% outcomes for victimization and bullying in both uncontrolled and controlled studies fell in the categories of negligible (i.e., effect size *r* between .00-.09) and negative.

Two more reviews of bullying prevention program evaluations have appeared since the publication of that first review.[5] Vreeman and Carroll (2007) reviewed the outcomes of 26 bullying prevention programs in four different categories: curriculum interventions implemented in classrooms, multidisciplinary whole-school programs, social and behavioural skills groups, and other. Their review indicated that 14% of evaluated programs yielded consistently positive outcomes on bullying and victimization rates, 38% yielded a mix of positive and non-positive outcomes (e.g., no change in self-reported bullying but small reduction in victimization), and 48% of the programs yielded zero or negative results. Finally, Baldry and Farrington (2007) reviewed 16 evaluations of bullying preventions programs. They classified the outcomes of 50% of these studies as producing desirable outcomes, 13% as producing mixed results, 24% as producing small or negligible results, and finally 13% as producing undesirable results. Despite some disagreement about the overall pattern of outcomes for bullying prevention programs among these three reviews, the authors concur that the effectiveness of these programs is not yet established and that further research is required to determine what kinds of interventions in what contexts can effectively reduce bullying

Two School Climates

Until that information becomes available, there remain interesting questions about how bullying prevention initiatives in some schools can succeed while in others have little or no positive impact. Researchers are increasingly considering the role that school climate may play in the success or failure of programs. I propose that a school climate founded on the principles of restorative justice is the type of climate in which bullying prevention programs will tend to succeed. In contrast, I speculate that the more traditional and still common punitive climate, which privileges punishment as a disciplinary policy, is not conducive to resolving bullying problems effectively in the long-term. Therefore, bullying prevention initiatives implemented in such a context are less likely to succeed. While there may be other types of school climates, I will focus on

---

[5] There is considerable overlap in the evaluation studies included in these three reviews. For example, 50% of the evaluations reviewed Baldry & Farrington and 27% of those reviewed by Vreeman & Carroll were included in Smith et al. review. It is important to note that each of these research teams relied on different analytic methods for their reviews, which may explain the divergence in some of their conclusions.

two these key types that seem relevant to modern schools. These climates are depicted here in their pure forms for illustrative purposes. In practice, they rarely exist in pure form but rather in differing degrees. For the purposes of my argument, schools exhibiting primarily punitive principles will be characterized as having a punitive climate, and schools exhibiting primarily restorative principles will be characterized as having a restorative climate.

As Figure 1 illustrates, a punitive climate is typified by high social control and low social support to community members (Wachtel & McCold, 2001). It is based on the presumption that people are motivated primarily to maximize pleasure and minimize pain and discomfort (i.e., hedonism) and that behaviour can be effectively regulated with rewards and punishment. It is individualistic and moralistic in its orientation and presumes that people are free to choose between right and wrong. The net effect is that social problems, such as bullying, are situated within individuals. This means that when things go wrong, someone must be blamed and corrective action in the form of punishment must follow. Typically, punishments isolate wrongdoers, normally through suspensions or expulsions. There is minimal consideration for causes of the bullying, beyond the moral failing of the child. The emphasis is on adherence to rules of conduct and restoration of order, and little attention is given to the experiences of victimized children. This highlights another principle operative in punitive climates, which is authoritarianism. In schools, adult authorities are in charge and make the rules, and it is the children's role to obey them. This inevitably creates a community built and regulated primarily on fear of authorities. Disciplinary policies arising from a punitive climate are often referred to as "zero-tolerance" policies. These policies typically stipulate specific and automatic consequences for various categories of misbehaviour, such as expulsion for wielding a weapon or suspension for cursing at a teacher, and are intended to provide retribution to student-offenders and deterrence for others inclined to act in such ways (Stinchcomb, Bazemore, & Rienstenberg, 2006). The Ontario Safe Schools Act (2001) is an example of this type of policy.

Two Approaches to School Discipline[a]

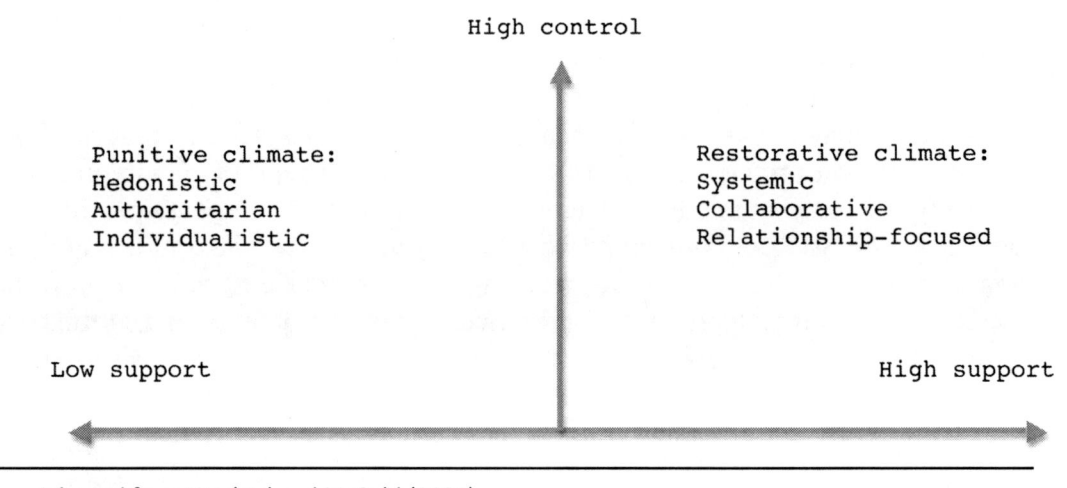

High control

Punitive climate:
Hedonistic
Authoritarian
Individualistic

Restorative climate:
Systemic
Collaborative
Relationship-focused

Low support   High support

a   Adapted from Wachtel and McCold (2001)

Chapter 6: Promoting a Positive School Climate

The restorative climate, although differing in many fundamental ways from a punitive climate, actually shares one important purpose, which is social regulation. It is recognized within this climate that communities must be orderly and individual rights respected, and therefore, social control is high, as is illustrated in Figure 1. However, this is best achieved by increasing support to wrongdoers rather than punishing and isolating them. This may take the form of problem-solving conversations between a teacher and students involved in a bullying incident. These discussions normally highlight the strengths wrongdoers bring to the resolution process and any recent successes that reveal their potential to be peaceful members of the community. Furthermore, notwithstanding the roles of individuals in the wrongdoing, there is a wider social context that must be considered. This systemic outlook on social problems permits a broader consideration of reasons for the misbehaviour with the intent of understanding, not blaming, the children involved. Fundamentally, misbehaviour within a restorative framework is seen as a violation of relationships, not rules. By implication, when wrongdoing occurs, those whose job it is to facilitate the resolution of the problem focus on how the people involved have been hurt, including the victim, the wrongdoer, and members of their communities and families. This extended group of affected individuals could include, for example, a friend who is worried about the victimized student's well-being, a teacher who is angry at the wrongdoer for injuring a vulnerable student in her care, and a parent who is discouraged about another setback for her child at school.

Ultimately, wrongdoers must be accountable for their misbehaviour, and they are expected to make amends to repair the hurt and damaged relationships resulting from their misbehaviour. Because solutions to social problems like bullying are derived collaboratively, members of the larger community (e.g., the classroom and school) are involved in developing codes of conduct that specify appropriate and meaningful consequences for misbehaviour. Finally, an important goal of making amends within a restorative framework, in addition to righting wrongs, is to re-integrate wrongdoers back into their communities. It is through the communities' efforts to rally around wrongdoers and to provide support and care, which is in contrast to the isolating effects of the punitive approach, that the seeds are planted for reducing bullying and developing positive relationships in the long-term.

Restorative Practices in the Classroom

Restorative justice has been a primary system of justice in many ancient societies. It has been revived in modern societies, driven in large part by work by the people in First Nations communities in North America (Adams, 2004). Restorative justice has also gained a foothold within the Canadian judicial system, and it is being increasingly used as an alternative to retributive justice in certain circumstances, particularly when aboriginal peoples are involved. However, its introduction into schools is relatively new, and its practices are less well developed than more traditional disciplinary systems within the school context (Drewery, 2004). Educators in New Zealand and Australia have been at the forefront of these developments over the last two decades. Canadian schools have been slower to formally embrace this approach to deal with aggression and bullying among children, although there are signs of growing interest in alternative approaches to zero-tolerance policies that became widely popular in the 1990s.

Whatever its conceptual allure as a potential means to deal with bullying problems in schools, it is critical that the effectiveness of the restorative approach to resolve school bullying be scrutinized empirically. Although data are very limited, early indications in the research literature suggest that restorative practices in school settings constitute a promising approach to dealing with bullying and other forms of aggression. For example, Morrison (2003) reported that a school-wide conflict resolution program built on restorative principles had a number of positive outcomes. At the end of the program, students displayed more adaptive ways of dealing with conflict and more respect and consideration for members of their school community, and they participated at higher rates in the activities of the community. McCold (2003) reported outcomes of an intensive educational program for delinquent and at-risk youth based on principles of restorative justice. The data revealed that the youth participants showed increases in self-esteem and social values at the end of the program. Additionally, there was a significantly lower rate of re-offending among participating youth in the six months following completion of the program. Finally, Stinchcomb et al. (2006) reported evaluation outcomes for a restorative justice pilot program implemented in several elementary and middle schools within the same school board. Pre/post quantitative measures revealed reductions in behavioural referrals to the principals' offices and in school suspensions. Qualitative findings indicated that stakeholders were often personally satisfied using the restorative approach to deal with bullying and conflict. Additionally, formal peace conferences (or circles) led by adults reportedly became less frequent over the three-year interval of the evaluation, as students and teachers integrated restorative principles into their daily interactions with one another. This led the authors to speculate that the climate of the schools had fundamentally changed following the intensive implementation of the restorative approach. These are encouraging preliminary results, but clearly more research on restorative practices in schools is required before final conclusions on the effectiveness of the approach can be made.

The more formal practices within the restorative justice approach, such as circles and conferencing, are beyond the scope of this chapter. (For a description of restorative conferencing used in schools, see Drewery, 2004.) However, as climate is manifested in the relationships in the school community and restorative justice is centred on relationships, there are ways to use restorative principles in the daily life of the school community when teachers are faced with student misbehaviour and have the task of restoring peace in the classroom and helping students mend damaged relations. The four questions set out and explained below are intended to guide teachers when they converse with students involved in bullying incidents. How these questions might be used by the teacher in such cases is illustrated in the example of Ben, a grade 4 boy, who has been accused of repeatedly taunting and threatening a classmate, Julia, while playing during recess.

Chapter 6: Promoting a Positive School Climate

1. *What has happened?* The teacher asks those involved in the incident what happened, fleshing out the details of the events and seeking clarification when necessary with each of the students. She could begin the dialogue by asking Julia, "What did Ben say to you during recess? What did you do or say after he said that to you?" She might then summarize what she has heard by saying, "Based on what I've heard so far, I understand that, Ben, you were sitting on the bench, and you overheard Julia and Karen talking about your friend Mike, and what they were saying upset you." Subsequently, she could ask Ben if Julia's account converges with his recollections by asking, "Is the way Julia described the events similar to what you remember happening, Ben? Is there anything you would add to or change in Julia's version of events?" It is likely that their accounts of events will differ, and the teacher should not take the divergences as proof that someone is lying. Differing perspectives lead people, children and adults alike, to experience the same events in different ways. When all accounts have been offered, the teacher can negotiate with the children a reasonable account of the events and finally summarize explicitly for the children her understanding of the events in question. Through this discovery process. It is critical that the teacher listen with curiosity and respect to all sides of the story and work hard to understand what the children are telling her.

2. *What were you thinking and feeling when this occurred?* This question is useful in exploring the context in which the misbehaviour occurred. The teacher in our example could ask Julia what it felt like to hear Ben's taunts and threats: "How did what Ben said affect you? You looked upset when you came in after recess. What were you feeling then?" While we are often (and correctly) compelled to focus on the wrongdoer's behaviour and the victimized child's feelings in response, it is important in the service of understanding the broader context of the bullying incident that the wrongdoer's feelings and the victimized student's behaviours are also explored. The teacher might ask Ben, "When you heard Julia say that about Mike, how did you feel on the inside when you heard that?" This creates opportunities for promoting personal accountability and responsibility, so that children learn that others do not "make them do it." This line of dialogue, if followed through to its conclusion, will also illuminate more appropriate ways for children to express the feelings that give rise to aggressive behaviour.

3. *Who has been affected and how has it affected them?* This question encourages teachers to consider the impacts of the misbehaviour on members the wider classroom or school community. There are direct effects of bullying that are relatively easy to observe, if one looks closely enough. A discussion with the victimized student(s) is usually sufficient to uncover these direct effects. In our example, the teacher could ask Julia how she is feeling now and whether or not she is scared about the things Ben said to her earlier. There may also be indirect effects of bullying on children who were peripherally involved in the episode: Other children may become more uncomfortable in the classroom with the aggressor present such that it disturbs their work and relationships within the class. These effects are usually less obvious and only emerge with additional probing. Inquires with Julia's friend, Karen, who witnessed the harassment, might reveal such effects. A complete understanding of these impacts is essential for deciding the most effective

ways by which a wrongdoer may make amends. Additionally, by exploring these effects, the teacher helps aggressors learn the true impact of their aggression.

4. *How can the misbehaviour be rectified?* One of the key elements of restorative justice is the necessity to set right the wrongs that have been committed. This is a critical step to restoring relationships and re-integrating the wrongdoer into the community. This necessarily requires input from those hurt by the misdeeds. There is any number of ways for amends to be made, and the key consideration is that the wrongdoer and those who were victimized or affected all feel that sanctions encourage healing. The teacher has an important role in determining appropriate sanctions in consultation with the children involved in an incident. In our example, the teacher might suggest that Ben write a letter of apology to Julia, and then ask Julia if she would accept this gesture of peace-making from Ben. The teacher would then supervise Ben so that he writes a letter in which he appropriately explains why he acted as he did, takes responsibility for his behaviour, apologizes for the hurt he caused Julia, and promises not to do so again.

An additional benefit of the restorative approach to dealing with bullying illustrated in the example above is that it can engender increased empathy in children who bully others. Empathy is a shared emotional response that reflects an individual's emotional and cognitive understanding of another person's distress (Feshbach, 1997, p. 35). A substantial volume of research indicates that, in general, empathy is positively related to prosocial behaviour, like comforting or helping others, and negatively related to aggression. Preliminary research suggests that bullying may be similarly remedied through empathy training (Espelage, Mebane, & Adams, 2004), and restorative practices like those described here represent one possible route to achieving this goal.

Conclusion

In summary, restorative justice is a set of principles and practices that promotes healing, moral learning, community caring, and personal responsibility. It is proposed that by implementing these ancient principles of justice, teachers can cultivate empathy and positive relationships among students and contribute to the development of a school climate in which all children flourish and thrive. As an alternative for schools that rely primarily on punitive principles and methods, a school climate founded on restorative principles offers valuable lessons to children involved in bullying about how to be responsible citizens. As conflict and wrongdoing are universal in human communities, teachers should not be frustrated when these issues arise in their classrooms but should see them as rich opportunities for learning about better ways for people to live in peace.

Chapter 6: Promoting a Positive School Climate

Key Messages

1. Effective solutions for bullying require, as a starting point, caring and respectful relationships among all members of the school community.

2. Restorative justice as a disciplinary approach privileges collaboration, inclusion, and accountability.

3. A punitive approach to discipline emphasizes punishment and exclusion of the misbehaving student.

4. A school whose climate integrates principles of restorative justice will likely be more successful at dealing effectively with bullying problems than a school with a punitive climate.

References

Adams, P. (2004). *Restorative justice, responsive regulation, and democratic governance.* Journal of Sociology and Social Welfare, 31, 3-5.

Anderson, M., Kaufman, J., Simon, T. R., Barrios, L., Paulozzi, L., & Ryan, G. et al. (2001). *School-associated violent deaths in the United States, 1994-1999.* JAMA: Journal of the American Medical Association, 286(21), 2695-2702.

Baldry, A. C., & Farrington, D. P. (2007). *Effectiveness of programs to prevent school bullying.* Victims and Offenders, 2, 183-204.

Canadian Initiative for the Prevention of Bullying (n.d). *What is bullying?* Retrieved February 7, 2006 from http://www.cipb.ca/aboutbullying/whatisbullying.html.

Cohen, J. (1988). *Statistical power for behavioural sciences* (2nd ed.). Hillsdale, NJ: Erlbaum.

Connolly, J., Pepler, D., Craig, W., & Taradash, A. (2000). *Dating experiences of bullies in early adolescence.* Child Maltreatment, 5(4), 299-310.

Craig, W. M., & Harel, Y. (2004). *Bullying, physical fighting and victimization.* In C. Currie et al. (Eds). *Young People's Health in Context: international report from the HBSC 2001/02 survey.* WHO Policy Series: Health policy for children and adolescents (Issue 4, pp. 133-144). Copenhagen: WHO Regional Office for Europe.

Craig, W. M., & Pepler, D. J. (2007). *Understanding bullying: From research to policy.* Canadian Psychology, 48, 86-93.

Craig, W. M., Pepler, D., & Atlas, R. (2000). *Observations of bullying in the playground and in the classroom.* School Psychology International, 21, 22-36.

Drewery, W. (2004). *Conferencing in schools: Punishment, restorative justice, and the productive important of the process of conversation.* Journal of Community and Applied Social Psychology, 14, 332-344.

Espelage, D. L., Mebane, S. E., & Adams, R. S. (2004). *Empathy, caring, and bullying: Toward an understanding of complex associations.* In D. L. Espelage & S. M. Swearer (Eds.), *Bullying in American schools: A social-ecological perspective on prevention and intervention* (pp. 37-62). Mahwah, NJ: Lawrence Erlbaum.

Feshbach, N. D. (1997). *Empathy: The formative years Implications for clinical practice.* In A. C. Bohart & L. S. Greenberg (Eds.), *Empathy reconsidered: Directions for psychotherapy* (pp.33-59). Washington, DC: American Psychological Association.

Glover, D., Gough, G., Johnson, M., & Cartwright, N. (2000). *Bullying in 25 secondary schools: Incidence, impact and intervention.* Educational Research, 42, 141-156.

Hanish, L. D., Kochenderfer-Ladd, B., Fabes, R. A., Martin, C. L., & Denning, D. (2004). *Bullying Among Young Children: The Influence of Peers and Teachers.* In D. L. Espelage & S. M. Swearer *(Eds), Bullying in American schools: A social-ecological perspective on prevention and intervention* (pp. 141-159). Mahwah, NJ: Lawrence Erlbaum.

McCold, P. (2003, May). *Evaluation of a restorative milieu: CSF Buxmont School/Day Treatment programs 1999-2001.* Paper presented at the Second International Conference on Violence in Schools, Quebec, QC.

Morrison, B. E. (2003). *Regulating safe school communities: Being responsive and restorative.* Journal of Educational Administration, 41, 689-704.

Nansel, T. R., Overpeck, M., Pilla, R. S., Ruan, W., Simons-Morton, B., & Scheidt, P. (2001). *Bullying behaviors among US youth: Prevalence and association with psychosocial adjustment.* Jama: Journal of the American Medical Association, 285, 2094-2100.

Olweus, D. (1993). *Bullying at school: What we know and what we can do.* Malden, MA: Blackwell.

Rigby, K. (2003). *Consequences of bullying in schools.* Canadian Journal of Psychiatry - Revue Canadienne de Psychiatrie, 48, 583-590.

Salmivalli, C. (1999). *Participant role approach to school bullying: Implications for intervention.* Journal of Adolescence, 22, 453-459.

Smith, J. D., Schneider, B., Smith, P. K., & Ananiadou, K. (2004). *The effectiveness of whole-school antibullying programs: A synthesis of evaluation research.* School Psychology Review, 33, 548-561.

Stinchcomb, J. B., Bazemore, G., & Rienstenberg, N. (2006). *Beyond zero tolerance: Restoring justice in secondary schools.* Youth Violence and Juvenile Justice, 4, 123-147.

Sutton, J., & Smith, P. K. (1999). *Bullying as a group process: An adaptation of the participant-role approach.* Aggressive Behavior, 25, 97-111.

Vaillancourt, T., Hymel, S., & McDougall, P. (2003). *Bullying is power: Implications for school-based intervention strategies.* Journal of Applied School Psychology, 19, 157-176.

Vreeman, R. C., & Carroll, A. E. (2007). *A systematic review of school-based interventions to prevent bullying.* Archives of Pediatrics & Adolescent Medicine, 161, 78-88.

Wachtel T., & McCold, P. (2001). *Restorative justice in everyday life: Beyond the formal ritual.* In H. Strang & J. Braithwaite (Eds.), *Restorative justice and civil society* (pp. 114-129). Cambridge: Cambridge University Press.

Chapter 7:

Best Practices in School-Based Bullying Prevention Programs: What Works?

Leslie M. Tutty
University of Calgary

Introduction

In the world of violence prevention, bullying is the "common cold". While most of us were not victims of child abuse and our current intimate relationships are neither physically nor emotional damaging, many of us can remember having been tormented with taunts on the schoolyard, excluded by a group of peers, or being a member of a group watching another being bullied. From the perspective of many individuals, bullying is simply a part of growing up; a rite of passage that tests the mettle of children and youth, preparing them for adulthood. Those who subscribe to this belief would never see the need to institute bullying prevention programs.

But the deaths of Jason Lang in Taber Alberta, shot by a fellow student and 15 year old Reena Verk, murdered by a mixed gender group of young teens in British Colombia, not to mention the tragedy in Columbine High school in Littleton Colorado, have led us to realize that childhood is not the idyllic period we hope it is. Our children and youth are impacted by many forms of violence (Tutty & Bradshaw, 2004). Youth who commit suicide have commonly been bullied by peers and the internet has provided new tools to harass other teens in public and humiliating ways called "cyber-bullying" (Patchin, & Hinduja, 2006; Li, 2006). While the internet as a venue is novel and permits expanded access to the audience to witness the humiliation of the child being victimized, the bullying techniques are no different (Beran & Li, 2005).

Over the past 30 years, numerous school-based violence prevention programs have been developed to address issues such as conflict resolution, child sexual abuse, dating violence, sexual harassment and sexual assault. Bullying programs have been introduced most recently. This chapter provides an overview of issues to consider when reviewing prevention programs, presents information specific to conflict resolution and bullying programs, suggests best practices in bullying prevention programs, and provides examples of programs with strong research evidence.

The programs were identified in a resource manual developed to assist schools and community agencies in making informed choices about school-based violence prevention programs (Tutty, Bradshaw, et al., 2005). Funded in 2002, by the Crime Prevention Partners Program of Justice Canada, the manual was updated in 2005 in collaboration with Drs. Claire Crooks and Peter Jaffe from the University of Western Ontario, with financial support from the Trillium Foundation of Ontario[6].

In part, the manual was developed in response to a survey of Calgary school personnel that were responsible for making decisions about which violence prevention programs their students would have access to (Tutty & Nixon, 2000). The 609 respondents reported receiving information on numerous programs. About one-third of the school personnel were confused about both choosing appropriate violence prevention programs, and evaluating what constitutes an effective program. One vice-principal mentioned that brochures for over 150 programs crossed his desk in a year. A number of school personnel commented that they lack the background to assess the programs and needed guidelines as to what to look for in a program that represents best practices.

In response, the project research team decided to investigate programs that reflect best practices. We searched for school-based prevention programs with research evidence through a variety of sources, in total, identifying over 100 prevention programs that met our criteria of being a formal program with research evidence. As bullying is the most frequently identified form of violence in schools and has prompted school-wide efforts to address this problem (Bauman & Del Rio, 2005; Craig, Pepler & Atlas, 2000; O'Moore, 2000), this chapter focuses on bullying and conflict resolution programs.

What is Violence Prevention?

Stopping violence before it occurs is the major goal of universal prevention programs. School-based violence prevention efforts for children/youth are based on the principle that education can change awareness and knowledge, and teach skills that may change behaviour. The hope is that such knowledge will empower children and youth to interact in positive and prosocial ways.

Prevention programs can be directed at a total population (universal or primary prevention), at a group considered 'at-risk' (secondary prevention) or at a group already experiencing violence either as victimizers or victims (tertiary prevention) (Kessler & Albee, 1975). Our focus in this chapter is on universal, school-based violence prevention programs, that is, those directed at all children/youth and delivered in the school setting. Most programs provide information in the hope of informing or changing attitudes with respect to problem behaviours, preventing bullying being an obvious example. Others teach about positive (prosocial) skills such as good communication or problem solving skills so that relationship problems such as dating violence do not develop in the first place. Still other

---

[6] 2002 edition available on-line: www.ucalgary.ca/resolve/violenceprevention/. To receive the 2005 edition, email tutty@ucalgary.ca

programs focus on personal factors such as self-esteem that are considered to protect against problems developing.

Given the different possible foci, a significant question is whether programs should focus on healthy or on problem relationships. Is it better to focus on healthy sexuality or describe sexual abuse/assault? Should programs focus on healthy peer relationships rather than bullying? Although there are no best practices with research evidence in the literature, from my perspective, one needs both, especially in primary prevention. Students need the skills for "normal" living: communication skills; problem solving skills; interpersonal negotiation skills. All programs should promote relationships forged on the basis of equal power and goodwill. Students also need to know, however, about the abuse of power, when they might need to ask for assistance or how they could help a friend who disclosed that they were being abused.

Who Delivers Prevention Programs?

Violence prevention programs are often offered in schools by an external agency with expertise in addressing a particular form of violence (Tutty, 1991; 1996). For example, sexual assault centers were the first to develop child sexual abuse prevention programs; dating violence prevention was first offered by staff from shelters for abused women. One advantage of externally offered programs is that those who present the program are most often professionals that know the material well and are comfortable with the topic. Staff from external programs can comfortably discuss the violence prevention concepts with children, thus relieving teachers of some of the responsibility to handle disclosures and potentially embarrassing material. Teachers are often reluctant to take a major role in violence prevention programs, perceiving such duties as beyond the scope of their jobs.

A disadvantage of external programs is that use of the program is voluntary; only a portion of the children in an area will have access to the program. Teachers or principals who invite the program may already be sensitized to the abuse issue and may have previously provided some information to their students. Those most likely to need the information, individuals who know little about the problem, are least likely to be aware of the programs. Another disadvantage of external programs is that staff are in the schools for a limited time.

Internal programs are integrated directly into the schools' curricula, for example, into health or family life education classes. Teachers both present the material and assume responsibility for leading role-plays and answering questions from children. Schools are a natural environment for prevention programs, addressing entire populations of children with an approach that fits with the purpose of the institution – providing education. Children may more likely disclose to teachers; however, training is especially important, as teachers, like most of the population, often feel uncomfortable discussing sensitive topics with children. In addition, teachers may, themselves, have been abused, and presenting information on interpersonal violence and bullying may be distressing.

Another advantage of internal programs is that teachers can integrate violence prevention concepts with other relevant topics, such as self-esteem and resolving conflict, or as issues emerge in the classroom between students. A disadvantage of school-based curricula, as mentioned previously, is that some teachers perceive these topics as beyond what they should be expected to teach. Despite having a prepared curriculum, teachers may feel uncomfortable presenting the material, a reaction that is likely communicated to students.

An option is integrating aspects of both external and internal programs. Staff from external agencies may present the prevention materials within the school and are responsible for leading student discussions. They provide supplementary materials for the teachers to utilize in follow-up discussions in their classrooms. Teacher training is a key component in integrating the two types of programs. One disadvantage of such an integrated approach is that collaboration is time-consuming and requires considerable co-operation. However, the result is a prevention program that targets its message to larger segments of the community.

Evaluating Prevention Programs

Evaluating prevention programs is no simple task. In 1981, Martin Bloom, an early advocate of prevention programs, referred to it as "the impossible science." It is difficult to evaluate the success of prevention programs because the goal is to stop a particular problem or behaviour from developing in the first place. If the prevention strategy is successful, the problem will not occur; but neither can one say with any certainty that the problem would have developed. Although, it is challenging to evaluate the effectiveness of prevention programs, it is, nonetheless, essential.

Most prevention research evaluates whether the program has met its goals in changing knowledge and attitudes. Ideally, we'd prefer to have research evidence about both. Also, ideally, we would like to know whether children's behaviour actually changes in response to a prevention program because improvements in knowledge and attitudes are not necessarily accompanied by actual behaviour change. For example, knowing that bullying is inappropriate might change the behaviour of some, but not all children. However, it is easier to collect information about knowledge and attitudes about bullying than to identify actual changes in youths' behaviour in reaction to a program, so behavioural change is the least likely to be evaluated of the three variables. Including observations of children's behaviour either in simulated situations or *in vivo* (i.e., on the playground), strengthens the research but is expensive and rare, exceptions being the evaluation of Second Step (Grossman, et al., 1997) and Steps to Respect (Frey, Hirschstein, Snell, Edstrom, MacKenzie, & Broderick, 2005), both programs of the Seattle Committee for Children.

Finally, even if youth improve their knowledge attitude and behaviours after participating in a prevention program, do they remember the material over time or revert to their original pre-program levels? Evaluations that include follow-up testing to assess maintaining these prevention targets are important.

Some research is methodologically stronger than others. The best is often published in academic journals. The process of publishing involves peer reviews by knowledgeable academics; often articles are revised or otherwise strengthened through the review process. Strong research evaluation designs include the use of pre-tests and post-tests, so that one can assess whether the students' attitudes, knowledge or behaviours change after the program in comparison to what they knew in the first place (Tutty, 1993). A further important design feature is including control or comparison groups (with students that did not participate in the program) so that one can assess that it was the program that made the difference not other factors such as the passage of time or a national TV show on violence. In the school-based manual, we also included evaluations with less-clearly interpretable findings such as pre-test-post-test evaluations with no control groups. While we included programs that utilized consumer satisfaction surveys that can provide important program information, these are so often highly complimentary that they are not sufficient evidence that programs work.

It is important to realize that the stronger the research design, the more likely one is to identify problems with programs. For example, using a research design with pre-test and post-test measures of knowledge of bullying, one might identify significant improvements after the program. If one added a control (non-program) group, however, we might discover that the students who did not participate in a program also improved their attitudes, suggesting that something other than the program was responsible for the change. Further, non-significant results could be due to factors other than the program, such as a measure of attitudes that is not reliable, or a poorly trained program facilitator. Interpreting research results is complex.

Cautions about Programs

What is a program? For the purposes of this chapter, a program is a set of materials, a curriculum that addresses a particular issue. While in-person school presentations from individuals that have, for example, experienced and overcome bullying are compelling and can be instructive, for the most part they complement rather than constituting programs. Standardizing materials and providing a manual or curriculum are the hallmarks of a program.

Before presenting the conflict resolution and bullying programs with strong research evidence, there are several caveats to consider. First, a program is not a solution. It would be tempting to promote a program as the answer to significant problems such as bullying, but a program is simply the first step in raising awareness and providing information about the issue. Much detailed and difficult work remains to repeat the message that bullying is not acceptable, including reviewing school policies with respect to bullying and finding ways to involve all school staff and students in the effort.

We did not include good programs that have not yet been evaluated. Notably, though, a positive evaluation is not the only mark of a good program. Evaluations take time to conduct and are seldom the priority of new programs that must focus on connecting with schools and refining their materials. As such, programs that have not been evaluated are not necessarily ineffective. However, the programs that are cited in the resources manual have taken the extra effort to assess whether and how their programs work. This initiative speaks to their conviction that their programs can make a difference to young people.

Further, evaluations take time to conduct, as does publishing the research results. We may have missed some programs because their evaluations were not yet completed or not yet accepted for publication. Even when evaluation results are positive, the programs may not be effective if implemented differently from in the research protocol.

A final caveat is that we are not endorsing any program. There are important similarities and differences across the programs. They vary in terms of level of school (age of student), cost, length, parent involvement and other factors. These will all be considerations for school personnel in choosing which program is the best fit for their students.

Conflict Resolution and Bullying Prevention Programs

The earliest violence prevention programs, many developed in the 1970's, focused on teaching pro-social behaviours such as conflict resolution and related problem-solving skills including programs for conflict resolution, peer mediation and peace-keeping programs (Johnson, Johnson, Dudley, & Acikgoz, 1994). Conflict occurs naturally in the process of decision making and working with others. Conflict, in and of itself, is not damaging, but how one deals with conflict can be. Conflict resolution refers to strategies that enable students to address arguments and disputes in peaceable and cooperative manners.

Peer mediation is a specific form of conflict resolution, whereby trained students act as neutral third parties in settling non-physical disputes between other students. Traditionally, peer mediation involves a selected group of students (cadre) who are trained in mediation skills and then offer their services in the playground or lunchroom (Johnson, Johnson, Dudley & Magnuson, 1995). More recently, peer mediators have been students who volunteer for this service after everyone in the school has participated in the conflict resolution skill building. The hope is that a peaceable school results when the values and skills of cooperation, communication, tolerance, positive emotional expression, and conflict resolution are taught and supported throughout the culture of the school.

Eleven conflict resolution and peer mediation programs with strong research support are listed in Table 1[7]. They are listed starting with three comprehensive programs starting with students in youngest grades that also address students through grades 9 to 12. However, aside from the first three, the majority of programs target students in two or three year groupings. All comprise teacher offered curricula of varying lengths and focuses: some include peer mediation components but the most common strategy is teaching conflict resolution techniques.

---

[7] Additional research and contact information is available from the 2005 School-based Resource Manual (email tutty@ucalgary.ca for a free copy).

Table 1. Published Conflict Resolution Control/Comparison Group Designs

Program	Grade	Results
Resolving Conflict Creatively Program	K to 8	Aber, et al. (1999; 2003). N = over 5000 & 11,000. Children receiving more (25+) RCCP lessons had significantly slower growth in self-reported hostile attributions, aggressive fantasies and aggressive problem-solving strategies.
Second Step: A Violence Prevention Curriculum (Seattle Committee for Children)	K to 9	Grossman et al. (1997): RCT with 790 Gr. 2-3 students. Behavioural observations: physical aggression decreased moderately for program children, increased in controls. At 6-months, program schools continued lower physical aggression. Neutral or prosocial behaviour significantly increased post-program; constant in controls. Taub (2002): rural school: Gr 3-5 students. At 4 months post, program students significantly increased prosocial & decreased antisocial behaviours; controls increased antisocial behaviours. Behavioural observations: program students significantly improved engaging with peers at 1-year.
Teaching Students to be Peacemakers	K to 12	Johnson & Johnson (2002): meta-analysis of 16 studies: Gr. 1-9. Trained students used mediation skills to resolve conflicts equally at home & school, had positive attitudes about resolving conflicts. Teachers saw classrooms as more positive and less destructive after the program. Parents saw students mediating conflicts at home.
STORIES (Teglasi & Rothman)	2 to 5	Teglasi & Rothman (2001): 59 Gr. 4 & 5 students (17 deemed aggressive). Less aggressive students improved in teacher-rated externalizing behaviours but aggressive children worsened. Aggressive students self-reported lower externalizing behaviour and beliefs supporting aggression. Rahill & Teglasi (2003): compared STORIES & a social skills program: Gr. 2-6 special education students (82 students; 19 controls). Program students increased cognitive growth & improved behaviour.

Chapter 7: Best Practices in School-Based Bullying Prevention Programs

Peacemakers	4 to 8	Shapiro et al. (2002): 1400 Gr. 4-8. Program students self-reported significant increases in knowledge of psychosocial skills & decreases in aggressive behaviours. Teacher-reports: program students had fewer disciplinary aggressive incidents, used fewer mediation services & got fewer suspensions for violent behaviour than control students.
Project WIN	5 to 8	Roberts, et al. (2004) 34 Gr. 5 (program N=19; control N=15). Program students reported greater liking of classmates & more positive attitudes to teamwork. At 2-month follow-up (Roberts & White, 2004): children's sense of community persisted, liking classmates increased, perceptions of trust increased, but not attitudes to teamwork.
SMART Team	5 to 9	Bosworth et al. (1996; 2000): 558 Gr. 6-8 students. Program students accessed SMART Talk software for 4 weeks & significantly increased knowledge, intentions to use non-violent strategies & beliefs about non-violent solutions.
Responding In Peaceful and Positive Ways (RIPP) (Meyer, et al. (2000).	6 to 8	Farrell, et al., (1996): 260 Gr. 6 program; 317 controls: significant decrease in physical fighting for program boys, not girls. Farrell, et al. (2001): 602 Gr. 6: program youth had lower rates of fighting, weapons at school, in-school suspensions, used peer mediation more & significantly increased conflict resolution knowledge. No significant pre/post differences on out-of-school suspension rates & self-reported behaviour & adjustment. Farrell, et al. (2003): program students: better attitudes to non-violent solutions to problems. Controls: higher rates of aggressive behaviours over two follow-ups.
Student Created Aggression Replacement Education (SCARE)	7 to 9	Herrmann & McWhirter (2003): 207 at-risk middle school students randomly assigned to SCARE or a vocational program. Program students self-reported less anger & less likely to feel angry at others after program. Not maintained at 8-weeks. Program students: less aggressive attitudes at 8 weeks and self-assessed as less aggressive than controls.

Violence Prevention Curriculum for Adolescents (Prothrow-Stith)	9 to 10	DuRant et al. (1996) compared this to Conflict Resolution (below): 209 Gr. 6-8 students. Students in both programs self-reported decreases in hypothetical violence, frequency of violence use & fighting (30-day period). DeJong et al. (1989): 347 students: significant decreased self-reported fighting for program students.
Conflict Resolution: A Curriculum for Youth Providers	7 to 9	See DuRant (1996) above: 209 Gr. 6-8 students. Students in both programs self-reported significant decreases in using hypothetical violence, frequency of violence use and fighting (30-day period). Students in Conflict Resolution: significantly fewer fights resulting in injury needing medical treatment.

What research evidence supports the efficacy of conflict resolution programs? The 11 programs listed in Table 1 all utilized strong pre-test/post-test research designs. Of these programs that all utilized solid research designs, Grossman et al.'s (1997) evaluation utilizing randomized clinical trials with 790 Gr. 2-3 students with independent observers on the playground, lunchrooms, and classrooms, is the strongest methodologically, providing evidence for the efficacy of the Second Step program. Other conflict resolution programs with exceptional research support are Resolving Conflict Creatively (Aber, Brown & Henrich, 1999; Aber, Brown & Jones 2003), and Teaching Students to be Peacemakers (Johnson & Johnson, 2002), both of which utilized very large samples and conducted multiple studies over time.

Recently, the focus of school-based prevention has largely shifted to programs that deal with bullying, a component of dealing with conflict, but not its entirety. Bullying is an abuse of power. Conflict resolution and peer mediation are useful for relationships of relatively equal power, but they are questionably as effective with children that bully and may manipulate these interventions and utilize them abusively. Rather, appropriately dealing with children/youth who bully involves adults using authoritative controls such as school policies and discipline procedures that hold children/youth who bully accountable for their behaviour and supports change, such as through counselling (Whitted & Dupper, 2005).

The Characteristics of Bullying Programs

Prevention programs on bullying typically take a different approach from the conflict resolution programs, teaching about the power differentials inherent in bullying. Dan Olweus from Norway was the pioneer of bullying prevention program development. In reaction to the suicides of several Norwegian children who were victimized, Olweus (1991) developed and implemented a comprehensive school-based program, the Bullying Prevention Program (BPP) for students from kindergarten to Grade 12. Most bullying prevention programs used Olweus' programs as a base.

Chapter 7: Best Practices in School-Based Bullying Prevention Programs

Bullying prevention programs teach students about the power inherent in bullying and ways that bystanders reinforce bullying behaviour by being silent or not protesting. In fact, changing bystander behaviour has become a focal point for a number of programs to break the bullying cycle (Jeffrey, Miller & Linn, 2002). One way to accomplish this goal is to change attitudes, such as intolerance for differences that underlie bullying.

Early on, the primary target audience for bullying prevention programs was younger children (up to grade 5). A broad definition of bullying that includes teasing and exclusion is not stressed in every program, while overt aggressive behaviour is always acknowledged (Tutty, et al., 2005). Expanding the definition of the power dynamics inherent in bullying, into related abuses of power such as sexual and racial harassment, has resulted in programs being created for middle and high school students. Commonly, most programs for students in Kindergarten to Grade 8 provide information on identifying feelings, managing anger, differences between individuals and conflict resolution strategies. Problem solving, cooperation and conflict resolution skills are not only promoted but also practiced.

Building on knowledge and skills learned previously, programs for high school students typically focus on the causes and effects of violence, attitudes that promote violent solutions to conflict, difficult interpersonal situations, and high-risk behaviours such as drug, alcohol and weapons use that are commonly associated with conflict escalating into violence.

Bullying prevention programs invite teachers to intervene when children's conflict is about power and control, not negotiation. Until recently, teachers have often ignored bullying, perceiving it as conflict that children can cope with themselves (Bauman & Del Rio, 2005; Tutty, Ogden & Costello, 2006). Craig and Pepler (1997) observed that teachers intervened in only 4% of the bullying episodes.

Most bullying prevention programs involve teacher-delivered curricula (rather than external programs). They utilize a multi-dimensional approach – a combination of individual, classroom, school-wide, and community initiatives with students, teachers, school staff, and parents. Bullying programs underscore the importance of looking at school policies and procedures with respect to bullying and developing procedures to respond quickly and consistently to bullying incidents. These can function as a strategy to involve parents, moving prevention beyond the school walls into the community.

Good programs model principles of non-violent conflict resolution and respect for diversity through school policies, procedures and activities that involve students, school staff and parents. In addition, though, schools need to become aware of local resources such as internal or external counselling programs that support children who have been victimized and provide intervention for children that use bullying behaviours.

Evaluating Bullying Prevention Programs

Most of the bullying prevention program evaluations reviewed reported some success in increasing knowledge and/or decreasing violence. The multitude of ways that were used to measure reductions in violence makes comparisons across programs challenging. The most common method that researchers utilized to measure decreases in physical aggression were self-report questionnaires about actual or intended use of aggression and incidents of witnessing bullying. However, others measured violence-related referrals to the principal, the frequency of fighting (observed, self-, teacher- or parent-reported), feeling safer at school; school suspensions; threats with a weapon; behaviour problems in classroom as reported by teacher; frequency and intensity of fights with siblings as reported by parents; and self-reported aggressive thoughts or fantasies.

Table 2. Published Bullying Program Control/Comparison Group Designs

Program	Grade	Results
Bully-Proofing Your School (Garrity, et al., 2000)	K to 8	Beran, et al. (in press) 197 grades 4 to 6 students: The frequency of self-reported witnessing of bullying significantly decreased at post-test for those receiving the program, but remained constant in the comparison group. Attitudes towards victims remained stable in the program group, but deteriorated in the no-program students. An unpublished pre-post control groups study (Brockenbrough, 2001) found no effects.
Get Real About Violence	K to 12	Meyer, et al. (2004) evaluated the curriculum in two Gr. 7 classrooms (168 students in intervention school; 125 in control school). Measures assessed the frequency and intent to commit verbal aggression, watching a fight, spreading rumours about a fight and engaging in a fight. While the scores of students in both conditions worsened over time, the program students' scores did not deteriorate to the same extent as those in the control group.
Peacebuilders (Embry, et al., 1996).	K to 12	Krug et al., (1997). PeaceBuilders schools significantly decreased injuries related to fights compared to comparison schools. Flannery et al. (2003): 8 schools: 4128 students in Gr. K-5. Teachers rated Gr. K-2 students significantly higher on social competence. Gr. 3-5 students rated less aggressive than non-intervention students & these changes were maintained over time. No changes observed in control schools.

The Sheffield Project	K to 12	Smith & Sharp (1994) in 27 schools: elementary students were bullied less often & were a bully less than control schools. Program students less likely to join in but no change in perceptions of teachers' abilities to stop bullying. Secondary students more likely to tell an adult if bullied. 80% of students felt the changes improved school climate.
Steps to Respect (Seattle Committee for Children)	3 to 6	Frey et al. (2005) 571 students observed on playground. At post-test, program students accepted bullying & aggression less, felt more responsible to intervene & saw adults as more responsive to reports of bullying than control students. Program students believed that assertive intervention behaviours were easier and reported less victimization.
Bullyproof (Sjostrom & Stein) / Expect Respect adapted Bullyproof	4/5	(also addresses sexual harassment) Sanchez, et al. (2001); Meraviglia, et al. (2003); Whitaker, et al. (2004). Some mixed results: Gr. 5's improved knowledge of sexual harassment but not bullying (Meraviglia et al). All 3 studies found program students increased knowledge of sexual harassment behaviours more than controls & increased awareness of bullying & sexual harassment behaviours in their school.

Table 2 presents seven bullying prevention programs that were evaluated with strong research designs. Three of the programs were developed for students from kindergarten to Grade 12; another one is for students from kindergarten to Grade 8. Similar to the conflict resolution programs presented earlier, six of the seven are teacher offered curricula. The additional program is co-presented by a teacher and a community agency representative from a sexual assault centre.

Of these, several stand out as both exemplary research and programs. Flannery et al. (2003) evaluation of eight school using Peacebuilders; Smith and Sharp's evaluation of the Sheffield Project students in 27 British schools encompassing both elementary and secondary level students and the evaluation of Steps to Respect (Frey et al., 2005) using independent observations of children's behaviours on playground similar to the research on the Second Step program reviewed in the conflict resolution section. Both programs were developed by Seattle Committee for Children.

The research results on several bullying prevention programs were mixed, suggesting the need for further examination. Meraviglia, Becker, Rosenbluth, Sanchez & Robertson (2003) found increases in knowledge of sexual harassment but not bullying. With respect to the Bullyproofing Your Schools program, one study (Beran, Tutty & Steinrath, 2004) supported knowledge gains but another researcher (Brockenbrough, 2001) concluded that the program was not effective.

Several observations about the evaluations of both conflict resolution and bullying programs research deserve mention. Although increasing prosocial behaviours was a stated objective of some programs, it was measured in few evaluations. Similarly, few evaluations assessed a reduction in verbal bullying or "excluding" behaviours: both expressions of bullying utilized by more girls than boys. Bullying prevention programs that concentrate only on physical acts of aggression miss the more covert expressions of bullying and, as result, may primarily measure changes in ways that boys bully.

Programs or the research evaluating them rarely addressed gender differences in either the expression of bullying or program results. Conducting a gender analysis on results from dating violence and sexual harassment is fairly standard, but only one evaluation of a conflict resolution program compared the behaviour of girls to boys (Farrell, Meyer & Dahlberg, 1996). In this analysis, while boys demonstrated a decrease in physical violence from pre- to post-test, girls did not.

Importantly, several school-based prevention programs with a central focus on another form of interpersonal violence also include material with respect to bullying. These programs include three with a central focus on child sexual abuse prevention: Good Touch, Bad Touch (K to 6) (Harvey, Forehand, Brown, & Holmes, 1988); Project Trust (Gr. 3-12), which is for a wide age range of students and also addresses dating violence using a peer model (Oldfield, Hays, & Megal (1996), and "Touching" (K to 8) (Tutty, 1992). While the published evaluations provided strong support for these programs, the research focus was on the child sexual abuse prevention concepts not bullying.

The Fourth R, a relationship program with strong evaluation support, also includes material on bullying prevention. This 21 week curriculum for middle school students incorporates information on sexuality and substance use (Wolfe, Wekerle, Scott, Straatman, Grasley, & Reitzel-Jaffe, 2003). Utilizing programs with information on multiple forms of violence makes sense given the strong connections of each form of violence to abuses of power and control.

Strengths and Challenges for Bullying and Conflict Resolution Programs

Researchers have provided support for several conflict resolution and bullying programs as positively impacting knowledge, beliefs and attitudes about bullying. Limited support suggests that such programs can improve students' behaviours and utilization of skills to address bullying when it occurs. Evaluations of prevention programs need to continue, with particular emphasis on follow-up; ensuring that changes in attitudes, knowledge and behaviours are maintained over time. While most evaluations report improvements in knowledge of and attitudes to bullying, does this translate into changes in behaviour, particularly on the part of bystanders? The next stage of research on prevention programs

Chapter 7: Best Practices in School-Based Bullying Prevention Programs

would be well advised to assess changes in actual peer participation in and observing bullying, since bystanders both reinforce and sanction bullying behaviour.

Bullying prevention programs have contributed a number of ideas that can strengthen other violence prevention initiatives. Broadening the prevention focus beyond children and youth to also examine the school climate and policies and community influence on bullying is impressive and provides an important additional context for other violence prevention programs to consider. Raising the issue of bystanders is an important broadening of perspective that acknowledges that all forms of violence take place in a social context that allows them to occur.

As already noted, bullying prevention programs are one of a number of school-based violence prevention programs developed over the last thirty years. Despite the fact that forms of violence are similar (i.e., bullying and sexual harassment) and that violence and bullying commonly involve an abuse of power, the literatures on various forms of violence tend to be separate and school personnel may have limited knowledge of the dynamics of other types of abuse. The strategies to address various forms of violence, conflict resolution, communication skills, improving self-esteem are similar.

What could the bullying field learn from these other efforts to prevent aggressive behaviours? The major themes of other prevention programs include socializing children by promoting non-violent values such as egalitarian behaviour and the right to be different, and developing the skills to put these values into practice. The skills that address violence across its varied forms include good communication; non-violent conflict resolution choices; the ability to understand and take the perspective of others into account; problem solving that includes learning about alternatives to violence; healthy relationships built on respect for self and others; and support- and help-seeking skills. This common skill set provides the opportunity to link, build-upon and reinforce learning from one violence prevention program to another.

As suggested by Thurston, Meadows, Tutty and Bradshaw (1999), addressing different forms of abuse at different ages ensures that the issues and skills are repeated. One program is unlikely to effectively address the multiple forms of violence that students potentially face. Programs must be developmentally appropriate and repetition over the years is recommended. Violence prevention is not a quick-fix (one show, one video, one curriculum), but multifaceted (Tutty & Bradshaw, 2004). Ideally, violence prevention programs in schools should begin early and interventions should be repeated regularly throughout the stages of child development. Schools need to offer a series of prevention programs and the responsibility for integrating the various pieces into a whole remains on the shoulders of the school teachers and administration.

Other prevention programs have created useful models to make programs more interactive in the hope of more effectively engaging children and youth. To truly decrease the incidence of bullying the children and youth themselves need to adopt the issue as their own. Programs must use approaches that engage young people using a variety of interactive techniques to capture their attention. Inviting students to take leadership is not a new idea; peer mediation approaches have used this strategy for over thirty years, although traditional peer mediation does not necessarily address bullying well.

Peer education models, commonly utilized in dating violence prevention programs (Tutty, et al., 2005), could take this one step further. Students could lead presentations or develop and offer plays to their peers, only two ways to more actively involve adolescents or children. The hope is that hearing the message from peers will seem more relevant and have a stronger impact to youth. A recent example of utilizing peers to address bullying and harassment is the Student Leader Workshops developed by Wessler and De Andrade (2006) in which students attend a one-day intensive training to discuss the impact of harassment and develop low-key and simple intervention strategies.

The previously described question of whether to focus on bullying or on pro-social skills is relevant to the current discussion. Some programs raise awareness of bullying without explicitly teaching children the skills to address their peers, either as the target of bullying or as a bystander. Both knowledge and skills are essential to comprehensively preventing the problem. In addition, even though the majority of children do not commonly use power and control tactics in their peer relationships, conflict resolution programs and peer-mediation programs have a place in assisting them to deal with the everyday playground conflicts that are not abuses of power but require resolution nonetheless.

Conceptualizing bullying as an abuse of power allows us to address a broader range of issues, several of which are commonly encompassed in bullying. Program personnel could easily expand the definition of bullying to address sexual harassment, homophobia and racism and include this as core content (Wessler & De Andrade, 2006). While sexist, homophobic and racist comments are integral in bullying at even elementary school levels, bullying programs do not necessarily note these sensitive issues.

What are the challenges of implementing strategies that either prevent bullying or intervene earlier and in a more successful manner? The next section lists several. Bullying prevention programs encourage school personnel to pay attention to bullying behaviours, but, how, more specifically, should teachers intervene? While some schools have no policies to address bullying, others may utilize "zero tolerance" policies that merely punish students, effectively using formal power and authority to punish the informal use of power and authority. Several authors suggest, instead of zero tolerance, using the "teachable moment" (Coloroso, 2003) or restorative justice techniques (Ahmed, & Braithwaite, 2006; Morrison, 2006). Teaching effective strategies that address bullying would be a valuable addition to teacher training, both within faculties of education and as post-graduation workshops.

Another potential challenge for bullying prevention programs having an impact on students is the extent to which teachers model appropriate behaviour about respectful non-power-based relationships? While the majority of teachers exemplify these ideals, a small number bully students, an issue that has received little attention in academic journals until recently (Twemlow, Fonagy, Sacco & Brethour, 2006). If some teaching staff themselves abuse power, incorporating programs into such classrooms will be a wasted effort. Would teacher's college courses on how to educate students without abusing power impact this dynamic? Is there a way to encourage peers to confront these colleagues in a supportive manner? This is an important area for further consideration, as teachers who use bullying behaviours against their charges create significant student problems.

Despite these considerations, given the potential serious impact of bullying on children and youth, including suicide and homicide, this first wave of bullying prevention programs shows promise. But it is not yet time to rest on our laurels. Let's continue to share ideas and integrate best practices from other prevention initiatives. While the potential dangers of bullying behaviours have generally been acknowledged, do children, youth, and teachers pay attention to the small acts of power and control that inhabit school halls and playgrounds daily? How can we best address new venues for bullying such as the use of the internet (cyber-bullying), which expand the venue and reach of bullying beyond schools? Until our children feel safe in their schools and homes, we must continue to identify, implement, and evaluate strategies, programs and policies to support them.

Key Messages

1. School-based bullying and conflict resolution programs can assist students and school personnel to more effectively prevent bullying or to intervene earlier when bullying occurs.

2. Good programs target school policies and staff: not just students.

3. Effective programs with strong research support are available to utilize in schools.

4. While schools are a logical venue to provide bullying prevention programs, the problem exists and must be addressed in the community.

References

Aber, J.L., Brown, J.L., & Henrich, C.C. (1999). *Teaching conflict resolution: An effective school-based approach to violence prevention.* New York, NY: National Center for Children in Poverty.

Aber, J.L., Brown, J.L., & Jones, S.M. (2003). *Developmental trajectories toward violence in middle childhood: Course, demographic differences, and response to school-based intervention.* Developmental Psychology, 39(2), 324-348.

Ahmed, E., & Braithwaite, V. (2006). *Forgiveness, reconciliation, and shame: Three key variables in reducing school bullying.* Journal of Social Issues, 62(2), 347-370.

Bauman, S., & Del Rio, A. (2005). *Knowledge and beliefs about bullying in schools: comparing pre-service teachers in the United States and the United Kingdom.* School Psychology International, 26(4), 428-442.

Beland, K. (1988). *Second Step, Grades 1-3: Pilot project 1987-1988 summary report.* Seattle, WA: Committee for Children.

Beran, T., & Li, Q. (2005). *'Cyber-harassment': A new method for an old behavior.* Journal of Educational Computing Research, 32(3), 265-277.

Beran, T., Tutty, L., & Steinrath, G. (2004). *An evaluation of a bullying prevention program for elementary schools.* Canadian Journal of School Psychology, 19(1-2), 99-116.

Bloom, M. (1981). *Primary prevention: The possible science.* Englewood Cliffs, N.J.: Prentice Hall.

Bosworth, K., Espelage, D.L., DuBay, T., Daytner, G., & Karageorge, K. (2000). *A preliminary evaluation of a multimedia violence prevention program for early adolescents.* American Journal of Health Behavior, 24(4), 268-280.

Brockenbrough, K.K. (2001). *Peer victimization and bully prevention among middle school students.* Unpublished doctoral dissertation, University of Virginia.

Craig, W. & Pepler, D.J. (1997). *Observations of bullying and victimization in the school yard.* Canadian Journal of School Psychology, 13, 41-60.

Craig, W.M., Pepler, D., & Atlas, R. (2000). *Observations of bullying in the playground and in the classroom.* School Psychology International, 21(1), 22-36.

Coloroso, B. (2003). *The bully, the bullied, and the bystander.* New York: Harpercollins.

DeJong, W., Spiro, A., Wilson-Brewer, R., Vince-Whitman, C., & Prothrow-Stith, D. (1989). *Evaluation summary: Violence Prevention Curriculum for Adolescents*. Newton, Massachusetts: Education Development Center.

DuRant, R.H., Treiber, F., Getts, A., McCloud, K., Linder, C.W., & Woods, E.R. (1996). *Comparison of two violence prevention curricula for middle school adolescents*. American Journal of Preventive Medicine, 12(5), 91-100.

Embry, D.D., Flannery, D.J., Ansonia, A.T., Powell, K.E., & Atcham, H. (1996). *PeaceBuilders: A theoretically driven, school-based model for early violence prevention*. American Journal of Preventive Medicine, 12(5), 91-100.

Farrell, A.D., Meyer, A., & Dahlberg, L.L. (1996). *Richmond Youth against Violence: A school-based program for urban adolescents*. American Journal of Preventive Medicine, 12(5 Supplement), 13-21.

Flannery, D.J., Liau, A.K., Powell, K.E., Vesterdal, W., Vazsonyi, A.T., Guo, S., et al. (2003). *Initial behaviour outcomes for the PeaceBuilders universal school-based violence prevention program*. Developmental Psychology, 39(2), 292-308.

Frey, K.S., Hirschstein, M.K., Snell, J.L., Edstrom, L.V.S., MacKenzie, E.P., & Broderick, C.J. (2005). *Reducing playground bullying and supporting beliefs: An experimental trial of the Steps to Respect program*. Developmental Psychology, 41(3), 479-491.

Garrity, C., Jens, K., Porter, W., Sager, N., & Short-Camilli, C. (2000). *Bully proofing your school* (2nd ed.). Longmont, CO: Sopris West.

Grossman, D.C., Neckerman, H.J., Koepsell, T.D., Liu, P. Y., Asher, K.N., Beland, K., Frey, K., & Rivara, F.P. (1997). *Effectiveness of a violence prevention curriculum among children in elementary school: A randomized controlled trial*. Journal of the American Medical Association, 277, 1605-1611.

Harvey, P., Forehand, R., Brown, C., & Holmes, T. (1988). *The prevention of sexual abuse: Examination of the effectiveness of a program with kindergarten-age children*. Behavior Therapy, 19, 429-435.

Herrmann, D.S., & McWhirter, J.J. (2003). *Anger and aggression management in young adolescents: An experimental validation of the SCARE program*. Education and Treatment of Children, 26(3), 273-302.

Jeffrey, L. R., Miller, D. & Linn, M. (2002). *Middle school bullying as a context for the development of passive observers to the victimization of others*. Journal of Emotional Abuse, 2(2/3), 143-156.

Johnson, R., & Johnson, D.W. (2002). *Teaching students to be Peacemakers: A meta-analysis*. Journal of Research in Education, 12(1), 25-39.

Johnson, D.W., Johnson, R., Dudley, B., & Magnuson, D. (1995). *Training elementary students to manage conflict*. Journal of Social Psychology, 135(6), 673-686.

Johnson, D.W., Johnson, R., Dudley, B., & Acikgoz, K. (1994). *Effects of conflict resolution training on elementary school students*. Journal of School Psychology, 136(6), 803-817.

Kessler, M., & Albee, G. (1975). *Primary prevention*. Annual Review of Psychology, 26, 557-591.

Li, Q. (2006). *Cyber-bullying in schools: A research of gender differences*. School Psychology International, 27(2), 157-170.

Meraviglia, M. G., Becker, H., Rosenbluth, B., Sanchez, E., & Robertson, T. (2003). *The Expect Respect Project: Creating a positive elementary school climate*. Journal of Interpersonal Violence, 18(11), 1347-1360.

Meyer, A.L., Farrell, A.D., Northup, W.B., Kung, E.M., & Plybon, L. (2000). *Promoting non-violence in early adolescence: Responding in peaceful and positive ways*. New York: NY, Kluwer Academic/Plenum Publishers.

Meyer, G., Roberto, A.J., Boster, F.J., Roberto, H.L. (2004). *Assessing the Get Real about Violence curriculum: Process and outcome evaluation results and implications*. Health Communication, 16(4), 451-474.

Morrison, B. (2006). *School bullying and restorative justice: Toward a theoretical understanding of the role of respect, pride, and shame*. Journal of Social Issues, 62(2), 371-392.

Oldfield, D., Hays, B.J., & Megal, M.E. (1996). *Evaluation of the effectiveness of Project TRUST: An elementary school-based victimization prevention strategy*. Child Abuse and Neglect, 20(9), 821-832.

Olweus, D. (1991). *Bully/victim problems among school children: Some basic facts and effects of a school-based intervention program*. In D. Pepler & K. Rubin (Eds.), The development and treatment of childhood aggression (pp. 411-448). Hillsdale, CA: Lawrence Erlbaum.

O'Moore, M. (2000). *Critical issues for teacher training to counter bullying and victimisation in Ireland*. Aggressive Behavior, 26, 99-111.

Patchin, J.W., & Hinduja, S. (2006). *Bullies move beyond the schoolyard: A preliminary look at cyber-bullying*. Youth Violence and Juvenile Justice, 4(2), 148-169.

Roberts, L., White, G., & Yeomans, P. (2004). *Theory development and evaluation of Project WIN: A violence reduction program for early adolescents*. Journal of Early Adolescence, 24(4), 460-483.

Sanchez, E., Robertson, T.R., Lewis, C.M., Rosenbluth, B., Bohman, T., & Casey, D.M. (2001). *Preventing bullying and sexual harassment in elementary schools: The Expect Respect model*. Journal of Emotional Abuse, 2(2/3), 157-180.

Shapiro, J.P., Burgoon, J.D., Welker, C.J., & Clough, J.B. (2002). *Evaluation of the Peacemakers Program: School-based violence prevention for students in grades four through eight*. Psychology in the Schools, 39(1), 87-100.

Sjostrom, L., & Stein, N.D. (1996). *Bullyproof: A teacher's guide about bullying and harassment for use with fourth and fifth grader students*. Boston, MA: Wellesley Centres for Women.

Smith, P.K., & Sharp, S. (Eds.), (1994). *School bullying: Insights and perspectives*. New York: Routledge.

Teglasi, H., & Rothman, L. (2001). *STORIES: A classroom-based program to reduce aggressive behaviour*. Journal of School Psychology, 30(1), 71-94.

Thurston, W. E., Meadows, L., Tutty, L. M., & Bradshaw, C. (1999). *A violence reduction health promotion model*. Report to Prairie Partners Community Foundation.

Tutty, L. (1991). *Child sexual abuse: A range of prevention options*. Journal of Child and Youth Care, Special Issue, 23-41.

Tutty, L. (1992). *The ability of elementary school children to learn child sexual abuse prevention concepts*. Child Abuse & Neglect, 16(3), 369-384.

Tutty, L. (1995). *The challenge of evaluating prevention programs: An example from child sexual abuse*. In A. Love (Ed.), Evaluation methods sourcebook II (pp. 104-118). Ottawa, ON: Canadian Evaluation Society.

Tutty, L. (1996). *Prevention education: An integrative review of the research*. In C. Bagley & W. Thurston with L. Tutty (Eds.), Understanding and prevention of child sexual abuse: Volume I. (pp. 369-389). Aldershot, England: Arena.

Tutty, L., & Bradshaw, C. (2004). *School-based violence prevention programs: How well do they work?* In C. Ateah & J. Mirwalt (Eds.), Within our reach: Policies, programs and practices to prevent abuse across the lifespan (pp. 47-60). Halifax, NS: Fernwood and RESOLVE.

Tutty, L., & Bradshaw, C., Thurston, W.E., Barlow, A., Marshall, P., Tunstall, L., Dewar, M.E., Toy-Pries, D., Thomlinson, D., Este, D., Meadows, L., Josephson, W., Dobko, S., Proulx, J., Perrault, S., McDonald, M., &. Nixon, K. (2005). *School based violence prevention programs: Preventing violence against children and Youth* (Revised Ed.). Calgary: AB: RESOLVE Alberta. Available Online at www.ucalgary.ca/resolve/violenceprevention/

Tutty, L., & Nixon, K. (2000). *ACAV Violence Prevention Coordinator Evaluation: Final report*. Calgary, AB: RESOLVE Alberta.

Tutty, L., Ogden, C., & Costello, J. (2006). *An evaluation of the More Than 4% Workshop: Building Capacity to Respond to Bullying and Harassment Workshop*. Calgary, AB: RESOLVE Alberta.

Twemlow, S.W., Fonagy, P., Sacco, F., & Brethour, J.R., Jr. (2006). *Teachers who bully students: A hidden trauma*. International Journal of Social Psychiatry, 52(3), 187-198.

Wessler, S.L., & De Andrade, L.L. (2006). *Slurs, stereotypes, and student interventions: Examining the dynamics, impact, and prevention of harassment in middle and high school*. Journal of Social Issues, 62(3), 511-532.

Whitted, K.S., & Dupper, D.R. (2005). *Best practices for preventing or reducing bullying in schools*. Children & Schools, 27(3), 167-175.

Wolfe, D.A., Wekerle, C., Scott, K., Straatman, A., Grasley, C., & Reitzel-Jaffe, D. (2003). *Dating violence prevention with at-risk youth: A controlled outcome evaluation*. Journal of Consulting and Clinical Psychology, 71, 279-791.

Chapter 8:

Engaging Community Champions in the Prevention of Bullying

Bonnie Leadbeater
University of Victoria

Introduction

Ideals for the development, evaluation, and dissemination of prevention programs for improving public health are changing. Often, prevention programs are generated in university settings, where up-to-date empirical knowledge is accessible to researchers who have the funding, expertise, and protected time necessary to solve puzzles of how to effect changes in the behaviours that threaten to compromise individuals' health, educational potential, or social relationships. Once generated, these programs are tried out in cooperation with potential knowledge users. Next, while monitoring the variability in the fidelity with which practitioners deliver the programs, researchers use longitudinal comparisons of randomly selected program and control groups to assess their effectiveness for individuals who are at risk for or exhibit the targeted problem. On the basis of statistically reliable evidence of their success, programs can be then manualized and made available to other practitioners. Practitioners learn about these programs in university or college courses, continuing education programs, training workshops, seminars, professional development days and so on. In this model, converting evidence-based knowledge into everyday actions requires models of effective teaching and learning.

However, the apparent simplicity of this "expert-driven dissemination model" (as I will call it to designate the production of prevention programs by experts who then disseminate them to practitioners) hides the enormous difficulties and complexity of engaging practitioners in using knowledge for social change, particularly when social problems with multiple determinants are the targets of change. Bullying is one such problem.

Unfortunately the dissemination of bullying prevention programs through the expert-driven model is generally ad hoc and sporadic. This stands in contrast to the dissemination of new medications that have been subject to random control designs to test their effectiveness and subsequently, mass-produced. Pharmaceuticals are distributed through formal, nationally regulated networks of physicians and pharmacists – organized and supported largely by government agencies and public funds. There is no similar system or support for overseeing the dissemination of prevention programs that target common public health problems in our schools or communities. Locally developed programs are hard to access and only very rarely disseminated. Even evidence-based prevention programs can be short-lived if champions do not emerge to sustain or carry them forward. As a result, approaches to bullying vary from school to school often depending more on the energy, preferences, and training of principals and teaching staff than on evidence of whether programs are effective or not.

Also, partly as a consequence of this absence of systematic models for disseminating prevention programs, researchers have generated and regenerated a great many programs. These are often based on our considerable empirical knowledge of the characteristics of children who bully their peers, the risks for and consequences of bullying for children and adolescents, and the protective factors that ameliorate these risks. As a result, many programs endeavor to promote the social competence, friendships, social skills, emotional regulation, and empathy thought to be lacking in children who bully others. Other programs aim to enhance parenting skills or to stem children's aggressive school behaviours through zero-tolerance, suspensions, restitution, or behavioural retraining.

In reality, however, most bullying prevention programs are not developed in the ivory towers of universities or with the control of drug trials. Rather, they are developed through collaborations among researchers and the intended users of the knowledge such as teachers, children, parents, mental health service providers, or not for profit groups. Nevertheless, the significant role of knowledge users in producing and evaluating prevention programs and in using them to enhance social action has only begun to be recognized and appreciated (Israel, Schulz, Parker, & Becker, 1998).

Reviews of the evaluations of these programs typically show some gains in targeted behaviours for some children at some ages; yet, overall we are often disappointed by the failure of these many efforts to halt bullying and by the persistence of bullying in classrooms, playgrounds, school halls, neighbourhoods and homes (Miller, Brehm, & Whitehouse, 1998; Nation, Crusto, Wandersman, Kumpfer, Seybolt, Morrissey-Kane, & Davino, 2003; Salmivalli, Kaukiainen, & Voeten, 2005; Smith, Schneider, Smith, & Ananiadou, 2004). Programs that isolate or aggregate aggressive children together may actually be doing more harm than good (Dodge, Dishion & Lansford, 2006). These results are hard to understand. Teachers point to insurmountable problems at home that undo the training children receive at school. Parents of victimized children point to schools' inability to control aggressive children. Researchers locate problems in inadequate implementation of programs by practitioners and practitioners decry the impractical, ivory tower approaches of university-based experts. And everyone is right. Research has shown that characteristics of classrooms, schools, neighbourhoods and families are all related to children's experiences of bullying and peer victimization. What is the solution?

In this chapter, I highlight the need to better recognize the value of collaborative, community-wide approaches to the development and dissemination of prevention programs for bullying. First, I briefly review empirical research showing that the determinants of bullying are frequently complex and located outside of individual children's skills and competence. Recent research suggests that bullying is embedded in a wide range of social problems such as multiple family moves and disruptions, high concentrations of adversities related to poverty in inner city schools, neighbourhood values that support violence, and high classroom levels of aggressive behaviours. I argue that these social contexts can and often need to be changed. However, the engagement and continued support of practitioners and community members who work with children and youth are needed for the development, evaluation, and dissemination of effective prevention programs for bullying. I describe a university-community collaboration that has culminated in the development and use of a relatively inexpensive peer victimization prevention program that involves emergency service providers (community police officers, firefighters and paramedics), student athletes, elementary school staff (including principals, teachers, playground supervisors, and librarians), parents and, yes, university-based researchers.

The "WITS Rock Solid Primary Program" was designed and locally implemented through a collaboration between a not for profit group (The Rock Solid Foundation, www.rocksolid.bc.ca), the Greater Victoria School District 61, and researchers from the University of Victoria's Centre for Youth and Society (www.youth.society.uvic.ca). The WITS acronym stands for "Walk away," "Ignore," "Talk it out," and "Seek help" but the program is not merely directed at teaching these conflict resolution skills to children; rather, this program aims to create responsive environments for the prevention of peer victimization. Although this program has considerable local uptake, I conclude by reconsidering questions about the possibility of engaging other communities for disseminating what I have learned. Will obstacles to knowledge use again keep other communities from reshaping this program to address their own concerns with peer victimization? What can PREVNet's national collaborative effort do to overcome these difficulties?

The Social Contexts and Determinants of Bullying

Our understanding of bullying is changing. A narrow conceptualization of bullying as an individual problem requiring solutions that target offending individuals, stands in contrast to the reality of bullying as an interpersonal, context-based, community problem needing cross context, interpersonal solutions (Espelage & Swearer, 2004). Recent research amply demonstrates that contexts created by children's friendships and peer groups, and by the norms of their families, classrooms and neighbourhoods all play roles in engendering, maintaining, promoting, or diminishing bullying (Leadbeater, in press; Dodge, et al., 2006).

Peer group influences are frequently blamed for and indeed appear to influence children's aggression. Reviews of research on the quality, direction of influence, and context of peer friendships among antisocial peers conclude that dyadic and group relationships can create contexts for the development of deviancy (Kupersmidt, Coie, & Howell, 2004). Segregated groups of aggressive youth appear to reinforce each other's aggressive behaviours and can train each other in valuing and using them (Dishion, Poulin, & Burraston, 2000). However, the layered ecologies of children's experiences (family, school, and neighbourhood) also appear to moderate peer influences. For example, in research with aggressive and non-aggressive dyads of 10-year-old boys, Bagwell and her colleagues found no significant differences for children's self-reports of the qualities of their friendships (closeness, help, security, conflicts) (Bagwell, 2004; Bagwell & Coie, 2004). However, Bagwell (2004) observed that a third of the aggressive boys' "best friends" lived within walking distance of their homes but did not attend the same schools. Compared to non aggressive youth, aggressive youth knew these neighbourhood friends longer and spent more time with them in unsupervised play. Bagwell (2004) suggests that whereas school-based friendships may be reorganized each year by new classroom groupings, the stability of these less supervised, neighbourhood friendships with aggressive friends may be important in maintaining aggressive behaviours.

The use of aggression against peers also appears to interact with social norms that support aggressive behaviours in schools, neighbourhoods, families, and communities (Aber, Jones, Brown, Chaudry, & Samples, 1998; Hoglund & Leadbeater, 2004; Kellam, Ling, Merisca, Brown, & Ialongo, 1998). In an evaluation of a classroom intervention (the Good Behavior Game) directed at reducing children's aggressive behaviours, Kellam et al. (1998) found that placement in first grade classrooms with higher aggregate levels of physically aggressive peers (as rated by teachers) contributed to boys' (but not girls') aggressive behaviours in middle school – independent of family- and school-level poverty. Similarly, Aber et al. (1998) investigated the effects of classroom and neighbourhood contexts on the effectiveness of a violence prevention program (Resolving Conflicts Creatively) for 5,053 second to sixth grade children in New York City. Findings showed that the positive effects of high levels of program lessons taught on limiting children's aggressive cognitions were diminished both for children in classrooms in which more of them rated the use of aggression as "perfectly OK", as well as for children who lived in poorer, more violent neighbourhoods.

Classifying sixth grade students as victims, aggressors, aggressive-victims and socially adjusted, Graham, Bellmore and Mize (2006) found that aggressive youth were more likely to attribute their poor adjustment to unfairness in school rules than the other groups. Their perceptions of the school context as unfair may be a function of aggressive youths' efforts to deflect blame and maintain self-esteem; however, they may also be accurate reflections of how these youth come to be treated in the school context. Aggressive youth are frequently subject to efforts to reduce the disruptiveness of their behaviours (e.g., setting desks apart from others in the class, restricting activities on the playground, and suspensions). These approaches may be perceived by aggressive youth as unfair or differential treatment and may serve to further marginalize and alienate them from conventional classroom norms (Leadbeater, 2000). Kupersmidt et al. (2004) have argued that, in an overall context of being rejected by school-based peers, the influence of aggressive or deviant friendships prevails.

Hoglund and Leadbeater (2004) examined the direct and interacting effects of differences in classroom, school, and family contexts on changes in children's behaviour problems (disruptiveness and aggression) across first grade. Increases in behaviour problems were greater for children who had more behaviour problems at the beginning of grade one, but also for children who had experienced multiple family moves or who attended schools with more children on income assistance (controlling for family income). Family moves may disrupt protective friendships and entering a new school may subject children to the tendency of others to exclude "new" children, both of which further reduce children's exposure to prosocial peers. High poverty neighbourhoods that feed into a single inner-city school can compound disadvantages related to poverty such as parenting stress, unemployment, inadequate access to after school supervision, etc.

Research also demonstrates that bystanders can create a context of tolerance for bullying in school playgrounds either through active support or as silent witnesses. Indeed, Craig and Pepler (1997) observed that peers were present in 85% of bullying episodes on school playgrounds and that in 81% of bullying episodes peers reinforced the behaviours of the children who were bullying. Salmivalli and her colleagues (Salmivalli, Lagerspetz, Björkqvist, Österman, & Kaukiainen, 1996) have argued that bullying should be viewed as a peer-group process and that efforts to intervene should be aimed at reducing peer group support for bullying by raising group awareness of bystander roles. Children who hold values against bullying may also require opportunities to practice acting against bullying through role playing and rehearsal of behaviours that discourage bullying (Salmivalli et al., 2005).

Exposure to family, school, classroom or neighbourhood contexts that support bullying has been largely overlooked as a target for prevention programs. Given this emerging picture of the social determinants of bullying, it is not surprising that school-based programs that have succeeded in increasing social skills and empathy in individual children have had less success in reducing bullying (Dodge et al., 2006; Salmivalli, et al., Voeten, 2005; Smith et al., 2004). Efforts to change the contexts that support bullying may require levels of school district, community, school and family support that are difficult to achieve, but these may be imperative to the success of prevention programs.

The Social Contexts of Prevention Research

Individuals or organizations working in parallel cannot realize solutions to most of our complex social and health concerns. Collaborations among a broad spectrum of partners may advance both empirical knowledge and its use (El Ansari, Phillips & Zwi, 2004; Landry, Lamari & Amara, 2001; Lasker, Wiess & Miller, 2001). University-community alliances for research have ushered in new methods for conducting research on sensitive social problems and on innovative or best practices for preventing or treating these problems. These alliances or partnerships typically comprise teams of university-based researchers from different disciplines and targeted members of the non-university community (e.g., policy makers, police, service providers, school boards, teachers, parents, and children or youth themselves) to address issues of mutual concern in ways that ensure relevant questions are posed and research findings are rapidly disseminated (Israel et al., 1998; Macaulay & Nutting, 2006).

How does this collaborative approach change the research process? Researchers engaged in community-based research spend considerably more time in the field consulting with partners at every point in the development, execution, and dissemination of the research program than has been typical of university-based research. The partnerships also serve as important vehicles for uncovering problems that need to be addressed. Community knowledge can be integrated into research questions, program development, and evaluation. Links between the partners also depend on discovering points of exchange beyond the inception stage to facilitate co-ownership of knowledge and its use. Research products grow over time and can be conceptualized as a "synthesis of a broad spectrum of knowledge rather than an individual study's findings" (Lomas, 2000, p. 142). Community-based research serves to further the exchange of ideas in ways that reach beyond the traditional training models of knowledge production and dissemination to experts.

The road to interdisciplinary collaborations is not always smooth. Reconciling differences between a scientific approach to knowledge production and an approach to knowledge production that emerges from the sometimes-unspecified wisdom of practice itself requires ongoing dialogue. Scientists' concerns with issues of validity, reliability and rigour in substantiating a program's efficacy often play a less important role for community members, whose strategies for knowledge use are embodied in action and are often taken for granted in practice. Meeting the challenges of collaboration requires acknowledging the existence of multiple types of expertise, recognizing the need for different strategies of knowledge use, and sanctioning the time and funding that permits the development of shared understandings. This requires attention to establishing and maintaining reasons to work together, formalized links, and active communication. It also requires community leaders who champion the value of addressing the target problem and who are willing to create and sustain the momentum of their constituents. Next I describe the process of a successful community-university collaboration that grew through seven years of interaction to develop and disseminate locally a promising program for the prevention of bullying.

The WITS Rock Solid Collaboration

WITS Conceptual Framework.

The WITS program is a coordinated initiative between elementary school educators, community groups and developmental psychologists that takes a comprehensive, multi-setting approach to reducing peer victimization and enhancing social competence at the school and classroom levels. This program is linked to the school district's mission of creating responsive and safe school environments that enhance students' social and emotional competence, social responsibility, and learning outcomes. "Using your WITS to Walk away, Ignore, Talk it out, and Seek help" can become code words with school-wide visibility and parent and community support. The ideal is to create school, classroom and family environments that speak with a uniform voice to promote positive conflict resolution strategies. The WITS program has multiple components (see Table 1) and is set out in an easily accessed manual that is available on our website, www.youth.society.uvic.ca. The manual provides resources that invite creativity. The program is non prescriptive and can be adapted to the needs and interests of a particular school and community

WITS Program Components
See website manual at www.youth.society.uvic.ca

Teacher & Librarian Curriculum	Directs teachers to a wealth of early childhood literature and activities that can be used to reinforce WITS messages in the classroom. The curriculum addresses the learning outcomes required for elementary school curricula concerning social skills and responsibility, personal planning, language and visual arts, and drama. It also includes information that is central to a librarian's curricula including effective literacy techniques used in the stories, vocabulary building, etc.
Emergency Services Curriculum	Walks police, fire fighters or paramedics through the swearing-in-ceremony where kindergarten to grade 3 children are "deputized" as police helpers to keep their school safe and help other children. A stuffed walrus mascot (Witsup) is given to each school. WITS activity books, bookmarks, etc. are given to the children as reminders and to take these messages home.
WITS Booklist	Details a list of popular picture books that are in print and are available in libraries or bookstores.
University Athlete Curriculum	Uses student athletes to provide positive role models from the community who advocate "using your WITS" in short visits to elementary school classrooms over the school year. The students are organized and supervised by a community liaison hired by the police group and are supported by the police officer assigned to the school.
W.I.T.S for Siblings and Friends	Guides parents in using WITS to resolve conflicts between siblings or children and their friends, using books and TV programs, to identify WITS strategies. Time outs prescribe "walking away" to think about good solutions to deal with problems.

History of WITS.

The collaboration grew out of common goals that originated from many sources. In 1998, there were many independent efforts to respond to highly published incidents of

Chapter 8: Engaging Community Champions in the Prevention of Bullying

youth violence that resulted in deaths or disabilities locally, provincially, and across North America. In British Columbia, police, policy makers at the Ministry of Education, school personnel, and University of Victoria researchers were scrambling for greater understanding of and solutions for a problem that appeared to be spiraling. In this context, the Rock Solid Foundation and an elementary school principal, Judi Stevenson, began collaborating to create an early intervention program to help young children solve conflicts peacefully by using their WITS. At the same time, the Ministry of Education of British Columbia was working on a social responsibility curriculum and schools were struggling for resources to help them implement these guidelines. The impetus from these converging communities priorities and challenges also fit with my own interest in peer victimization and mental health concerns when I joined the University of Victoria's Psychology Department in 1997. These many individual concerns were drawn together gradually by the newly forming University of Victoria's Centre for Youth and Society – which was holding forums with researchers and community to discuss priorities for research that were relevant to our community. Finally, requests for proposals for innovative community-university research alliances were launched by the Social Sciences and Humanities Research Council of Canada and by the innovative Community Alliances for Health Research (CAHR) program of the newly formed Canadian Institutes for Health Research. The puzzle pieces and players were in place but the steps to their intersection were spurred on by the confluence of several events.

The Rock Solid Foundation was developed in the fall of 1997 by several police officers in conjunction with a popular local lacrosse team, the Victoria Shamrocks. At this time they were presenting an interactive program to high school students, urging them to understand that they had rights to protection from peer assaults and threats of violence. Unfortunate circumstances in the community as well as growing partnerships led to the expansion of the Foundation activities that included the WITS program.

On November 14th 1997, the Greater Victoria Region was devastated by the tragic murder of a 14-year-old girl. Reena Virk was badly beaten and ultimately drowned by a group of her peers beneath a bridge in the city core. This horrific incident created tremendous media attention and raised questions about what types of youth violence prevention programs existed, with many questions directed to the Foundation. After Reena's death, members of the Foundation spoke to over 500,000 young people in grades 4 to 12 about pro-active solutions to peer violence, threats, intimidation and harassment. A video documenting this initial program ("Rock Solid Children Youth and Families: Creating Responsive Environments for the Prevention of Youth Violence") was created in collaboration with the Centre for Youth and Society at the University of Victoria and it was distributed to schools both within and outside of our local community. The video and accompanying manual aimed to help communities find their own solutions to peer violence. After viewing this program, many educators in the local school district stated that these messages would have a greater impact if they also targeted children in the primary grades. Consequently, a partnership was formed between the Foundation, educators from the Greater Victoria School District, and the Centre for Youth and Society to advance a primary educational program.

WITS Classroom Component.

In the late 1990's, under the leadership of Judi Stevenson (principal of a local elementary school), a committee of teachers was formed to develop curricula for books to show how the WITS acronym could be incorporated into the primary grades. Other teachers, particularly teacher librarian Sonia Engstad, added new books and curricula to the available resources. Through these books, WITS is integrated into the school district's learning objectives for language arts, interpersonal understanding, and social responsibility for Kindergarten to grade 3 children. Teachers are directed to a wealth of early childhood literature in which child characters resolve interpersonal conflicts by using one or more components of the WITS message (WITS story books). The manual identifies which WITS message(s) the storybook promotes and provides ideas for creative classroom activities which teachers can complete with students to reinforce the WITS messages. Activities include role-playing, drawing, and creative writing that help children to use their imagination to identify ways for using their WITS to help resolve peer conflicts. The program is not intended to be prescriptive in terms of the number of WITS storybooks read or activities teachers complete per month. Rather, the program encourages teachers to select WITS books for their story times, incorporate activities that focus on WITS messages into daily lesson plans, display students' art and creative writing projects that illustrate WITS messages, recognize children for using their WITS, and capture the "teachable moments" that deal with conflicts as they occur between children (e.g., asking children how they used or could have used their WITS when they had a conflicted interaction).

School teachers, principals and playground assistants initially participated in a two-hour in-service training in February of 2000 lead by Judi Stevenson and Tom Woods (co-author and Director of the Rock Solid Foundation). "Training" centered on rallying schools to adopt the child-friendly WITS program and on discussing ways to deliver the program to students throughout the whole school and to incorporate it into existing classroom curricula (rather than as an add-on program that created extra work for teachers). Teacher champions from the original curriculum development group populated most schools and served as onsite advocates for the program's use. Curriculum manuals are made available to local schools in CD format upon request and are available on-line, www.youth.society.uvic.ca.

WITS Emergency Service Providers' Component.

The primary goal of this component is to bring helping adults who can be recognized by their uniforms (city police, RCMP, fire fighters, and paramedics) into schools to reinforce that WITS messages. They talk to students about using their WITS outside school and emphasize the importance of telling adults whenever they are faced with a concern about their own safety. Police school-liaison officers initially delivered the WITS messages to young children after attending on-site demonstrations in schools led by Tom Woods. As the program grew, other emergency service personnel have become involved.

A short manual describes ideas for the participation of emergency service workers and again these people have offered new ideas about how to be involved in the WITS program.

Chapter 8: Engaging Community Champions in the Prevention of Bullying

At the beginning of the school year, an initial police visit is held in the school auditorium and all kindergarten to grade 3 students are "sworn-in" as "WITS Special Constables" to keep their school safe and to help other children. During this visit children are read story of how Witsup, the Walrus (the WITS mascot), used his WITS to get his friends' advice on how to help a child who was being bullied. They are taught how to salute and stand at attention like a WITS recruit, how to give the secret WITS handshake and password ("huddy, huddy"). Each child is given a "WITS Special Constable" badge at the initiation ceremony, and is advised that the emergency service worker will be back to visit to see how the new deputies are doing using their WITS. Teachers, principals, and other school personnel are encouraged to attend this swearing-in ceremony

Ideally, the time commitment for the emergency service workers is approximately one hour per school for the initial swearing-in-ceremony and approximately 10 minutes per class for 10 to 15 follow-up visits. These visits ideally occur about once a month over the course of the entire school year. The follow-up visits are intended to be informal, flexible, fun, and absorb little time or resources. These visits maintain the momentum of the program by encouraging the children to use their WITS and reinforce that the WITS messages are also important outside the school context. The emergency service visitors leave every child a WITS "gift-reminder" (including book marks, pencils, activity books, zipper pulls) as a reminder to use their WITS and to help take the WITS messages home. These small items are corporately sponsored and cost approximately $2 per child per year.

Varsity teams from the University and local athletic groups are also encouraged to take part by adopting a class or even an entire school for WITS visits. Using the same format, and in conjunction with the police, athletes visit can classes regularly to provide other positive, community role models who reinforce the WITS messages or can come over lunch periods to play soccer, basketball, or other games with the students and ask them about using their WITS.

The Parent Component.

In addition to the "gifts" that are given to children to take home, parents are encouraged to use the WITS language and books at home through contacts with the school and through posters in classrooms and hallways. Children sometimes receive "awards" acknowledging success in using their WITS. Finally, a pamphlet: "WITS Resources for parents" (printed by the Rock Solid Foundation) is sent home to help parents use WITS messages to resolve conflicts at home. A WITS "time out" can be instituted where children are advised to walk away, ignore, and when they are able, to come back to talk about the conflict with the parents' help.

Overall annual costs to administer the program are relatively low (about $2.00 per child) because of the commitment from local police departments to support the program. A part-time coordinator, employed by the Rock Solid Foundation, liaises with local volunteers from emergency services to schedule the swearing-in-ceremonies and assign schools to police and community volunteers. The development of program materials and the evaluation of the program were funded through research grants, and research evidence supporting the preliminary effectiveness of the program has spurred its local adoption and continued support. Ongoing, extensive fund raising activities of the Rock Solid Foundation and the participation of the local school-based police liaisons, together with parents and teachers, keep the costs of the program low and commitments and visibility high. Recently the university-community research collaboration has risen to the challenge of extending the WITS programs across all grades in elementary schools with the creation of the WITS Leadership (WITS LEADS) program. The latter focuses specifically on reducing relational aggression and increasing prosocial leadership skills among 4th and 5th grade students.

Consistent with other evaluations of comprehensive school-based programming (Aber et al., 2003; Comer, 1985; Olweus, 1993), results of our preliminary three-year longitudinal evaluations suggest that peer victimization can be reduced through this whole school program – particularly in inner-city schools (Leadbeater, Hoglund, & Woods, 2003; Leadbeater & Hoglund, 2006). Although the exact mechanism of action of these multiple components (that are often adapted to local use by enthusiastic champions) cannot be determined, creating school, family, and community cultures that speak with a uniform voice about peaceful solutions to peer conflicts may hold promise for reducing peer victimization.

How does a Community-Engagement Model of Dissemination Differ from a Traditional Expert-Driven Model?

Knowledge producers in expert-driven dissemination models for prevention programs can have considerable control over the production, ownership, and distribution of these programs. Manuals are generated that prescribe actions for these evidence-based programs to enhance confidence in the fidelity of program delivery. Expert trainers and frequent follow up or supplementary training sessions can also add to the certainly that the program will be delivered in ways that are consistent with approved actions. Program developers provide credential for trainers and the trainers are paid for their expertise in teaching the new program to knowledge users. If programs are faithfully delivered to groups of children who are much like those involved in the original program testing, they can be expected to have similarly positive results in changing public health risks. Following this model of dissemination, the program developers (often university-based researchers) continue to be recognized as outside experts who own and disseminate the program, and need to be involved as the program is extended to new communities. Practitioners who take on the program are assured in knowing what to do to attain the desired outcomes.

Knowledge producers in a community engagement model share control over the production, ownership, and dissemination of prevention programs. The WITS collaboration relied on and continues to rely on community champions among emergency service providers, parents, and school district personnel who have local visibility, trust and respect. They

Chapter 8: Engaging Community Champions in the Prevention of Bullying

are recognized for their leadership and often their tenacious dedication to a cause. Program resources and manuals are generated and regenerated to describe resources and innovative approaches that could be adopted by program users. Indeed, champions of the WITS programs in individual schools have developed new resources including songs, playground programs, poems, awards, and classroom role-playing activities. These resources and new activities personalize the program, but they also carry it beyond the boundaries delimited by the fidelity demands of disseminating expert-driven programs. Actions can even go beyond the intended principles of the program as happened in one school visit where I witnessed a child being suspended for not using his WITS. In this community engagement model, rights to program ownership, rights to its modification, and rights to dissemination are loosely held and may be informally agreed upon or even tacitly understood in the activity of the collaboration. Program uptake depends on the mobilization and enthusiastic leadership of a committed group of community advocates or champions. In the WITS program, these have included teachers, principals, counselors, parents, sports teams, city police, RCMP, fire fighters, and paramedics. Few of these champions are paid outside of their usual work and many work as volunteers. The ongoing fundraising and active support of the Rock Solid Foundation supports some staff training and use of program resources and books by participating teachers and emergency service providers, but monitoring how the program is actually implemented in schools will require onsite observers.

Balancing scientific rigour for program development and evaluation with community enthusiasm and actions that adapt, add to, and revise the program may require a loss of certainty in and control of program fidelity. It may be that research is needed to better understand the nature of community investments in "making a prevention program your own" and the necessary, but perhaps guided flexibility, needed for adoption and implementation. In fact, it may be that program changes instituted by community champions, which may challenge "fidelity' of knowledge application from the expert position, may themselves be the mechanism of knowledge uptake that we are seeking!

With the local success in disseminating the WITS Programs, we seem to have come full circle. Have we once again created a local program with local evidence of effectiveness and local support that will now bump up against the barriers created by the lack of provincial or national systems for the dissemination and evaluation of promising local programs to prevent bullying? What is needed to connect the dots of research groups that have already produced and reproduced "innovative" approaches that use the best of empirically-based theory and research strategies to engage communities in comprehensive approaches to reduce bullying?

Major research centres studying peer bullying and victimization are dispersed across Canada, the United States, and Europe. The physical distances between them have given rise to knowledge gaps including a lack of consensus in defining the key components of non-physical bullying, a lack of indicators for assessments, and a lack of age and gender appropriate targets and approaches to prevention and intervention. In an effort to stem the tide of research inconsistencies and the costly proliferation of program efforts that are not theoretically grounded or empirically-based, there is a clear need to bring together key university-based researchers and their community partners to inform, manualize, and disseminate high quality, integrative, empirically-based and economical approaches to the prevention of peer bullying and victimization.

As PREVNet (Promoting Relationships and Eliminating Violence Network) leaders Drs. Wendy Craig and Debra Pepler have noted, there is also a need to develop a national strategy for the prevention of bullying and to create a one-stop information site that can identify theory and research-based, best practices for the prevention and treatment of aggression. A recent World Health Organization survey ranked Canada a disappointing 26th in bullying, and 27th in victimization, among the 35 countries assessed. The continued geographic isolation and interdisciplinary and cross-professional fragmentation in understanding and preventing peer victimization and bullying from kindergarten to high school is costly and ineffective. We need to learn more about how promising, locally established programs can be moved to national action and how nationally recognized programs can be relevant to and disseminated at the local level. New networks of researchers and knowledge users (e.g., school districts, police, NGOs, etc.) may be able to champion the dissemination and large-scale evaluation of promising programs. However, dissemination depends not only on the existence of research-based knowledge, but also on the receptiveness and capacity of practitioners to use it. Considerable effort is needed to increase the capacity of communities and schools to "pull" into use the knowledge and opportunities that are disseminated or "pushed" by research teams, and to support community champions who are already engaged in this pull. Programs developed through university-community collaborations may also be adopted more easily by new groups because they have already been vetted and monitored for practical relevance and feasibility for implementation.

The foundation for involving user groups outside of academic settings has begun to be laid through PREVNet partnerships. Funded by a four-year Networks of Centres of Excellence – New Initiative grant, PREVNet has already engaged leaders in 42 **national, non-government organizations to launch a national initiative to help schools and communities adopt more scientific – and proven – approaches to respond to bullying, victimization and aggression among children and youth. These partner organizations include the** Canadian Association of Principals, Canadian Coalition for the Rights of Children, Kids Help Phone, Girl Guides of Canada, Canadian Association of Social Workers, Canadian Parks and Recreation, Red Cross, and The Hospital for Sick Children. These groups are already championing the needs of Canadian children for safe, happy environments in which to grow. As they step into the arena of preventing bullying, let's hope university-based researchers and the research funding agencies are ready to work with community partners and support their enthusiasm and leadership. It takes this level of collaboration to make communities safe havens for children and youth.

Chapter 8: Engaging Community Champions in the Prevention of Bullying

Key Messages

1. Bullying is an interpersonal, context-based problem needing context-based, interpersonal solutions. The contexts created by children's friendships, peer groups, and the norms of families, classrooms and neighbourhoods and communities play roles in engendering, maintaining, promoting, or diminishing bullying.

2. The prevention of bullying in children requires solutions that target relationships in a variety of the contexts where children interact with others.

3. Community champions are needed to facilitate the development, evaluation and dissemination of these context-relevant prevention programs.

References

Aber, J. L., Brown, J. L., & Jones, S. M. (2003). *Developmental trajectories toward violence in middle childhood: Course, demographic differences, and response to school based intervention.* Developmental Psychology, 39, 324-339.

Aber, J. L., Jones, S. M., Brown, J. L., Chaudry, N., & Samples, F. (1998). *Resolving conflict creatively: Evaluating the developmental effect of a school-based violence prevention program in neighbourhood and classroom context.* Development and Psychopathology, 10, 187-214.

Bagwell, C. L. (2004). *Friendships, peer networks, and antisocial behavior.* In J. B. Kupersmidt and K. A. Dodge (Eds.) *Children's Peer Relations: From Development to Intervention.* (pp. 37-57) Washington, DC: American Psychological Association.

Bagwell, C. L. & Coie, J. D. (2004). *The best friendships of aggressive boys: Relationship quality, conflict management, and rule-breaking behavior.* Journal of Experimental Child Psychology, 88, 5-24.

Bellmore, A. D., Witkow, M. R., Graham, S. & Juvonen, J. (2004). *Beyond the individual: The impact of ethnic context and classroom behavioral norms on victim's adjustment.* Developmental Psychology, 40, 1159-1172.

Bukowski, W. M., & Sippola, L. K. (2001). *Groups, individuals, and victimization: A view of the peer system.* In J. Juvonen & S. Graham (Eds.), *Peer harassment in school: The plight of the vulnerable and victimized* (pp. 355-377). New York: Guilford Press.

Craig, W., & Pepler, D. (1997). *Observations of bullying and victimization in the schoolyard.* Canadian Journal of School Psychology, 2, 41-60.

Comer, J. P. (1985). *The Yale-New Haven Primary Prevention Project: A follow-up study.* Journal of the American Academy of Child and Adolescent Psychiatry, 24, 154-160.

Crick, N., & Grotpeter, J. K., (1996). *Children's treatment by peers: Victims of relational and overt aggression.* Development and Psychopathology, 8, 367-380.

Dishion, T. J., Poulin, F., & Burraston, B. (2000). *Peer group dynamics associated with iatrogenic effects in group interventions with high-risk young adolescents.* In D. W. Nangle & C. A. Erdley (Eds.), *The role of friendship in psychological adjustment. New directions for child and adolescent development* (No. 91) (pp. 79-92). San Francisco, CA: Jossey-Bass Inc.

Dodge, K. A., Dishion, T. J., & Lansford, J. E. (2006). *Deviant peer influences in intervention and public policy for youth.* Social Policy Report, XX(1), 3-19.

El Ansari, W. E., Phillips, C. J., & Zwi, A. B. (2004). *Public health nurses' perspectives on collaborative partnerships in South Africa*. Public Health Nursing, 21(3), 277-286.

Espelage, D. L. & Swearer, S. M. (2004). *Bullying in American Schools A Social-Ecological Perspective on Prevention and Intervention*. Mahwah New Jersey: Lawrence Erlbaum Associates.

Graham, S., Bellmore, A.D., & Mize, J. (2006). *Peer victimization, aggression, and their co-occurrence in middle school: Pathways to adjustment problems*. Journal of Abnormal Child Psychology, 34, 363-378.

Hanish, L. D., & Guerra, N. G. (2000). *Predictors of peer victimization among urban youth*. Social Development, 9, 521-543.

Hawkins, J. D., Catalano, R. F., Morrison, D. M., O'Donnell, J., Abbott, R. D., & Day, L. E. (1992). *The Seattle Social Development Project: Effects of the first four years on protective factors and problem behaviors*. In J. McCord & R. E. Tremblay (Eds.), Preventing anitsocial behavior: Interventions from birth through adolescence (pp. 193-161). Proceedings from the 10th Biennial Meeting of the International Society for the Study of Behavioral Development, Jyvaeskylae, Finland.

Hoglund, W. L., & Leadbeater, B. J. (2004). *The effects of family, school, and classroom ecologies on changes in children's social competence and emotional and behavioral problems in first grade*. Developmental Psychology, 40, 533-544.

Israel, B. A., Schulz, A. J., Parker, E. A., & Becker, A. B. (1998). *Review of community-based research: assessing partnership approaches to improve public health*. Annual Review of Public Health, 19, 173-202.

Kellam, S. G., Ling, X., Merisca, R., Brown, C. H., & Ialongo, N. (1998). *The effect of the level of aggression in the first grade classroom on the course and malleability of aggressive behavior into middle school*. Development and Psychopathology, 10, 165-185.

Kupersmidt, J. B., Coie, J. D., & Howell, J. C. (2004). *Resilience in children exposed to negative peer influences*. In K. Maton, C. Shellenbach, B. Leadbeater, & A. Solzar (Eds.) Investing in Children, Youth, Families and Communities: Strengths-based research and policy (pp. 13-30). Washington: American Psychological Foundation.

Landry, R., Amara, N., & Lamari, M. (2001). *Utilization of social science research knowledge in Canada*. Research Policy, 30, 333-349.

Lasker, R. D., Weiss, E. S., & Miller, R. (2001). *Partnership synergy: A practical framework for studying and strengthening the collaborative advantage*. The Milbank Quarterly, 79(2), 179-205.

Lavis, J. N. (2006). *Research, public Policymaking and knowledge translation processes: Canadian efforts to build bridges.* The Journal of Continuing Education in the Health Professions. 26, 37-45.

Leadbeater, B., (in press). *Matching the prevention of social aggression to critical developmental and contextual transitions in middle school.* In (Eds.)Understanding Girls and Aggression.

Leadbeater, B. J., (2000). *Can restorative justice approaches be used as alternatives to elementary school suspensions?* Advocate Vol 23, 1, 6-8.

Leadbeater, B., & Hoglund, W. (2006). *Changing the social contexts of peer victimization.* Journal of the Canadian Academy of Child and Adolescent Psychiatry, (15)1, 21-26.

Leadbeater, B., Hoglund, W., & Woods, T. (2003). *Changing contexts? The effects of a primary prevention program on classroom levels of peer relational and physical victimization.* Journal of Community Psychology, 31, 397-418.

Lomas, J. (2000). *Connecting Research and Policy.* ISUMA: Canadian Journal of Policy Research, Spring, 140-144.

Macaulay, A. C. & Nutting, P. A. (2006). *Moving the frontiers forward: Incorporating Community-based participatory research into practice-based research networks.* Annuals Of Family Medicine, 4(1), 4-7.

Miller, G. E., Brehm, K., & Whitehouse. S. (1998). *Reconceptualizing school-based prevention for antisocial behavior within a resilience framework.* School Psychology Review, 27, 364-379.

Nation, M., Crusto, C., Wandersman, A., Kumpfer, K. L., Seybolt, D., Morrissey-Kane, E., & Davino, K. (2003). *What works in prevention: Principals of effective prevention programs.* American Psychologist, 58, 449-456.

Olweus, D. (1993). *Bullying at school: What we know and what we can do.* Oxford, UK: Basil Blackwell.

Rudolph,K. D., & Clark A. G. (2001). *Conceptions of relationships in children with depressive and aggressive symptoms: Social cognitive distortion or reality?* Journal of Abnormal Child Psychology, 29, 41-56.

Salmivalli, C., & Kaukiainen, A., & Voeten, M. (2005). *Anti-bullying intervention: Implementation and outcome.* British Journal of Educational Psychology, 75(3), 465-487.

Salmivalli, C. Lagerspetz, K., Björkqvist, K. Österman, K., & Kaukiainen, A. (1996). *Bullying as a group process: Participant roles and theri relations to social status within the group.* Aggressive Behavior, 22, 1-15.

Smith, D. J., Schneider, B. H., Smith, P. K. & Ananiadou, K. (2004) *The effectiveness of whole-school antibullying programs: A synthesis of evaluation research*. School Psychology Review, 33, 548-561.

Solomon, D., Watson, M., Battistich, V., Schaps, E., & Delucchi, K. (1996). *Creating classrooms that students experience as communities*. American Journal of Community Psychology, 24, 719-748.

Vitaro, F., Brendgen, M., Pagani, L., Tremblay, R. E., & McDuff, P. (1999). *Disruptive behavior, peer associations, and conduct disorder: Testing the developmental links through early intervention*. Development and Psychopathology, 11, 287-304.

Author Notes

This research was supported by grants from the Canadian Institutes of Health Research (#CAR-4327), the Social Sciences and Humanities Research Council of Canada (410-2000-0748) and from the PREVNet partnership.

Chapter 9:

The Fourth R:
A School-Based Program to Reduce Violence and Risk Behaviours among Youth

David A. Wolfe, Claire V. Crooks, Ray Hughes, Debbie Chiodo
CAMH Centre for Prevention Science
Peter G. Jaffe
University of Western Ontario

Introduction

There has been much concern about the adolescent triad of risk behaviours – violence, substance use, and sexual behaviour. We begin our discussion of prevention by recognizing that many adolescents experiment with high-risk behaviours such as drinking, and that exploring sexuality is a major aspect of their development. Unfortunately, many also develop abusive or violent methods to control their peers or dating partners, which is not surprising given the strong pro-violence messages entwined with entertainment and advertising media aimed at this age group. Consequently, we do not expect adolescents to eliminate all risky activities entirely. One way or the other, they need to develop their choices, values, and skills concerning these potential perils to be prepared for a successful transition to adulthood. In this regard, developing relationships and social competence is critical for establishing habits to ensure their health and well-being.

Our definition of success in terms of experimental risk behaviours among teens is based on what we want adolescents to do, not merely what we want them to avoid. From this vantage point, healthy adolescent outcomes incorporate strong relationship skills, self-awareness and knowledge about one's boundaries, high levels of self-efficacy, and good citizenship skills. At the same time, we hope to see a decrease in health-damaging behaviours through a combination of delayed onset, safety strategies pertaining to particular behaviours (such as condom use and not driving if drinking alcohol), and better help-seeking strategies. Finally, we believe success is reflected by youth engagement,

---

[8] Portions of this chapter appeared in Wolfe, Jaffe, & Crooks, (2006). Used with permission.

measured by attitudes, awareness, and involvement of youth in shaping their school climate and peer norms. In effect, we envision an outcome that incorporates healthy adolescent functioning in a range of domains and is consistent with a more holistic notion of well-being. With this goal of preparing youth in mind, we discuss the specifics of an integrated prevention model that involves comprehensive programming, skills-based approaches, and a relationships focus. We illustrate this discussion with examples from our school-based program for building healthy relationships, the Fourth R.

The Fourth R (for Relationships) is a comprehensive school-based program designed to promote healthy relationships and prevent risk behaviours among adolescents. It grew out of the Youth Relationships Project (YRP), a dating violence prevention program developed for youth with family backgrounds of maltreatment and violence. The YRP's success in demonstrating changes in violence-congruent attitudes and abusive behaviours of youth at risk for violent relationships resulted in widespread interest in adapting the program for use with all youth, regardless of risk status (Wolfe et al., 2003).

The cornerstone of the Fourth R is a 21-lesson skill-based curriculum that promotes healthy relationships and targets violence, high-risk sexual behaviour, and substance use among adolescents. Physical and Health Education teachers who deliver the curriculum receive specialized training. Our contention is that relationship skills can be taught in much the same way as the first three r's (reading, 'riting, and 'rithmetic), and establishing these skills as a fundamental part of the high school curriculum is equally essential. Furthermore, given the abundance of negative relationship models available to teens, it is crucial that they be exposed to healthy alternatives and equipped with the skills to engage in healthy relationships themselves. The *Fourth R* is comprised of three units: peer and dating violence, healthy sexuality, and substance use. Together, these three units are considered to address the triad of adolescent risk behaviours (i.e., violence, substance use and sex) that are connected to each other in terms of co-occurrence, but also rooted in the peer and dating relationships experienced by youth. Each unit contains similar themes of value clarification, provision of information, decision-making and an extensive skill development component. Connections among the three units are emphasized throughout.

Clarifying values allows adolescents the opportunity to think about their own boundaries and comfort levels, and about the decisional balances involved in each of these behaviour areas. This process is ongoing and integrated into skill development. Adolescents receive ample practice role playing ways to resolve conflict, both as participants and in the role of bystander. In addition to practice, seeing their peers role play solutions is an important part of the program, and one of the most effective ways to increase self-efficacy.

There are three other key components in addition to the 21 curriculum lessons, addressing school, parents, and larger school community. School interventions include staff and teacher awareness education, information about the program, and supplementary activities by the student led Youth Safe Schools (YSS) committees to increase links between community partners. For example, the YSS committee organizes guest speakers, field trips, and agency open houses to raise the profile of violence prevention in their school. Parents receive regular updates about the program through a newsletter and meetings and are provided with developmental information and strategies relevant to parenting adolescents. In brief, the Fourth R was designed to operationalize the best practice principles identified and discussed in our recent book (Wolfe, Jaffe, & Crooks, 2006): skill development within a relationship context, positive youth development initiatives, and comprehensive coverage of target and related issues.

Strengthening Relationship Skills

The importance of skills has emerged as a fundamental principle of best practice in prevention programs, regardless of the actual behaviour(s) being targeted. Conceptualizing skills in adolescence is complicated—not only are skills important, but they are affected by decision-making processes that precede these skills. Teens require the behavioural ability of knowing how to do something, as well as the decision-making capability of knowing and choosing when to use these skills.

The Information Motivation Behaviour Skills (IMB) model is particularly useful for conceptualizing how to bridge the gap between knowing what to do and doing it (Fisher, Fisher, Mischovich, Kimble, & Malloy, 1996). In simple terms, to promote the development of skills that will actually be used, adolescents need a strong foundation of accurate information, the building blocks of effective behavioural responses in difficult situations, and the blueprint of motivation to use these skills. The following sections elaborate on the importance of each of these components, as well as the way they fit together.

Accurate Information

The most widely used strategies in promoting healthy choices tend to be information-based. However, in the case of some risk behaviours such as smoking, it is clear that information about the health-damaging consequences of smoking is not sufficient to invoke individual change. Everybody knows that smoking is harmful, yet people continue to do it. In some countries, there has been a move to include increasingly graphic pictures of damaged lungs and throats on cigarette packages to illustrate the potential negative effects in the hopes of deterring smokers. If these tactics have had an impact on smokers, it has been minor. Although smoking rates overall are down slightly, the number of adolescent girls starting to smoke continues to rise, and a significant minority of North Americans continue to smoke cigarettes on a regular basis (U.S. Surgeon General, 2004).

Although not sufficient in and of itself, accurate information about the risks associated with particular behaviours is clearly an essential foundation for healthier choices. There are numerous examples of successful public health campaigns—such as those targeting seatbelt use or not drinking during pregnancy—where providing accurate information has had a significant impact on rates of use (in the former case) or abstinence (in the latter). Best practices identified for reducing risky sexual behaviour include providing accurate information about the risks of unprotected intercourse and methods of avoiding unprotected intercourse (Kirby, 1999). Likewise, information about specific substances is an important part of substance use prevention (Botvin & Kantor, 2000). Perhaps the surprising thing in today's world of sexually sophisticated youth culture is that teens don't know as much as we think they do. For example, the Kaiser Family Foundation found that young people generally feel uninformed about STIs, HIV, and contraception (KFF, 2003).

The Fourth R uses a number of strategies to increase the salience and interactive nature of the information component. One of the exercises in the Sexual Health part of the program is a Question Box where students submit anonymous questions for teachers to answer to the whole class. There is often a wide range of questions that underscore the lack of clear and accurate information common among adolescents. The issue of salience is addressed by having students themselves generate the questions. In some cases, teachers of girls' classes trade questions with teachers of boys' classes, and read and answer the questions submitted by opposite sex classes. This trading of questions is perceived very positively by the students and contributes to the material being seen as relevant. Cognitive authority is addressed by involving older adolescents in a number of ways. For example, the Teen Panel—a group of teenage parents who speak about contraception, choices, and the realities of teen parenting—is always very well received by the grade 9 students. In addition, older peers (typically grade 11 or 12 students from the Leadership Class) are used to assist in the grade 9 classes. Within the context of the high school peer hierarchy, using older students is a highly effective avenue for increasing cognitive authority and salience of information.

In sum, although accurate information is critical, it is widely recognized that information alone is not sufficient for behaviour change. Furthermore, the manner in which we attempt to transmit information is critical—there is consensus that passive information and knowledge transfer, such as lectures or group discussions, should not be the main mechanism of change. Recognizing the social context of information is also important, because the source of a message can have a significant impact on the extent to which the message is acknowledged and integrated into people's beliefs.

Behavioural Skills

Virtually every successful prevention program has a skills building component. Improving social and emotional competence is a hallmark of effective prevention programs (Greenberg, Domitrovich, & Bumberger, 2000). Adolescents need the opportunity to learn new skills, such as assertiveness, communication, and problem-solving, and practice applying them in different situations. Without skills, accurate information by itself offers poor protection in the face of pressure from peers and dating partners.

Adolescent self-efficacy is an important target in increasing skills. Self-efficacy stems from having particular skills, but also having the confidence that those skills will actually work in a real situation. Four key strategies to increasing self-efficacy (Bandura, 1986) include (1) providing a successful mastery experience; (2) providing an opportunity to witness others have successful mastery experiences; (3) creating these opportunities in a way that is not overly anxiety-provoking; and (4) providing immediate feedback. Simply being instructed in skills, discussing them, or even writing out responses are not likely to increase skills and self-efficacy -- to foster skill development it is critical to provide realistic opportunities to practice and receive feedback. By analogy, a teen who practices lay-ups at a basketball hoop day after day and perfects her form may have particular skills, but is unlikely to feel much self-efficacy because she has not tested those skills in a game situation and is uncertain of the outcome when she tries them. By the same reasoning, an adolescent who practices being assertive in front of a mirror with no feedback from others is unlikely to have much confidence in her strategies working in a "game situation." Adolescents need to practice these skills in as realistic a situation as possible to increase their feelings of self-efficacy that these skills will actually work when called upon in situations of conflict.

This analogy can also be applied to the example of learning to intervene as a bystander when witnessing abusive behaviour. Most adolescents have been in a situation where they see someone getting bullied or harassed. We know from the broader literature on bullying, that the majority of children and youth are distressed by witnessing these interactions. However, for youth (or adults) to attempt to intervene in such a situation, they need to have the expectation that taking action will lead to a desired outcome, that is, a resolution of the situation that does not endanger or humiliate the person intervening. Otherwise, even though they may be highly distressed by what they witness and motivated to intervene, they are unlikely to act. This example shows the importance of competence and skill building—too often it is assumed that whether or not someone takes action is simply a matter of motivation.

Successful programs use a range of active skill development strategies, such as:

- They provide hands-on experiences that increase participant skills;

- They help participants develop assertiveness and resistance skills;

- They increase communication skills; and

- They provide ample opportunities for written and verbal practice of these skills (Nation et al., 2003).

Role plays can be extremely effective but they need to be carefully planned, introduced, and debriefed. A role play activity that gets out of hand can be a failure experience and counterproductive, or so anxiety-provoking that the experience is aversive. In the Fourth R students role play a range of conflict situations relating to peer and dating relationships. Because the process of responding to a provocative situation, such as bullying or pressure to use drugs, is difficult, role-plays are broken down into small steps. Students are given actual scripts for the first few exercises to reduce their discomfort and ease them into action one step at a time. Over time students practice brainstorming solutions, trying responses, trying responses in the presence of other people, trying responses in the face of resistance, and analyzing what worked well and what did not. Importantly, they have ample opportunities to see their peers attempt to navigate similar scenarios, and discuss what they liked or didn't like about particular approaches. Through feedback from their teachers and peers, they are able to handle increasingly complicated and difficult situations as the program continues.

One of the innovative components of the Fourth R includes ways to integrate these learning opportunities into the daily fabric of high school life. For example, during a recent classroom visit to a grade 9 boys' Physical Health Education class, one of the authors (our National Education Coordinator who is also a Physical and Health Education teacher) set up a quick role play with three boys as they threw the football around. One of the boys took on the role of having been out with a girl on the weekend and wanting to talk about the sexual behaviour that occurred in a way that clearly objectified the young woman. The second boy encouraged the first to tell more details and reinforced the first boys' objectification. The third boy role-played being a friend of the young woman in question, feeling uncomfortable with the situation, and trying to intervene to challenge his friends and redirect the conversation. The role play went smoothly, with the rest of the class observing and debriefing afterwards. The whole activity took less than five minutes. The success of this in vivo role play built upon the boys' previous experience in structured classroom role plays as part of the Fourth R -- attempting a role play like this from scratch would be difficult. The boys' feedback from the experience was positive and they indicated the situation was realistic, which increases the likelihood that learning experiences will generalize to the boys' lives. Furthermore, attempts to resolve the situation provided the rest of the class with a model for an alternate response to a common situation.

Interpersonal skills—effective communication, assertiveness, and conflict resolution—are critical for adolescents to be able to make healthy choices, although without an accompanying sense of self-efficacy such skills are less effective. Youths need to have confidence that their skills will lead to a desired outcome. Building skills that translate to higher self-efficacy depends on them having the opportunity to practice the skills in as realistic a setting as possible, observe others practicing these skills, get feedback from adults and peers on their skills, and do all of these in a manner that is not so anxiety-provoking as to be aversive.

Motivation

Even with accurate information and the behavioural skills to make healthy choices, motivation is often a critical missing piece in preventing unsafe choices. Youth can know that smoking causes cancer and have reasonably good assertiveness skills, but still choose to smoke when pressured by their peers. Motivation to behave in a certain way or make specific choices is a critical determinant of outcomes. Previous attempts to motivate teens have often relied on scare tactics, or emphasizing the cost of not changing. As we have seen this approach is rarely successful, especially for those most likely to experiment, and is particularly ill-suited to adolescents' stage of cognitive development. Furthermore, adolescents are hypersensitive to adult hypocrisy (Bradley & O'Connor, 2002). Being exposed to adult role models who engage in the behaviours they are encouraging youth to avoid adds an impediment for motivation. To create motivation there needs to be a multi-pronged approach focusing both on the individual and on the peer culture.

Information and skills increase self-efficacy, which in turn strengthens motivation. Being aware of alternative choices and having confidence to follow through on his or her choice, even in hypothetical or contrived situations, establishes a healthy pattern that is likely to be reinforced and repeated. Although scare tactics alone have not been very successful in changing risk behaviour, adolescents need the opportunity to discuss in depth both the positive and negative consequences of various behaviours. Outcome expectancies, or what someone believes will happen if he or she behaves a certain way, are related to the motivation to engage in health protective practices. For example, with respect to condom use outcome expectancies can be related to physical (pleasure), social (partner's reaction), and personal implications.

Consistent with the notion of decisional balance, teens need to be able to discuss the positive consequences of high-risk behaviour. What positive physiological, social, and/or emotional benefits do adolescents derive from using alcohol or other substances? They may find that alcohol helps them overcome anxiety in social situations or that it helps them gain acceptance with a particular peer group. Although adults would prefer that teens not resort to alcohol to achieve those goals, ignoring the potential benefits experienced by adolescents does not make those benefits disappear. Recognizing there are benefits experienced by teens who use alcohol and other drugs creates an environment where individuals can engage in rational decision-making. Allowing individuals to consider the pros and cons of particular behaviours increases motivation, as shown in studies with resistant clients in substance abuse treatment (Miller & Rollnick, 2002). These motivational interviewing techniques empower individuals to take responsibility for their health and make decisions, rather than having the onus fall on the therapist or teacher to "talk someone into" healthy choices.

The Fourth R targets motivation at the peer level in a number of ways. For example, each school's Youth Safe Schools committee involves students from different grades, and is generally youth-driven. These committees or clubs serve multiple purposes: They provide a public face and forum for students interested in social action work, and they create media campaigns for the school that specifically target peer level influences. Previous campaigns have included segments on peer pressure—some have even targeted the aforementioned gap between what students think their peers are doing and what they are actually doing. The issue of cognitive authority is addressed by using the club to develop and implement these campaigns, since youth are much more likely to see information from their peers as relevant and useful compared to messages perceived as adult-driven. Student club members also present information or assist with role plays in younger grades in the capacity of peer leaders. Similarly, motivation can be socially constructed at the community level, such as hosting an annual violence prevention leadership awards night for students who have excelled in violence prevention and gender equity activities.

Ensuring Comprehensive Participation

We have emphasized that comprehensive programming is a best practice principle for effective prevention strategies. Programs that address the various contexts within which youth function and the different factors that affect youth behaviour are more likely to be successful than those that focus on one specific context or determinant of behaviour. In the case of violence, substance use, and high-risk sexual behaviour education and prevention with high school students, considerations for comprehensive programming include age-appropriate inclusion of parents, school-wide activities, and teacher involvement.

Age-Appropriate Inclusion of Parents

A comprehensive approach dictates inclusion of parents, although deciding how to include parents is tricky in light of this developmental stage. Developing an identity autonomous from their parents is a major developmental task for adolescents, but at the same time they need to balance this newfound autonomy with ways of staying connected to parents. Although the individuation process is taking place, youths who maintain this connectedness tend to fare better. Another consideration for the type and extent of parent involvement is the logistics of program delivery in the school setting. Although parent-youth sessions may be feasible in programs run through community mental health agencies, there are clear limitations to the types of involvement for parents within the school setting.

We opted to use a primarily information-dissemination strategy with parents. Parents receive a presentation about the program at the orientation night for prospective high school students and their parents in the spring of grade 8. Once students are at a school that offers the Fourth R, their parents are sent newsletters designed to be a user-friendly reference covering a range of topics, including information about the changes adolescents experience, the trends for various behaviours, and what their adolescents will learn in the program. We are currently building on the newsletters by developing a manual for parents that will underscore the importance of parent-adolescent communication, and provides parents with many tips for increasing healthy communication with their adolescents about the sensitive areas of violence, substance use, and sexual behaviour. The manual also contains many other references, such as parenting books and websites for those seeking more information on particular topics.

Teacher Involvement

Teachers need sufficient training to successfully implement a program such as the Fourth R. Similar to the discussion of the IMB model of behaviour change for adolescents, teachers need training that addresses all three of these areas: information, motivation, and behavioural skills. Without adequate training and booster sessions for teachers, the most innovative (and effective) components of programs can get dropped. Our teacher training uses the same principles as our program: teachers are provided with sufficient background information, and given opportunities to practice and receive feedback on their attempts to facilitate role plays.

The same considerations for information transfer discussed earlier in this chapter with respect to schools apply to teacher training. Teachers must have faith in the people doing the training to attach importance to the information. We have found that training using a combination of researchers and teachers is most effective. Typically, researchers provide the background orientation to the literature and teachers do the actual training for the curriculum. Although many of us who are psychologists have extensive experience facilitating role plays and training others to facilitate role plays, experience, and feedback indicate that teachers feel very strongly about non-teachers trying to tell them how to teach. In other words, we are considered credible for providing background information and explaining the research design, but we have less cognitive authority when it comes to teaching the actual skill of teaching. By partnering with experienced teachers who have extensive training skills, we are able to maximize the effectiveness of the whole training experience.

In motivating teachers we have found that it is imperative to gear the message to the audience. It needs to be made clear why a particular prevention program will benefit teachers as well as students. For example, teacher and student morale, and the relationship between students' feelings of school safety and their achievement scores, provide a good basis for capturing teachers' interests in the Fourth R. Focusing on some of the immediate benefits of implementing such a program, such as having a ready-made curriculum that meets state or provincial guidelines, is likely to have more of an impact on teacher motivation than identifying a long-term outcome that will not directly affect their teaching experience. It is not that teachers do not care about the long-term well-being of their students; rather, in the current educational climate where many teachers feel overwhelmed and demoralized, immediate benefits will be much more salient. The training and implementation issues of these programs are absolutely critical to their success,

Being Gender Strategic

Prevention with adolescents requires an understanding of the gender forces they are facing, and programming to match their world view about these gender realities (Crooks, Wolfe, & Jaffe, in press). High school students are developmentally at a stage where notions of gender tend to be very rigid. The typical high school environment rewards behaviours consistent with the male "jock" ideal, while devaluing activities seen as more feminine, leading to an aggressively homophobic culture. At the same time, adolescents report that girls hit boys as or more often than boys hit girls in their relationships. Because they lack the gendered understanding of important differences in the nature of this violence, both boys and girls will be hypersensitive to messages that they hear as "boy bashing" (Tutty et al., 2002). The challenge is to understand this reality, yet increase awareness of adolescents' understanding of gender and societal constructs of gender. In the Fourth R we target gender awareness through media deconstruction activities, discussions about different expectations and standards for boys and girls, and sometimes using different activities for boys and girls. Opportunities to discuss these issues in single sex groupings may also provide increased comfort while debating sensitive issues.

With respect to teachers, there is a wide range of awareness, comfort, and skill in relation to gender and violence issues. Some teachers have already sought out specialized training in the area and are skilled facilitators. Others find the topic awkward or even irrelevant. We know that statistically there will also be a subset of teachers delivering the program who perpetrate or experience violence in their own intimate relationships. Teacher buy-in is critical, and engaging them in the program requires identifying benefits to them.

In sum, building skills that support adolescents to make healthy choices is a multidimensional endeavour. Although information is the component that tends to be targeted most often, it is typically presented in a way that fails to appreciate issues such as cognitive authority of the information source and the importance of interactive delivery. Effective behavioural skills training requires practice and opportunities to see others practice to increase both competence and self-efficacy. Motivation, which can be targeted individually or through the use of peers, helps adolescents put all the pieces together to make healthy choices in their peer and dating relationships. Most of all, adolescents require ongoing opportunities to practice resolving difficult situations in a range of areas, as well as in the face of realistic resistance.

Research Findings

Our research team has completed the Phase I evaluation of the Fourth R, conducted with 10 intervention and 10 control schools (a total of 1896 students). A cluster randomized design was used to assign the 20 high schools (i.e., clusters) to the intervention or control condition. Phase I includes pre- and post-testing conducted in September and March of the students' Grade 9 year. Phase I results examine gains in mediators of change, such as attitudes, knowledge, and engagement in the classroom exercises related to the central issues of relationship violence, sexual health, and substance use/abuse measured soon after students complete the program. However, this initial phase of the evaluation does not examine behavioural outcomes per se because the time frame is too short to assess actual changes in self-reported risk behaviours. We will be reporting follow-up findings on this sample in 2009 to determine the extent to which students in the program have reduced their overall risk behaviours two years following program delivery, relative to those in control schools.

Phase I findings indicate that Fourth R students learned the materials and had significant gains, relative to controls, in knowledge and attitudes pertaining to violence, substance use, and sexual health. We also found that the students in the intervention schools enjoyed their physical health education classes more than students in the other schools, and found the exercises and activities to be very engaging. Finally, and perhaps most importantly, we found significant gains in skill acquisition among students from intervention schools, using a convenience sub-sample of 200 students (100 per condition). To assess skill acquisition under realistic circumstances, we created a behavioural analog using peer actors. The actors invited students (two at a time) to a party, and pressured them to engage in risk behaviours (e.g., to bring alcohol, drugs, money, etc.). Blind raters coded these 5-minute paired interactions in terms of student demonstration of skills taught in the program (i.e., negotiation, delay, refusal) as well as their extent of yielding and compliance to these negative pressures. The findings support our contention that the students do acquire important skills in the program. For example, Fourth R students were 2.2 times more likely than controls to show at least one negotiation skill during role-play interaction (p=.013); 4.8 times more likely to show at least one delay skill during role-play interaction (p=.05) (girls only); and were 50% less likely to yield to the pressures. Further details on the design and findings are available in Wolfe et al. (submitted).

In a related investigation, we examined the relationships between multiple forms of child maltreatment and violent delinquency in adolescence. Prospective data from the same students were used to examine the additive influence of individual-level (i.e., childhood maltreatment; parental monitoring, sex), and school-level variables (i.e., students' sense of safety across the entire student body) assessed at the beginning of grade 9 on engagement in delinquency four to six months later. Results at the individual level identified being male, experiencing maltreatment in childhood, and poor parental nurturing as important predictors of violent delinquency. School climate also played a significant role in predicting delinquency: schools in which students felt safe had fewer grade 9 students engaging in violent delinquent behaviours. Notably, the impact of cumulative forms of childhood maltreatment on risk for engaging in violent delinquency was greater among those schools that had not participated in the Fourth R, suggesting a school-wide buffering effect for the most vulnerable students. Interested readers are referred to the forthcoming paper by Crooks, Scott, Wolfe, Chiodo, and Killip (2007).

In sum, the Fourth R is a promising strategy for establishing universal, school-based curricula for educating youth about risk behaviours. To date we have shown that a skills-based, interactive program delivered by school teachers can address multiple risk behaviours that occur in relationship contexts for adolescents. The focus on embedding the program into curricula that meets the guidelines for mandatory classes in secondary schools provides a vehicle for widespread dissemination and sustainability far beyond that which can be achieved by an add-on program. We are now turning our attention to introducing these important topics of healthy relationships at a younger grade, with increasing knowledge and practice introduced in core courses from elementary through high school. We have developed the program for Grade 8 students, and have expanded the high school curricula to Grade 10 and Grade 11 English courses (see www.thefourthr.ca for information on these strategies).

Chapter 9: The Fourth R

Key Messages

1. Youth need information that will help them make good decisions, and to be shown positive relationship models that will demonstrate alternatives to the negative examples they frequently see in the world around them.

2. Involving all adolescents in education about safety and risk, rather than just those who show problems, builds resilience for future difficulties. A universal approach precludes the need for identifying youth and reduces the stigma of being labeled high risk.

3. Through the *Fourth R* program, all students are better equipped with the skills they need to build healthy relationships and to help themselves and their peers reduce risky behaviours.

4. Relationship knowledge and skills can and should be taught in the same way as reading, writing, and arithmetic, and therefore we refer to the classroom-based curriculum as the **Fourth R (for *Relationships*) core program**. This curriculum consists of 21 skill-based lessons that meet the Ontario Ministry of Education's learning expectations for grade 9 health education.

5. The Fourth R core program addresses adolescent risk behaviours by focusing on relationship goals and challenges that influence their decision-making.

References

Bandura, A. (1986). *Social foundations of thought and action: A social cognitive theory*. Upper Saddle River, NJ: Prentice-Hall.

Botvin, G. J., & Kantor, L. W. (2000). *Preventing alcohol and tobacco use through life skills training: Theory, methods, and empirical findings*. Alcohol Research & Health, 24(4), 250-257.

Bradley, M. J., & O'Connor, C. (2002). *Yes, your teen is crazy! Loving your kid without losing your mind*. Gig Harbor, WA: Harbor Press.

Crooks, C., Scott, K., Wolfe, D. A., Chiodo, D., & Killip, S. (2007). *Understanding the link between childhood maltreatment and violent delinquency: What do schools have to add?* Child Maltreatment, 12, 269-280.

Crooks, C. V., Wolfe, D. A., &. Jaffe, P. G. (in press). *School-based adolescent dating violence prevention: Enhancing effective practice with a gender strategic approach*. In Intimate Partner Violence (K. Kendall-Tackett & S. Giacomoni, Eds.), Kingston, NJ: Civic Research Institute.

Fisher, J. D., Fisher, W. A., Mischovich, S. J., Kimble, J. D., & Malloy, T. E. (1996). *Changing AIDS behavior: Effects of an intervention emphasizing AIDS risk reduction information, motivation, and behavioral skills in a college population*. Health Psychology, 15(2), 114-123.

Greenberg, M. T., Domitrovich, C., & Bumberger, B. (2000). *Preventing mental disorders in school-aged children: A review of the effectiveness of prevention programs*. Washington, DC: Substance Abuse and Mental Health Services Administration, US Department of Health and Human Services.

Kaiser Family Foundation. (2003). *National survey of adolescents and young adults: Sexual health knowledge, attitudes, and experiences*. Menlo Park, CA: Kaiser Family Foundation.

Kirby, D. (1999). *Reflections on two decades of research on teen sexual behavior and pregnancy*. Journal of School Health, 69(3), 89-94.

Miller, W. R., & Rollnick, S. (2002). *Motivational interviewing: Preparing people for change*. New York: Guilford.

Nation, M., Crusto, C., Wandersman, A., Kumpfer, K. L., Seybolt, D., Morrissey-Kane, E., et al. (2003). *What works in prevention - Principles of effective prevention programs*. American Psychologist, 58(6-7), 449-456.

Tutty, L., Bradshaw, C., Thurston, W. E., Tunstall, L., Dewar, M. E., Toy-Pries, D., et al. (2002). *School based violence prevention programs: A resource manual to prevent violence against girls and young women*. Calgary, AB: RESOLVE Alberta.

U.S. Surgeon General (2004). *The health consequences of smoking*: A report of the Surgeon General. Washington, DC: Author.

Wolfe, D. A., Crooks, C. V., Chiodo, D., Hughes, R., Ellis, W., & Jaffe, P. (submitted). *Effectiveness of a school-based program to prevent violence and related risk behaviors among adolescents: Initial gains in knowledge and skills*. Journal of Adolescent Health.

Wolfe, D. A., Jaffe, P., & Crooks, C. (2006). *Adolescent Risk Behaviors: Why Teens Experiment and Strategies to Keep Them Safe*. New Haven: Yale University Press.

Wolfe, D. A., Wekerle, C., Scott, K., Straatman, A., Grasley, C., & Reitzel-Jaffe, D. (2003). *Dating violence prevention with at-risk youth: A controlled outcome evaluation*. Journal of Consulting and Clinical Psychology, 71, 279-291.

Chapter 10:

Engaging Aboriginal Youth in School-Based Violence Prevention: A Comprehensive Evaluation Perspective

Claire V. Crooks
CAMH Centre for Prevention Science and
University of Western Ontario Centre for Research and Education
on Violence Against Women and Children

Introduction

A growing body of literature suggests that successful school-based violence prevention programs share several key features (Wolfe, Jaffe, & Crooks, 2006; Greenberg, Domitrovich, & Bumberger, 2000). Effective programs are comprehensive with respect to addressing multiple contexts or settings that are important to children and adolescents. These programs extend beyond information delivery and passive forms of teaching to include interactive skills-based instruction, preferably providing sufficient opportunity for youth to role-play and practice skills. Successful programs tend to have youth empowerment or leadership components. They are implemented for an adequate duration of time for meaningful changes to occur among individuals and the larger school setting. Effective programs are holistic in addressing the whole youth (e.g., simultaneously addressing the adolescent risk behaviours triad of violence, substance use and sexual behaviour), within the context of positive youth development and healthy relationships (Wolfe et al. 2006).

Although there is some agreement among researchers and educators about these critical features, there is also an emerging awareness that effective programs are not one-size-fits-all. In particular, there has been a call for meaningful adaptation to increase the cultural relevancy of programs. Prevention models that meet the needs of ethnically, culturally, and geographically diverse communities are necessary to ensure the health and well-being of all Canadian adolescents. Unfortunately, despite this call for culturally relevant programs, Aboriginal youth remain an under-studied and under-served segment of the population who experience disproportionate levels of interpersonal violence and related risks.

Chapter 10: Engaging Aboriginal Youth in School-Based Violence Prevention

The purpose of this chapter is to describe a multi-component school-based prevention initiative for Aboriginal youth that has emerged through a partnership of researchers, educators, community members, and youth over the past four years. This initiative has included several youth-developed video resources, a peer mentoring program, and an expanded and adapted curriculum (based on the *Fourth R* program). Specifically, using a comprehensive evaluation framework, the need, theories, and process associated with the initiative are discussed. Finally, several emerging lessons regarding engaging youth and community partners are highlighted.

Comprehensive Program Evaluation

Although program evaluations often begin from the successful implementation of the program, a case can be made for documenting the successes and challenges of innovative programs long before they get to that stage. A comprehensive evaluation framework recognizes that there are numerous steps required in empirically examining the development and implementation of a program. That is, well before a program can be tested for efficacy in a randomized control trial, there are a number of key components that require evaluation. These components include identification of need for a particular program, examination of theory, and assessment of process, followed by evaluation of outcome, efficacy and efficiency of intervention (Rossi, Freeman, & Lipsey, 2003).

Within a comprehensive framework, the first stage of evaluation concerns the *need* for the program. In other words, it is necessary to establish that the program provided is meeting a need or filling a gap in the community. Data relevant to answering this question include documented needs of particular target groups, and community stakeholder involvement and support. In addition, locally identified needs can be considered at this stage. The second stage involves scrutiny of the *theory* behind the program. As argued by Lipsey and Cordray (2000), evidence must be gathered to determine if the conceptualization and design of a program reflects valid assumptions about the nature of the targeted problem and its resolution. A range of data may support underlying program theory, including research on components of successful programs and approaches with a particular target group. In the third stage of program evaluation, the *process* of intervention must be examined to evaluate whether the program can be reasonably implemented in a way that meets the needs of the target client group and community stakeholders. Client satisfaction surveys, community feedback meetings, and participant retention rates are all relevant to this level of evaluation. It is only after these first three levels have been addressed that issues such as efficacy and efficiency can be evaluated. All too often these critical foundation pieces are overlooked in the final reporting of a research study.

This chapter applies a comprehensive program evaluation framework to the *Aboriginal Fourth R* initiatives. Emphasis is placed on evaluation at the first three levels (i.e., need, theory, and process). In particular, I address the following questions: 1) Is there a need for culturally-specific violence prevention programs for Aboriginal youth? 2) What do theories tell us regarding essential program components? and, 3) Is there evidence that a prevention program based on these theories meets the needs of Aboriginal youth and educators?

1) Is there a need for culturally-specific violence prevention programs for Aboriginal youth?

Evidence supporting the need for prevention programs for Aboriginal youth can be drawn from the literature documenting difficulties experienced by these youth in general. The health of Aboriginal[9] people in Canada and especially their children has been designated a national priority by numerous policy makers. There exists a long history chronicling the abusive conditions to which indigenous people were subjected. From the 1800s onward, Aboriginal children were often removed from their parents' homes and communities, and placed in residential schools that were operated by the federal government. Compounding the trauma of being away from home at such a young and vulnerable age, the schools viewed Aboriginal peoples and cultures as vicious or violent and would not allow the expression of Aboriginal cultures and languages in any form. Residential schools also were responsible for pervasive sexual and physical abuse, isolation, and neglect (Blackstock, Clarke, Cullen, D'Hondt, & Formsma, 2004; Milloy, 1999). The legacy of residential schools was widespread trauma and generations of children who were not raised by their families within their communities, which set the stage for high rates of social problems evident today.

This disconnect from cultural traditions and identity continues to be a major stressor for many contemporary Aboriginal communities. Communities that have somehow retained or re-established a sense of cultural identity and tradition have fared better. For example, an analysis of the variation in suicide rates across First Nations communities showed that the extent to which a community had achieved a sense of cultural identity, and more specifically autonomy, was directly related to lower suicide rates (Chandler & Lalonde, 1998).

Health indicators for Aboriginal peoples are worse than for any other groups in Canada (Young, 1994). Aboriginal peoples have the lowest life expectancies, highest infant mortality rates, substandard and overcrowded housing, lower education and employment levels, and the highest incarceration rates. Aboriginal adolescents experience higher rates of physical, sexual and emotional abuse, leaving school, and involvement in violent behaviour and delinquency.

In summary, although there is variability across individual communities, Aboriginal children as a group, continue to experience unacceptable and disproportionate levels of risk across all identified dimensions: Poverty, substance misuse, education, youth suicide,

---

[9] The use of the term Aboriginal in this section is not intended to over generalize about the significant cultural differences across the multitude of First Nations, Inuit and Metis peoples. Rather, most of the research and policy documents being cited do not distinguish amongst these groups. Where research has been more specific, the appropriate term is used.

accidental injury, child welfare, sexual exploitation, and youth justice (Blackstock et al., 2004). Clearly these rates of health problems demonstrate a need for a comprehensive approach that includes a full spectrum of strategies ranging from primary prevention to clinical intervention. Policy makers have suggested that there is a critical need for funding to develop and implement both national and community based prevention strategies that provide holistic support to First Nations children, youth, and families (Blackstock et al, 2004; Royal Commission on Aboriginal Peoples, 1996).

To date, few prevention programs have been adapted, implemented and evaluated for use with Aboriginal youth (Hawkins, Cummins, & Marlatt, 2004). Programs that do exist are often not documented with enough detail for other communities to use (Hawkins et al., 2004). There have been some programs that implement culturally-relevant teachings, but these have been mostly evaluated based on anecdotal evidence and small case studies (Blackstock et al., 2004). As part of a larger national project on culturally relevant programming, our research group conducted an audit with 15 partners across the country. The results of these interviews suggested that our partners unanimously felt that there is a lack of programs that have been documented, let alone evaluated (Chiodo, Crooks, McShane, Formsma, & Gosnell, 2006).

In addition to the broader need for prevention programming for Aboriginal youth in Canada, our research team identified two specific needs based on our local involvement with students and educators. The first observation was that in our experience implementing the *Fourth R* program across the Thames Valley District School Board, First Nations youth virtually never self-identified as leaders in violence prevention within the schools. Although student-led Safe Schools Committees were developed at every secondary school in the school board, Aboriginal youth did not show up on these committees, even at the three secondary schools that have the highest numbers of First Nations youth.

The second locally specific need was identified by our Aboriginal Advisory Board, which we convened in spring 2004 to guide our work in this area. The committee, comprised of First Nations Counsellors and administrators, consultants, community members and researchers, noted that the transition to secondary school was very difficult for many local First Nations students. In particular, students living on the neighbouring reserves who attended schools in their own communities until grade 8 are subsequently bused into the city to attend urban secondary schools in grade 9. These students have to contend with becoming a visible minority at school for the first time, and onerous transportation arrangements (i.e., 90 minute bus rides are not uncommon), in addition to all of the typical stressors associated with starting high school. The educators and First Nations Counsellors strongly expressed the concern that this difficult transition places youth at risk of school failure or drop-out before they have had the opportunity to really connect with their new schools. Thus, in addition to the needs of Aboriginal youth documented in the literature, our local group identified the need to identify and foster youth in violence prevention leadership roles, as well as the need to support youth in making a successful transition into high schools.

2) What do theories tell us regarding essential program components?

Existing research about successful prevention programming with Aboriginal youth has identified numerous core components that are the same as with mainstream youth. Effective substance use prevention programs, for example, include life and behavioural skills development, build self-efficacy and self esteem, target attitudes, and increase community involvement (Gilchrist, Schinke, Trimble, & Cvetkovich, 1987; Schinke, Botvin, Trimble, Orlandi, Gilchrist, & Locklear, 1988). Similarly, suicide prevention programs emphasize the importance of holistic, comprehensive, skills-based intervention within a cultural identity framework (Gary, Baker, & Grandbois, 2005). It is worth noting that most of these larger trials have been conducted in the US, and the extent to which they apply to Aboriginal youth in Canada is unclear. Thus, they provide a starting point for considering appropriate programming innovation, but may not be completely relevant.

Although existing literature and theory dictate that successful prevention programs for Aboriginal youth include many components found in the broader field of prevention, there is also recognition that these approaches are necessary but not sufficient. Two concepts in particular are useful in understanding the paradigm shift that is required to make prevention programs culturally relevant. At the individual level, bicultural competence has been identified as an important outcome for youth. Bicultural competence refers to the attitudes, behaviours, and coping strategies necessary to be successful in both the Aboriginal and White communities (Hawkins et al., 2004). Specific components of bicultural competence include: Knowledge of cultural beliefs and beliefs, positive group attitudes, bicultural efficacy, communication competence, role repertoires, and groundedness in both cultural identities (LaFromboise, Coleman, & Gerton, 1993). Mainstream programs that provide opportunities to explore these concepts in the dominant culture must also provide a parallel focus on Aboriginal culture to increase bicultural competence.

The other important element of adaptation relates to the community as the level at which problems should be understood and addressed. Although community involvement is a general best practice principle for violence prevention, the degree to which and meaning of community ownership is significantly different in culturally relevant programs. Hawkins and colleagues note that community emphasis refers to the process by which programs are likely to be successful and adopted (i.e., with significant and meaningful community collaboration at each step), as well as the focus on the contributors to problems (e.g., looking at structural contributors to violence rather than simply focusing on individual or family risk factors). Because of the importance of community, culturally relevant programs must seek to involve the community and increase connections among youth and community resources at every opportunity.

To summarize, considering the components of theoretically sound programming for Aboriginal youth requires an appreciation of both content and context. With respect to content, the prevalence and centrality of youth suicide as a challenge faced by many First Nations communities is grounds for explicitly addressing suicide with the rest of the adolescent risk triad (i.e., violence, substance use, and sexual behaviour). In addition, the National Aboriginal Health Organization (NAHO) has identified a need for culturally appropriate education materials (e.g., videos, pamphlets) to facilitate prevention (e.g., suicide prevention; NAHO, undated). With respect to context, an appreciation of community and historical contributors to risk and protective factors provides an appropriate framework rather than situating all problem behaviours within the individual or family. Furthermore, the overarching importance of cultural identity at the community level and individual level (especially as it pertains to bicultural competence) must be integrated as an organizing principle. On the basis of these principles, our partnership of educators, community members, and researchers has developed a number of initiatives including several video projects, a peer mentoring program, and a culturally-relevant curriculum. Each of these is described briefly in turn, with an emphasis on the more innovative aspects.

Video Projects

Our first project was the development of a video resource based on First Nations youth demonstrating different interpersonal skills in the face of peer pressure and conflict. Over a four week period, 23 youth came together to discuss youth issues, identify conflicts, script scenarios, and make a video. Youth identified many salient conflict areas relevant to all youth (e.g., dating violence, peer pressure to use drugs), as well as some that were more culturally specific (e.g., racism, peer pressure to not date someone from another culture). After the first video resource, subsequent projects incorporated non-Aboriginal students (at the recommendation of the first group of youth) and focused on expanding the diversity of conflict scenarios experienced by the youth (e.g., gang violence, cyber-bullying). A third video was developed specifically to demonstrate help-seeking strategies. A final shorter project specifically adapted materials related to setting fires as part of a mainstream arson prevention program. Throughout all of the video development projects there was a dual focus on process (e.g., understanding the process by which youth become engaged in the activity; understanding youth's experience of the project) as well as outcome (e.g., developing culturally relevant resources for violence prevention programming). To date, there have been 46 youth involved in making four different videos.

Peer Mentoring Program

Another component of the initiative is an *Aboriginal Peer Mentoring Program*. The peer mentoring program connects younger secondary students with peer mentors from older grades who have made a strong commitment to school. This link with an older student who is experiencing school success was intended to help smooth the transition from elementary to secondary school for the younger individual. In the original pilot, pairs were matched on the basis of shared interests. Peer mentoring pairs met at lunch on a weekly basis for approximately 3 months. They were encouraged to pursue their own activities, but also provided with optional activities that include a focus on holistic and culturally-relevant models of healthy youth. In addition, as a way to increase community involvement and connectedness, an adult from the local First Nations community (identified by the Advisory Board) attends the peer mentoring group every three weeks to provide a cultural teaching and facilitate a sharing circle. The program is supported in the schools by the First Nations Counsellors who check in with peer mentors each week for an update on the session and to provide support for any difficult issues that may have arisen. As of January 2008, four cycles of the peer mentoring program have been run in each of three secondary schools, with approximately 110 participating students.

Over the two years that the mentoring program has been running, there have been several innovations. For example, as the program evolved, some schools found that a group-based approach was more successful than the traditional mentoring dyad. In addition, we have now developed a "stacked course" curriculum in which grade 9 students and grade 11 students work towards different credits in the same classroom (a general study skills credit for the former and a leadership credit for the latter). Much of the peer mentoring work has been integrated into this stacked course, such that students are now able to obtain course credit for their involvement. The stacked course is being piloted in the same three secondary schools during the 2007-2008 academic year. Finally, we now host a conference for grade 8 Aboriginal students to prepare them for the transition to secondary school. In addition to participating in other activities and hearing a keynote address, grade 8 students learn about the mentoring program and stacked course as options available to them to smooth their transition from grade 8 to grade 9. Several experienced mentors from the program participate in a panel at the conference to answer the younger students' questions and address particular anxieties they may be experiencing in relation to their upcoming transition to secondary school.

Aboriginal Perspective Fourth R Curriculum

The violence prevention curriculum was based on the *Fourth R* curriculum and developed in collaboration with an Aboriginal educator with extensive experience bringing an Aboriginal perspective to curriculum documents that meet Ontario Ministry of Education guidelines. Additional input was obtained from our other partners, including a group of youth consultants who reviewed the document as part of summer employment and made recommendations specifically pertaining to the relevancy and completeness of the role play scenarios.

The curriculum adds a cultural identity framework for youth and situates some of the issues facing Aboriginal youth in a historical context. Notably, the *Aboriginal Perspective* curriculum draws links between residential schools and the widespread effects of trauma in communities. There is a focus on holistic models of healthy youth development and relationships with an emphasis on the connection to sexual decisions and substance use. Youth have opportunities to identify individual and community strengths within their cultural framework that will support them in making healthy choices. Suicide prevention is addressed explicitly with a safety planning lesson. Cultural myths about substance use are directly countered. Teaching strategies have been adapted to include the use of sharing circles and bringing community members into the classroom. Additional educational materials (including the videos described above) and role-play examples support the curriculum by demonstrating healthy relationship skills in situations relevant to youth (e.g., racism at school, inter-cultural relationships).

The curriculum has been implemented once at the Alternative Education program of the Thames Valley District School Board (located on the Chippewas on the Thames Reserve). Based on this implementation the curriculum was revised for a second local implementation. In addition, it is being implemented in Saskatchewan during the 2007-2008 school year. It is anticipated that there will be significant adaptation to incorporate appropriate cultural content when the program is used in different communities.

In summary, a range of initiatives have been developed over the past few years. Although these initiatives differ in terms of focus, duration, and number of youth involved, they share an emphasis on incorporating cultural traditions and increasing community connections. Furthermore, positive youth development and leadership opportunities are key components of each initiative.

3) Is there evidence that a prevention initiative based on these theories meets the needs of Aboriginal youth and educators?

This chapter has outlined several related initiatives designed to promote healthy relationships and prevent violence among Aboriginal adolescents through skills-based, relationship-focused programming within a larger cultural identity framework. Is there evidence that these approaches are meeting the needs of the youth and communities they are intended to serve? This question can be considered from the vantage point of the various stakeholders involved with the program – youth leaders, peer mentoring participants, students receiving the curriculum, and educators and community.

Youth involved as leaders in the video projects and as peer mentoring clearly have been engaged in the process and demonstrated commitment to the initiatives over time. For example, of the 24 youth who began our largest video project, 23 completed the project, which is a higher retention rate than for most of our non-Aboriginal projects. Furthermore, approximately 60% of youth (excluding those who graduated) have been involved in subsequent projects. More recently we were able to hire one of the graduates as a part-time Youth Liaison Coordinator while she undertakes further education at college. Many of our educational partners have commented positively on the level of commitment from the youth in our projects, in light of the previous absence of these same youth from similar initiatives.

What accounts for the success? Pre- and post-interviews and surveys have identified a number of critical factors in achieving youth engagement. Most notably, youth identified the potential to meet new people, the fact that they were initially approached by adults with whom they had strong relationships (typically the First Nations Counsellor in the schools), and the opportunity to counter prevailing attitudes and stereotypes about First Nations youth (e.g., by being seen to provide something positive to the community) as their primary reasons for becoming involved in the project (Rawana, Crooks, Chiodo, Hughes, & Pereira, 2006). Interestingly, some youth identified their main reason for getting involved (versus not doing so in the past) as simply the fact that they were directly and personally invited to be involved, underscoring the importance of an active recruitment strategy based on pre-existing relationships.

The peer mentoring program has had some preliminary evaluation based on interviews, a sharing circle (from which participant comments were transcribed), and a facilitated brainstorming exercise with First Nations Counsellors and administrators from the schools (Rawana, Pereira, Chiodo, Crooks, & Hughes, 2006). Initial reflections provided positive support for the program including reports of increased involvement of youth in school activities, personal growth in the youth, improvements in relationships among youth and with project stakeholders, increased awareness about Aboriginal community organizations, and learning Aboriginal traditional customs and knowledge. For instance, youth reported that, "I liked the fact that you get into such a close bond with your mentee and that she was someone I would have never met if it wasn't for the peer mentoring program...I think I got as much out of it as she did because I got a new friend". Another youth reported "a lot of Native kids probably come [to school] and they are scared and they don't know anybody but then they see that grade 11's and 12's have made it this far, and they have stayed in school and all that probably gives them hope".

The curriculum has been piloted only once with a group of youth in the Alternative Education program, so the comments offered about the implementation process are very preliminary. However, the educator and assistant who oversee the program have noted that attendance was higher during the *Aboriginal Perspective Fourth R* being implemented, and that individual students showed up more consistently than for their other classes. Participation in the interactive activities was noted to increase greatly over the course of the program (as noted by the educators who typically teach there as well as the educator who came in specifically to teach the course). In addition, the students responded extremely favorably to the video resources (that were developed by other youth as part of the initiative), suggesting that those videos were relevant and helpful, at least for this group of youth.

In terms of feedback from the larger community and educational system we have surveyed these stakeholders after every project to gain their perspective on the successes and challenges of the initiatives and found the feedback to be positive. Our partners have continued to show their commitment and endorsement of the initiative through their ongoing participation with the Advisory Board. The school board has committed significant additional resources to the project by paying a teacher to pilot the curriculum in a reserve school. In terms of community endorsement, in October 2006 the Fourth R team was honoured with the Chippewas on the Thames' *Educator of the Year Award* at an educational awards night. We hope that is a reflection of the successful partnerships that have emerged over the past four years.

Looking back... and moving forward

Reflecting on the past few years and the progress we have made in the area of violence prevention programming with Aboriginal youth, there are a number of lessons we can identify from our successes and challenges. These lessons relate to developing and maintaining partnerships, establishing program direction and achieving youth engagement, and conducting research. Ten of the most salient lessons are outlined here in the hopes that they may provide some assistance to other community-research partnerships facing similar challenges.

Developing and maintaining partnerships

1. *Patience is a virtue.* When we consider our progress in the area of developing prevention programs for Aboriginal youth, we are simultaneously proud of our progress, and also astounded by how quickly time has passed! In the first year of our partnerships, we had many stimulating discussions and debates, but our only completed activity was one small video project. It has taken more than three years to get to the point where our programs are ready for evaluation. The time and resources that have gone into developing strong partnerships has significant implications for timelines and funding proposals, because very few funders would be willing to fund a complete year of discussion and partnership-building. We have had to be creative in finding bridge funding to keep partnerships developing. A significant area of learning for the research was coming to understand the culture, governance structures and education systems of the three First Nations communities involved with the project. Gaining this understanding and knowledge takes time and emerges though conversations, attending community events, and the willingness of our partners to share their local customs and history.

2. *Partnership building and maintenance has to be a priority not an afterthought.* In our experience, working from existing relationships was an important piece of getting started. Some of our partners questioned why we were focusing on Aboriginal youth in schools, when those youth are lower risk than many of the youth who have left school and are in the larger community. We chose to begin in the schools because of our existing relationships with the board and our understanding of the system. We are now increasingly becoming involved with the broader communities as an outgrowth of our work in the schools. There is a balance between having enough partners at the table to get started and being over-inclusive to the point where it is difficult to move forward because of the inability to schedule meetings. Regular meetings with our advisory committee have been an effective way to keep partners involved. We have had difficulties in the past largely when we have hurried to go in a direction (e.g., for funding) when there was not sufficient time to consult with partners and make decisions as a group. Underlying all of our relationships is the theme of making sure there is the time and opportunity for trust to develop, both among adult partners, and with the youth involved in the initiatives.

3. *Recognize difference in mandates and conflicting priorities.* Each of our partners brings different perspectives and mandates to the table, and it has been important for us as researchers to develop an appreciation of these different realities. For example, in planning a video resource project, the First Nations Counsellors wanted to include as many youth as possible, the project facilitators had a specific number in mind to optimize the group dynamics, the researchers had limits with respect to funding availability, and the school administrators had concerns about how much school the youth would miss and felt strongly that only those youth with strong attendance records should be considered. We have been most successful when we have provided ample opportunity for everyone to identify specific concerns and brainstormed solutions as a group. As researchers, launching our projects and collecting appropriate data may be our priorities. However, the school system's primary mandate is not the facilitation of program research and it is important to recognize and respect these differences. A fundamental challenge related to mandates is the difference in availability of research and programming funding. As researchers, we are able to obtain funding specifically to develop, implement and evaluate a project. Our educational partners may be more concerned with widespread implementation and sustainability of a program, even before it has been evaluated. Working together to identify resources for both research and programming, and trying to build sustainability into programs from the outset has been an important direction.

Establishing program direction and achieving youth engagement

4. *Goals jointly determined with partners have been the most successful.* Although our research team had a vision of how the project might evolve at the outset (which was necessary for obtaining funding), the process has been highly flexible in terms of responding to the direction of our Advisory Committee. Not surprisingly, the initiatives that arose directly from needs identified by the Advisory Committee have been arguably the most successful, partly with respect to sustainability. For example, the peer mentoring program that was developed to address the difficult transition for many First Nations youth from elementary school on the reserve to secondary school in the city has been integrated into the role of the First Nations Counsellors in the school.

5. *Engaging Aboriginal youth requires specific and targeted strategies.* Our experience in the larger Thames Valley District School Board over the past six years has been that First Nations youth did not volunteer or self-identify to participate in leadership roles for mainstream violence prevention initiatives. Our success with initiative and sustaining youth engagement in our Aboriginal violence prevention programs demonstrates that many of these youth are highly interested in participating and in making their schools and communities safer for other youth. Engaging them has required specific strategies that have at times entailed multiple steps (such as meetings with the First Nations Counsellors, meetings with the research team, and individual interviews). Clearly the passive invitation to participate in the form of a school flyer will not be as successful. With a targeted focus on youth engagement, we have developed a core group of

talented and inspirational youth leaders who have made a multi-year commitment to these projects.

6. *Different youth will be engaged through different pathways.* Different youth may have very different reasons for becoming involved in a particular project and all of the pathways to engagement are equally valid. For example, in describing their reasons for volunteering for the video project demonstrating healthy conflict resolution skills by and for First Nations youth, self-described reasons for involvement ranged from wanting to counter racism and improve the situation of First Nations youth:

> *"This project opened people's eyes to how Native people feel, even teachers may look down at you because you're Native and they think that you will drop out of school"*

> *"I am really glad that someone is trying to bring attention to situations Native Youth go through and I would really like to be a part of this project"* (First Nations student)

To interest in the technical aspects of video production:

> *"I have never really done anything like it... make a movie... could lead to doing more of it or even a job in the future"*

To simply responding to an overture from an adult:

> *"I have never been asked to do anything like this before."*

As these quotes indicate, pathways to involvement may differ, but each constitutes a valid point of engagement for that particular youth. Notably, many of the factors that we expected to be attractive to youth at the outset (e.g., financial incentives, pizza), were not the factors identified by youth as key in their decision to become involved.

7. *Identify and recruit youth through their pre-existing relationships.* Our success with recruiting youth leaders and participants has been completely predicated on their strong existing relationships with their First Nations Counsellors, particularly for the first project. Once youth are involved, they tend to self-select for future projects, but the initial participation was highly related to being invited and encouraged by their counsellors. Youth identified the importance of this relationship in their pre- and post-interviews after the video projects and peer mentoring. As the momentum of the project has increased, additional youth have become involved on the basis of peer referral, but adult relationships were especially key in the early stages.

8. *Youth leadership does not mean completely youth run.* Even as youth have taken on increasing roles as leaders in the direction of the project, the need for extensive organizational and logistical support has not diminished. Some of the required

supports are typical of many youth projects, while others stem from culturally-related demographics. The most notable requirement is extensive planning and provision of transportation for youth who live on reserves. Because there are no late buses, projects have to occur during lunch hour, school time, or alternate transportation arrangements are required. Flexibility was also a crucial element in accommodating youths' participation. For example, a summer project that had been scheduled to run during the day had to be re-scheduled to evenings and weekends to accommodate the number of youth who had daytime summer employment.

Considerations for conducting research

9. *First Nations youth are the focus of much research.* There is consensus among our First Nations partners that their youth have been over-researched, without any clear benefit to the youth themselves or any practical implications arising from the research. In many cases, the adults described the phenomenon known as "drive-by research" where youth have completed surveys or interviews and never heard from the researchers again in terms of results or implications. We have attempted to address this research fatigue through two avenues. First, we have listened to the specific nature of our partners' complaints; namely, that much of the research has been problem-focused and documented deficits for First Nations youth without a corresponding focus on strengths. As a result, we have developed a research strategy focusing on more positive elements of youth development including engagement, youth assets, and self-perception / identity. Second, we have tried to involve our partners more directly in the research process to create an environment whereby they see themselves as collaborators rather than research "subjects." This dialogue about the role and importance of research continues to be a challenge and we recommend that new partnerships begin to have these discussions early in their work together. The Ownership, Control, Access, and Possession guidelines published by NAHO provide useful guidance in negotiating these relationships (Schnarch, 2004).

10. *Methodology and measures need to be adapted.* Even if all partners are convinced about the importance (or necessity) of research, there are significant barriers to identifying and measuring appropriate outcomes. Because of our concerns about some of the available self-report measures that were not developed for this population, we have used these cautiously, while relying more heavily on interviews and feedback surveys. Our early experience was that one-to-one interviews did not capture the feedback that was spontaneously emerging as part of the closing circle of various projects. As a result, we have been experimenting with recording and transcribing talking circles as a modified focus group idea.

As our programs have begun to stabilize and we move into a more formal outcome-based research phase, there are a number of challenges that lie ahead. Identifying (or developing) appropriate outcome measures remains is one such challenge. Some measures, such as the Harter Self-Perception Profiles for Adolescents have at least been adapted for use with American Indians, and are potentially suitable for Aboriginal youth in Canada. In other areas, suitable measures are clearly lacking. For example, although bicultural competence is a highly sought after outcome, there is not currently an assessment tool for measuring this construct. The challenge of appropriate control groups is also a daunting one. Because of the community-focused nature of the process of developing and implementing prevention programs, it is difficult to identify a control group within the same community. As the same time, differences across communities are such that a between communities design would be based on untenable assumptions of homogeneity. Clearly there is a need for creative research designs that combine quantitative and qualitative methodologies.

With respect to programming, the process of localization will be important to document. Aboriginal communities across Canada represent highly diverse cultural and linguistic groups, and the usefulness of the programs described in this chapter for other communities will be variable. Although every attempt has been made to incorporate elements of Aboriginal cultures that are more ubiquitous, such as the medicine wheel and Seven Grandfather Teachings, there are cultural groups that do not incorporate these traditions. As other communities begin to adapt and implement the peer mentoring program and curriculum, it will be important to document the process of localization. Significant challenges remain in maintaining the balance between preserving program elements that appear to benefit all youth, incorporating a cultural identity to make the program salient for each community of Aboriginal youth, and documenting the implementation and outcomes of each step of the process. Although challenging, this work represents a critical piece in moving away from one-size-fits-all violence prevention solutions to providing meaningful programs for all Canadian youth.

Key Messages

Over the past four years, our research team has worked in close partnership with Aboriginal and non-Aboriginal educators and youth from the Thames Valley District School board, along with other Aboriginal members of the larger community to develop a series of initiatives for Aboriginal youth. These initiatives aim to extend our school-based work in promoting healthy relationships and preventing violence with adolescents in general to be more culturally-relevant for Aboriginal youth. We have been very successful in engaging Aboriginal youth as leaders and participants in these initiatives. The following points are lessons we have learned that may help other organizations build on their work with Aboriginal youth

1. <u>Engaging Aboriginal youth requires specific and targeted strategies.</u> All of our projects have been implemented in mainstream secondary schools where there were similar pre-existing initiatives for which all youth (including Aboriginal youth) are eligible. It was not until we begin to specifically and proactively work to connect with Aboriginal youth that we were able engage them in significant numbers. Reaching a critical mass of Aboriginal students involved with these projects (rather than attracting one or two interested students) has provided important momentum for the project, even when challenges were encountered.

2. <u>Different youth will be engaged through different pathways.</u> Youth involved in our projects have identified a range of factors that influenced their decisions to become involved, including relationship-based factors, personal career goals, and specific interests. Using a range of approaches in identifying and recruiting potential participants will increase the number and diversity of the participants.

3. <u>Identify and recruit youth through their pre-existing relationships.</u> Many of the youth in our initiatives became involved through a personal invitation from an adult with whom they had a strong connection. In particular, the First Nations Counsellors in the schools were paramount in encouraging students to attend even an information session, and providing support as students contemplated becoming involved. Students identified their early contact with researchers and project staff as other important factors in deciding to commit to the project. Face-to-face meetings may be particularly important for these youth, rather than relying on information sheets and letters.

References

Blackstock, C., Clarke, S., Cullen, J., D'Hondt, J., & Formsma, J. (2004). *Keeping the promise: The convention on the rights of the child and the lived experiences of First Nations children and youth*. Ottawa, ON: First Nations Child and Family Caring Society of Canada.

Chandler, M. J. & Lalonde, C. E. (1998). *Cultural continuity as a hedge against suicide in Canada's First Nations*. Transcultural Psychiatry, 35, 193-211.

Chiodo, D. G., Crooks, C. V., McShane, M., Formsma, J., & Gosnell, G. (2006). *Successes and challenges in violence prevention programming with Aboriginal youth: The critical role of youth engagement*. London, ON: CAMH Centre for Prevention Science.

Gary, F., Baker, M., & Grandbois, D. (2005). *Perspectives on suicide prevention among American Indian and Alaska Native children and adolescents: A call for help*. Online Journal of Issues in Nursing, 10.

Gilchrist, L. D., Schinke, S. P., Trimble, J. E., & Cvetkovich, G. T. (1987). *Skills enhancement to prevent substance abuse among American Indian adolescents*. International Journal of the Addictions, 22, 869-879.

Greenberg, M. T., Domitrovich, C., & Bumberger, B. (2000). *Preventing mental disorders in school-aged children: A review of the effectiveness of prevention programs*. Washington, DC: Substance Abuse and Mental Health Services Administration, US Department of Health and Human Services.

Hawkins, E. H., Cummins, L. H., & Marlatt, G. A. (2004). *Preventing substance abuse in American Indian and Alaska Native youth: Promising strategies for healthier communities*. Psychological Bulletin, 130, 304-323.

LaFromboise, T. D., Coleman, H. L. K., & Gerton, J. (1993). *Psychological impact of bicultural competence: Rationale and application*. Psychological Bulletin, 114, 395-412.

Lipsey, M. W., & Cordray, D. S. (2000). *Evaluation methods for social intervention*. Annual Review of Psychology, 51, 345-375.

Milloy, J. S. (1999). *A national crime: The Canadian government and the residential school system 1879-1986*. Winnipeg, Canada: University of Manitoba Press.

National Aboriginal Health Organization (NAHO; undated). *Acting on what we know: Preventing youth suicide in First Nations. The report of the advisory group on suicide prevention*. First Nations Centre National Aboriginal Health Organization Briefing Note #FNC03-007. Ottawa: Author.

Rawana, J., Crooks, C. V., Chiodo, D., Hughes, R., & Pereira, J. (2006, March). *Engaging Aboriginal youth in school-based violence prevention*. Banff International Conference for Behavioural Science, Banff, AB.

Rawana, J., Pereira, J., Chiodo, D. G., Crooks, C. V., & Hughes, R. (2006). *The development and preliminary evaluation of a school-based mentoring program for Aboriginal youth*. Unpublished manuscript.

Rossi, P. H., Freeman, H. E., & Lipsey, M. W. (2003). *Evaluation: A systematic approach* (7th ed.). London: Sage.

Royal Commission on Aboriginal Peoples (1996). *Volume 3: Gathering strength, Chapter 5: Education*. Retrieved 03 June 05 from http://www.ainc-inac.gc.ca/ch/rcap/sg/si43_e.html#2.%20The%20Framework:%20Lifelong,%20Holistic%20Education.

Schinke, S. P., Botvin, G. J., Trimble, J. E., Orlandi, M. A., Gilchrist, L. D., & Locklear, V. S. (1988). *Preventing substance abuse among American-Indian adolescents: A bicultural competence skills approach*. Journal of Counselling Psychology, 35, 87-90.

Schnarch, B. (2004). *Ownership, control, access, and possession (OCAP) or self-determination applied to research: A critical analysis of contemporary First Nations research and some options for First Nations communities*. Journal of Aboriginal Health, 1, 80- 95.

Wolfe, D.A., Jaffe, P.G., & Crooks, C.V. (2006). *Adolescent risk behaviors: Why teens experiment and strategies to keep them safe*. New Haven, CT: Yale University Press.

Young, T. K. *(1994). The health of Native Americans: Towards a bicultural epidemiology*. Oxford: Oxford University Press.

Author Notes

The author wishes specifically to acknowledge the contributions of the First Nations Counsellors, administrators, and educators from the Thames Valley District School Board; members of the Advisory Board; fellow researchers and program developers from the CAMH Centre for Prevention Science; consultant Darren Thomas from the Six Nations Reserve; and the youth who have been involved in the different initiatives. This work has been funded by the Public Health Agency of Canada, the Government of Ontario through the Ministry of the Attorney General, and the London Community Foundation.

Chapter 11:

The Norwegian Manifesto Against Bullying: Opportunities, Challenges And Results On A National And School Level

Midthassel Unni Vere and Roland Erling,
Centre for Behavioural Research University of Stavanger

Introduction

The purpose of this chapter is to describe some of the opportunities, challenges, and results of the Norwegian Manifesto against bullying on a national and school level. The Manifesto was initiated by the Norwegian government. We review the national context, and the opportunities, and challenges that the Manifesto represented as well as discuss the prevalence of bullying during the Manifesto period. As part of the Manifesto, the Ministry of Education supported two anti-bullying programs. At the school level we will concentrate on the challenges of implementing the programs. To demonstrate the challenges, we use a case study of the work done in two schools who participated in the anti-bullying program Zero.

The Norwegian Manifesto Against Bullying

In September 2002, the Prime Minister of Norway launched the Manifesto Against Bullying. This initiative was not the first time the central authorities in Norway had taken action to reduce bullying. The first national initiative came in 1983 lead by two researchers, Dan Olweus and Elrling Roland, as a response to two suicides caused by bullying. The aim of this first initiative was to enhance competency in schools to deal with bullying. All elementary and lower secondary schools in Norway received a booklet (Olweus & Roland 1983) on bullying and what schools could do to reduce bullying behaviour. A film was also made available to all schools. The major achievement of this first national campaign however, was a survey conducted in 1983. For the first time ever, national data on bullying were collected. Two follow-up studies were conducted: Olweus conducted a study in schools in the city of Bergen, and Roland conducted a study in the county of Rogaland. Olweus reported positive effects of the intervention two years later (Olweus,

1991). In contrast, results from the Rogaland survey showed that schools were finding it difficult to commit to long-term anti-bullying strategies (Roland, 1989). One explanatory factor for these differences may be that the schools in Bergen had received visits from the researcher, giving them feedback and discussing further work with them, whereas no follow up had been given to the Rogaland schools.

The next national initiative to prevent bullying began in 1996. This initiative was motivated by several headlines and articles in the newspapers about severe bullying in schools and questions by the public regarding what the authorities were doing to combat this problem. A national representative survey conducted by the Centre for Behavioural Research (CBR) indicated that bullying was still a problem in Norway. The Centre was asked to design a strategy for anti-bullying work in schools, with the primary aim of building competence in children and youth, while at the same time supporting professionals in schools. The focus was broader this time with a stronger focus on prevention (Roland & Vaaland, 1996). For example, material was created for students' councils in schools emphasizing the role of the bystander. Furthermore, a network of 350 professionals was trained to support schools. There were some challenges with this model of trained trainers supporting the schools. The trainers were dependent on schools' contacting them for help. As many of the trainers were teachers themselves, there was no time scheduled for their work with other schools. Therefore, support from these trainers varied greatly (Midthassel, 1997).

The Manifesto launched by the Prime Minister in 2002, differed in significant ways from previous initiatives. First, the Manifesto was a partnership venture, with collaborations between both governmental and nongovernmental organizations. The partnership consisted of the Government, the Union of Municipalities, the Teachers' Union, the Parents' Union and the Ombudsman for Children. Together they signed the Manifesto stating that they would cooperate on a "zero vision" of bullying. According to a "zero vision", bullying is not tolerated in any form and has to be dealt with in a constructive but firm way.

The partnership involved a much broader focus compared to the previous initiatives. All the partners initiated anti-bullying measures intended for their target groups. The Manifesto period was stipulated to last for two years and was led by the Ministry of Education. The Minister established an expert group who met regularly and who also had meetings with the Manifesto partners several times a year. The aim of this was to report on the work and to discuss important matters related to the Manifesto. One central initiative was to support two anti-bullying programs, namely the "Olweus program" developed by the Olweus group at the University of Bergen and the "Zero program" developed at the CBR at the University of Stavanger. Schools were encouraged to participate in one of these programs. Both of these Norwegian programs were based on the work by Olweus and Roland (1983).

National, representative data from primary and secondary schools on bullying are available from 1995 to 2004. The CBR collected these data by questionnaires to pupils in spring 1995, 1998, 2001 and 2004. These data indicated a worrisome trend, bullying and victimization were increasing over time. In 1995, the number of students being bullied or bullying others weekly or more often was about 5%, which had been a national level for a long period (Olweus 1993; Roland 1999). For some unknown reason, the number of both children and youth reporting either being victimized or bullying others increased approximately 35% from 1995 to 1998. The curve continued to climb steeply and the result from 2001 showed an increase of approximately 70% from 1995. This result was subject to heavy media exposure and added fuel to a call for a strong national initiative, which became the Manifesto Against Bullying. Both His Royal Highness King Harald and the Prime Minister, in their New Year speeches, expressed concern about the alarming increase in bullying.

During the first Manifesto period, 2002-04, the bullying trend data shifted. The 2004 data indicated a 30% reduction in both bullying and victimization rates. The Prime Minister, announced these findings in a national conference aimed at summarizing the work as a result of the Manifesto. It is not possible, of course, to attribute this reduction to the Manifesto. There is evidence however that indicated a positive effect from the national initiative. According to CBR data, between 70% and 80% of schools increased their efforts to combat bullying during the Manifesto period. A report describing the national and local activities has been published (Tikkanen & Junge, 2004).

Opportunities and challenges at school level

The Manifesto gave schools the opportunity to focus on bullying. Programs, material, and funding were made available and the national expectations and support were emphasized. Research however has shown that a top-down approach needs a bottom up response to be successful (e.g., Fullan 2001; Stoll, MacBeath, Smith & Robertson, 2001). Although a well documented program with user friendly material and external support provides significant resources to schools, the implementation process depends on the involvement of staff, students, and parents. Such a whole school approach however, is challenging. Research in Norway has shown more variation between teachers within schools than between schools in their involvement in school development activities (Midthassel, Manger & Torsheim, 2002). Even when all staff members participate, the level of engagement differs within schools (Midthassel & Bru 2001).

Overcoming the challenges of whole school involvement is vital to the success of the work. These challenges exist at both the individual and organizational level. Individual and organizational elements have proved to be of importance for teacher involvement in development projects (Larsen, 2005; Midthassel 2004). The figure below shows some of the challenges and their assumed relationships.

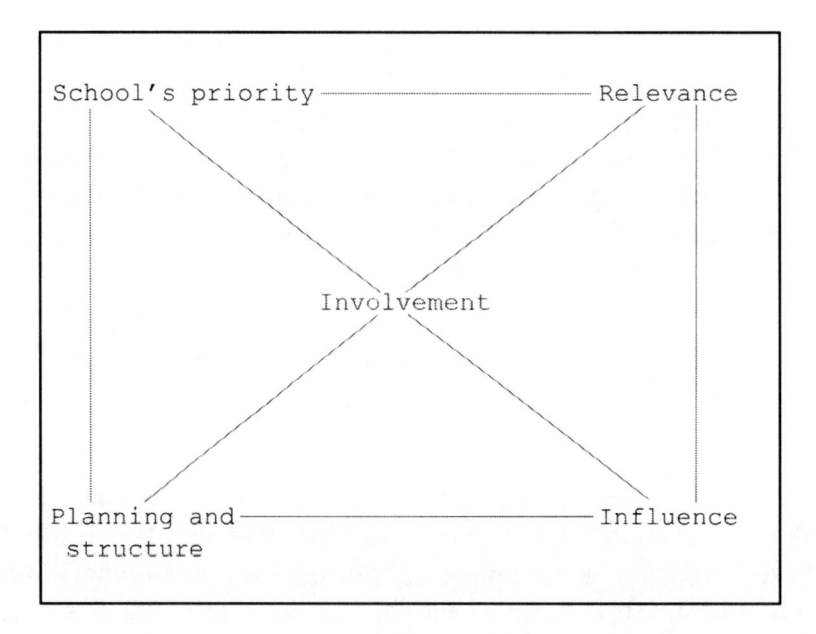

```
School's priority ─────────── Relevance
         ╲              ╱
          ╲            ╱
           ╲          ╱
            Involvement
           ╱          ╲
          ╱            ╲
         ╱              ╲
Planning and ─────────── Influence
structure
```

Schools' Priorities

Teachers and schools in most countries experience multiple initiatives and demands for improvement and change. The danger associated with these demands is the teachers become overloaded and programs may be fragmented (Hargreaves & Hopkins, 1994; Fullan, 2001; Midthassel, 2004). To avoid these problems, the school and principal need to prioritize projects (Midthassel, Bru, & Idsoe, 2000; Midthassel & Bru, 2001; Midthassel & Ertesvåg accepted). With the Norwegian Manifesto, the authorities had instructed schools to prioritize anti-bullying work and the two programs supported by the central authorities were offered to the schools. Nonetheless, it is important to consider the degree to which the school's own priorities would be in line with this priority. In his book of 1991, readiness is one of the themes Fullan holds as important in the initiation of a change. Readiness encompasses capacity and need. If the school is already engaged in other projects, its capacity to carry out another program introduced from outside sources may be limited. Furthermore, there is a question of need within the school. For example, how well does the program fit or match the current needs at the school? Readiness to engage will be compromised if the needs are not met by the program proposed.

Planning and Structure

A whole school approach requires that everyone is involved in the planning and the activities. In an ordinary school day the planning and structures mostly are concerned with the core activities: teaching classes and monitoring students' work. Although collaboration between colleagues has increased over the years, traditionally, it is one teacher executing her/his planning in the classroom. Researchers have characterized schools and professional organizations as loosely coupled systems (Weick, 1976; Mintzberg, 1979; 1989) that often find innovation challenging to address and implement. A whole school approach requires planning and cooperative work across classes, between staff, and between parents and the school. Consequently, structures are needed that support work beyond the normal collaboration groups. This organization also requires ongoing monitoring, and follow-up as well as strong leadership to ensure that planned activity takes place. Without such structures, routines, and follow up, the principal may have misperceptions of the level of staff involvement (Midthassel & Bru 2001; Larsen, 2005).

Relevance of the Program

Teachers tend to be more involved in projects if they think their investment will pay off compared to projects where they believe the investment will have a limited impact (Midthassel, 2004). In Norway, the central initiative and the new legislation made anti-bullying work more relevant than in previous years. Anti-bullying work was a high priority on the agenda and teachers could be held responsible for not investigating bullying incidents. We also know however, that teachers tend to engage in activities which will be a direct help in their classrooms (Fullan 2001; Louis & Kruse,1998; McLaughlin 1990; Midthassel and Bru 2001). Therefore, how they perceive bullying or a negative climate among students is likely to influence their judgement of how relevant this anti-bullying work is. Furthermore, the school's culture of innovation has been identified as an important element of change (e.g., Stoll et al. 2001; Midthassel, Bru & Idsøe, 2000). Teachers' perception of the innovation culture influences teachers' involvement in school development activities (Midthassel 2004).

Influence

Being able to influence work makes it more meaningful and therefore increases motivation (Midthassel, 2006). Although research indicates that programs with user-friendly materials are an advantage in the implementation process (Reynolds 1998), one might assume that teachers' sense of ownership of the program will increase if their professional knowledge and experience will have some influence on the work (Fullan 2001; Stoll et al. 2001). Furthermore, research has shown that loyalty to a program is another challenge and there seem to be a balance between loyalty and the freedom to adapt programs to the actual situation (Larsen, 2005).

Experiences from Two Schools – A Case Study

To show how the different challenges might affect schools, we draw on experiences from one combined school and one secondary school that participated in the Zero-program from May 2003 until September 2004. We consider the schools' priorities, planning and structure, relevance, influence, and involvement. We also report changes in bullying behaviour among the students at the two schools from 2003 to 2004.

The combined school was situated in a rural coastal area, a municipality with 2000 inhabitants. The school had 220 students from first to tenth grade and 28 teachers. This school had a female principal who had been in her position for one and a half years when the school started the program. The secondary school was situated in a large inland municipality with 24000 inhabitants. The school had 270 pupils from 8th to 10th grade and 25 staff members. This school had a male principal who had been in his position one and a half years when this school started the program. The two schools were part of a larger case study including six schools. We have chosen these two schools to show differences in the way schools handled the program.

Data collection

Group interviews were conducted with the project groups in the two schools in November 2003 and March 2004. Additionally, telephone interviews with the principals were carried out in February 2004. In all schools participating in the program, six professionals were asked to answer a questionnaire in June 2004 about the anti-bullying work going on during the program period. The professionals who completed the questionnaire comprised representatives from: the leadership, the teacher union's, the safety deputy, and three ordinary teachers. Although reminders were sent to the schools, the numbers of returned questionnaires differed. From the two schools in this study four professionals from the secondary and only two professionals from the combined school returned the questionnaires. Therefore, data from this survey are used with caution and only to shed further light on data collected through interviews. As part of the program, all students at the schools answered anonymously one questionnaire about bullying in school in May 2003 and another in May 2004 (Roland, Bru, Midthassel & Vaaland submitted). The themes for the questionnaires were bullying behaviour, places where bullying behaviour occurred, who they would tell about the bullying, and perceived safety and happiness at school. In this chapter, only the variables "bully others" and "being bullied" are presented. Each variable consists of four items: one global item concerning bullying behaviour and three items describing specific bullying behaviours: teasing, isolating and hitting/kicking. A student who responded positively to one or more of the four items was counted as one person (bully / victim). In the questionnaires, the students were given this definition of bullying: *"By bullying we mean physical and/or mental aggression towards a victim, carried out by individuals or groups. Bullying assumes an unequal relationship of strength between the victim and the bully and episodes which are repeated over time"* (Roland & Vaaland 1996). The students were asked to mark one of the following categories: 'never', 'once in a while', 'weekly', 'every day' (computed from 1-4). Descriptive computing mean and frequencies were used. To compare results from 2003 to 2004 comparison of means and comparison of frequencies for the weekly and every day bullying behaviours are reported.

Results

School's Priority

Results from the interviews showed that at the combined school the Zero-program was the only project this year and therefore, highly focused. The principal was the leader of the project group and highlighted her role in pushing the program forward. She was a former school leader at district level and felt that she was clever at leading processes. She also described her staff as being very loyal to decisions made. Moreover, she perceived her task to be easy with a lot of enthusiasm from the parents. At this school, they signed a local version of the Manifesto which was reported in the local paper. This picture of a highly prioritized program was also supported by the two professionals who returned their questionnaire in June. They perceived very few obstacles to implementing the program.

Also, at the secondary school the principal was the leader of the project group. From his perspective, the program was important and in the autumn he had a lot of plans. His engagement came into conflict however, with his wish not to push his staff too hard since they also had other urgent things to focus on, for example, a low rank on the academic ranking list. The four professionals who returned their questionnaire in June reported the activities among students, parents, and teachers to be moderately prioritized throughout the year. At this school, the obstacles to carrying out the program were relatively high compared to other schools; the main obstacles being shortage of time, lack of response from the students' council and difficulties integrating the program into everyday school life.

Planning and Structure

As part of the Zero-program all teachers attended a one-day course on bullying and the project group within the school attended five additional seminars. The schools received results from a survey on bullying in the school prior to the program, identifying the challenges for each school. Furthermore, the schools were entitled to assistance and advice from professionals in Zero throughout the 14 months of the program. The project groups were supposed to make plans for the work in school and put in place structures for following up the work. As the Zero Program is guided by principles rather than a manual, it required an active project group and firm leadership planning the work in school. The schools received material for use by teachers, for the students' council, and for parents. They also received a detailed description of how to make an action plan against bullying through an extended process involving all staff.

Results from the interviews showed that in the combined school the project group planned the work throughout the year and had regular meetings. When questioned one year after the initiation of the program, the two professionals from the staff perceived the project group to have an important role in the anti-bullying work. The staff worked on the action plan in line with the descriptions given, which implied that discussions in colleague groups had priority in the staff's time for planning throughout the winter. Moreover, the anti-bullying work was integrated into daily activity. For instance, in this school they had already established a gathering for all students once a week. Once the program started, they used time in these gatherings to focus on preventing bullying. They also used sports activities and excursions to focus on building positive relationships.

At the secondary school there were no regular meetings of the project group and the survey among staff suggested that the project group's role was moderate. There were a significant number of plans, but these were not followed up with the exception of the use of reflective vests. This practice became a routine. Feeling that the description of the action plan was too extensive, the principal planned a smaller version involving all staff at a seminar and assigned two teachers the responsibility of completing the plan. Although the project group described the seminar as successful, the completion of the plan was drawn out and it was not finished by the last interview in March.

Relevance

Results from the interviews revealed that at the combined school there had been a severe bullying case some years earlier. This incident had involved the whole school and much of the community. The case had been exposed in the media and the school had been criticized for their handling of the problem. This unpleasant experience led to systematic anti-bullying work involving staff, parents, and students and they contacted experts to help them with the work. Since then the school had a new principal who continued the anti-bullying work. When the school received the invitation from the Zero-program the principal discussed this invitation with her staff and the conclusion was that even though they were already working systematically on anti-bullying work they recognized the importance of this invitation. They wanted to ensure that they did the right things and felt that participation in the program would help them to institutionalize their anti-bullying work. In addition, the parents' council strongly supported becoming involved in the program.

Also at the secondary school bullying had been a problem. From the interviews, we learned that they had experienced a great deal of bullying and other unacceptable behaviour the year prior to the program. The principal felt the lack of competence among staff as well as lack of routines contributed to the high prevalence of bullying, consequently he applied to be involved in the program. However, the students responsible for most of the behaviour problems had left school soon after the program started and by the autumn of 2004 the remaining students did not have the level of behavioural problems that were challenging the teachers. Consequently, it is uncertain whether the teachers now felt the same need for more competence.

Influence

Although the program provided materials, and courses and seminars, the schools were requested to plan their local activity based on local challenges. Even if the program prescribed preventative work in class, there was no manual for this work. The teachers could find ideas in the material, but there was room for local influence. In the Zero-program, the work on the action plan was supposed to involve all staff and the work procedures described aimed at securing teacher influence.

The interviews showed that in the combined school, which followed the description on the action plan, allowing the individual teachers to be heard, the staff reported that they were content with the process and the plan. At the secondary school, which minimized teacher involvement on the plan, the staff reported to being only moderately satisfied with the process and the result.

Involvement

From the interviews, we got the impression that at the combined school there was significant activity among students, parents, and staff. They reported high levels of engagement among parents in the parents' council. The parents' council initiated activities among the students and informed all the parents of the program at parents' evenings in the different class groups. The two parents in the project group were active and very enthusiastic about the opportunity for the school to participate in this program. They gave important support to the principal and ensured that the work was done. Together with the school leadership, the parents also involved the driver of the school bus, since incidents of bullying had taken place on the bus. The two students in the project group visited all classes and talked about the program and ensured that the students' council was involved, using the material created for them and discussing themes in the classes. All staff used reflective vests when on duty as part of the program and they were supposed to follow up the program in lessons and in meetings with individual students and their parents.

At the secondary school the situation was quite different. While the opportunities were the same, the interviews revealed that the challenges were greater than in combined school. In spite of some attempts from the principal, the parents did not become involved in the program, either in the project group or through activities. The principal suggested that the leader of the parent council was too busy and that the majority of parents were not interested in addressing bullying. There were three students in the project group who had irregular participation in the project groups' seminars. In spite of this, the three students were enthusiastic and had a lot of plans, for example, a seminar for the students' council and for a system of pupil guards in the playground. None of their plans were put into effect, with the exception of the use of reflective vests and the seminar when the staff worked on the action plan. The project group did not know much about the anti-bullying work in their school, because it was entirely up to the individual teacher in their classes. The principal did not follow up on what work was conducted in the classrooms.

Changes in Bullying Behaviour in the Two Schools from 2003 to 2004

At both schools, bullying behaviour and victimization decreased during the first year of the program. At the combined school the mean score of 'bully others' decreased from 1.51 to 1.36, $F = 6.42$, $p = .012$. At the secondary school the decrease was from 1.84 to 1.75, $t = 1.51$, $p =$ ns. For the variable 'being bullied' the decrease at the combined school was from 1.71 to 1.52, $F = 5.26$, $p = .022$. Corresponding results at the secondary school were 1.69 to 1.55, $F = 4.06$, $p. = .05$). 'Being bullied' weekly or more often went down 33% at the combined school, from 13.7% to 9.1% and 28% at the secondary school, from 11.5% to 8.3%. Results from a test of differences in change scores between the two schools showed no differences between the schools.

Discussion

The results suggest differences between the two schools in the elements which are assumed to influence involvement, as well as in actual involvement in the program. Although both schools had experienced severe bullying, which should have made participation in the program relevant, the two schools' addressed the problem differently. At the combined school, the experience resulted in systematic anti-bullying work that began before attending this program. Furthermore, when the program was offered to the school, the principal saw this as an opportunity to continue and institutionalize their anti-bullying work. Moreover, it is assumed that their previous work made the planning and the required structures in the program period more easily obtainable. Consequently, the Zero Program did not require significant energy from the staff. For instance, while many schools experience difficulties concerning parental involvement in programs, the parents in the combined school acted as a motivating force for the school. Prioritizing this program was agreed upon among staff and parents and the staff was given the opportunity to influence the program through the work on the action plan. In line with the assumption that these elements are critical for involvement, the interviews at both times revealed significant activity involving staff, parents, and students in this school.

An overall impression from the interviews at the secondary school was that the challenges in the school paralyzed the anti-bullying work and it is uncertain whether the staff really wanted to put any significant effort into the program. The interviews indicated that the principal wanted to increase the staff's competence in addressing bullying and hoped that using this program would be helpful. He was aware of the instructions from the central authorities and he also knew that his staff needed to develop greater competence in this area. His aims to increase the staff's competence however, may have come in conflict with his wish not to push his staff too hard on this issue since the school's low academic ranking was also a problem. This hesitant role may have limited the success of the program. The principal did not succeed in signalling the program's importance nor did he use the project group to plan and carry out activities which would have given the staff and students influence in the process. In fact, the lack of follow-up activities may have inadvertently signalled that this was a low priority project. These signals together with fewer behaviour problems from the students during the relevant school year and a lack of pressure from the parents might have reduced the staff's sense urgency regarding anti-bullying work.

Although the two schools' implementation of the program was very different, their change in bullying behaviours did not vary significantly. This might be surprising and needs comment. Given the level of involvement and activity in the combined school, a decrease in bullying behaviour could be expected whereas this was not expected at the secondary school. There is reason to believe that the natural departure of a group of challenging boys can partially explain the result. Therefore, while we can assume that the implementation of the program had some impact on the result achieved at the combined school it is likely that there were other explanations and factors at work in the secondary school.

Summary

The Manifesto provided an important window of opportunity for anti-bullying work in Norwegian schools, however, our experience indicates significant challenges remain to the implementation of the Manifesto. A program needs to be research-based and provide user-friendly material of a high standard, as well as, being delivered appropriately (Fullan 2001; Greenberg, Domitrovich, Graczyk and Zins, 2002). Program developers may be able to control these elements. The real challenges for a program may be in interacting with a school system and the professionals such as teachers. Our study highlights the importance of the role of the schools context, the school system, and the challenges associated with whole school involvement. The successful implementation of programs relies on learning how the new competence is used, and we only have limited information on this.

It is not possible to say precisely whether and in what way the Manifesto helped schools in their anti-bullying work. There is evidence however, that between 70% and 80% of schools increased their efforts to address bullying in their schools. A strong national concern supported by the government and the Ministry of Education is important for the effort. The leap from this support to the quality implementation of the identified programs is a long step. The quality of implementation is influenced by the resources available to support the program. The Manifesto contributed resources by subsidising the cost for schools of adopting either the Olweus Program or the Zero Program. Quality, however, also is about knowing how to prevent and intervene, and how to bring about successful implementation. The Manifesto partners relied on a long and strong Norwegian research tradition on bullying and on well-developed programs being accessible. Subsequently, they profited from reasonably well-informed principals and teachers on bullying issues (Roland 2000). Latent competence in the schools was activated by the Manifesto. Our case studies, however, indicate that schools differ in their ability to implement a program to combat bullying among the students and these differences in prioritizing, involvement, monitoring, and follow-up may be important elements in successful programs to prevent bullying.

Key Messages

1. A national initiative creates important opportunities for bullying prevention work in schools.

2. A national initiative is not a guarantee for the successful implementation of bullying prevention work in schools.

3. The successful implementation of bullying prevention work requires prioritizing of the work; involvement of all staff, parents, and students; and monitoring that the work is being done.

References

Chan, J. H. F. (2006). *Systemic patterns in bullying and victimization. School Psychology International*, 27(3), 352-369.

Fullan, M. (2001). *The new meaning of educational change* (3 ed.). New York: Teacher College Press.

Greeenberg, M. T., Domitrovich, C. E., Graczyk, P. A., & Zins, J. E. (2001). *A conceptual model of implementation for school-based prevention interventions: implications for research, practice and policy*: Draft copy.

Hargreaves, D. (2001). *A capital theory of school effectiveness and improvement.* British Educational Research Journal, 27(4), 487-503.

Hargreaves, D., & Hopkins, D. (Eds.). (1994). *Development planning for school improvement.* London: Cassell.

Larsen, T. (2005). *Evaluating principals' and teachers' implementation of second step.* University of Bergen, Stavanger.

Louis, K., & Kruse, S. D. (1998). *Creating community in reform: images of organizational learning in inner-city schools.* In K. Louis & S. Kruse (Eds.), *Organizational learning in schools.* The Netherlands: Swets & Zeitlinger.

McLaughlin, M. (1990). *The Rand Agent Study:Revisited: Macro Perspectives and Micro Realities.* Educational Researcher, 19(9), 11-16.

Midthassel, U. V. (1997). *KUFs ressurspersoner mot mobbing - erfaringer og idéskisse.* Stavanger: Senter for atferdsforskning, Høgskolen i Stavanger.

Midthassel, U. V. (2004). *Teacher involvement in school development activity and its relationships to attitudes and subjective norsm among teachers: A study of Norwegian Elementary and Junior High school teachers.* Educational Administration Quarterly, 40(3), 435-456.

Midthassel, U. V. (2006). *Creating a shared understanding of classroom management.* Educational Management Administration & Leadership, 34(3), 365-383.

Midthassel, U., & Bru, E. (2001). *Predictors and gains of teacher involvement in an improvement project on classroom management. Experiences from a Norwegian project in two compulsory schools.* Educational Psychology, 21(3), 229-242.

Midthassel, U., Bru, E., & Idsøe, T. (2000). *The Principal's role in promoting school development activity in Norwegian compulsory schools*. School Leadership and Management, 20(2), 147-160.

Midthassel, U. V., & Ertesvåg, S. (accepted). *Schools implementing Zero. The process of implementing an antibullying program in six Norwegian schools*. Accepted for publication in Journal of Educational Change.

Midthassel, U., Manger, T., & Torsheim, T. (2002). *Community effects on teacher involvement in school development activity: a study of teachers in cities, smaller towns and rural areas in Norway*. Reserearch Papers in Education, 17(3), 293-303.

Mintzberg, H. (1979). *The structuring of organizations*. Englewood Cliffs NJ: Prentice-Hall.

Mintzberg, H. (1989). *Mintzberg on Management*. New York: The FreePress.

Norway, S. (1994). *Standard classification of municipalities 1994*. Oslo: Statistics Norway.

Olweus, D. (1993). *Bullying at school: what we know and what we can do*. Oxford: Blackwell.

Olweus, D., & Roland, E. (1983). *Mobbing - bakgrunn og tiltak*. Oslo: Kirke- undervisnings- og forskningsdepartementet.

Olweus, D. (1991). *Bully/victim problems among school children: Basic facts and effects of a school-based intervention program*. In D. Pepler & K. H. Rubin (Eds.), *The development and treatment of childhood aggression*. Hilldale, NJ: Erlbaum.

Reynolds, D. (1998). *"World class" school improvement: An analysis of the implications of resent international school effectiveness and school improvement research for improvement of practice*. In A. Hargreaves, A. Lieberman, M. Fullan & D. Hopkins (Eds.), *International Handbook of Educational Change*. London: Kluwer Academic Publisher Group.

Roland, E. (1989). *Tre år senere*. Stavanger: Centre for Behavioural Research.

Roland, E. (1999). *School influences on bullying*. Stavanger: Rebell forlag.

Roland, E. (2000). *Bullying in school: Three national innovations in Norwegian schools in 15 years*. Aggressive Behavior, 26(1), 135-143.

Roland, E., Bru, E., Midthassel, U. V., & Vaaland, G. S. (submitted). *Anti-bullying efforts in Norway 2001-2004*.

Roland, E., & Vaaland, G. S. (1996). *Mobbing i skolen. En lærerveiledning*. Oslo: Kirke-Undervisnings- og Forskningsdepartementet.

Stoll, L., Macbeath, J., Smith, I., & Robertson, P. (2001). *The change equation*. In J. Macbeath & P. Mortimore (Eds.), *Improving school effectiveness*. Buckingham: Open University Press.

Tikkanen, T., & Junge, A. (2004). *Realisering av en visjon om et mobbefritt oppvekstmiljø for barn og unge*. Stavanger: RF- Rogalandsforskning.

Weick, K. (1976). *Educational organizations as loosely coupled systems*. Administrative Science Quarterly, 21, pp.1-19.

Chapter 12:

Bullying in Kindergarten and Prevention

Françoise D. Alsaker and Christof Nägele
University of Berne

Introduction

Studies addressing the issue of bullying during the preschool years or in kindergarten are still extremely rare, especially as compared to the growing literature in this domain regarding older school children. The questions typically asked by parents, teachers, and even researchers concerning bullying in kindergarten can be summarized as follows: Can bullying already occur at this age? Are there valid and reliable ways to measure it? And if the first two questions are answered positively, the next question to arise is: are we really talking about the same phenomenon as in older children?

Our own earlier studies and a few other studies tell us that bullying occurs in preschool and kindergarten. Bullying has been observed, for example, in day-care centers in Norway (Alsaker, 1993a, 1993b), in kindergarten in the United States (Kochenderfer and Ladd, 1996) and in Switzerland (Alsaker, 2003; Alsaker & Valkanover, 2001). However, we still need more precise knowledge concerning the similarities in bullying between younger and older children, the impact that bullying and victimization has on younger children's well-being, and the stability of the roles before and during the transition to elementary school.

The study of bullying and victimization in kindergarten opens up new opportunities to understand early processes in the pathways to victimization, and to investigate different social and individual risk factors and their interactions in the very beginnings of bullying behaviour patterns. Furthermore, knowledge of early risk factors may contribute to the improvement of prevention programs and especially add to our arguments regarding the implementation of such programs in kindergarten and elementary school. In order to answer the above mentioned questions, a longitudinal project, "Pathways to Victimization", was launched by the first author in the canton of Berne, Switzerland, in 2003. The project is still ongoing and aims at addressing a very broad range of issues such as: the possible impact of biological or medical problems, personality and cognitive factors, social skills, family variables, classroom settings, teachers' attitudes and behaviours; as well as the possible negative outcomes, such as depressive symptoms and psychosomatic complaints. In the present chapter, we limit our presentation to findings that may provide information about similarities and differences in the bullying experiences of kindergarten as compared to older school children. In addition, we present the prevention program that was used in 36 kindergartens and some preliminary results regarding its effectiveness.

Three Central Features of Bullying and Research Questions

One of the agreed-upon features of bullying is that it is an aggressive behaviour systematically oriented against specific children (Rigby, Smith, & Pepler, 2004) and that it lasts for extended periods of time. Consequently, in studies involving school children, authors have often used a rather strict criterion to categorize children as involved in bullying others or in being victimized: bullying or victimization should occur at least once a week (see Smith et al., 1999). Thus, the first question we want to examine in the present chapter is whether it is possible to categorize children according to this criterion in kindergarten and how percentages match existing results for older children. Although frequency is not necessarily the main criterion for negative outcomes - as less frequent bullying also may harm children who are especially vulnerable (Kochenderfer-Ladd & Ladd, 2001) - it may be an appropriate criterion in order to compare the occurrence of bullying in different age groups. While Kochenderfer and Ladd (1996) clearly demonstrated the existence of bullying in kindergarten, their use of an averaged score did not permit a direct comparison with the common frequency-oriented results. In the study conducted by the first author in 18 kindergartens (n = 344) in the city of Berne in Switzerland in 1997, the frequency criteria were used in questionnaires given to the teachers (Alsaker & Valkanover, 2001). The results showed that teachers were able to designate or identify children who bullied others or who were victimized at least once a week during a three-month period and their reports corresponded well with children's nominations of children who fit these same designations, as explained later in this chapter (Alsaker & Valkanover, 2001; Perren & Alsaker, 2006). Furthermore, as will be presented in the following sections, we found highly comparable percentages of victimized students among kindergarten and older school children (Alsaker, 2003). Still we wanted to test whether these earlier results could be replicated in a much larger and more diverse sample six years later. Also, as the peer-nomination interview was very time consuming, we wanted to develop a new procedure for teachers and compare results from both studies.

A second central issue focuses on role-differentiation. Most researchers differentiate between "bullies" (bullying others and are not victimized), "passive victims" (are victimized and do not bully), and "bully-victims" or "aggressive victims" (are victimized and bully others) (e.g., Olweus, 1993a; Salmivalli, Lagerspetz, Björkqvist, Österman, & Kaukiainen, 1996; Rigby, 1996; Schwartz, 2000). In this chapter, we examine whether we can find comparable roles in kindergarten. In order to do so, we address individual characteristics of children endorsing the different roles and their acceptance in the group. As we know from earlier studies, children who bully and those who both bully and are victimized are characterized by aggressive behaviour, but these two groups seem to differ in terms of the type of aggression they display. Children involved only in bullying are supposed to be more instrumental, whereas those involved in both bullying and being bullied use aggressive behaviour reactively (Pellegrini, 1998). In fact, Salmivalli and Nieminen (2002) reported school-aged children who both bullied and were victimized to be the most aggressive children of all, both in terms of proactive and reactive aggression. These dually involved children have also been found to show more oppositional defiant behaviour (Kokkinos & Panayiotou, 2004). In our earlier study, kindergarten teachers reported children who both bullied and were bullied to use physical aggression even more often than those who only bullied, whereas these two groups of aggressive children did not differ in their use of other forms of aggression (Perren & Alsaker, 2006). As to acceptance by peers, in terms of being liked or rejected, most studies have found victimization and rejection by peers (in terms of sociometric status) to be highly correlated (see Salmivalli & Isaacs, 2005). For example, Ladd and Troop-Gordon (2003) reported rejection to be predictive of later victimization and victimization of later peer rejection. In most studies, which have been primarily conducted with school-age samples, there has been no differentiation between those children who are only victimized and those who are both victimized and bully others.

Results from a variety of studies seem to suggest an association between being dually involved in bullying and victimization and some neuropsychological impairments (Olweus, 1999) or at least symptoms of ADHD, especially in terms of hyperactivity (Kumpulainen et al, 1998; Schwartz, 2000). Again, these results were obtained in studies on school-aged children. As a result of their hyperactivity, victimized aggressive children might act in rather disturbing ways and break social norms in the peer group to a larger extent than other aggressive children. In kindergarten, our first results indicated that victimized aggressive children had problems with maintaining attention on different tasks and their parents reported more perinatal problems (Alsaker, 2003). Thus results from different studies seem to converge and draw a picture of victimized aggressive children as rather different from both children involved only in bullying others or in being bullied. Since most studies of bullying among younger children (e.g., Crick. Casas, & Ku, 1999; Kochenderfer & Ladd, 1996; Monks, Ortega, & Torrado, 2002) have not differentiated between passive and aggressive victimized children, little is known about victimized aggressive children at a younger age. As noted by Schwartz, Proctor, and Chien in 2001, we do not yet have an accurate description of victimized aggressive children. One of the major aims of the ongoing study is to provide a fairly detailed picture of these children before they enter school.

The third and final issue to be addressed in this chapter – before we turn to the prevention program - regards the psychological wellbeing of children who are directly involved in bullying, either in bullying others or in being victimized. The negative consequences of victimization in schoolchildren are well documented (Rigby, 2003). Among other things, school- aged children who are victimized (including victimized aggressive children) are generally more depressed than children who bully without being victimized and non-involved children (Alsaker, 2006). Also in the first Bernese Kindergarten study, teachers reported both types of victimized children as seemingly unhappy (Alsaker, 2003). A Swedish study also strongly suggested that early victimization had causal long-term effects on the individual's propensity to experience depression, independent of victimization experiences in adulthood (Olweus, 1993b). In this chapter, we want to address the negative impact of victimization in terms of depressive symptoms.

How do We Measure Bullying in Kindergarten?

Research on bullying among older school children is typically based on self-report questionnaires. As demonstrated in two earlier studies (Alsaker & Valkanover, 2001; Kochenderfer & Ladd, 1996), self-report techniques are not really appropriate in assessing victimization in kindergarten. Young children typically see themselves as having been victimized (around 70 to 75%), while they are rather reticent to tell about their role in bullying others. Another problem arises in assessing victimization by means of peer nominations. The very first study conducted with 120 preschool children in Bergen, Norway in 1990 (Alsaker, 1993a), demonstrated that children were not able to designate children who were victimized when asked directly. They could easily nominate children who systematically bullied other children, but when asked: "are there children who get bullied by others", they often could not nominate any child. The teachers, however, were able to indicate typical victims.

In our earlier Bernese study, teachers rated each child on four victimization and four bullying items (physical, verbal, property-oriented, and exclusion), using a 5-point rating scale (never, seldom, once or several times a month, once a week, several times a week). In order to compare our findings with previous research with older children, our young students were categorized as primarily "bullying" when they reportedly bullied other children at least once a week in one form or another, but were not victimized. Students categorized as having been victimized met the opposite criteria, and children who met both criteria were classified as victimized aggressive students. Children were interviewed individually so that the interviewers explained the term bullying by means of four drawings, each depicting a different form of bullying (physical, verbal, property-related, or exclusion; see also Alsaker & Valkanover, 2001). Using photographs of all children in the class, we asked each child to nominate children who bullied others and to indicate the targets of these aggressive behaviours. This was never a problem. Children knew very well who the targets of the bullying were, when asked in this manner. The nominations received – for children who bullied and were victimized - were transformed into percentages of possible nominations in the class and – in order to make scores comparable across classes – they were standardized (z-scores according to the class and the whole sample). Children were categorized as being victimized or as bullying when their standardized scores were higher than one standard deviation above the mean for their class and for the whole sample. The two measures (teachers' reports and peer nominations) were then combined. Only 18 children could not be categorized due to major non-agreements between teachers' reports and peer nominations. Interestingly, detailed analyses of the non-agreements showed that the teachers' reports seemed to give the most accurate information (Alsaker, 2003).

A usual statistical problem in research on bullying and victimization problems is that the number of children who are categorized as bullying others or being victimized is relatively low compared to non-involved children. For the present study, we wanted to conduct in-depth interviews of children who were involved in some role, either bullying others, being victimized or both, we decided to screen children prior to interviews. In order to screen a large number of children, we had to decide on a more cost-effective assessment method than the one described above. Another issue that urged us to develop a more economical measure was the frequent requests from practitioners concerning "easy-to-use" measures to assess bullying in different settings.

On the basis of our earlier findings concerning the correspondence between peer nominations and kindergarten teachers' reports and the superiority of teachers' reports in cases of disagreement, we decided to use teachers' reports. However, even if the results generally indicated that teachers' reports were valid, some caveat remained. It seemed that teachers had difficulties in distinguishing bullying from conflicts (Alsaker, 2003). Therefore, the method had to be refined. Thus, in the ongoing study, prior to data collection, teachers were offered a workshop (one workshop for all teachers participating in the study in every community included in the project), during which they received information about bullying. This workshop corresponded to the first module of our prevention program: sensitizing teachers to the phenomenon of bullying, instructing them in depicting indicators of bullying situations and in some observation techniques. We also pointed out the differences between bullying behaviour and conflicts. The teachers were invited to read the questionnaires and make comments on the items, ask clarifying questions etc. They then took the questionnaires with them, one for each child. This procedure clearly added to the validity of our measure, since we wanted to assess bullying and victimization and not conflicts in general. It also added to the reliability of the measure since all teachers using the instrument were provided with the same background information. But, this procedure also means that all teachers in the study were given some "treatment" within our prevention program, since the information can be regarded as equivalent to our first module.

The Participants and the Data Collection Procedure

Kindergartens were recruited community wise, according to geographical and socio-economic criteria in order to generate a fairly representative sample of communities located in the surroundings of the city of Berne (radius of approximately 40 kilometers) and belonging to the German speaking part of the canton of Berne. The study was conducted in 67 kindergartens. From all children registered in these classes, 1,090 children (47.9% girls) were allowed to participate (informed consent from 97.5% of the parents). Due to difficulties in recruiting teachers in some communities, data collection had to be conducted in two phases (the first phase during the 2003-2004 school year and the second phase during the 2004-2005 school year), using two samples of children. The samples were defined by enrollment in kindergarten; that is, on both occasions children were enrolled in the first or second year of kindergarten. All results have been tested for differences between samples and yielded no differences. The samples were considered equivalent and treated as such in the analyses.

Concerning the first sample of children (n = 692), teachers reported on bullying and some behaviour variables by the end of November 2003. These data were used to screen children who would be tested intensively. Also, teachers filled in more detailed questionnaires concerning the children who were categorized as involved in bullying others or in being victimized and a group of children drawn randomly from the non-involved children. In addition, children who were not chosen for the in-depth tests were interviewed using a very short procedure. The decision to conduct these short interviews was based on two grounds. First, we wanted to get additional data from the children themselves on bullying, popularity and social clusters in the kindergarten groups. Second, we did not want to produce any kind of stigmatization, especially because all children were very excited about the "human researchers" wanting to talk with them about going to kindergarten. Because the second sample included fewer children (n = 398), the interview procedure was shortened and there was no screening.

At the end of the school year (June 2004 or June 2005), teachers filled out questionnaires on all children and children were interviewed again, using the short interview procedure. On both occasions, teachers also filled out questionnaires on their own work situation, their attitudes towards different facets of bullying and victimization and among other things, on how confident they felt in dealing with bullying when it occurs.

We also asked parents to fill out questionnaires about their children, their family and themselves. We obtained questionnaires back from 73% of the parents.

To What Extent does Bullying Occur in Kindergarten?

Results from the first Bernese study on bullying in kindergarten clearly demonstrated that teachers were able to designate children who bullied other children or who were victimized in one or another way on a regular basis, i.e., at least once a week over a three-month period. This finding was replicated in the on-going study. As shown in Figure 1, of the children being victimized, only the prevalence of those categorized as passive (or non-aggressive) victims were consistent across studies at 6%. The percentages were identical for girls and boys. In Figure 1, we also included results from school children obtained in Switzerland and Norway in 1994. Children in this earlier study were in 4th through 9th grade. These results have been chosen as a basis for comparison, because the self-report questionnaires given to the students were designed in the same manner as the questionnaires given to the teachers in the present kindergarten study and the criteria to categorize the children were exactly the same (Alsaker, 2003; Alsaker & Brunner, 1999). As can be seen in Figure 1, the percentage of victimized children is almost identical in kindergarten and in school. The percentage of victimized aggressive children differs substantially between kindergarten and school.

Percentages of Children Involved and not Involved in Bully/Victim Problems

Bar chart showing Kindergarten 1997, Kindergarten 2003 & 2004, and School CH/N 1994:
- Passive Victims: 6, 6, 7
- Aggressive Victims: 10, 7, 3
- Bullies: 11, 12, 5
- not-Involved: 47, 55, 36

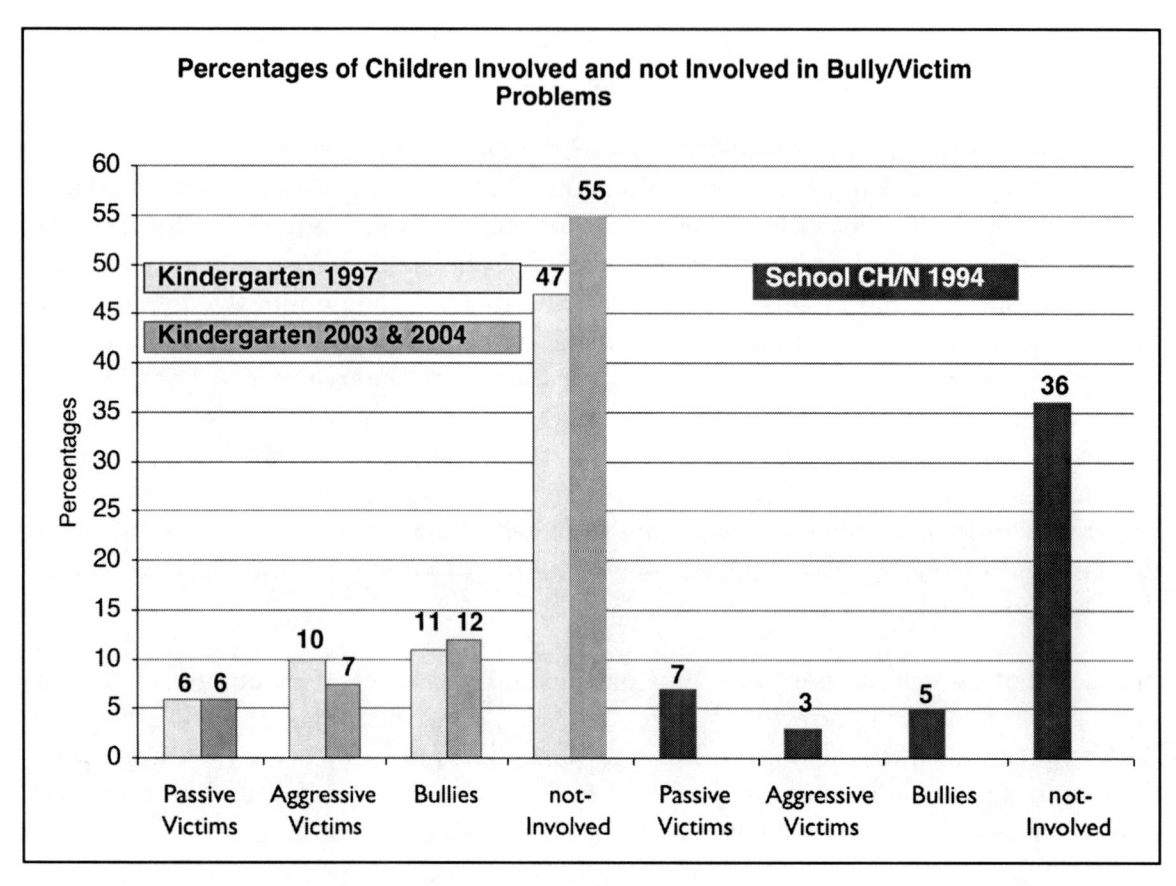

Comparison of percentages of children involved and not involved in bullying in two kindergarten samples and a school sample (N = Norway and CH = Switzerland)

First, we want to comment on the difference between the 1997 and the 2003/04 studies. Analyses of the 1997 data seemed to indicate that teachers sometimes had difficulties in differentiating bullying, conflicts, and fights. Therefore, we concluded that the rather high percentage of victimized aggressive children (10%) could have been inflated by this lack of differentiation and that children who were involved in many conflicts might have been falsely categorized as victimized aggressive children. The slightly lower percentage (7%) obtained in the present study may indicate that our new procedure, providing differentiated information to the teachers prior to data collection, has worked in the expected direction. However, the percentage of children assigned to the victimized aggressive category (7%) is high as compared to school children (usually around 3%, as in the school study mentioned above).

The higher prevalence of the victimized aggressive children will be discussed at the end of the chapter. There was a substantial and statistically significant gender difference as to the prevalence of this category: 3% of the girls and 12% of the boys were categorized as victimized aggressive children. This gender difference corresponds well with the 1997 study and the school study. In the latter study 1.3% of girls and 4.2% of boys were classified as victimized aggressive children. As to children who bullied, the two kindergarten studies yielded similar results and also higher percentages than school children. This difference might be due to the general decline in the use of aggression over the years between preschool and adolescence (Tremblay, Hartup, & Archer, 2005) and, to some extent, to a certain unwillingness to declare oneself as bullying when self-report is used. Nevertheless, researchers in Germany have reported percentages in school children to vary between 4% and 12% depending upon the criterion of frequency they used (Lösel & Bliesener, 1999). All in all, we might conclude that the present study confirms that bullying and victimization are part of kindergarten children's daily lives and that it concerns as many or even more children in a direct way than it does in elementary school. The next question is whether we are speaking about the same phenomenon.

Characteristics of the Children Involved in Bullying

Aggressive Behaviour

Children who bully and those who both bully and are victimized have one characteristic in common: they behave more aggressively than other children and they do so on a regular basis. This was one of the criteria to be met in our definition of the categories. However, as noted in the first section of the chapter, there are good reasons to expect victimized aggressive children to be even more aggressive than those who only bully, especially in terms of physical aggression. Besides the specific items on bullying, we also asked teachers to answer three items on overt aggressive behaviour that are often used in the literature to assess fighting, biting, and destroying things (see Ladd & Profilet, 1996). The results were as expected (see Figure 2). Both in girls and in boys, victimized aggressive children were the most overtly aggressive children in the group, that is, they were even significantly more aggressive than the children who were only involved in bullying.

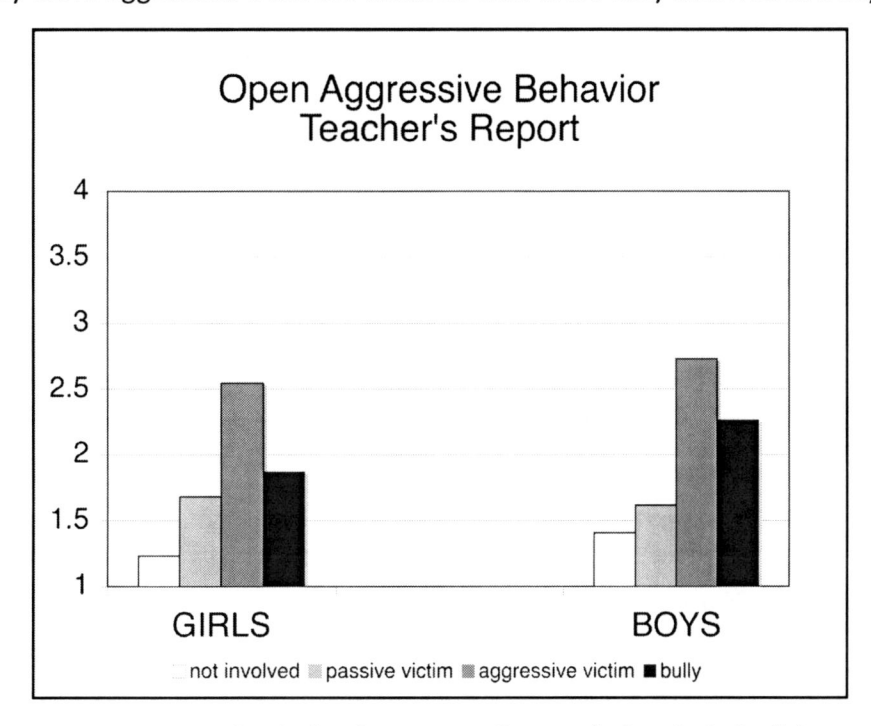

Scores on open aggressive behaviour according to their role in bullying patterns

As we had asked teachers four different questions concerning bullying, we were able to compare those children involved only in bullying and victimized aggressive children on their use of different forms of aggressive behaviour. Whereas 30% of the children who bullied used physical aggression at least once a week, 75% of the dually involved children did so. Interestingly, 21% of the children who bullied never or seldom used physical means (indicating their bullying behaviour was nonphysical), while this was the case for only 4% of the victimized aggressive children. The dually involved children also destroyed other children's property significantly more often than those who just bullied (25% versus 8%) but they did not differ in terms of verbal aggression (around 65% used it frequently in both groups). And last but not least, children who only bullied used exclusion significantly more frequently when they bullied others compared to the victimized aggressive children (63% and 31%, respectively).

These results confirm our hypothesis concerning the disturbing and norm-breaking behaviour of victimized aggressive children and clearly show that findings from school aged samples can be replicated in kindergarten children. The results, however, are based on teachers' reports. Therefore, in the next section we focus on the perceptions of the children, themselves, and report on analyses concerning the social status of the different groups of children. Who are the most and least liked children in the kindergarten group?

Popularity in the Peer Group

As illustrated in Figure 3, a cardboard bus was used to assess how well liked the children were in their kindergarten group.

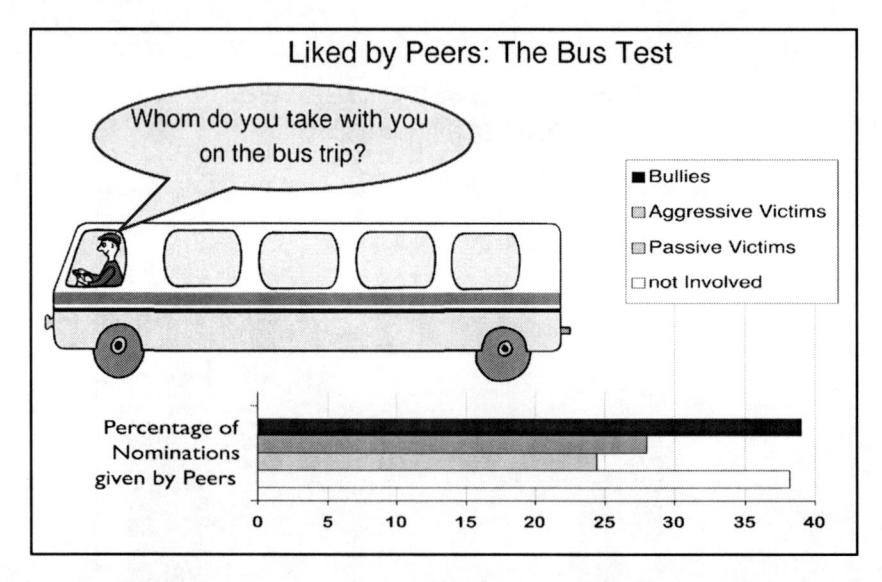

Children's popularity in the class according to their role in bullying patterns

After some introductory chat we asked children the following question: "You are going on a bus trip. Which children from the kindergarten group do you want to take with you?" Again, using photographs of all children in the class, the child could choose up to six peers.

Nominations were transformed into percentages of possible nominations in the group. As shown in Figure 3, while children who bullied and non-involved children received almost 40% of possible positive nominations on average, victimized children and those involved in both bullying and victimization received significantly fewer nominations (24% and 28%, respectively). This finding replicates our earlier finding in kindergarten and fits well with earlier studies in school-age samples. As noted above, in most studies these two types of victimized children have not been differentiated. Our data show, that they actually do not differ in terms of popularity. The findings on the low acceptance of dually involved children, as compared to those only involved in bullying and to non-involved children may very well reflect their high level of aggressive behaviour. However, the results concerning the low acceptance of the victimized children remain puzzling. Until now, there are no findings to our knowledge that could certainly explain why they should be less liked by their peers than other children. Actually, these children act in prosocial ways, helping and comforting peers and also sharing their belongings with others (Alsaker & Gutzwiller-Helfenfinger, in press). Our earlier findings (Perren & Alsaker, 2006) suggest that their generally lower ability to assert themselves in the group and to set limits lead to a low status in the peer group, making them vulnerable to victimization, and that this in turn contributes to their poor status. This interpretation would be in line with Ladd and Troop-Gordon's (2003) findings.

The high acceptance of children who bully also needs further attention. Our results correspond well with Boulton and Smith's (1994) study and our own findings in the first Bernese kindergarten study (Alsaker, 2003). They may very well reflect the position held by Sutton, Smith, and Swettenham (1999) stating that children who bully and have well developed social-cognitive skills may be able to manipulate peers' attitudes towards themselves. As presented in the above section, they often use social aggression (exclusion) and seldom use overt aggressive behaviour. We should also keep in mind that part of the positive nominations they receive may come from other aggressive peers, as aggressive children have been found to cluster together as early as in kindergarten (Perren & Alsaker, 2006).

Behaviour Associated with ADHD

As mentioned above, the hypothesis of an association of ADHD with victimization, especially for children who are dually involved in bullying and victimization has been put forward by several authors. The line of reasoning can be explained very simply: Children with certain types of ADHD will behave in fairly disturbing ways to the group. Their impulsivity and hyperactivity may jeopardize their integration into the peer group. The assessment of ADHD is complex and requires clinical observations, tests and interviews. In our study, we did not aim at a diagnosis of ADHD. We wanted to assess variables associated with ADHD that could be of importance for the child's behaviour and acceptance in the group. In the present chapter, we present results on inattention, impulsivity, and hyperactivity, as reported by the teachers. Each of these variables was assessed using four to five items corresponding to symptoms listed in DSM-IV and chosen from different instruments on the basis of discussions with neuro-pediatricians. Some sample items are given here: Inattention "He/she has trouble concentrating on tasks"; Impulsivity "He/she has trouble awaiting his/her turn"; Hyperactivity "He/she is not able to sit still".

The results were generally as expected regarding all three variables, children involved in both bullying and victimization always had the highest scores. As to impulsivity and hyperactivity, boys showed significantly more problems than girls, but there were no interactions with the bullying roles. The victimized aggressive children had higher scores on *impulsivity* than all other children, i.e., also significantly higher than the children who bullied only. Children who bullied only, however, were also high on impulsivity, significantly higher than the non-aggressive victimized children and the non-involved children. The dually involved children also had the highest scores on *hyperactivity*, but they did not differ significantly from the children who bullied. Both groups scored much higher than the non-aggressive victimized children and the non-involved children. That is, even if the results are in line with our expectations as to the victimized aggressive children, they draw a picture of children who only bully – in the teacher's eyes – who also display much impulsive and hyperactive behaviour.

In regards to *inattention*, the picture was somewhat different in girls and in boys. In boys, the victimized aggressive boys were more inattentive than all other children, but the boys who bullied were also more inattentive than non-involved children. As to girls, those who bullied only had more attention problems than non-involved children but they were clearly better than both types of victimized girls. In statistical terms, the girls who were victimized and nonaggressive did not differ from girls who were both victimized and aggressive. It may well be that some of these girls have attention deficits without hyperactivity, which is more common in girls than in boys (Barkley, 1998). As a consequence, they might display some behaviour that is not well suited in girls' groups, or in some way renders them more vulnerable to victimization. These differential findings in girls and boys also indicate that pathways to victimization may differ in boys and girls as early as in kindergarten.

In sum, the clearest finding is that victimized aggressive children are highest on all problems that could be associated with ADHD or at least with a lack of behavioural regulation. This finding corresponds well to hypotheses and results in school age populations of children. The children who bully, in our kindergarten sample were not very well regulated either, and the female victims shared problems of inattention with the girls who were involved in both bullying and victimization. These findings may indicate that children involved in bullying their peers in kindergarten differ from those who continue to show this behaviour at an older age.

Depressiveness

In our study, teachers were asked to answer two items, depicting depressive expressions in the child (The child seems to be unhappy, saddened; the child looks a little sad). This is not equivalent to measuring depression, but it is one of the typical characteristics of depression in childhood (Groen & Petermann, 2002) and may serve as an indicator of depressiveness. In addition, they answered an item depicting being worried. All three items were highly correlated (reliability coefficient of .87) and a mean score of depressiveness was computed for each child. The results are similar to those found for school-aged boys: Both types of victimized boys have significantly higher scores than all other boys. In girls, teachers perceive only the victimized girls to be more sad, unhappy, and worried than all other groups of girls.

Be-Prox - Prevention Program against Bullying in Kindergarten and School

The first version of the Bernese Program against bullying was developed in 1998 in the frame of a research project (Alsaker, 2003, 2004; Alsaker & Valkanover, 2001). It was based on well-known principles used in school bullying prevention programs (e.g., Olweus, 1993a; Smith, & Sharp, 1994) and in various programs for social–cognitive skills training. The basic principle of the program was to enhance teachers' capability of handling bullying. On the basis of an evaluation of the program during the project period (including a pre- and posttest evaluation) and upon using the program in different settings after the project period, we refined the procedures and worked on reducing the costs. In the mean time, we published a manual for teachers, a poster, information for parents, and a film to be used in schools (Valkanover, Alsaker, Svrcek, & Kauer, 2004). This prevention "package" has since been employed in courses and counselling meetings with teachers and in the implementation of Be-Prox in the present project.

Basic Principles

Be-Prox can be characterized as a *systemic and value oriented approach*. It does not aim directly at changing individuals, but at changing the system, the kindergarten class, composed of all children and the teacher(s). Be-Prox also aims at enhancing or introducing positive values that are central for healthy social interactions in the class.

From a methodological perspective, the program is based on *transfer of knowledge* and *support*. Knowledge about bullying is still limited or even insufficient for all too many teachers. Therefore, developing awareness and understanding still plays a central role in the program. However, knowledge does not suffice. Our experience over the years has demonstrated that children who bully can be very good at arguing and explaining their actions so that teachers feel very insecure about how to interpret the situation. All in all, teachers' insecurity about their right to intervene or their ability to discover and to solve bullying problems prevents them from taking action. They need counselling and support from colleagues to overcome their feelings of insecurity. Therefore, "group sessions" are still an integral part of the prevention program. Also, over the years we have learned that it was of great help to have a consultant team composed of a psychologist and a teacher. This team adds very much to the acceptability of the program.

Furthermore, we emphasize the importance of *cooperation and participation*. Therefore, we behave as models in our work with the teachers: We "propose" specific elements, motivate teachers to use them and work together with the teachers on preparing their implementation in the class. Participation also means that the implementation of the program has to be flexible and adaptable to the very different needs encountered by teachers. This is necessary to maintain teachers' motivation to take part in the course and to apply the various elements of the program.

As we want to ensure that teachers *implement* the elements of the program, and not only learn about them, we meet them over a long period of time, usually around four to five months. In the present project, we usually organized six group sessions and gave the teachers specific tasks to work on between the meetings during a five-month period (see also Alsaker, 2004 for a detailed presentation of the first version of Be-Prox).

The Central Elements of Be-Prox

Beside the basic principles presented above, all elements of Be-Prox are based on empirical knowledge about bullying, that is: 1) Bullying is a social phenomenon, all children are involved, 2) it may be difficult to recognize bullying, especially when subtle forms are used, 3) nobody talks about it, and it is often trivialized, 4) children who are victimized cannot defend themselves adequately and have little support, 5) bullying has tremendous psychological consequences.

The first module is called *sensitization*. As described in an earlier section of this chapter, specific aspects of victimization were presented and the differentiation between conflicts and bullying was emphasized. The task given to the teachers in the weeks between the first and second meeting is called *"Look at it"*. They were invited to observe their class and to fill out the questionnaires on each child. In other settings they are free to decide how they want to document their observations.

The second module is called *"Talking together about bullying and victimization"*. The importance of discussions about bullying and victimization together with all children, different manners to address the issue in the class etc. are in focus. During this session an emphasis is put on values and children's rights. Teachers are urged to think about their own attitudes towards children involved in bullying and/or victimization and to make a commitment to values against bullying before addressing it with the children. The task for the teachers is called *"Talk about it"*. For many teachers this step is difficult and in some it produces anxiety. Our experience is that many teachers need some additional support and counselling to take this step.

The aim of the third module is to urge teachers to elaborate a *behaviour code* in collaboration with the children. The importance of rules, limits, and structure for children's development is discussed. Also, the central role of the so-called non-involved children is addressed. Civil courage is in focus. The task for the teachers is called *"The contract"* and represents the first step of concrete actions to be taken against bullying.

The topic of the fourth module is the importance of consistent teacher behaviour, of positive and negative sanctions, and the use of basic *learning principles*. Previous experiences (see Alsaker, 2004) showed how important it is to discuss these issues in-depth. Teachers' insecurity about bullying and also about their role as teachers often inhibits any kind of consistent action. The task given to the teachers is: *"Take Action"*, meaning "use positive and negative sanctions, remind children about the contract when needed, reinforce positive behaviour". At this point, we now start motivating teachers to talk to parents, to organize information meetings, etc.

Social skills, empathy and *positive activities* are the focus during the fifth meeting. Here again, civil courage is discussed. Teachers are invited to enhance children's ability to take the perspective of victimized children, to say stop, to report on bullying behaviour when they cannot help themselves, that is, in general to engage in helping and supporting each other in difficult situations. We also invite the teachers to include physical activities and body awareness as part of the planned positive activities. They are asked to train children in differentiating between aggression and strength. Teachers are asked to find or elaborate adequate teaching material and use it with the children.

The final meeting is now called *"Consolidation through own prevention goals"*. This last meeting gives teachers an opportunity to reflect on the work they have done, to discuss their attitudes toward aggression, toward victims, and to formulate goals for their work during the next school year.

Evaluation

Using a pre- and posttest design with a control and a prevention group, we are able to analyze our data for changes in a wide range of variables. As shown in the previous Bernese study (Alsaker, 2004; Alsaker & Valkanover, 2001), the most interesting source of information with respect to changes in occurrences of bullying, is provided by the children themselves. This part of the data is still being processed; therefore we will concentrate on 1) the evaluation of the courses by the teachers, 2) reports from the children about implementation of program elements and their own behaviour in bullying situations, and 3) possible changes in basic attitudes and feelings of insecurity in the teachers.

As described in the previous section, the program was implemented in 36 kindergarten classes. In some kindergartens, two teachers shared the job and both teachers took part in the prevention meetings; all in all 46 teachers participated. Twenty-one kindergartens served as control classes.

In considering the evaluation of the effects of our prevention program, we recognize that the sensitization of all teachers prior to the project means that all teachers were given some "treatment". This, in turn, means that we have no "non-treatment" control group with which to contrast the prevention group. As such, if effects are found, they reflect the improvements beyond the first module.

Participants' Evaluation of the Be-Prox program

All teachers participating in the Be-Prox program were asked to evaluate the courses on the last day. The evaluation was unanimously positive. This feedback was important as it gives information about the acceptance of contents and instructors. The positive evaluation of the course is a prerequisite for a positive transfer of the different elements of the program into the daily work of the teachers. Of course, a positive bias should be expected when a course is evaluated by the participants, especially when they committed themselves to take part in six meetings and to work with the children in the time between meetings. Therefore, we must point out, that this information is not to be considered an evaluation of possible effects of the program, it is an indication of the acceptability of the program.

Among other things, the competence of the consultants was rated 3.98 on a scale from 1 (not at all satisfying) to 4 (very satisfying); the quality of the preparation of the instructors was rated 3.92, the atmosphere during the sessions was rated 3.83, the gain in knowledge on bullying was rated 3.79. That is, the Be-Prox program received a very positive evaluation from the participants.

This extremely positive feedback is a valuable information as it shows that the Be-Prox prevention program is highly accepted by teachers, even if they often were confronted with discussions concerning own values and their understanding of their profession, or were urged to talk about topics they would have liked to avoid.

The Children's perspective

First of all, we wanted to know whether central program elements had been implemented and whether children had taken notice of it. Therefore, by the end of the school year we asked children whether they had discussions about bullying and victimization problems in the class. The good news is twofold: first, 63% of the children in the prevention group answered the question positively and this was significantly more than in the control group. The second good news is that 45% of the children in the control group also said that bullying had been discussed in class. We conclude that the sensitization prior to the data collection might have had an effect. Teachers could easily obtain information about how to handle or prevent bullying. Among other things, our prevention "package" is distributed by the editors of most school materials in Switzerland. Also, even if the prevention and control groups were chosen in different communities, all communities were in a radius of 40 km distance from Berne and teachers in the same canton have many opportunities to meet.

Regarding the contracts, or specifically rules against bullying, the results were also very encouraging. 81% of the children in the prevention kindergarten classes and 64% of the other children could report that there were clear "rules" against bullying in their class. The difference was significant.

Since enhancing empathy and understanding for the victims was part of the program, we also asked children about what they would do if their best friend was to bully another child. Only 9% of the children in the prevention kindergarten said they would join in, this was significantly less than in the control kindergarten (16%). Furthermore, we compared emotional reactions reported by the children when witnessing another child being victimized. There were no differences at pretest: 61% of all children reported adequate reactions (angry or sad) and 27% reported inadequate reactions (happy or disinterested). At posttest, there were more children in prevention kindergarten reporting adequate reactions (74% as compared to 65% in control kindergarten), and correspondingly fewer children reporting inadequate reactions (19% as compared to 26%. There was no change in control kindergartens, but a significant change in the prevention group.

Teachers' Attitudes and Feelings of Insecurity

It has repeatedly been shown that victimized children cannot defend themselves efficiently. Hence, a central message of the Be-Prox program is that intervention by adults is needed. One of the statements teachers had to respond to was formulated as follows: "A child who is being victimized should defend her/himself". Teachers in both groups rated the question similarly prior to the intervention: On a scale from 1 (no, not true at all) to 4 (yes, absolutely true) the mean was 1.9. At post-test, the value had dropped to 1.57 for the teachers in the prevention, whereas it had remained constant for the teachers in the control group. We conclude that the Be-Prox intervention showed the intended effect.

Teachers often feel overwhelmed when confronted with victimization. Therefore, it was a major aim of the program to enhance teachers' feelings of adequacy and competence when facing difficult situations, such as bullying. Our data shows that participation in the program did matter. Teachers responded to the following statement: "I am insecure about how to react when bullying occurs in my class". Before the implementation of the program, teachers from the control group agreed slightly more often with the statement than their colleagues in the prevention group (mean values were 2.4 and 2.2, respectively). At post-test the values had dropped to 1.5 in the prevention group, but remained about the same in the control group.

All teachers agreed that it is important to talk with the parents when a child is victimized or bullies others. No differences were found between the prevention and control groups. We had also asked teachers about their feelings when they had to contact parents because of a child's problems in the class. We asked whether or not 1) they hesitate to get in touch with the parents, 2) they feel competent and secure to contact the parents, 3) they seek support from school authorities, and 4) from colleagues. There were no changes at all between pre- and post-test. This is an interesting finding, because it shows that the effects were confined to the issues we had worked on with the teachers.

Conclusions

The general similarity or at least correspondence of the results comparing school aged children (usually aged between 10 and 16) and kindergarten children aged 5 through 7 is impressive. Especially, considering that the data differ in regards to the source of information and the procedures used (self-report, teachers' reports, peer-nominations). The reliability of the findings indicates that bullying – as we know it from research with school-aged children - really exists in kindergarten. Even the percentages of non-aggressive victimized children are similar.

The higher percentage of victimized aggressive children may simply reflect development and the reality of social life in this age group. As aggressive behaviour, especially physical aggression usually decreases at this age (Tremblay et al., 2005), it might be that boys who still behave highly aggressively (as do the victimized aggressive children) experience more retaliation and eventually victimization, as a reaction to their non-normative and highly disturbing behaviour. If this is the case, we could expect some of these victimized aggressive kindergarten children to develop the ability to control their aggressive behaviour during their kindergarten years and to become better accepted by their peers upon entry to elementary school. Still a number of these children could develop into persistently aggressive children. With regard to this issue, the information we collected on impulsivity and hyperactivity (including several tests that were not presented here) will be of great value when analyzing the longitudinal data. We also noted that kindergarten children involved only in bullying their peers were reported to be rather impulsive and very active.

The present data suggest that the most important difference between the two types of children who bully is their ability to control their physical aggression. The use of social aggression by children who only bully indicates that they may be more manipulative than dually involved children and have rather well developed social understanding, including knowledge about norms, when to break norms and when not to. Children involved in both bullying and victimization seem to be rather inefficient and possibly deregulated aggressors, as proposed by Perry, Perry, and Kennedy (1992), whereas children involved in bullying only could be rather controlled and efficient aggressors (see Sutton et al., 1999). Further analyses will be conducted, especially including data from different tests tapping social skills and social disinhibition.

Some findings also pointed out that pathways to victimization may differ for girls and boys. Attention deficits were clearly related to the status of being victimized only in girls, whereas it was not in boys. Here also we will need to include data from different tests to clarify whether this difference is due to some attention deficit, and what kind of behaviour might be associated with this deficit that renders inattentive girls vulnerable to victimization.

Bullying is typically a social phenomenon that requires both the presence of aggressive children in the group and the passivity of other children and adults in order to develop into a chronic pattern. Nevertheless, some individual deficits seem to increase children's vulnerability to becoming victimized. The differences we found between the groups of children involved in bullying problems are of great significance for the early detection of vulnerable children and also for further refinements of the prevention program. It is probable that highly aggressive children who are not well regulated and hence become victimized by their peers are to be considered as a high-risk population. These children can, almost certainly, draw only limited benefit from general bullying prevention programs addressing the whole group. In such cases, individual counselling of the teacher and some treatment or support for the child are needed.

The findings with regard to Be-Prox confirm that the prevention works. Among other things, we found changes in teachers' attitudes towards victimized children, we reported that they had gained in security concerning how to handle bullying and we found several positive changes in children's reactions in the prevention group. We find this especially encouraging because all teachers had received some treatment, as they all went through the first module of the program. The high percentage of children in the control group reporting about several elements of the program also indicates that the control group teachers had not been inactive. Therefore, the changes we found in the prevention group as compared to the control group indicate that our concept of group counselling over several months has clear benefits. Especially the gain in "feelings of security when faced with bullying" allows for hope that these teachers will be competent observers and that they will continue acting adequately in order to prevent bullying or to stop such patterns in their beginning.

The discussions during the first meeting with the teachers and data collected at pre-test showed that there are still too many teachers who do not know how to recognize bullying in an early phase and too few who know how to handle bullying situations. In the present study, we could replicate an earlier finding and demonstrate that victimization is associated with depressiveness as early as kindergarten. This is in line with results from studies among school-aged children and adolescents up to 16 years of age. Repeated victimization may elicit intense emotional experiences, including feelings of worthlessness and helplessness (Alsaker & Olweus, 2002). These experiences may result in negative expectations towards peers and school and in turn make the child more vulnerable to victimization, as it may result in less adequate interactions with peers (Alsaker, 2004). Therefore, it is important that prevention of victimization starts in preschool contexts. But it is likely important that it does not stop there. Bullying prevention means "looking at it, talking about it, and acting against it" over all years of schooling.

Key Messages

1. Be aware of covert forms of bullying – they already occur in kindergarten.

2. Talk with the children about good and bad things happening in the kindergarten group.

3. Talk about the unfairness of bullying and provide children with alternative behaviours

4. Give children an opportunity to feel competent and teach them to say no!

5. Encourage children who are not directly involved in bullying to intervene when they witness such situations. They may be trained to stop bullying behaviour, to ask the teacher to help or to include the victim in play situations.

References

Alsaker, F. D. (1993a). *Bully/victim problems in day-care centers: Measurement issues and associations with children's psychosocial health.*

Alsaker, F. D. (1993b). *Isolement et maltraitance par pairs dans les jardins d'enfants: comment mesurer ces phénomènes et quelles en sont leurs conséquences?* Enfance, 47, 241-60.

Alsaker, F. D. (2003). *Quälgeister und ihre Opfer. Mobbing unter Kindern - und wie man damit umgeht.* Berne: Huber Verlag.

Alsaker, F. D. (2004). *The Bernese program against vicitmization in kindergarten and elementary school (Be-Prox).* In P. K. Smith, D. Pepler, & K. Rigby (Eds.), *Bullying in schools: How successful can interventions be?* (pp. 289-306). Cambridge: Cambridge University Press.

Alsaker, F. D. (2006). *Psychische Folgen von Mobbing.* In H.-C. Steinhausen (Ed.), *Schule und psychische Störungen.* (pp. 35-47). Stuttgart: Kohlhammer.

Alsaker, F. D., & Brunner, A. (1999). *Switzerland.* In P. Smith, K, K. Morita, J. Junger-Tas, D. Olweus, R. Catalano, & P. Slee (Eds.), *The nature of school bullying: A cross-national perspective.* (PBS Record: 14690 ed., pp. 250-63). London: Routledge.

Alsaker, F. D., & Gutzwiller-Helfenfinger, E. (in press). *Social behavior and peer relationships of victims, bully-victims, and bullies in kindergarten.* In S. R. Jimerson, S. M. Swearer, & D. L. Espelage (Eds.), *The International Handbook of School Bullying.* Mahwah, New Jersey: Lawrence Erlbaum Associates

Alsaker, F. D., & Olweus, D. (2002). *Stability and change in global self-esteem and self-related affect.* In T. M. Brinthaupt, & R. P. Lipka (Eds.), *Understanding the self of the early adolescent.* (PBS Record: 9720 ed., pp. 193-223). New York: State University of New York Press.

Alsaker, F. D., & Valkanover, S. (2001). *Early diagnosis and prevention of victimization in kindergarten.* In J. Juvonen, & S. Graham (Eds.), *Peer harassment in school: the plight of the vulnerable and victimized.* (pp. 175-95). New York: Guilford Press.

Barkley, R. A. (1998). *Attention-deficit hyperactivity disorder: A handbook for diagnosis and treatment* (2nd ed.). New York: Guilford Press.

Boulton, M. J. & Smith, P. K. (1994). *Bully/victim problems in middle-school children: stability, self-perceived competence, peer perceptions and peer acceptance.* British Journal of Developmental Psychology, 12, 315-29.

Crick, N. R., Casas, J. F., & Ku, H.-C. (1999). *Relational and physical forms of peer victimization in preschool*. Developmental Psychology, 35, 376-85.

Groen, G., & Petermann, F. (2002). *Depressive Kinder und Jugendliche*. Göttingen: Hogrefe.

Kochenderfer, B. J. & Ladd, G. W. (1996). *Peer victimization: Manifestations and relations to school adjustment in kindergarten*. Journal of School Psychology, 34, 267-83.

Kochenderfer-Ladd, B., & Ladd, G. W. (2001). *Variations in peer victimization. Relations to children's maladjustment*. In J. Juvonen, & S. Graham (Eds.), *Peer harassment in school. The plight of the vulnerable and victimized*. (pp. 25-48). New York: The Guilford Press.

Kokkinos, C. & Panayiotou, G. (2004). *Predicting bullying and victimization among early adolescents: Associations with disruptive behaviors disorders*. Aggressive Behavior, 30, 520-33.

Kumpulainen, K., Räsänen, E., Henttonen, I., Alqvist, F., Kresanov, V., Linna, S.-L., et al. (1998). *Bullying and psychiatric symptoms among elementary school-age children*. Child Abuse & Neglect, 22, 705-17.

Ladd, G. W. & Profilet, S. M. (1996). The Child Behavioral Scale: a teacher-report measure of young children`s aggressive, withdrawn, and prosocial behaviors. Developmental Psychology, 32, 1008-24.

Ladd, G. W. & Troop-Gordon, W. (2003). *The role of chronic peer difficulties in the development of children's psychological adjustment problems*. Child Development, 74, 1344-67.

Lösel, F., & Bliesener, T. (1999). Germany. In P. Smith, K, K. Morita, J. Junger-Tas, D. Olweus, R. Catalano, & P. Slee (Eds.), *The nature of school bullying: A cross-national perspective*. (pp. 224-49). London: Routledge.

Monks, C., Ortega Ruiz, R., & Torrado Val, E. (2002). *Unjustified Aggression in Preschool*. Aggressive Behavior, 28, 458-76.

Olweus, D. (1993a). *Bullying at school. What we know and what we can do*. Oxford: Blackwell.

Olweus, D. (1993b). *Victimization by peers: Antecedents and long-term outcomes*. In K. Rubin, H, & J. Asendorpf, B (Eds.), *Social withdrawal, inhibition, and shyness in childhood*. (pp. 315-42). Hillsdale, NJ: Erlbaum.

Olweus, D. (1999). *Sweden*. In P. Smith, K, K. Morita, J. Junger-Tas, D. Olweus, R. Catalano, & P. Slee (Eds.), *The nature of school bullying: A cross-national perspective*. (pp. 7-27). London: Routledge.

Pellegrini, A. D. (1998). *Bullies and victims in school: A review and call for research*. Journal of Applied Developmental Psychology, 19, 165-76.

Perren, S. & Alsaker, F. D. (2006). *Social Behaviour and Peer Relationships of Victims, Bully-victims, and Bullies in Kindergarten*. The Journal of child Psychology and Psychiatry and Allied Disciplines, 47, 45-57.

Perry, D. G., Perry, L. C., & Kennedy, E. (1992). *Conflict and the development of antisocial behavior*. In C. U. Shantz, & W. W. Hartup (Eds.), *Conflict in child and adolescent development*. (pp. 301-29). New York: Cambridge University Press.

Rigby, K. (1996). *Bullying in schools: And what to do about it*. London: Jessica Kingsley.

Rigby, K. (2003). *Consequences of bullying in schools*. Canadian Journal of Psychiatry, 48, 583-90.

Rigby, K., Smith, P. K., & Pepler, D. (2004). *Working to prevent school bullying: key issues*. In P. K. Smith, D. Pepler, & K. Rigby (Eds.), *Bullying in schools. How successful can interventions be?* (pp. 1-12). Cambridge, UK: Cambridge University Press.

Salmivalli, C. & Isaacs, J. (2005). *Prospective relations among victimization, rejection, friendlessness, and children's self- and peer-perceptions*. Child Development, 76, 1161-71.

Salmivalli, C., Lagerspetz, K., Björkqvist, K., Österman, K., & Kaukiainen, A. (1996). *Bullying as a group process: participant roles and their relations to social status*. Aggressive Behavior, 22, 1-15.

Salmivalli, C. & Nieminen, E. (2002). *Proactive and reactive aggression among school bullies, victims, and buly-victims*. Aggressive Behavior, 28, 30-44.

Schwartz, D. (2000). *Subtypes of victims and aggressors in children's peer groups*. Journal of Abnormal Child Psychology, 28, 181-92.

Schwartz, D., Proctor, L. J., & Chien, D. H. (2001). *The aggressive victim of bullying: emotional and behavioral dysregulation as a pathway to victimization by peers*. In J. Juvonen, & S. Graham (Eds.), *Peer harassment in school: the plight of the vulnerable and victimized*. (pp. 147-74). New York: Guilford Press.

Smith, P. K., Morita, K., Junger-Tas, J., Olweus, D., Catalano, R., & Slee, P. (Eds.). (1999). *The nature of school bullying: A cross-national perspective*. London: Routledge.

Smith P. K. & Sharp S, (Eds). (1994). *School bullying: insights and perspectives*. London: Routledge.

Sutton, J., Smith, P. K., & Swettenham, J. (1999). *Bullying and 'Theory of Mind': A critique of the 'Social Skills Deficit' view of anti-social behaviour.* Social Development, 8, 117-27.

Tremblay, R. E., Hartup, W. W., & Archer, J. (Eds.). (2005). *Developmental origins of aggression.* New York: The Guilford Press.

Valkanover, S., Alsaker, F. D., Svreck, A., & Kauer, M. (2004). *Mobbing ist kein Kinderspiel. Arbeitsheft zur Prävention in Kindergarten und Schule.* Bern: Schulverlag.

Author Notes

The on-going project from which we present some results in this chapter "Pathways to Victimization and a Multisetting Intervention", is conducted with financial support from the Swiss National Science Foundation, National Research Program 52, Grant Nr. Nr. 4052-69011.

Chapter 13:

School Bullying in Italy: Nature and Functions from Childhood to Adolescence and Related Interventions

E. Menesini
University of Florence

Introduction and Historical Overview

In Italy, attention to school bullying was raised by a series of studies on bullying carried out at the University of Florence starting in the early 1990s. In 1997, the first Italian survey on the nature and the extent of the problem across different geographical areas was published (Fonzi, 1997). In this book, bullying was reported at a more substantial level than had been found in other European and Western countries, more than 30% of primary school pupils and 22% of middle school students admitted to being victimized (see table 1 for a comparison with other European countries). Newspapers and television amplified these data raising awareness in schools and communities. Researchers, headmasters and teachers began to study and to confront the phenomenon.

Table 1. Comparison in the rate of bullying between Italy and other countries

	% Who Bully	% Who are Victimized	Frequency category
Fonzi & coll. (1997) – Italy	9	13	1/week or more
	23	30	sometimes or more
Whitney & Smith (1993) – UK	4	10	1/week or more
	12	27	sometimes or more
Olweus (1993) – Norway	7	9	Now and then or more
Almeida et al. (1999) – Portugal	17	21	sometimes or more
Junger-Tas & V.Kesteren (1999) NL	20	22	Regularly

Given this high proportion of bullying in our country, attention to the problem has been particularly high. For example, from 1995 to 2005 more than 10 books have been published on this topic (Fonzi, 1997; 1999; Marini & Mameli, 1999; Menesini, 2000; 2003; Genta, 2002; Lazzarin & Zambianchi, 2004; Castorina, 2003; Caravita, 2004; Buccoliero & Maggi, 2005) and several papers and chapters appeared in national and international books and journals. To better comprehend the meaning of the Italian data, we decided to work on the cultural meaning of this behaviour across languages and contexts by asking the following questions:

Does the Word Bullying Have the Same Meaning across Different Languages and Cultures?

Is it possible that Italian children are more aggressive than their European peers or simply do some types of bullying have a different meaning in different countries? This chapter provides a summary of some of the issues we tried to address which relate to definitional issues and to the cultural meaning of the problem.

What is Bullying?

At scientific level, there is general consensus on the following definition: "Bullying is a subcategory of aggressive behaviour; but a particularly vicious kind of aggressive behaviour, since it is directed, often repeatedly, towards a particular victim who is unable to defend himself or herself effectively…." (Smith, Morita, Junger-Tas, Olweus, Catalano , Slee, 1999). According to several authors (Olweus; 1999; Smith et al. 1999), three elements are particularly relevant in this definition:

1) *Intentionality*: the bully deliberately brings damage to the victim

2) *Persistency*: it is not a matter of isolated, but repeated episodes acted by the bully against a particular schoolmate

3) *Imbalance*: there is an imbalance of power and of authority between the two actors, the bully and the victim

This is a more complex definition than it may appear at first sight, as it does not refer to a single action, but to a relational situation regarded in its temporal progress. It does not include occasional negative actions done in jest or in a burst of anger, but it is used like a sort of script, that is a conventional sequence, in which the actors play set roles (Smorti, 2003).

Given this definition, we may ask ourselves whether it is shared by children, as direct protagonists of bullying, and by people living in different countries and cultures. To this purpose we carried out a first study with 30- to 55-year-old parents of children aged 6-13 years within a European network of five different countries: Italy, Spain, Portugal, England and Japan (Smorti, Menesini, & Smith, 2003). In this study, target terms were selected using focus groups of children. Participants were presented with 25 stick-figure cartoons showing different types and contexts of bullying and related behaviours. They were asked to evaluate whether the cartoons could be described or not by one of the target terms. Cluster analysis identified 6 clusters of cartoons characterised by specific behaviours from non-bullying to different types of bullying: non-aggressive, fighting, severe physical aggression, verbal aggression, exclusion, and severe exclusion. On the basis of these clusters, there were clear differences across terms and countries regarding both the width of the semantic area of a term and its closeness to the usual scientific definition of bullying (see Figure 1). As we can see in Figure 1, we have clusters of behaviour on the X axis and percentages of inclusion in that word by the five countries samples on the Y axis. Looking at the distribution, we can notice that severe exclusion and severe physical aggression do not have the same meaning in the five words used to translate bullying. In summary, we found that there were clear differences across terms and countries regarding the definition usually used for bullying.

We can assume, therefore, that differences in the semantic fields across languages might have affected the way the problem has been investigated in a cross-cultural perspective and may partly account for differences in the rates of bullying reported in each country, even when the same questionnaire was used. For example, if "bullying" for the Italians is largely meant as arrogance, and it is not so for other countries, this requires caution when we compare data from different nations on the basis of a single criterion. For instance, in the UK, being bullied in the last 2-3 months ranged from 27% to 10% respectively in primary and secondary school (Smith, et al. 1999). In Italy, where the more inclusive term *prepotenze* was used, the percentages were about twice as high, with figures of 13% once a week or more often and of 30 % if we consider sometimes or more often (Fonzi et al. 1999).

An implication of these results is that, in cross-cultural research on bullying (as in other areas) there should be a clear understanding of the varying meaning profiles of words used to translate bullying (or aggression, violence, etc). This is crucial when rates of the phenomenon are being compared, although it also applies to comparisons of behaviours based on sample characteristics (i.e., age differences, sex differences).

Figure 1. Percentage of parents who included the cartoons in each cluster as part of the "definition" of that term.

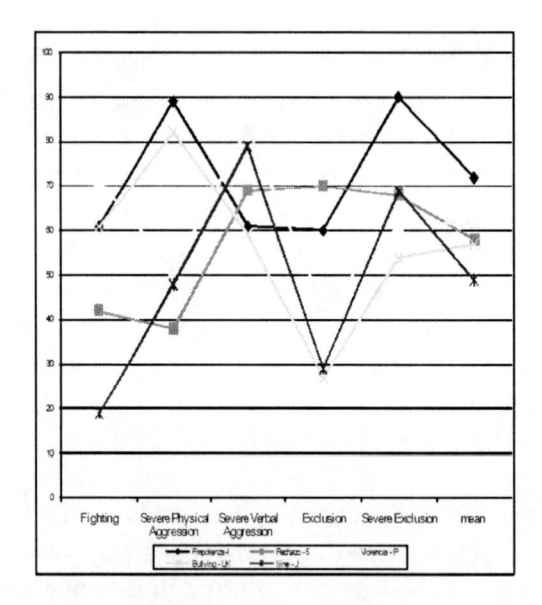

Some differences may be also related to different informants. For example we might ask whether children understand bullying according to its scientific meaning and whether teachers and parents perceive bullying in the same way as students do. Another study I conducted with colleagues (Menesini, Fonzi and Smith 2002) highlighted how divergent students' and teachers' perspectives can be when describing situations which may be considered as bullying. In particular, we found that the dimensions of social exclusion, gender exclusion, and verbal bullying depicted in the cartoon situations are those in which teachers systematically apply the terms less often than do students. We might infer that in these specific contexts, teachers are often unaware of the conflicts and of the negative behaviours occurring among students.

Explanatory Models and Risk Factors

The Italian research sheds new light on the main risk factors related to "social and cultural factors" and to "moral and socio-cognitive mechanisms" underlying bullying behaviour. Some studies conducted in Naples highlight social and cultural factors related to bullying (e.g., Bacchini & Valerio, 1997). What seems to influence the vast variability of the phenomenon in Naples is not so much the social class that the children belong to, but the ecological environment and the city district in which they live. The rates of bullying are significantly different for those children residing in quarters of high mafia density compared to children living in other areas. In the high density areas, we found an extremely high level of bullying and pervasive attitudes to justify bullying problems. Students in these areas often underestimate the seriousness of bullying problems as compared to other delinquent actions and offences often observed in the community. In this context, the values of the culture seem to be crucially important to explain the rate and the extent of bullying problems.

Moral reasoning and emotions are individual factors that relate to the likelihood of bullying. Children who bully tend to have lower levels of moral reasoning than either children who are victimized or non involved children. We investigated moral disengagement among these groups of children (Menesini, Fonzi & Vannucci, 1999). We found that children who bullied had the highest scores, particularly with regard to the process of dehumanisation (see Figure 2). This mechanism was identified by Bandura (1990) as one that enables perpetrators to treat their victims cruelly without feeling guilty. In a subsequent study, we investigated the emotions surrounding a bullying situation. In this study we presented a bullying scenario and asked different participants in bullying situations to report how they would feel. Compared to the other participants, children who bullied their peers reported feeling more indifferent or proud when they took the bullying role in the story. In terms of values and goals, children who bully appear to experience an asymmetry between themselves and other people: although they seem able to perceive others' intentions and needs, they value themselves more than other people (Menesini, Sanchez, et al., 2003). Feelings of indifference are also present in the case of children who play pro-bullying roles (giving support to peers who bully) as well as in bystanders, those who try to escape from the situation and don't do anything to stop bullying.

Figure 2. Differences in moral disengagement as a function of classification as bullies, victims, or outsiders

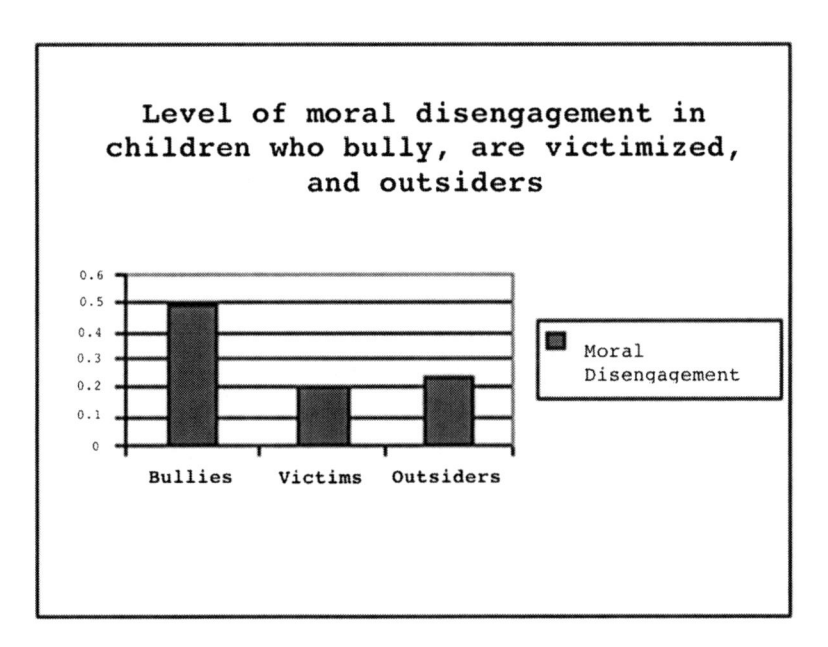

In a third study, (Camodeca and Menesini, 2007), we investigated how children who bully or are victimized report feeling guilty and ashamed in relation to morally relevant situations. We found that children who bully reported to feeling less guilty and ashamed than prosocial and not-involved children in moral contexts when their behaviour caused harm or distress to someone else. This is a confirmation that children who bully may be guided by egocentric reasoning and lack of a sense of responsibility, which, in turn, makes them indifferent to the victims' sufferings (Arsenio & Lemerise, 2001; Menesini et al.,

2003). They do not feel responsible for the harm caused, and, therefore, lack feelings of guilt or shame in moral situations.

From these studies, we can conclude that the area of moral behaviour, reasoning and emotion is a critical one for children who bully. Therefore bullying prevention programs should address these issues either directly or through preventive and indirect approaches such as that of enhancing students' personal responsibility for their peers.

Intervention and Prevention Programs of the First Period

Before examining potential intervention strategies, we should ask ourselves whether adults are aware of the problem and whether victimized children feel confident of their help. Often we have had the impression that adults – parents and teachers- underestimate the importance of children's sufferings and adopt a strategy of deafness and indifference, instead of taking responsibility for them.

Both English and Italian studies (Whitney & Smith, 1993; Fonzi, 1997) have emphasized that only 50% of victimized children report the problem to their teachers and/or parents. This percentage diminishes with age, so that secondary school pupils are even less likely to disclose their victimization. Teachers are less likely to be approached than parents: for example, in Italy only 51% of primary school and 35.5% of secondary school pupils talk with their teachers about bullying, whereas 65.4% and 50.9%, respectively, tell their parents about it (Menesini, Fonzi & Smith, 2002). From cross-cultural research conducted in England and in Italy, it emerges that teachers hardly ever intervene to stop bullying, though the victims themselves consider their potential action very effective (Menesini et al., 1997).

These data point to a "culture of silence", which is the real danger to be faced: it removes and denies the shameful events and nullifies the roles of each person involved as they are dispersed in a general ethos relieving individuals of their responsibilities. A first step for the prevention of this phenomenon is, therefore, to engage the different systems involved with the child, particularly schools and families. Special attention should also be devoted to discussion and communication opportunities for teachers, parents, and pupils in order to improve awareness of bullying and ensure a shared definition of the problem. With regard to intervention, some of the documented Italian experiences (Menesini, 2000; 2003; Menesini and Modiano, 2003) include:

1) Interventions at school level (educational projects; whole school policies)

2) Intervention at group-class level (curricular and cross-curricular approaches which focus on developing social abilities and cooperation)

3) Intervention based on peer support models (befriending and mediation models).

Most of these school interventions have been implemented and evaluated in several areas of the country and their effectiveness was tested over a short period. In the majority of the cases, these intervention-studies were implemented with three steps: 1) teachers' training; 2) school or classroom interventions and 3) pre-and post-test evaluations.

The most popular types of intervention in Italy are based on the curricular approach at the class group level. This approach usually consists of a variety of integrated activities across several areas of the curriculum. Many bullying prevention programs for Italian schools have been developed in the following areas: literature, history, audiovisual education, role-playing and drama, empathy training, communicative skills and mediation training (Menesini, 2003). This approach has been extensively validated, enriched and adapted in many schools across the country. Generally curricular and short-term interventions seem to raise awareness about bullying and change the attitudes towards the problem, but often they are less effective in modifying individual behaviour and in bringing long-lasting effects on the school climate.

Another type of intervention against bullying is that of peer support, which aims to enhance students' responsibility to take action against bullying and to improve school and class climate. The most popular approach, especially for primary and middle schools in Italy, is the "befriending model" defined as "operatore amico" in Italian. Usually two or three students in the class volunteer in turn for 2-3 months to help other children in their social, emotional and learning needs. There have been two evaluation studies of befriending as a bullying prevention strategy: one carried out in two middle schools from Central Italy (Menesini, Codecasa, Benelli & Cowie, 2003) and the other carried out in two primary and four middle schools in the Venice area (Menesini, 2003; Lazzarin and Zambianchi, 2004). In general, the evaluations showed a positive effect on the experimental classes, preventing a normative increase in bullying and pro-bullying behaviours, especially among boys, and reducing bystanders' attitudes of apathy and indifference (see Figure 3).

Figure 3. Differences on bullying scale between experimental boys and girls and the students of the control classes at two data collection points

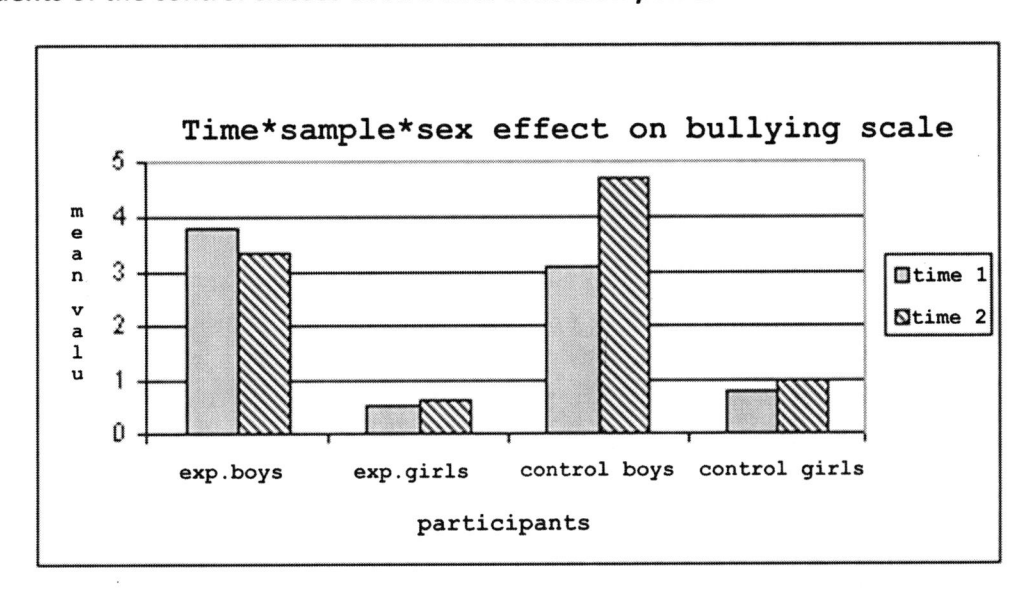

The whole school approach has not been frequently implemented in Italy. Teachers are often reluctant to introduce this approach in schools, since they tend to prefer class-level interventions which are easier to implement and do not require extensive resources and organization. There are, however, some well documented studies showing that this approach can be particularly effective in reducing bullying in schools. Even within Italy, the most significant results were obtained by interventions at the school level. For instance an experience in two middle schools reported by Menesini (2000) showed a strong decrease of the phenomenon estimated at more than 50% in six years (see Figure 4). This experience started as a curricular intervention and after four years teachers and principals decided to develop a school anti-bullying policy to frame and support the work done at the class level. This program focused on involving different levels of the school system: principals, teachers, students, and parents and the results, as depicted in Figure 4) showed that this systemic approach can affect bullying in the long term.

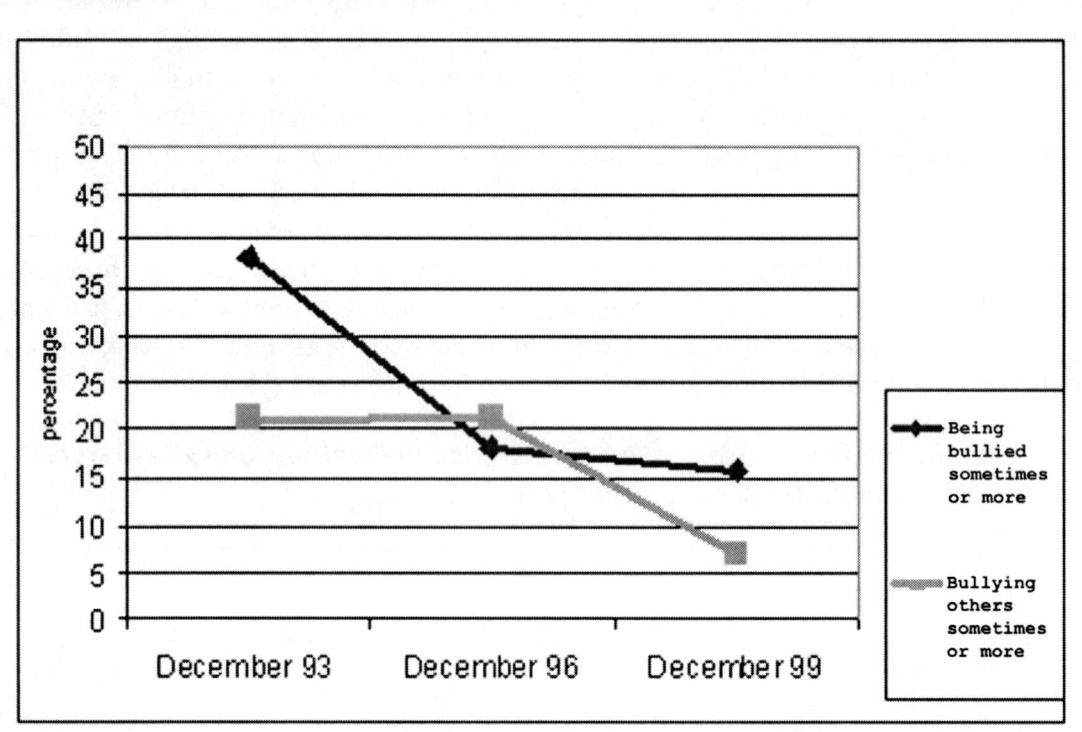

Figure 4. Mean values of being bullied and bullying others at three different data collection times

As Gini (2004) pointed out, intervention programs in Italy show an overall good level of success in modifying pupils' attitudes and in reducing the incidence of victimization. However, the need emerges for a more comprehensive and systemic approach to achieve more effective results and to support the anti-bullying policy in the long term.

The Current Attention to Adolescence

Since most of the intervention research done in Italy has focused on students of primary and middle schools, some scholars have recently turned their attention to a deeper analysis of bullying in adolescence. In our view, in fact, the meaning of bullying is strongly intertwined with that of development both in terms of continuity and discontinuity of experiences and of contexts where these interactional patterns take place across developmental stages. Secondly, bullying compared to the other forms of aggressive behaviour, is persistent over time, takes place in the context of a group of peers and most children are aware of it. Even if not attacking the victim or joining in the harassment, the silent majority of classmates play a significant role in what is going on. These two features of bullying, development and contexts, can be considered as two key factors which have influenced research and interventions in our country.

In relation to literature, there are currently two opposite hypotheses on bullying and violence in adolescence. Some authors stress the decreasing trend of this behaviour with age (Olweus, 1993; Smith et al. 1999); conversely, others stress the increase of violence and antisocial behaviour during the same period (Moffitt, Caspi, Rutter & Silva, 2001; Stattin and Magnusson, 1989; Loeber and Hay, 1997). Although not all adolescents and children involved in bullying are antisocial, we might ask whether different types of aggression, frequently observed at this age, are related to each other and belong to the same latent variable or are simply separate manifestations of aggression. These are some of the issues we would like to address using data from studies carried out in more recent years. Pepler and colleagues (2001) drawing from a developmental-contextual approach, hypothesized that bullying among older students is not restricted to the school context, but it pervades other relevant social relationship contexts. Bullying has been defined as a social behaviour in its most intimate nature. Whereas among younger children the elective context of display is represented by the class group, among adolescents it moves to the more spontaneous relationship contexts that teens have, such as within groups of friends and cross-sex relationships. Some authors consider bullying as part of a more general aggressive pattern.

Olweus (1993) underlined how bullies are often characterized by psychotic personality, they show positive attitudes towards violence, and bullying is often associated with antisocial and deviant behaviour (Farrington, 1993). Andershed, Stattin and Kerr (2001) tried to verify whether the people involved in school bullying were also involved in violence in the streets. They collected data on sample of almost 3,000 14-year-old students in Sweden, and showed that bullying was strongly linked to street violent behaviour and weapon-carrying both in boys and girls. Results were discussed within the mechanism of social selection which can be relevant for explaining continuity across different contexts and patterns. Rutter (2005) and Moffitt et al. (2001) in fact suggested that these aggressive individuals have a high probability of selecting situations and environments that favour antisocial behaviour. Consistent with this, Baldry (2001) and Baldry and Farrington (2000) show that, although bullies are considered at risk for deviant and transgressive behaviour in later years, they also present a concurrent risk of being involved in deviant behaviours.

During adolescence, cross-sex relationships emerge as another context for aggressive behaviour in the form of sexual harassment and dating aggression. From a relational and developmental perspective, the social contacts with cross-sex peers become more and more salient in pre-adolescence and adolescence. According to Pellegrini (2001), dating and access to heterosexual peers are important resources for adolescents; therefore, youth with a tendency to bully frequently use bullying and sexual harassment to be dominant in their peer group. Others have found that sexual harassment is mediated by dating experiences: those youth who bully and are highly involved in dating experiences or are more precocious tend to sexually harass other peers (Connolly, Pepler, Craig & Taradash, 2000; Wekerle & Wolfe, 1999).

In 2002, we started a longitudinal study on bullying and victimization in adolescence. To this purpose we followed a cohort of 1,300 students of a city in Tuscany for three years during secondary high schools (Menesini & Nocentini, 2006). The aims of this study were to answer the following questions:

- How frequent is bullying during adolescence?

- Which types of behaviours are more frequent at this age compared to younger ages?

- How stable is bullying?

- How much is bullying related to other types of aggressive and antisocial behaviour such as violence in the street, sexual harassment, dating violence and drugs use ?

By means of several self-report measures we have obtained relevant results which show that in high schools there appear to be some specific characteristics of bullying as follows:

1) A clear decrease in the prevalence compared to rates in primary and middle schools, with a figure ranging from 10 to 20%, as well as significant differences across school types (peaks in vocational schools as compared to technical and classical schools).

2) Higher reports of perpetration compared to victimization experiences.

3) Cross-age nature of the problem: At this stage, bullying seems to be present not only with same-age students as in previous stages, but also in the interactions between older and younger students. In Italy, this is referred to as "nonnismo" (similar to hazing of young recruits in the army). Younger students frequently reported experiences of victimization at the hands of older students in school, as well as before and after school.

4) A high prevalence of bullying and violence outside schools on buses and trains (19.8%), on the street (34.6%), and in groups of friends or crowds (37.5%); paradoxically the prevalence of bullying outside schools was higher compared to the rate of school bullying.

5) Some bullying takes the form of sexual harassment towards cross-sex peers (3.1% bullying and 8.2% being bullied) or same-sex peers (16.1% bullying and 6.3% being bullied). Often the same students can be involved in other types of violence such as dating violence or violence in the streets.

In this study, we could also investigate the relation between bullying and other antisocial or risk behaviours. The main findings were:

- Youth who bullied or were involved in both bullying and victimization were at greater risk for patterns of aggressive and other antisocial behaviours, such as drug use.

- Youth who bullied or were involved in both bullying and victimization were more likely to be involved both in the role of perpetrators and victims of physical aggression and sexual harassment in their dating relationships. These findings confirm our hypothesis, that in adolescence, coerciveness in peer interactions, such as that represented by bullying, can be transferred to dating and cross-sex relationships.

- Youth who bullied or were involved in both bullying and victimization were also often involved in the double role of the perpetrator and victimized individual in other contexts; they experienced both internalizing and externalizing symptoms and were at higher risk for dating violence.

- All these findings highlight the role of social selection in adolescence: the continuity of problems for youth who bully or are involved in both bullying and victimization can be related to specific environments which reinforce individuals' behaviours. This hypothesis seems particularly relevant for adolescents who are more pro-active in their relationships and can easily prefer similar friends

Although bullying is often the result of the interaction between contextual factors, which can easily explain the social dynamic of phenomenon, (Salmivalli et al. 1996), and personality factors, social selection processes seem to be particularly relevant, especially during the adolescent stage and in the case of aggressive behaviour (Rutter, 2005; Moffitt et al., 2001). In middle childhood, bullying behaviours are exhibited by a large portion of the population and participation in this form of aggression is variable in terms of percentages and the children involved. In adolescence, however, a progressively deviant track seems to be established and maintained both across different contexts and within the same persons.

We can also look at the problem of continuity across domains, relationships, and typologies from the perspective of victimized youth. The majority of the aforementioned studies have focused on continuity between different types of behaviour in the case of perpetrators. Is it possible to find continuity also in the case of the victimized youth? How much do personality versus contextual variables play a role in the individual development of victimized adolescents?

Although there is a paucity of research on the associations among different types of victimization (in school, in the street, and/or in an intimate relationship), there are several studies on the health consequences of victimization from childhood to adulthood for school bullying. The research is generally consistent in finding that children and youth who are victims of peer bullying are at high risk for the development of internalizing symptoms. From our study, however, it seems that victimized youth are significantly less consistent in their problematic behaviour compared to those who are involved in bullying their peers (Menesini and Nocentini, 2006).

New and Future Directions for Interventions

Based on this discussion of the problem of bullying in adolescence, we propose the following new directions for intervention projects in secondary schools:

1) *Addressing bullying between older and younger students.* To reduce the likelihood that older students will bully the new students in a school, we recommend a "Welcoming peer group" for incoming students. Several projects on peer welcoming have been developed and published (Cowie & Wallace, 2000). These are peer support models designed to prevent negative attitudes towards younger students and to give them support and mentoring. In these experiences, peer supporters, who are usually older students, are involved in a series of interventions with the incoming classes to introduce the new students to the system and to have a specific responsibility to care for and respect the new students. One such project was carried out in 2001-2002 in three secondary schools. These interventions were evaluated at the European level within The Connect project "Violence in Schools" (Menesini, 2003).

2) *Addressing bullying among cross-sex and same sex interactions.* To prevent the emerging forms of bullying in cross- and same-sex relationships, we have developed sexual harassment and dating violence prevention programs. A pilot program within a high school in Tuscany (Menesini & Nocentini, 2005) was designed to improve students' skills in interpersonal communication in order to prevent and solve problems which might occur in dating experiences. The focus of the program was on raising awareness about sex roles and stereotypes, developing understanding of emotion communication signals of the other, improving conflict mediation skills, and understanding mutuality and empathy in romantic relations.

3) *School Mediation Projects.* This model of mediation has been implemented in some schools in Rome (Baldry, 2004) and in some projects supported by European Union (Buccoliero & Maggi, 2005). The basic tenet of these projects is to help students understand what a conflict is and which strategies can be implemented to solve conflicts. In some cases, a group of students and adult mediators have been trained to resolve disputes and conflicts. In other cases, the approach is mainly focused on students and the aim is to develop and implement formal and informal peer mediation among them.

In all these experiences carried out in high schools the emphasis is on peer involvement and participation. Within these programs, peers are regarded as a school resource which can be activated to prevent and address problems, and to enhance empathic skills and group cooperation.

Conclusion

Based on the wide range of findings in the present chapter, we can draw two general conclusions. First, from the overall evaluation of the research on the nature and prevention of bullying, it is clear that significant strides have been made in the last 10 years. Within this body of research, there is a common thread: an effort to improve students' responsibility, respect and citizenship. In recent years, in Italy we have observed the development of a public ethos based on indifference and private gains in contrast with the sense of common good. The bullying prevention initiatives are designed to break this wall of indifference and egocentrism and to promote a new sense of responsibility and respect towards others. Within the approaches that focus beyond individual children and youth and extend to the community, bullying prevention programs aim to promote "A way of living together". From a broader social perspective, these programs promote "a new ethic of responsibility and caring" in young generations and in this way may contribute to social-cultural change.

Secondly, it is important to note that although substantial research and intervention efforts on bullying started almost 15 years ago and has been well documented, further efforts are required. In particular, there is a need for more coordinated national strategies, and perhaps international strategies to prevent violence and bullying among young people. With respect to interventions in Italy, there appears to be a sharp contrast between the large number of local studies reported and the absence of a specific national policy. The comparison between these two institutional levels highlights the need for stronger cooperation between different systems working to support the healthy development of children and youth: schools, universities, political committees, and NGOs. As O'Moore (2004) reported, the problem of bullying is so complex that individual school efforts alone are not enough to combat the problem. Therefore, a commitment of the governments will be required as suggested by World Health Organization report (2002) on violence and health and also by the United Nations report (2006) on violence and violence prevention.

Key Messages

1. The construct of bullying is understood differently by different linguistic groups and cultures and caution should be exercised when comparing the prevalence of bullying and victimization across cultures.

2. Compared to their peers, children who bully obtained the highest scores for moral disengagement, particularly with regard to dehumanisation - a process that enables cruelty without guilt (Bandura, 1990). Children who bullied their peers also reported feeling more indifferent or proud than did other students when they were asked to imagine taking the bullying role in a story.

3. In Italy, the prevalence of bullying among primary school students is greater than among secondary school students, and interventions to date have focused on primary school students. Adolescents who bully or are involved in both bullying and victimization pose a significant concern because we found they were more likely than their peers to engage in concurrent drug use, sexual harassment, dating aggression, and street violence. Victimization among adolescents did not appear to show the same continuity across contexts, although long term mental health risks are consistently reported in the literature.

4. Curricular and peer support approaches at the class level are the most common bullying prevention approaches used in Italy. These short-term approaches seem to raise awareness and change attitudes, but often are less effective than school level programs in modifying individual behaviour and bringing long-lasting effects on school climate. A national bullying prevention policy, the commitment of government, and greater cooperation between the education system and other systems working with children and youth are necessary to support healthy development.

References

Almeida A.M (1999) *Portugal*. In P.K. Smith, Y. Morita, J. Junger-Tas, D. Olweus, R. Catalano, and P. Slee (a cura di) *The Nature of School Bullying. A Cross-national Perspective*, London & New York: Routledge, pp.174-186.

Arsenio, W. F., & Lemerise, E. A. (2001). *Varieties of childhood bullying: Values, emotion processes, and social competences*. Social Development, 10, 59-73.

Andershed, H., Stattin, H., & Kerr, M. (2001). *Bullying in school and violence on the streets. - Are the same people involved?* Journal of Scandinavian Studies in Criminology and Crime Prevention, 2, 31-49

Bacchini D., Valerio P. (1997). *Napoli: l'arte di sopravvivere tra conflitto ed affiliazione*. In A. Fonzi, *Il bullismo in Italia*, Giunti, Firenze.

Baldry A. (2001). *Italy*. In R. Summers, A. Hoffman (eds.) Teen violence: Global perspective. Greenwood: Publishing: Westport.

Baldry A. C. (2004) *La mediazione scolastica: principi e metodi*. In R. G. Ardone e A.C. Baldry (a cura di) *Mediare i conflitti a scuola*. Roma: Carocci, 117-138.

Baldry, A., Farrington, D. (2000). *Bullies and delinquents: Personal Characteristics and Parental Styles*, Journal of Community and Applied Social Psychology, 10, 17-31

Bandura, A. (1991). *Social Cognitive Theory of moral thought and action*. In J. Kurtines, & W. Y. Gewirtz (Eds.). *Handbook of moral behaviour and development, Vol. 1: Theory*. New York: Lawrence Erlbaum Associates.

Buccoliero E. Maggi M. (2005) *Bullismo, bullismo*. Milano: F. Angeli.

Camodeca M. , Menesini E., (2007) *Approccio contestuale al senso di colpa e alla vergogna: Validazione di uno strumento*. Età evolutiva (in press)

Caravita S. (2004) *L'alunno prepotente*. Brescia: La scuola editore.

Castorina S. (2003) *Fantasie di bullismo. I racconti di bulli e vittime al test proiettivo dell'abuso infantile*. Milano: F. Angeli.

Connolly J.A., Pepler D., Craig W., Taradash A. (2000). *Dating experiences of bullies in early adolescence*. Child Maltreatment: Journal of the American Professional Society on the Abuse of Children, 5, 299-311.

Cowie H., Wallace P. (2000). *Peer support in action. From bystanding to standing by*. London: Sage Publication.

Farrington D.P. (1993). *Understanding and preventing bullying*. In Tonry M, Morris N. (eds): "*Crime and justice: An annual review of research. Vol.17.*" Chicago, IL: University of Chicago Press, pp. 381-458.

Fonzi A. (1997) (ed.) *Il bullismo in Italia. Il fenomeno delle prepotenze a scuola dal Piemonte alla Sicilia. Ricerche e prospettive d'intervento*. Firenze: Giunti.

Fonzi, A. (1999) (ed.). *Il gioco crudele: compagni vittime e compagni oppressori*. Firenze: Giunti.

Fonzi A., Genta M.L., Menesini E., Bacchini D., Bonino S., Costabile A., (1999), *Italy*. In P.K. Smith, Y. Morita, J. Junger-Tas, D. Olweus, R. Catalano, and P. Slee (a cura di) *The Nature of School Bullying. A Cross-national Perspective*, London & New York: Routledge, pp.140-156.

Genta M.L. (2002) (ed.). *Il bullismo. Ragazzi aggressivi a scuola*. Roma: Carocci.

Gini, G. (2004). *Bullying in Italian schools: an overviewof intervention programmes*. School Psychology International, 25 (1), 106-116), 2004.

Junger-Tas J. (1999). *The Netherlands*. In P.K. Smith, Y. Morita, J. Junger-Tas, D. Olweus, R. Catalano, and P. Slee (a cura di) *The Nature of School Bullying. A Cross-national Perspective*, London & New York: Routledge, pp.205-223.

Lazzarin M.G., Zambianchi E. (2004) *Pratiche didattiche per prevenire il bullismo a scuola*. Milano: F. Angeli.

Loeber R. , Hay D. (1997) *Key issues in the development of aggression and violence from childhood to early adulthood*, Annual Review of Psychology, 48, 371-410.

Marini F. , Mameli C. (1999) *Il bullismo nelle scuole*, Roma: Carocci.

Menesini E. (2000) *Bullismo, che fare? Prevenzione e strategie di intervento nella scuola*. Firenze: Giunti.

Menesini E. (2003) (ed.) *Bullismo: le azioni efficaci della scuola*. Trento : Erickson Edizioni.

Menesini E., Codecasa E., Benelli B., Cowie H. (2003) *Enhancing children's responsibility to take action against bullying: evaluation of a befriending intervention in Italian middle schools*. Aggressive Behavior,29, 1-14

Menesini E., Eslea M., Smith P.K., Genta M.L., Giannetti E., Fonzi A., Costabile A. (1997) *A crossnational comparison of children's attitudes towards bully/victim problems in school*, Aggressive Behavior, 23,1-13 .

Menesini E., Fonzi A., P.K. Smith (2002) *Attribution of meanings to terms related to bullying: a comparison between teacher and pupil perspectives in Italy*. European Journal of Psychology of Education, XVII, 4, 393-406.

Menesini E., Fonzi A. Vannucci M. (1999) *Il disimpegno morale: la legittimazione del comportamento prepotente*. In FONZI A *(a cura di) Il gioco crudele. Studi e ricerche sui correlati psicologici del bullismo*. Firenze: Giunti, pp.39-53.

Menesini E., Modiano R. (2003) *A Multi-faceted Reality: A Report from Italy. P.K. Smith (ed.) Violence in schools: the response in Europe*, Routledge Falmer Ed. , pp.153-168.

Menesini E. e Nocentini A. L. (2006). *Bullismo e comportamenti a rischio in adolescenza. Percorsi di continuità e discontinuità in un campione di studenti delle scuole superiori*. Lucca: Edizioni Provincia di Lucca.

Menesini E., Nocentini A. (2005) *Educazione affettiva e relazionale con l'altro sesso. Percorso di intervento per la prevenzione dell'aggressività e delle molestie nei rapporti interpersonali*. Internal Report – Department of Psychology – University of Florence.

Menesini E., Sanchez V., Fonzi A., Ortega R., Costabile A., Lo Feudo G. (2003) *Moral emotions and bullying. A cross-national comparison of diffenrences between bullies, victims and outsiders*. Aggressive Behavior, 29, 515-530.

O'Moore, M. (2004). *A guiding framework for policy approaches to school bullying and violence. Taking fear out of the schools.* (Organisation for Economic Co-operation and Development), OECD Conference, Stavanger, Norway, 5-8 settembre 2004.

Moffitt, T.E., Caspi A. , Rutter M., Silva P. A. (2001) *Sex differences in antisocial behavior*. Cambridge : Cambridge Univ. Press.

Olweus, D. (1993). *Bullying at school. What we know and what we can do*. Oxford: Blackwell.

Olweus D. (1999) *Sweden*. In P.K. Smith , Y. Morita , J. Junger -Tas , D. Olweus , R. Catalano and P. Slee (a cura di) *The Nature of School bullying. A cross national Perspective*, London: Routledge, pp. 7-27.

Pepler D, Craig W, Connolly J, Henderson K (2001): *Bullying sexual harassment, dating violence and substance use among adolescents*. In Werkele C, Wall AM (eds): "The violence and addiction equation." New York: Brunner-Routledge, pp.153-168.

Pepler, D., Craig, W., Yuile, A., & Connolly, J. (2004). *Girls who bully: A developmental and relational perspective*. In M. Putallaz & J. Kupersmidt (Eds.) *Aggression, antisocial behavior, and violence among girls*. Pp. 90-109. New York: Guilford Publications.

Pellegrini A. D. (2001). *A longitudinal study of heterosexual relationships, aggression, and sexual harassmentduring the transition from primary school through middle school*, Journal of Applied Developmental Psychology, Vol 22 (2), 119-133

Rutter M. 2005 *Multiple meanings of a developmental perspective on psychopathology*. European Journal of Developmental Psyhcology, 23, 221-252.

Salmivalli, C., Lagerspetz, K., Björkqvist, K., Österman, K., & Kaukiainen, A., (1996) *Bullying as a group process: participant roles and their relations to social status within the group*. AggressiveBehavior, 22, 1-15.

Smith, P.K., Cowie, H., Olafsson, R. & Liefooghe, A.M. (2002). *Definition of bullying: a comparison of terms used, and age and sex differences, in a 14-country international comparison*. Child Development, 73, 1119-1133.

Smith, P.K., Morita, Y., Junger –Tas, J., Olweus, D., Catalano, R. & Slee, P. (1999) (eds). *The Nature of School bullying. A Cross National Perspective*. London: Routledge.

Smorti A. (2003) *Bullying e prepotenze: ricerche sul significato*. Nucleo monotematico. Età evolutiva, 74, 48-50.

Smorti A., Menesini E., Smith P.K (2003), *Parents' definition of children's bullying in a five-country comparison*, Journal of cross-cultural psychology, Vol. 34,4, 417-432.

Stattin H. , Magnusson D. (1989) *The role of early aggressive behavior in the frequency, seriousness and types of later crime,* Journal of Consulting and Clinical Psychology, 1, 312-321.

U.N. (2006). *Violence against children*. United nations Secretary- General's study. New York, United Nations Organization.

Wekerle C., Wolfe, D.A. (1999). *Dating violence in mid-adolescence: Theory, significance, and emerging prevention initiatives*. Clinical Psychology Review, 19, 435- 456.

Whitney I., Smith P.K. (1993), *A survey of the nature and extent of bullying in junior/middle and secondary schools*, Educational Research, 35, 3-25.

WHO (2002). *World report on violence and health*, Geneva, World Health Organization.

Chapter 14:

Preventing School Bullying: The Irish Experience

Professor Mona O'Moore
Anti-bullying Research and Resource Centre,
School of Education,
Trinity College

Introduction

Who cares if someone gets a little hurt? We Were Men.

We never thought we would go too far.
We were doing him a favour.
He would get nowhere in life if it wasn't for us.
Each punch was like a lesson,
As he cowered and tried to shield himself from us
We would taunt and jeer at his failings.
And yes, on that final day
As he ran and fell, we pummelled him like putty.
Each punch, each call, each stumble, each fall
Made us that bit older and stronger. Honourable.
And yes we were great, powerful and on top of the world.
We Were Men.

That was until the next day,
When a stone cold, little, blue body got pulled out of the canal.

This verse was written by a schoolboy Jack Fox after an awareness raising campaign to stop school bullying and violence. The verse I believe reflects the progress that schools in Ireland have made to raise the awareness among our school-going population of the potential cost to individuals, families, and societies of peer aggression, bullying and violence. While much has been achieved since the first European Seminar that was held on School Bullying in Norway (O'Moore,1990), the most recent international survey carried out by the WHO (2004) in 35 countries indicated that there is no room for complacency within or outside of Europe. Only 35% of all young people (age 11 to 15 years of age) were not involved in any fighting, bullying or victimization. The WHO report (2004) highlights that peer aggression and victimization is a significant obstacle to healthy educational, social, and emotional adjustment and without intervention, the young people involved "are likely to be trapped in a snowballing pattern of negative interaction with family, teachers, peers, and romantic partners" (WHO, 2004, p.143). It is clear that the cost of this to individuals, families, schools, and society makes the necessity even greater for effective prevention of school violence.

Due to the complex and multi-faceted nature of school violence, it is well recognized that action from schools alone may not be sufficient to counteract the problem. To make a difference, action is undoubtedly required at a local, national, and international level (O'Moore, 2004). This is not however, to undermine the role of the school in prevention and intervention of school bullying. There is growing evidence to indicate that schools have the potential to reduce significantly the level of peer harassment, bullying, and violence (Vettenburg, 1999, Smith, Pepler & Rigby, 2004, Minton & O'Moore, 2004a). Evidence also is available to indicate that the earlier the intervention is introduced to children, the greater its effectiveness (Rigby, 2002). The added value of early intervention is that it is also more cost effective (OECD, 2004).

However, there is as yet no universal agreement as to which elements of intervention are the best predictors of change. In order to arrive at a consensus greater attention will have to be paid to criteria for evaluating effective prevention programs. The three criteria given the most weight by Blueprints for Violence prevention (Institute of Behavioural Science, University of Colorado, 2005) are: 1) a strong research design, 2) sustained effect, and 3) multiple site replications It is encouraging that the Olweus Bullying Prevention Program, has met these criteria and as a result has been judged a Blueprint program (Olweus & Limber, 1999). It is not surprising therefore the Olweus Bullying Prevention Program has been applied more or less directly in several countries. It is worthy of note, however, that the ability of the program to reduce the level of bullying can vary considerably from one intervention study to the next (Smith et al.2004). Thus, it is necessary to continue to develop and evaluate programs to prevent and address school bullying and violence.

As teachers are in the forefront of intervention in school violence, all programs that involve schools will by necessity have to incorporate teachers to a greater or lesser extent. For example, the intervention programs included in Smith, Pepler, and Rigby (2004) have all included opportunities to train teachers to "orient them to the concerns and strategies for bullying problems."

All the independent intervention studies reported on in Smith et al. (2004) have had varying degrees of success. Roland (2000) suggests that the success of intervention programs is very much dependent on the commitment of teachers. From my own experience of working with teachers at pre and in-service education levels, it would appear that the lack of commitment tends to be associated with inaccurate perceptions of school bullying and violence, as well as, an inability to deal effectively with incidents as they arise. This view has been echoed by members of the British-Irish Anti-Bullying Forum (2003). This is perhaps not surprising in view of the lack of pre-service training available to teachers world-wide on the subject of prevention and management of bullying and violence in schools. (O'Moore, 2000a; Vettenburg, 1999; Benbenisty & Astor, 2003). There is little doubt that initial teacher education on school bullying and violence would better sensitize teachers to the problem and ensure a greater level of competence to apply prevention and intervention strategies. Nicolaides, Toda and Smith (2002) found that trainee teachers would strongly welcome an input on school bullying in their basic training course. Indeed, the majority of the teachers in their study viewed it as essential to their training. The components that they identified as most important were those that are associated with secondary prevention, namely the measures to deal effectively with the students who are involved in school bullying.

Thus, to be effective, prevention programs for teachers whether at pre-service or in-service level need to pay particular attention to the teacher training element of the program. If one examines the different prevention programs that have been evaluated (Minton & O'Moore, 2004a, Smith et al. 2004), there are considerable differences in the amount of time that is given to sensitize teachers to the programs to be implemented in their schools. There are also considerable differences in the approaches to training. Some programs are more focused on the specific problem of bullying than others. Galloway and Roland (2004) support a more holistic approach since it will be more likely to support sustainable change.

In Ireland, as a result of a nationwide study of school bullying (see Table 1) that was conducted during 1993-1995 (O'Moore et al, 1997), it became clear that initiatives were needed on a national scale to prevent and reduce and counter school bullying.

Nationwide Study Primary & Post-Primary Schools

	Primary (N =9599)	Post Primary (N =10,843)
Children who Bully	12.3%	10.8%
Children who are Victimized	17.1%	11.5%
Children who both bully and are victimized	14.1%	4.1%
Total Involved	43.5%	26.5%

In planning the Irish National Initiative, consideration was given to existing programs. This process was facilitated by a conference on school bullying held at Trinity College Dublin in Oct. 1996 (O'Moore, 1997). The lessons that contributed to the development of a future model of prevention for Irish schools at that conference broadly included:

- Adopt a whole school approach inclusive of the community (Tattum, 1997; Byrne, 1997)

- Develop a school policy consulting as widely with the school community as possible (Smith, 1997, Mellor, 1997)

- Develop resources for teachers, parents, and pupils (Olweus, 1997; Roland & Munthe, 1997)

- Develop measures at the school, classroom, and individual level that are integrated into the day to day management of the school (Olweus, 1997; Roland & Munthe, 1997)

- Develop measures that are not just teacher directed (Rigby, 1997)

- Develop a network of professionals who assist in the implementation of a program on a regional and national basis (Roland & Munthe, 1997)

- Commitment of teachers is critical to the success of a program (Roland & Munthe, 1997)

An effort was made to incorporate all of these elements into the pilot project that was to be the basis of a nation-wide project to prevent and address with bullying, harassment and violence in Irish schools (O'Moore & Minton, 2004b). As a result, the bullying-prevention program adopted a multi-level whole school approach inclusive of the wider community. While the program had as its focus school bullying, it did not exclude violence. The view was taken that violence is not restricted to physical force but takes in aggression beyond physical aggression (O'Moore,2000b).

The pilot program adopted a structural framework that was similar to the second Norwegian national program of 1996 that was developed by Roland and Munthe (1997). Essentially, a network of professional teachers was trained who in turn provided training for teachers in schools which aimed to implement the program. This model increasingly referred to as "train-the- trainer" model had the advantage of being both cost effective and inclusive of all staff in a school, thereby enhancing the cooperation of everyone and avoiding the setting up of an 'elite' group. The project was named the Donegal Anti-Bullying Program because the evaluation took place in the County of Donegal, Ireland. Once the evaluation was complete, there was an expectation to implement the program on a national scale. Each Region in Ireland has an Education Centre which has the responsibility for the professional development of teachers. It was expected that each Education Centre in Ireland would nominate two teachers for training, one primary and one post-primary that would be a resource for their region. Also there was to be provision for accrediting teachers for their participation either by way of a Post Graduate Diploma and/or a M.Ed. in Aggression Studies (awarded by Trinity College, Dublin) with the potential to advance to Doctorate level.

Selection of Schools

All Primary schools in Area 1 of the County of Donegal (one of 26 Counties in the Republic of Ireland) were invited to participate in the study. In total 42 out of a possible 100 accepted.

Program Methodology

The program was carried out in 3 stages and each stage was evaluated. The first stage involved the training of a network of 11 teachers. The second stage involved the training of: a) the teachers and members of the board of management of the schools aiming to implement the anti-bullying program and b) the parents & members of the wider community of the schools involved in the project. The third stage involved the implementation of the program.

Stage 1: Training of the Network of Professionals

Eleven teachers were trained through a program of workshops and seminars, to provide education and support for boards of management, staff, pupils and parents in the prevention and management of bullying behaviour in their school communities. The training was conducted in 12 weekends over six months in the local Education Centre in Donegal town. On a few occasions the training took place in the local Health Board's Centre in Letterkenny. The Director of the Donegal Education Centre (Sally Bonnar) and the Education Officer of the North Western Health Board (Ann McIntyre) were instrumental in facilitating and providing ongoing support to the Network of trainers. Indeed the success of the project undoubtedly owes much to their unstinting efforts

The Training Program

The areas covered in the training program were: definitions of bullying, the myths of bullying, the extent of bullying, the signs of victimization and bullying, the ill-effects of bullying, and the causes of bullying behaviour, preventative strategies and strategies to deal with incidents of bullying. The need to include these elements were crystallised for me after a tragic suicide in Ireland which appeared to have its roots in school bullying (O'Moore, 2000a) and are supported by research (Nicolaides et al., 2002)

Rarely do teacher prevention programs provide information on the course content much beyond listing the areas that were covered in the training of the teachers (Smith, Pepler, & Rigby, 2004). Galloway and Roland (2004) argue that the approach that is taken in training teachers is a determinant of the success of a prevention program. Details of the content of the course can be obtained from the training manual that has been developed to accompany the national teacher prevention program (O'Moore & Minton, 2004a).

Stage 2: Training Of the Teachers

On completion of the training of the members of the Network, they were given the responsibility of 3 to 5 primary schools each. A launch of the program was arranged so that the principals of the project school had the opportunity to learn more about the program and meet the trainers. In attendance and giving their support were representatives from the Government's Department of Education & Science, the local Health Board and local Education Centre. A dinner and a true Irish evening followed the formal proceedings.

Subsequent to the launch, the trainers arranged the in-service days for the training of the staff at the 42 participating schools. One hundred and ninety-seven teachers took part in the in-service training. There were 14 groups in all with the size of the groups ranging from 10 to 20 teachers. Some of the smaller schools arranged to go together for the training. The trainers covered the following topics: Definition of bullying; Myths of bullying; Types of bullying behaviour; Profile of children who are victimized and children who bully; Effects of bullying; Developing a multi-level whole school approach, inclusive of a school policy; Classroom strategies for prevention of bullying; and Intervention – what to do when bullying happens.

In drawing up a school policy for addressing bullying behaviour, the staff were encouraged to draw on the Guidelines on Countering Bullying Behaviour in Primary and Post Primary Schools (Department of Education and Science, 1993). The elements of the policy are as follows:

1. To create a school ethos which encourages children to disclose and discuss incidents of bullying behaviour.

2. To raise awareness of bullying as a form of unacceptable behaviour with school management, teachers, pupils, parents/guardians.

3. To ensure comprehensive supervision and monitoring measures through which all areas of school activity are kept under observation.

4. To develop procedures for noting and reporting incidents of bullying behaviour.

5. To develop a program of support for those affected by bullying behaviour and for those involved in bullying behaviour.

6. To work with and through the various local agencies in countering all forms of bullying and anti-social behaviour.

7. To evaluate the effectiveness of school policy on anti-bullying behaviour.

The staff were also urged to underwrite their behaviour policy with that of a non-violent sanctions policy (Foster & Thompson (1991) that included using Restorative Approaches such as the No Blame approach (Robinson & Maines, 1992) and the Common Concern Method (Pikas, 1975). There was an understanding that 'No Blame' did not mean 'No Responsibility'. Indeed, the reverse was the case (O'Moore & Minton, 2004). As well as giving the teachers an understanding of the specific strategies to address bullying, there also was a strong emphasis on the importance of applying the principles of positive teaching and assertive discipline in the management of their classrooms (Merrett & Wheldall, 1990; Canter & Canter, 1992).The aim was to work towards helping children develop self-discipline. In addition, there was an emphasis on the crucial role of staff as models of behaviour (Rutter et al., 1979; O'Moore & Minton 2006; Robinson et al., 2006). Thus, the standards that were set for the pupils were to apply also to the staff. Attention was also given to the role of self-esteem in the prevention of bullying. While the relationship between self-esteem and bullying is still controversial (Farrington & Baldry, 2005), the data from O'Moore and Kirkham (2000) points to a very strong relationship. Thus, teachers were encouraged to take every opportunity to enhance the feelings of self- worth among their pupils. Attention also was directed to the benefits of enhancing the self-esteem of teachers (Dunham.1992).

In addition, the staff was introduced to the principles of co-operative learning (Johnson & Johnson, 1994) as a means to help create a more caring community in each classroom. The value of peer tutoring and peer support was also introduced as a potential resource to strengthen pro-active behaviour among peers (Cowie & Wallace, 2000)

Parent Evening

The parent evenings were held to increase awareness, which was also summarized in a flyer (O'Moore, 1999). Essentially, parents were made aware that their school would recognize that: a) Individual differences should be valued and respected; b) Every child has a right to an education that is free from fear and intimidation; c) Bullying behaviour is unacceptable and should not be tolerated. The following information was also provided: what is bullying; types of bullying, signs and symptoms of bullying; if your child is being bullied; if your child is engaged in bullying behaviour; the relationship of self-esteem and bullying; and making contact with the school. The objective of the parent training was to encourage them to contact their school if they suspected or had evidence that their child or indeed another child was being bullied. Particular emphasis was also given to the risks associated with allowing bullying behaviour to go unchallenged for children who bully (Olweus 1993). In other words, parents were told that they would do their child no favours by not challenging their child's unacceptable behaviour. Also, where at all possible, the parents were encouraged to assist schools to correct the inappropriate behaviour. Taking the research evidence into account that high levels of self-concept acted as a deterrent to subsequent bullying behaviours (Salmivalli, Kaukiainen, Kaistaniemi, & Lagerspetz., 1999; O'Moore & Kirkham, 2000), consideration also was given to the role of self-esteem in victimization and bullying.

Stage 3: Implementation of the Whole School Approach Inclusive of the Wider Community

Once completing the in-service day, the role of the staff was to work towards creating a zero tolerance/acceptance of bullying. The development of a School Policy, and School Charter was to facilitate this process. In order to increase ownership over the policy and the charter it was recommended that all interest groups within the school community be invited to participate in their development. The school community as a whole should ideally extend beyond the school management, teaching and non-teaching, pupils and parents, to members in the local community, who come in contact with the pupils, e.g., drivers of school buses, traffic wardens, shopkeepers.

To facilitate the development of a School Charter the staff were introduced to the following example:

- *Every child has the right to enjoy his/her learning and leisure FREE from bullying, both in the school and in the surrounding community.*
- *Our school community will NOT tolerate any bullying, even if the unkind actions were not intended to hurt.*
- *Pupils should support each other by reporting ALL instances of bullying.*
- *Bullying will be dealt with SERIOUSLY.*
- *We are a Telling School. Bullying is too serious not to report.*

Critical to the program was that all teachers created a climate in their own classes that did not accept bullying behaviour. Teachers were encouraged to develop class rules similar to those recommended by Olweus (1993): 1) We shall not bully other pupils; 2) We shall try to help pupils who are bullied; and 3) We shall include pupils who become easily left out. Age-related handbooks and videos on bullying were provided to the teachers to assist them in their awareness raising exercises. It should be pointed out, however, that the videos available at the time did not have children that characterised the Republic of Ireland's school –going population.

In raising awareness of bullying behaviour with the pupils teachers were encouraged to work through the medium of art, music, drama, and literature. A weekday (Open Day) was to occur where children could have their anti-bullying work exhibited for parents and members of the local community.

Evaluation of the Donegal Anti-Bullying Program

The evaluation of the effectiveness of the anti-bullying program was made by a comparison of the pupil responses at pre-test (before the program was implemented) and at post-test (after the program was implemented) based on pupils' responses to the modified Olweus Bully/ Victim Questionnaire. Teacher's responses were assessed by the Rigby Questionnaire.* Pre-testing was conducted (763 pupils in 42 schools) in the autumn term of 1998 when the training of the professional network started. The intervention in schools began during the summer of 1999 and the program was to be implemented during the academic year of 1999-2000. Post-testing (822 pupils in 35 schools) was conducted towards the end of the summer term of 2000.

At the time of analysis it was possible to match pre-test and post-test data from only 22 schools, due to anomalies in the administration of the questionnaires by the schools.

Characteristics of Schools and Students

The number of pupils in the 22 schools ranged from 21 to 280; the mean was 92. The average teaching class size ranged between 3 and 28, the mean was 13.9 pupils per class. In three of the smallest schools the classes were combined to form a single teaching class. Most of the schools with the exception of one were situated in villages (< 1,000 inhabitants) or open country. The socio-economic background of the pupils varied widely between, and within, the schools.

Results

The Prevalence of Victimization

There was a significant reduction of 19.6% in reports of being victimised in the last term ($x^2 = 5.77$, 1df, p<0.02). See Table 2.

Percentage of pupils who reported being bullied during the last school term.

How often:	Before	After
Not at all	63.3	70.5
Occasionally (once or twice)	18.6	17.4
Moderately (sometimes)	10.7	8.5
Frequently (once a week or more)	7.3	3.6

From Table 2, frequent victimization (i.e. being bullied once a week or more often) also was reduced significantly from pre-testing to post-testing (e.g., a reduction of 50%, $x^2 = 6.43$, 1df, p<0.02).

---

* Only the pupil responses will be reported on in this paper. Details of the teachers' responses can be gained from O'Moore & Minton (2005).

The Prevalence of Bullying Others

Percentage of pupils who reported taking part in bullying other pupils during the last school term.

How often:	Before	After
Not at all	72.9	77.6
Occasionally (once or twice)	17.7	18.2
Moderately (sometimes)	6.7	3.3
Frequently (once a week or more)	2.7	0.8

The data in Table 3 show that fewer pupils reported bullying others within the last school term after the implementation of the program than before. However, the reduction of 17.2% was only of marginal statistical significance ($x^2 = 2.89$, 1df, $p<0.10$). However, there was a strongly significant reduction of 69.2% in relation to frequent bullying (that is bullying others once a week or more often) ($x^2 = 7.93$, 1df, $p<.01$).

Pupil Intervention

After the implementation of the program pupils reported that they would be significantly less likely to take passive role when they were witness to another pupil being bullied. (See Table 4) After the program, just 9.2% of pupils reported that they would "do nothing, it's none of my business" when they saw another pupil of their own age being bullied as compared to 15.9% prior to the program ($x^2 = 10.58$, 1df, $p<0.01$).

Percentages for what pupils responded that they usually do when they see a pupil of their own age being bullied at school.

Response:	Before	After
Nothing, it's none of my business	15.9	9.2
Nothing, but I think I ought to help	22.2	19.3
I try to help her or him in some way	61.8	71.4

Teacher Intervention

Percentages of pupils' perceptions as to how often teachers try to put a stop to it when a pupil is being bullied at school.

How often:	Before	After
I don't know	39.4	34.6
Almost never	8.0	7.0
Sometimes	17.2	12.8
Almost always	35.4	45.6

Table 5 indicates that after the intervention, there was an overall improvement, though of marginal statistical significance (x^2 = 3.70, 1df, p<0.10) of the frequencies of their teachers attempts to put a stop to bullying. However, it was encouraging that there was an increase of 28.8% in the level to which teachers were perceived by their pupils to almost always intervene.

Who is told about Bullying?

There was no increase in the reporting of bullying to the teachers (see Table 6), in fact a slight decrease in reporting can be observed.

Percentages of bullied pupils reporting being bullied to teachers.

Response:	Before	After
No, I haven't told them	48.7	52.0
Yes, I have told them	51.3	48.0

Discussion

The evaluation findings were encouraging with regard to the implementation of the whole school/community approach to prevent and counter school bullying. The evaluation indicated that the program was effective with children of primary school age in reducing the level of victimization and bullying. Most importantly, there was a strong reduction in the level of frequent victimization (50%) and of bullying others (69.2%). These findings compare very favourably with the high profile program of Olweus (2004). Also encouraging and in contrast to Pepler et al., (2004), there was the significant improvement (41%) in the pupils' readiness to intervene when they are witness to bullying. The level of teacher intervention as perceived by pupils also was positive, although the 21% increase in the level of intervention reported by the pupils was not as high as expected. This is especially so when the findings are compared to the teachers own perceptions of their level of intervention of bullying incidents (O'Moore & Minton 2005). For example there were 97.6 percent of teachers in the study who reported that they "always" tried to stop bullying.

O'Moore and Minton (2005) have argued that the reported differences in teacher intervention between pupils and teacher reports may be due, at least in part, to how students and teachers define bullying. It is also possible that teachers do 'put a stop to all bullying' that they know about. However, it is the reluctance on the part of the pupils to report the bullying to teachers that may influence their perceptions of teachers appearing not to intervene. The failure in the present study to increase the level of reporting of bullying behaviour was a cause of concern. But the finding may not be as indicative of failure as it first seems. While there is evidence from the pupils qualitative responses that they do not feel that it is safe to tell (O'Moore & Minton, 2003), it may be as has been pointed out by Eslea & Smith (1998) that a bullying prevention program allows for greater pupil assertion and therefore there is less need to report incidents. Not withstanding this, it was felt that the issue concerning the reluctance of children who were victimized to report bullying did merit greater consideration in the subsequent nation-wide project.

The methodological approach used in the present study while similar to other prevention programs for teachers has strengths and limitations. There is little doubt that the pre- and post tests provide opportunities to measure change. Although the study controlled for the natural age related decreases in reports of being victimized found in large scales studies (O'Moore et al., 1997; Smith et al., 1999), it has been asserted by Harachi, Catalano & Hawkins (1999) that the lack of control groups does not allow for a definite conclusion.

A second limitation is that the promising results in the study may reflect the self selection of the schools involved in the project. However, in the subsequent nation-wide study (see below), there are identified control schools. All the schools in the Donegal project were primary school and due to factors outside the control of the research; most of them were small in size. There were four schools that served small towns, and the rest were situated in villages or open country. These factors also will be specifically assessed in the nation-wide evaluation.

The nation-wide program is entitled The ABC Whole School Response to Bullying. The ABC is the acronym for the fundamental principles of the program: *Avoid Aggression, Be Tolerant, and Care for Others.* Since the implementation of the ABC program, a DVD based Resource Pack, "Silent Witnesses" has been developed and launched by the Anti-Bullying Research and Resource Centre (TCD, 11th October, 2006). Silent Witnesses provides an engaging and powerful set of visual tools for secondary teachers and parents to educate young people on peer aggression, bullying and violence. It is the first professionally produced DVD dramatizing peer aggression, bullying, and violence in an Irish setting, with Irish voices. It has sub-titles in the native Irish Language. While 'Silent Witnesses' can be used as an independent awareness raising exercise in any bullying prevention curricula it is hoped that it will strengthen our ABC program in years to come.

To conclude, this Irish study provides considerable evidence that interventions to prevent and reduce school bullying can be successful. The study demonstrates that teachers play a pivotal role in the prevention and intervention of school bullying and violence. The strong commitment among the trainers throughout the program together with the political commitment undoubtedly contributed to the success of the program. Roland and Munthe (1997) have asserted that commitment of teachers is key to the success of an intervention program. Similarly. Benbenisty & Astor (2003) suggest that to prevent school bullying and violence "one of the most promising ideas is to create a teacher group that specialises in bullying and is a resource for programs in their region." Most importantly the present findings strongly support the need for comprehensive bullying prevention curricula at the initial teacher training level. The earlier teachers develop the confidence to deal effectively with problems of bullying and violence, the greater should be the reward in seeing a reduction in peer aggression, bullying and violence.

Key Messages

1. Challenge the myths that promote and reinforce bullying and violence.

2. Build trust and make it safe for children and young people to report bullying and violence.

3. Apply whenever possible restorative approaches when dealing with aggressive behaviour.

4. Involve all partners in a School Community to help build a Whole School Approach which says *NO* to Bullying and Violence.

5. Advocate for a module on *aggressive behaviour* for all teachers in training.

References

Benbenisty, R. & Astor, R.A. (2003) *Violence In Schools: The view from Israel. In: Smith, P.K (Ed.) Violence in Schools, the response in Europe*, London. Routledge-Falmer.

Byrne, B. (1997) *Bullying: A Community Response*, The Irish Journal of Psychology, 18, 2, 258-266.

Canter, L.& Canter ,M.(1992) *Assertive discipline: positive behaviour management for today's classroom*. Lee Canter & Associaties, C.A.,Santa Monica,

Cowie, H.& Wallace, P.(2000) *Peer Support in Action*, London, Sage.

Department of Education and Science (1993).*Guidelines on Countering Bullying Behaviour in Primary and Post Primary Schools*. Dublin. The Stationery Office.

Dunham,J.(1992) *Stress in Teaching*, London, Routledge.

Eslea, M. & Smith, P.K. (1998).*The long term effectiveness of anti-bullying work in primary schools*. Educational Research, 40, 203-18.

Farrington, D.& Baldry,A.C. *Individual risk factors for school violence in school violence*. In: Proceedings of 1X International Meeting on the Biology and Sociology of Violence,Oct.6-7,2005.Valencia,Queen Sofia Centre for the Study of Violence.

Galloway, D. & Roland, E. (2004). *Is the direct approach to reducing bullying always the best?* In: Smith, P. Pepler, D., and Rigby, K. (2004) (Eds), *Bullying in Schools. How Successful can Interventions be?* Cambridge, Cambridge University Press.

Harachi, T.W, Catalano, R.F. & Hawkins, J.D. (1999) *Canada*, In: Smith, P.K, Morita, Y., Junger-Tas, J., Olweus, D., Ratalano, R & Slee, P.(Eds), *The Nature of School Bullying: A Cross-National Perspective*: London, Routledge.

Institute of Behavioural Science, University of Colorado, Boulder, (2005) www.colorado.edu/cspw/blueprints

Johnson,D.W.& Johnson,R.T.(1994) *Learning Together and Alone, Co-operative, Competitive & Individualistic Learning*. New Jersey, Prentice-Hall.

Mellor, A. (1997) *Bullying: The Scottish experience*. The Irish Journal of Psychology, 18, 2, 248 - 257

Merrett,F.&Wheldall, K. (1990) *Effective Classroom Behaviour Management:Positive Teaching in the Primary School*, London, Paul Chapman.

Minton, S.J & O'Moore, M.,(Eds) (2004a) *A Review of Scientifically Evaluated Good Practices of Preventing and Reducing Bullying at School in the EU Member States.*, European Union, Commissioned by the European Commission (Directorate-General Justice & Home Affairs),

Minton, S.J. & O'Moore, M. (2004b) *Teachers – A Critical focus group in both schools based and workplace anti-bullying research: Perspectives from Ireland.* Paper presented to the 4th International Conference on Bullying Harassment in the Workplace. Bergen, Norway, June 28 – 29th. Proceedings.

Nicolaides, S., Toda, Y., & Smith, P.K (2002) *Knowledge and Attitudes about school bullying in trainee teachers.* British Journal of Educational Psychology, 22, 105 – 118.

OECD (2004) *Taking Fear Out Of Schools: International Policy & Research Conference on School Bullying & Violence*, Stavanger University College, Stavanger, Norway, 5th-8th Sept, 2004, edited by OECD & Norwegian Ministry of Education, 2004

Olweus,D.(1993) *Bullying at School: What we know and what we can do.* Oxford and Camridge.Blackwell.

Olweus, D. (1997) *Bully/victim problems in school, knowledge base and an effective intervention program.* Irish Journal of Psychology, 18, 170-190.

Olweus, D. & Limber, S. (1999) *Blueprints for violence prevention.* Bullying Prevention Program. Institute of Behavioural Science, University of Colorado, Boulder, U.S.A

O'Moore,A.M.,(Guest Ed.)(1997), Irish Journal of Psychology, 18, 2,

O'Moore, M. (1999) *Bullying; What Parents need to know.* Dublin, Trinity College, Anti-Bullying Research & Resource Centre.

O'Moore, M. (2000) *Critical Issues for teacher training to counter bullying and victimization in Ireland.* Aggressive Behaviour, 26, 99 – 111.

O'Moore,A.M.(2000) *Defining violence. Towards a pupil based definition.*Turin,Italy,1999-1577001-INO Project. www.commune.torino.it/novasres

O'Moore,A.M, (2004) *Guiding Framework for Policy Approaches to School Bullying & Violence*, Paper presented at Taking Fear Out Of Schools: International Policy & Research Conference on School Bullying & Violence, Stavanger University College, Stavanger, Norway, 5th-8th Sept, 2004.

O'Moore,A.M.&Kirkham(2001)*Self-Esteem and its relationship to bullying behaviour*, Aggressive Behaviour,27,269-83

O'Moore, M., Kirkham,C. &.Smith,M,(1997) *Bullying Behaviour in Irish Schools: A Nationwide Study*, Irish Journal of Psychology, 18, 141-169

O'Moore,M. & Minton,S., (2001) *Report to the Department of Education on the Project to Evaluate the Effectiveness of a Proposed National Program to prevent and counter Bullying Behaviour in Irish Schools* undertaken in Donegal Primary Schools. , Dublin, ABC, Trinity College Dublin,

O'Moore, M & Minton, S.J. (2003) *The Hidden Voice of Bullying.* In Shevlin, M. & Rose, R.(Eds..) *Encouraging Voices: Respecting the insights of young people who have been marginalised*, Dublin, National Disability Authority.

O'Moore, M & Minton, S.J, (2004a) *Dealing with Bullying in Schools: A Training Manual for Teachers, Parents and Other Professionals*, London, Paul Chapman Publishing.

O'Moore, M. & Minton, S.J. (2004b) *Ireland: The Donegal Primary Schools Anti-Bullying Project*, In: Smith, P.K., Pepler, D. & Rigby, K.(Eds) *Bullying in Schools: How successful can Interventions be?* Cambridge, Cambridge University Press.

O'Moore, M. & Minton, S.J. (2005) *Evaluation of the Effectiveness of an Anti-Bullying Program in Primary Schools*, Aggressive Behaviour,31, 609-622.

O'Moore,M.& Minton,S.J.(2006) *Making the School Environment Safe.* In: Gittins,C(Ed). *Violence Reduction in Schools- how to make a difference.* A Handbook. Strasbourg, Council of Europe Publishing.

Ortega,R. & Lora, M.J. (2000) *The Seville Anti-Bullying in School project.* Aggressive Behaviour, 26, 113-23.

Pepler,D.J., Craig,W.M., O'Connell,P. ,Atlas,R., Charach,A.(2004) *Making a difference in bullying:evaluation of a systemic school-based program in Canada.* In Smith,P.K.,Pepler ,D.&Rigby,K(Eds). *Bullying in Schools: How Successful Can Interventions Be?* Cambridge, Cambridge University Press.

Pikas,A.(1989) *The Common Concern Method for the treatment of mobbing.* In Munthe,E.& Roland,E.(Eds.). *Bullying :An International Perspective.* London;Routledge.

Rigby,K. (2002) *A Meta-Evaluation of Methods and Approaches to Reducing Bullying in Pre-Schools and Early Primary School in Australia.* Commonwealth Attorney Generals Department.

Robinson,G.&Maines,B.(1997) *Crying for Help: The No Blame Approach to Bullying.* Bristol, Lucky Duck.

Robinson,G.;Maines,B.&Hromick,R.(2006) *Supporting School Staff.* In Gittins, C(Ed.).*Violence Reduction in Schools-How to make a difference. A Handbook.* Strasbourg,Council of Europe.

Roland, E. (2000) Bullying in School: *Three National Innovations in Norwegian Schools in 15 years.* Aggressive Behaviour, 26, 135 – 43.

Roland, E. & Munthe, E. (1997). *The 1996 Norwegian program for preventing and managing bullying in schools.* Irish Journal of Psychology, 18, 233 – 47.

Rutter,M.,Maughan,B.,Mortimore,P.,Ouston,J.&Smith,A.(1979) *Fifteen thousand hours, Secondary Schools and their Effects on Children*, Cambridge, M.A .Harvard University Press.

Salmivalli,C.,Kaukiainen A.,Kaistaniemi,L,Lagerspetz,KMJ,(1999).*Self-Evaluated, self-esteem and defensive egotism as predictors of adolescent's participation in bullying situations*, Pers Soc Psychol Bull.25,1268-1278.

Smith, P.K. (1997) *Bullying in Schools: The U.K experience and the Sheffield Anti-Bullying project.* The Irish Journal of Psychology, 18, 2, 191 - 201

Smith, P.K, Morita, Y., Junger-Tas, J., Olweus, D., Ratalano, R & Slee, P. (Eds.). (1999) *The Nature of School Bullying: A Cross-National Perspective*: London, Routledge.

Smith, P.K., Pepler, D. & Rigby, K. (Eds.) (2004) *Bullying in Schools. How Successful can Interventions be?* Cambridge, Cambridge University Press.

Tattum, D. (1997) *A Whole school response: From crisis management to prevention.* The Irish Journal of Psychology, 18, 2, 221 - 232

Vettenberg, N. (1999) *Violence in Schools: Awareness raising, prevention, penalties* General Report Council of Europe,Publishing.

World Health Organization (2004) *Young people's health in context: Health Behaviour in School–aged Children (HBSC) study: Intermediate report from 2001/2002 survey.* Health Policy for Children and Adolescents. No.4

Author Notes

I wish to thank the Calouste Gulbenkian Foundation and the Government of Ireland's Department of Education and Science for their financial support and encouragement of the Donegal project. I am especially grateful to the network of professionals, principals, teachers and parents of the schools involved in the study. I wish to thank also the Irish Research Council for the Humanities and Social Science for their financial support of the nationwide intervention program to prevent and counter bullying, harassment and violence in Irish primary and post-primary schools. Finally I wish to thank Stephen James Minton for help with the data analysis of the Donegal Project and for his subsequent role of Director of Training of the ABC Whole School Response to Bullying.

Chapter 15:

School-based Intervention Research to Reduce Bullying in Australia 1999-2007: What Works, What Doesn't, and What's Promising?

Donna Cross, Therese Shaw, Natasha Pearce, Erin Erceg,
Stacey Waters, Yolanda Pintabona, Margaret Hall

Introduction

Given schools have finite resources and capacity to address student bullying, it is of growing importance to conduct research to identify the most parsimonious model of whole-of-school strategies and processes that can consistently and successfully reduce bullying victimization and perpetration experienced by school-age children.

Since 1999 to 2007 the *Friendly Schools and Families* (FS&F) research team at the Child Health Promotion Research Centre, Edith Cowan University has conducted a succession of longitudinal research projects with over 6,000 children, to systematically and empirically test in an Australian setting the effectiveness of theoretical and other evidence-based and promising processes to address mechanisms of bullying behaviour change. This iterative research began with a comprehensive formative trial to identify and validate with expert international researchers, contemporary research evidence of strategies to form part of universal, indicated and, selective interventions. This year-long formative study informed the intervention design of a four-year randomised group efficacy trial called *Friendly Schools (FS)*. The FS trial was used to confirm, alter, and extend the theoretical model and guidelines for practice generated from the initial formative research. Impact and process findings from this efficacy trial were then used to design a more 'real-world' three-year randomised effectiveness trial, called *Friendly Schools Friendly Families (FSFF)*, of those components found to be the most 'active' and missing from the efficacy trial. The results of the effectiveness trial have been used to rewrite and refine parts of the program for national dissemination. Currently this revised program called *Friendly Schools and Families* is being disseminated for adoption at a system level throughout Australia and internationally.

This paper describes the sequential trialling, development and refinement of the whole-of-school intervention components that formed the basis of these trials, to produce the *Friendly Schools and Families* bullying prevention program.

Background

Evidence of effective school-based bullying interventions has been sporadic (Salmivalli, Kaukiainen, & Voeten, 2005) and research in this area risks being criticised for failing to demonstrate a consistent effect on bullying behaviour. This inconsistency of results can be attributed to bullying behaviour's multi-level causality and the complexity and number of social, behavioural, and environmental factors that can influence its occurrence. Consequently, there is a need to determine the range of 'active ingredients' - empirical, theoretical and promising mechanisms - necessary to reduce the likelihood of bullying in schools (Stevens, De Bourdeaudhuij & Van Oost 2001).

Until recently in Australia, no empirical research had been conducted to investigate the effectiveness of interventions to address bullying behaviour in primary schools, yet reported prevalence of bullying with this age group was among the highest in the world (Rigby, 1997). Bullying is defined here as a repeated, unjustifiable behaviour that may be physical, verbal, and/or psychological. It is intended to cause fear, distress, or harm to another and is conducted by a more powerful individual or group against a less powerful individual who is unable to effectively resist (Olweus, 1994a; Smith, 1991). In Australia, approximately one in six school students report being bullied at least once a week and one in 20 report bullying others in the past six months (Rigby, 1997; Zubrick et al., 1997).

While primary school children of both genders report being bullied more frequently than secondary school students (Rigby 1997; Rigby, 1997, 1998), social skills based interventions to ameliorate the harm from or reduce bullying in schools have been found to be more successful with this age group as they tend to be more supportive of a student who has been bullied than older children (Slee & Rigby 1992, 1994; Smith, 1991; Zubrick et al., 1997). They are also more pro-social and are more likely to want bullying to stop (Olweus, 1994b; Slee & Rigby 1992; Smith, 1991).

Given however, that bullying does not occur equally in all primary schools, our research initially sought to determine the risk and protective factors associated with bullying and what some primary schools were doing better than others to address these, and how these mechanisms were affecting positive change in the primary school environment.

Stage 1 - Formative Trial:
Principles for School-based Bullying Prevention and Management (1999)

Our research began in 1999 with a formative study to compile a comprehensive and practical summary of evidence-based practice, with exemplar case studies, to guide schools' assessment, selection or development and implementation of whole-school strategies to reduce bullying,

The year-long formative trial comprised four major phases. Phase One involved the compilation and review of empirical evidence from school-based bullying interventions and theoretical foundations for bullying prevention. A major challenge in this stage was the many differences between study designs, evaluation methods, measurement and definitions of bullying. Also, different interventions had been tested with differing theoretical models, targets and age groups. Hence, it was not possible to derive definitive evidence based guidelines from the research. Instead the major outcomes of this phase were a summary of the most salient risk and protective factors found to mediate bullying behaviour (see Figure 1) and of the gaps in knowledge.

Figure 1: Mediating variables for bullying prevention

Demographic Variables
- Gender
- SES
- School size

Attitudes to Bullying
- Pro-victim attitudes
- Outcome expectancies of bullying
- Social norms and normative behaviours

Interpersonal Variables
- Peer support
- Social competence
- Number of friends
- Loneliness

Knowledge and understandings about bullying behaviour

Perceptions of School
- Happiness of school
- Liking school
- Teachers take action to discourage bullying

Bullying Experiences
- Being bullied
- Types of bullying
- Bullying others
- Reporting of bullying of self and others

Psychological Health
- Depression
- Anxiety
- Peer relations self concept
- General self concept

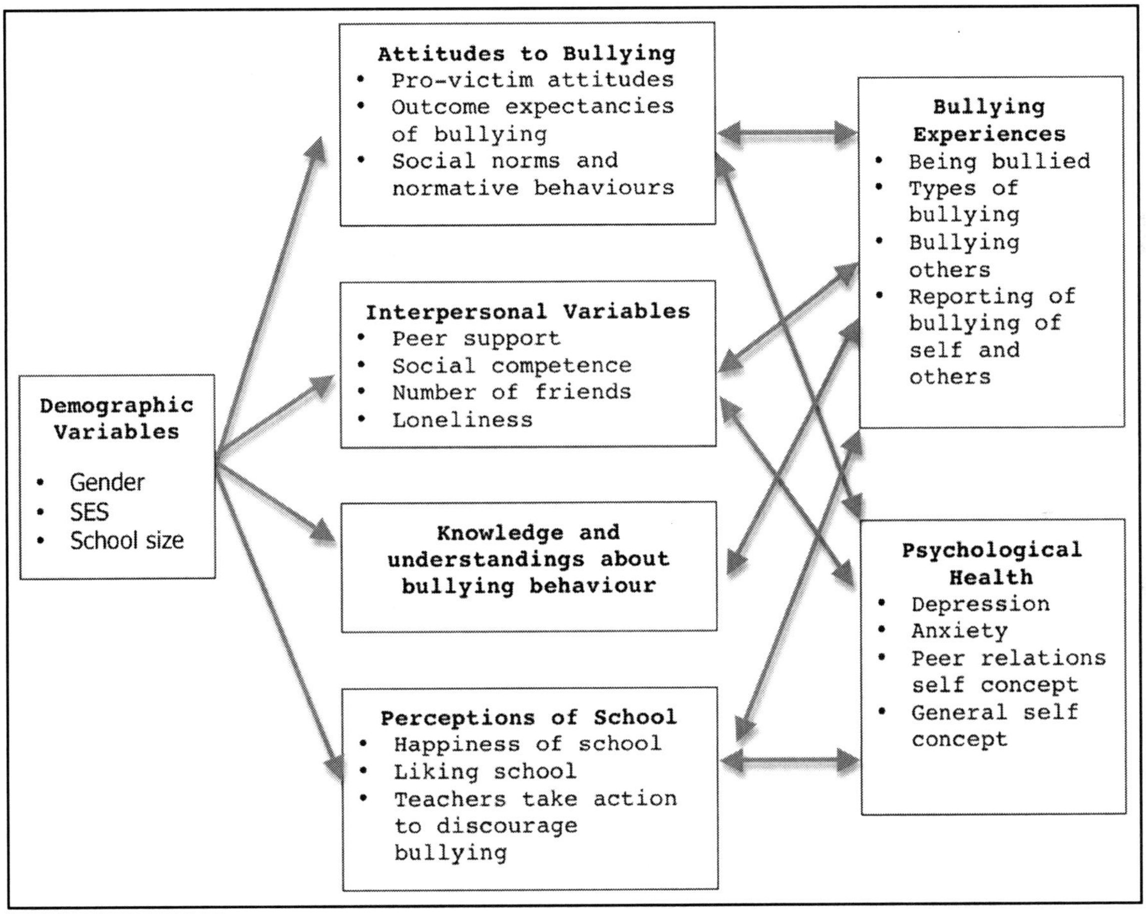

The key mediators (or risk and protective factors) hypothesised as amenable to change and affecting students' experiences with bullying behaviours included their attitudes and beliefs about bullying; the quality of their relationships with others; their knowledge and understandings about bullying and how to cope with it; and how they feel about their school.

This comprehensive literature search also contributed to the design of a draft set of principles of effective policy and practices to address these theoretical mediators and in turn the bullying experienced by children. These policies and practices were distilled into the six inter-related domains of the WHO Health Promoting School (HPS) model (WHO/UNESCO/UNICEF, 1991). These domains included the formal curriculum; school ethos (or social environment); the physical environment; policies and practices; school health services; and the school-home-community interaction (Booth & Samdal, 1997).

Phase Two involved structured consultation using the Delphi Technique (Delbecq, Van de Ven, & Gustafson, 1986; Miller, 1990) with an expert panel of 20 researchers and practitioners from England, Canada, Norway, the USA and Australia who were working to reduce bullying in schools. This phase was used to assess the accuracy, completeness and appropriateness of the evidence-based principles proposed in the conceptual model. Structured consultations enabled convergent validation and drew on the current knowledge of the expert panel members to debate and exchange evidence not identified in the initial literature search and helped to achieve group consensus and facilitate anonymous, active and equal participation from all members of the panel (Miller, 1990; Sumsion, 1998). After three questionnaire rounds of input the panel concurred that the revised principles described the current 'state-of-the-art' for successful practice to reduce bullying in schools. Table 1 provides a summary of the conceptual model and the final set of policy and practice principles.

Table 1.
Overview of the principles for school bullying prevention and management (Cross et al., 2004)

Health Promoting School Model Domains	Overview of the Principles
Policy and Practice	Establish a group, with members representative of the whole-school community, including the Principal, to coordinate the implementation of the Guidelines and key actions. Assess the prevalence and general awareness of student bullying. Provide the whole school with common understandings and consistent responses understood by the whole staff Write a whole–school Behaviour Management Plan (BMP) which includes the reduction and management of bullying. Senior staff demonstrate commitment to supporting staff and students through the implementation of the BMP. Implement the BMP consistently within and by the school community. Identify, assess and develop skills required by staff, students and parents to implement the BMP. Use positive approval, praise and encouragement to modify behaviours. Treat reports or observations of bullying seriously and with clear consistent action. Objectively and reliably evaluate the school's action to discourage and manage bullying.

Classroom Management and Curriculum	Use cooperative learning methods learning activities that actively engage students in developmentally appropriate ways to address bullying and enhance personal development and social skills
	Provide teachers with professional development opportunities.
	Provide students with learning activities to enhance their personal development.
	Use curriculum activities that foster positive relations among students and between students and teachers.
	Use encouragement and positive recognition to manage student behaviour.
	Use cooperative learning methods to promote pro-social behaviour.
	Teachers use the classroom situation, the curriculum and their knowledge of students, to help those who are bullied.
	Help students who engage in bullying behaviour to develop more appropriate modes of behaving and show positive ways to use the leadership and interpersonal skills that these students may possess.
School Ethos	Demonstrate the school principal's and senior staffs' commitment to taking action to discourage and manage bullying and maintaining this action.
	Provide a positive school environment that provides safety, security and support for students and promotes their well being.
	Mobilise bystanders, adults (especially parents and teachers) and students.
	Use the peer group to provide support for students who are bullied and use positive peer pressure to discourage bullying.
	Provide adult example and experiences that are congruent with the BMP and the formal curriculum.
	Raise student awareness that they have the right to seek help to resolve bullying incidents.
	Invite, encourage and value the participation of the whole school community to address bullying.

School-Home, Community Links	Establish close cooperation between staff and parents.
	Encourage (through many channels of communication) parents and the wider community to present a consistent message about bullying across the home, school and community.
	Develop positive strategies to deal with bullying in collaboration with parents.
	Use many channels of communication to ensure participation and knowledge of school action to reduce bullying.
	When appropriate contact parents of children involved in bullying.
	Seek assistance of community professionals especially for families who may require more intensive support.
	Provide opportunities for professional development for parents and the community.
	Increase parent and community awareness of the signs and symptoms of bullying and appropriate follow-up.
Student Services Teams	Use student services teams, school health services, outside agencies and chaplaincy services to help reduce bullying.
	Increase the student services team's and other school service's awareness of the signs and symptoms of bullying and appropriate follow-up.
Physical Environment	Provide appropriate monitoring and action for bullying when supervising outside the classroom.
	Identify bullying 'hot spots' in collaboration with students.
	Provide safe and well supervised areas in the school yard.
	Provide a stimulating school yard to encourage a wide range of structured and semi-structured activities for students, especially those who feel threatened in the school yard.
	Provide structured activities that promote adherence to social rules.
	Encourage positive ways of behaving in the playground.
	Provide equity of access to developmentally appropriate play areas and sufficient equipment for all students.

Following this expert review process, Phase Three involved key education system representatives identifying schools that had school policies or practices that matched at least one of the revised whole-of-school principles. Case studies from 80 of these schools were compiled to operationalize the principles with practical examples of how schools had implemented aspects of these policies and practices. The final phase (4) of this formative trial involved the pilot testing of these principles in six schools to obtain subjective judgments from school staff of their workability and usefulness. The formative research process that led to the development of these principles is described in more detail elsewhere (Cross, Pintabona, Hall, & Hamilton, 2004).

Stage 2 - Efficacy Trial: Friendly Schools Project (2000-2002)

The formative trial principles provided guidelines, legitimacy and a focus for the design of a whole-of-school socio-ecological approach to reducing bullying. The *Friendly Schools* (FS) efficacy trial aimed to review and extend the principles and theoretical model developed in the formative trial. It involved a cohort of 1,968 Grade 4 children and their parents and teachers, recruited from 29 randomly selected schools in Perth, Western Australia, tracked for three years, from 2000 to 2002 (from age 9 to 12 years). Fifteen schools were randomly assigned to the intervention group and 14 to the comparison group. The design and student baseline results are described in more detail elsewhere (Cross et al., In submission).

The FS intervention comprised three levels of intervention – the classroom, family and whole-school. Grade 4 children were targeted because in Australia this age is immediately prior to the age when bullying is most prevalent among Australian students (Rigby, 1997). This timing ensured the cohort was exposed to the intervention when information and skills were most likely to have relevance and practical application.

The *Friendly Schools* intervention was delivered at three levels:

1. Whole school level - school policy, organization, ethos and environment;

2. Classroom level - formal curriculum, teaching and learning; and

3. Family level - school-home-community link activities

Whole School Level

In each intervention school a team comprising the principal, student services staff, and other interested teachers, was trained to coordinate and facilitate their whole-school response to bullying. The teams received a detailed whole-school practices manual and were trained for four hours in each of the two intervention years to maintain their commitment and to strengthen their capacity to effectively address bullying within their schools. The whole-school practices manual and training aimed to address all the hypothesised mediators, but especially students' perceptions of school safety and the staff actions to discourage bullying, and students' sense of belonging and enjoyment of school. The manual included:

- Processes for reviewing and revising policy and school organization to reduce bullying, including sample school policies;

- Whole-of-school organization and ethos strategies to promote pro-social behaviour, social problem solving and to mobilize social pressure to discourage bullying;

- Ideas to enhance the quality of the school environment and break times to reduce bullying;

- Responses to manage bullying incidents, such as the Pikas 'Method of Shared Concern' (Pikas, 1989); and

- Case studies of successful school-based practice

Classroom Level

The *Friendly Schools* self-contained curriculum was designed to provide 18 hours of classroom teaching and learning (9 hours per year). It identified key learning outcomes, core activities and provided background information, cross-curricular learning activities and all resources required to teach the lessons, such as game pieces and videos. The learning activities aimed to address all mediators but especially students' attitudes, beliefs and understandings about bullying, and their interpersonal skills development.

Grades 4 and 5 classroom teachers each received six hours of professional learning to improve their comfort, confidence, and skills to teach the FS program and to manage student bullying behaviour. Interactive techniques were modelled by the trainers and teachers were given opportunities to practice and review these new skills. The theory and rationale supporting the program was emphasized and time was provided for teachers to share problems with and solutions to the program's implementation. All were asked to prepare a school-based implementation plan in an attempt to maintain their implementation after the initial enthusiasm from the training diminished.

The teacher training and classroom manual addressed:

- An understanding of what behaviours constitute bullying, why bullying is unacceptable;

- Students' ability to talk about bullying with each other and adults;

- Adaptive responses to being bullied, including reporting bullying, seeking support and responding assertively;

- Social skill development and social problem solving;

- Empathy building;

- Positive social norms and normative expectations to discourage bullying; and

- Peer support for students who are being bullied.

The learning activities provided opportunities for students to build empathy for individuals being bullied and to practise social and intra-personal skills including making friends, conflict resolution, self-efficacy to cope with bullying incidents, decision making and assertive communication. Other lower-level cognitive-based strategies addressed social support, reinforcement, and outcome expectancies. The specific content and titles of the learning activities are shown in Table 2.

Table 2. The Friendly Schools Grades 4 and 5 learning activities.

2000	Grade 4 Learning Activities	2001	Grade 5 Learning Activities
Term 2	**Information About Bullying** What is bullying behaviour? Developing an action plan Getting support	Term 2	**Cooperation Crusade** Equality in a Friendly School Cooperation in a Friendly School Friendly School cooperation game
Term 3	**Feeling Good About Myself and Others** The bystander Self esteem: What is it? Self esteem character study	Term 3	**Working it out Together** Bystander choices Decision making Skill building role plays
Term 4	**Cooperation in a Friendly School** Children's rights in a Friendly School Values in promoting *Friendly Schools* Friendship skills	Term 4	**Friendly Schools Playmates** Challenging negative thoughts Planning for positive advocacy Cross year level advocacy activity

Family Level

To reinforce and support classroom learning of social and cognitive skills, each of the 18 classroom learning activities (9 in each of Grades 4 and 5) included a home-based skill building activity for students to complete with their family. Home activities were designed to take approximately 10 minutes each to complete. Also, to actively involve all members of each intervention school's whole-school community in efforts to reduce bullying, 16 skills-based newsletter items (eight for each year of the study) were developed and disseminated. Each newsletter item provided the school community with a brief overview of research information followed by actions and tips to help them to deal with issues, such as what to do if their child is being bullied and/or bullying other children.

Data Collection

Self administered questionnaires were administered to the students, their teachers and parents at the start of the program and then at the end of each study year to measure students' knowledge, attitudes and beliefs about bullying and other mediators described previously, as well as the frequency and type of bullying they experienced. A more detailed explanation of the variables measured and the instruments used can be found elsewhere (Cross, 2004).

Data Analyses

All but one of the dependent variables (frequency of their experiences of being bullied and of bullying others, telling if they were bullied and whether they observed another student in their grade or younger being bullied) were analyzed as multi-category. Multinomial logistic regression models were fitted in Stata 8 to model the categorical dependent variables using robust estimation of standard errors to account for school level clustering. Cross-sectional ANCOVA-type analyses were conducted for each dependent variable where a separate model was fitted to each post-test time point, which included the baseline values of the dependent variable, gender and demographics.

Use of the Stata package made it possible to include all observed data in the analyses. Bonferroni adjustments were made to significance levels to account for the multiple comparisons of the dependent variable categories. For consistency, the binary dependent variable was also analyzed using the ANCOVA approach, utilizing random effects models (with random intercepts only).

Overview of the Main Student Results for Friendly Schools

At baseline the Grade 4 student cohort comprised 1,968 8-9 year olds. A third (67.6%, n=1,330) of these students completed each of the three follow-up questionnaires at the end of 2000, 2001 and 2002. In total 592 students (30.1%) were lost to follow-up from Baseline to Post test 3, of these 93 (4.7%) were lost at Post test 1, 215 (10.9%) were lost at Post test 2 and 284 (14.4%) were lost at Post test 3. All available data were included in the analyses.

Frequency of being bullied

Significant differences were found between the study conditions in the first year of the study at the end of Grade 4 (p=0.020) and in the third year for the data collected at the end of Grade 6 (p=0.024). At post test 1, when students were at the end of Grade 4, those in the intervention group were 1.5 times more likely not to be bullied occasionally (p=0.007) than the comparison group. No differences with regard to being bullied regularly were observed at this time point. At post test 3 when students were in Grade 6, students in the comparison group were 1.5 times more likely than the intervention group students to be bullied regularly rather than occasionally (p=0.013) and rather than not bullied (OR=1.5, p=0.030 approaching the adjusted significance value of 0.017). No differences were found between the study conditions with regard to the likelihood of being bullied when they were in Grade 7.

Frequency of bullying others

No differences were found between the groups in terms of the frequency of bullying others.

Telling someone if bullied

One of the objectives of the intervention was to encourage students who were bullied to seek help by speaking to someone about the bullying. All students answered this question in the questionnaire and thus it is possible to determine not only differences in students' tendencies to talk to someone if they were bullied but also to compare likelihoods of being bullied.

At almost every follow-up, the comparison students in the study were more likely to have told no-one that they were being bullied. At the end of Grade 4 these differences were significant (p=0.001), and comparison students were 1.7 times more likely to be bullied and not tell anyone than were the intervention group students. According to the responses to this question, students exposed to the intervention were also less likely to report being bullied at the end of Grade 4.

Whether observed another student being bullied

Comparison group students had significantly higher odds of reporting seeing another student being bullied at the end of Grade 4 after one year of the intervention (p=0.013), at post test 2 or when in Grade 5 (p=0.005) and Grade 6 (p=0.001). At the end of the first (OR=1.4), the second (OR=1.5) and the third year (OR=1.7) of the intervention, the comparison group students were approximately <u>one and a half times</u> more likely than intervention group students to indicate that they saw another student in their grade level or younger, being bullied.

Process Data

The FS process data collected via interview and self administered questionnaires from members of the whole-school teams showed that the majority of intervention schools, by the end of the two years, had completed less than 30% of the recommended whole-school program. In contrast, the mean proportion of classroom activities implemented over the two years of the project was 67%. A lack of teacher time and capacity support (e.g., skills, structures, resources and commitment), appear to have contributed to the under-implementation of the whole-school (and some parts of the classroom curriculum) intervention. Further, teachers found that the majority of home activities were completed and returned by less than a third of parents. Some also commented that the time and energy taken to follow-up with parents to complete the home activities discouraged them from sending further copies home.

Hence, while the FS efficacy trial showed some promising results, the process data suggest the program experienced some implementation failure or Type III error (Basch, Sliepcevich, Gold, Duncan, & Kolbe, 1985) in two of its three levels of intervention: at the whole school and family levels.

Stage 3 - Effectiveness Trial: Friendly Schools Friendly Families Project (2002-2004)

Process data from the *Friendly Schools* trial indicated that schools took almost two years to engage the whole school community in policy and practice initiatives to reduce bullying. FS intervention school staff reported competing demands on their time and energy and a lack of resources such as funding, staff and time, and a lack of support for staff implementing programs such as training and administration support, as reasons why they had not been able to implement more of the program. To respond to this feedback, the *Friendly Schools Friendly Families* effectiveness trial incorporated a unique capacity building component to support schools in implementation and sustainability of the whole school level of implementation and to increase their capacity to intervene more successfully at the family level. Hence, this research aimed to test strategies to more effectively engage parents.

Unlike FS that targeted a Grade 4 cohort only, the *Friendly Schools Friendly Families* project targeted the whole school community Grades 1 to 7 and collected data from a cohort of Grades 2, 4 and 6 students and their teachers and their parents/carers, the other school staff as well as a whole school project team (4-5 staff) from 20 randomly selected primary schools (not previously involved in the FS project) in the Perth metropolitan area.

Friendly Schools Friendly Families Study Design

Friendly Schools Friendly Families (FSFF) was a three-year group randomized intervention trial conducted from 2002 to 2004, immediately following the FS efficacy trial. This effectiveness trial was designed to experimentally manipulate the potential mechanisms of behaviour change that were not successfully implemented during the FS trial, via three study conditions (high, moderate, and low) of intervention delivery. The *high* intervention group received comprehensive training and support materials to address revised strategies for all three levels of intervention (whole school, classroom, and family) with a particular focus on the family intervention component. The *moderate* intervention group received support to implement strategies at only the whole school and classroom levels and the *low* (comparison) intervention group received a copy of a simplified version of the materials with no training to deliver any aspect of the program. Schools were randomly assigned to one of three intervention conditions.

While the FSFF intervention was similar to the FS program, strategies not found to be effective and others requiring more support were built into the whole school, classroom, and family levels FSFF intervention, particularly strategies to involve students' families.

Friendly Schools Friendly Families Intervention

As for the FS program the FSFF intervened on similar mediators that formed part of the theoretical model developed during the formative trial. The FSFF trial however, intervened at three levels - the whole school, classroom, and family - using a study design that could measure the relative impact of the two previously poorly implemented whole-school and family level components. As described below, the FS intervention was modified considerably for the FSFF trial.

Whole School Level

At the whole school level for the FSFF trial, a more comprehensive manual and training to support the implementation of the whole school components was developed. Feedback from the FS trial indicated that teachers required far greater capacity assessment and support and a more detailed implementation support manual with checklists, ideas, case studies and tools to guide and monitor their implementation, including a comprehensive needs assessment to help schools tailor and prioritize their actions. The whole-school level training provided eleven hours of active contact with each high intervention school. This comprised a nine hour training plus ongoing passive support to the whole school project team, and a two-hour training for classroom teachers and other school staff. In the first year the moderate condition schools received eight hours of training. During the second intervention year high and moderate intervention teachers were provided with a three-hour training on behaviour management techniques.

To enhance the FSFF whole school implementation high and moderate schools were asked to form a whole-school project team to facilitate the project's implementation. As part of their training, the teams were asked to assess their current capacity as a group using a series of questions that aimed to help predict the likelihood of successful program implementation. An individualized school capacity building report was produced that summarized the whole school project team's discussion and key actions identified by the team to increase their capacity to implement the FSFF program. Passive coaching was provided by the research team during the year culminating in a team meeting at the end of each of the two intervention years, to assess their capacity development and associated level of program implementation and identify critical factors that may influence implementation success

Family Level

.At the family level, in addition to simplifying the home activities used in FS for Grades 4 and 5, additional strategies and methods were devised to help messages and information penetrate families, particularly to reach the second parent/carer. This component, given to the high intervention group only, included an additional half-day training for the whole-school project team, resources to facilitate communication with parents (parent meeting presentations, family fair, student performance ideas including prepared assembly items, newsletter snippets with parenting tips, a self-help parent communication book and home activity sheets) and other specific capacity building strategies identified by each whole-school project team to increase the level of parent engagement

Classroom Level

.At the classroom level the activities that teachers reported during FS to be less interactive or too time consuming or difficult to implement where modified accordingly and provided to the FSFF cohort of Grades 2, 4 and 6 students. Also, approximately five hours per grade level of additional developmentally appropriate activities were prepared for all students from Kindergarten (age 4) to Grade 7 (age 12) in each high and moderate intervention school

Data Collection

The instruments, data collection and data analyses for the FSFF program was similar to that used in the Friendly Schools program except that the analyses involved three study conditions and three cohort groups (Grade 2, 4 and 6 students). Additional data were collected from school staff via a self-administered questionnaire about individual staff capacity. Each school's project team was responsible for the implementation of the program within their school. This questionnaire assessed the level of project implementation, level of project success and how the school team perceived the school's capacity to engage parents in the bullying reduction intervention.

Data were also collected from the cohort students, their parents and teachers using self-report questionnaires. Two different questionnaires were used to collect data from the students' parents/carers, one for the main parent/carer who talked with them about bullying and a shorter questionnaire to be completed by their other parent/carer.

Overview of the Main Student Results for Friendly Schools Friendly Families

Described below is an overview of the two-year post-intervention, bullying-related outcomes for only the cohorts of Grade 4 and 6 students, following two years of intervention support. Four dependent variables were considered, namely frequency of their experiences of being bullied and of bullying others, telling if they were bullied, and whether they had observed another student in their grade or younger being bullied. As for the FS study, the models were fitted in Stata 8 using multinomial logistic regression with robust SE estimation.

Frequency of being bullied

Significant differences were found for the Grade 4 cohort at the end of the first year of the intervention (p=0.001) but not at the end of the second year i.e., when the students were in Grade 5 (p=0.763). At the end of the first year of the study, students in the high intervention group were less likely to be bullied occasionally and less likely to be bullied regularly (every few weeks or more often) than those in the moderate (OR=0.63, p=0.002) and low (OR=0.55, p=0.012) intervention groups. If bullied, the high intervention group of students were 1.5 times more likely to be bullied occasionally (1-2 times a term) rather than regularly, than were those in the low intervention group (OR=1.5, p=0.000).

With regard to the Grade 6 cohort, significant differences existed between the study conditions, both at the end of Grade 6 (p=0.048) and at the end of the second year when the students were in Grade 7 (p=0.013). At both time points, the high intervention group were less likely to be bullied regularly (every few weeks or more often) than the moderate and low intervention groups. In particular at the end of Grade 6, the low intervention group were 1.9 times more likely than the high intervention group to be bullied regularly (p=0.005) whilst the moderate intervention group were 1.5 times more likely (p=0.029, approaching the adjusted level of significance of 0.017). After two years of the intervention (when the students were in Grade 7), the differences were as follows: Compared to the high intervention group students, the moderate intervention students had 2.3 times higher odds of being bullied regularly than not bullied (p=0.012). Similarly, the low intervention group were at 1.9 higher odds of this occurring, although this last comparison was not statistically significant (p=0.092). In addition, the students in the high intervention group were 2.7 times more likely to report being bullied 1-2 a term rather than regularly (p=0.001), when compared with the moderate intervention group students at the end of Grade 7.

Frequency of bullying others

Based on the students' self-report of the frequency that they had bullied others in the previous term, intervention effects were observed for the Grade 6 cohort (p=0.001), after one year of the intervention i.e. towards the end of Grade 6. No differences were found for the Grade 4 cohort. After one year of the intervention, the students in Grade 6 in the low intervention group were 1.5 times more likely to bully others occasionally when compared with the high intervention group students (OR=1.5, p=0.005).

Telling if bullied

No intervention effects were found for the Grade 4 cohort with regard to their frequency of telling if bullied, however some differences were observed for the Grade 6 cohort. At the end of the first year of the study, the Grade 6 students in the low intervention group were twice as likely than those in the high intervention group to report not telling anyone if they were bullied (OR=2.0, p=0.012) and 1.7 times less likely not to have been bullied (OR=0.6, p=0.014) than the high intervention students. At the end of the second year of the study (when the students were at the end of Grade 7), the students in the low intervention group were still two times less likely to tell someone of they were bullied, than those in the high intervention group (OR=2.0, p=0.000).

Whether observed another student being bullied

No differences were found between the groups regarding seeing a student in their grade or younger being bullied at school

Summary

While the Grade 4 cohort results for the FSFF effectiveness trial were somewhat equivocal, it would appear that the capacity building, multi-level program positively and significantly affected the Grade 6 cohort children in the high intervention group that is the group who received support for all three levels of intervention. These results were significant for those students who reported they were bullied and those who bullied others occasionally, as well as the proportion of students who reported they told someone if they were bullied. Importantly, these program effects sustained in this age group and strengthened following two years of intervention. A summary of results is provided in Table 3. It is reasonable to suggest that the capacity building model and family level intervention components were necessary to achieve positive change in bullying behaviour.

Summary of significant FSFF program effects for primary dependent variables

	Grade 4 cohort	Grade 6 cohort
Frequency of being bullied regularly		
1-year follow-up	(OR=0.55, p=0.012)* (OR=0.63, p=0.002) #	(OR=1.9, p=0.005)*- (OR=1.5, p=0.029)#-
2-year follow-up	-	(OR=1.9, p=0.012)*- (OR=2.3, p=0.005)#--
Frequency of bullying others occasionally		
1-year follow-up	-	(OR=1.5, p=0.005)*
2-year follow-up	-	-
Telling if bullied		
1-year follow-up	-	(OR=2.0, p=0.012)*
2-year follow-up	-	(OR=2.0, p=0.000)*

* High versus low intervention
\# High versus moderate intervention

While both the FS and FSFF trials demonstrated some positive outcomes, further analyses are currently being conducted using program implementation data. Program implementation in both studies was measured using several converging methods (triangulation) including teacher logs and self-report questionnaire, student recall, and face-to-face interview. These multiple measures are being used to generate an overall implementation index assigned to each student. These dose-response analyses will be used to determine which of the key Health Promoting Schools (HPS) components appear to contribute to the greatest amount of change in bullying behaviours and the hypothesised mediators of this change.

Process data

Qualitative structured interviews were conducted with members of the whole-school project teams at the beginning and end of each of the two intervention years. These structured interview discussions aimed to assess whole school capacity (skills, structures, resources and commitment), whole school level of implementation, and to identify critical success factors for building school capacity to implement whole school strategies and to engage parents in bullying reduction strategies. Briefly, these process data indicated that the capacity building approach made the committee focus on their barriers to program implementation and sustainability. School project teams reported that once issues such as staff time and workload were discussed often solutions were identified by the team. For example, building the program outcomes into staff work plans meant that the staff time spent on this program was acknowledged by the school even if it was outside of official work hours.

Stage 4: Program dissemination (2005 -)

During the FSFF effectiveness trial other schools in Australia began to contact the research team to obtain copies of the Program. These schools were promised access to these materials and training following the conclusion of the FSFF trial. During 2004 the process data collected from this trial was used to again rewrite and refine the intervention components for more widespread dissemination. The revised program was called Friendly Schools and Families (FS&F). The National demand was so great for FS&F that dissemination occurred at each state/territory level, such that key system level education staff were trained to support school/teacher adoption of the program. However, no evaluation of the effectiveness of the national dissemination of this program has been conducted. Since February 2005, over 1500 schools have purchased the program materials and training. Income from the sale of the FS&F materials and training will be used to fund further research.

Discussion

The Principles of Successful Practice to Reduce Bullying in Schools were found to be important for the development and potential effectiveness of the *Friendly Schools* and the *Friendly Schools Friendly Families* programs. This systematic and detailed review and validation of the evidence ensured that only strategies showing promise, empirically or theoretically, to reduce bullying behaviour were included and tested. Because school-based bullying interventions are complex and expensive, thorough formative evaluations, followed by robust efficacy and effectiveness testing are necessary to ensure the best outcomes can be achieved.

The findings from this series of these RCT trials suggest the principles that underpinned the bullying prevention programs tested show promise. Moreover, they indicate that multi-level whole-school, classroom and family interventions - implemented with capacity support for schools - appear to provide sufficient program dose to reduce bullying, and that these effects can be sustained and enhanced over a two-year period of implementation among older primary school students.

Nevertheless, more research is needed to understand the complex interplay between whole school, classroom, and family levels of intervention and to fill the empirical gaps in the theoretical models tested. Future research is also necessary to confirm the value of the approaches used, to clarify optimal mixes of these intervention levels, and strategies within these levels, and to identify barriers to implementation and strategies to overcome these. Lastly, we also need to better understand the critical developmental windows for delivery of these interventions and for whom the program is most effective and under what conditions – how do the policies and practices for example, generate particular processes in children in a school?

Key Messages

1. Secure the Principal's commitment to reduce bullying and establish a group within the school with members' representative of the whole-school community to coordinate the implementation of whole-school strategies to reduce bullying.

2. Provide common understandings of bullying behaviour and consistent responses understood by the whole school community.

3. Use cooperative learning activities that actively engage students in developmentally appropriate ways to address bullying and enhance personal development and social skills.

4. Demonstrate in an ongoing manner the school principal's and senior staff's commitment to taking action to discourage and manage bullying.

5. Mobilise bystanders and adults (especially parents, teachers and students) to use the peer group to provide support for students who are bullied and use positive peer pressure to discourage bullying.

6. Establish close cooperation between staff and the parents and communicate regularly through many channels to parents and the wider community to present a consistent message about bullying across the home, school and community.

7. Use student services teams, school health services, outside agencies to help reduce bullying.

8. Provide safe, well supervised and stimulating, structured and semi-structured areas for students, especially those who feel threatened in the school yard during breaks.

References

Basch, C., Sliepcevich, E., Gold, R., Duncan, D., & Kolbe, L. (1985). *Avoiding type III errors in health education program evaluation: A case study*. Health Education Quarterly, 12(4), 315-331.

Booth, M., & Samdal, O. (1997). *Health-promoting school in Australia: models and measurement*. Australia and New Zealand Journal of Public Health, 21(4), 365-370.

Cross, D., Hall, M., Hamilton, G., Pintabona, Y., Erceg, E. (2004). *Australia: The Friendly Schools Project*. In P. K. Smith, Peplar D., Rigby K. (Ed.), *Bullying in Schools: Global Perspectives on Intervention*. Ambridge: Cambridge University Press.

Cross, D., Pintabona, Y., Hall, M., & Hamilton, G. (2004). *Validated guidelines for school-based bullying prevention and management*. International Journal of Mental Health Promotion, 6(3), 34-42.

Cross, D., Shaw, T., Pintabona, Y., M., H., Hamilton, G., Erceg, E., et al. (In submission). *Social, attitudinal, psychological and school adjustment factors associated with bullying behavior in Australian primary school children*.

Delbecq, A. L., Van de Ven, A. H., & Gustafson, D. H. (1986). *Group techniques for program planning: a guide to nominal group and Delphi processes*. Middleton: Green Briar Press.

Miller, D. A. (1990). *Research through the Delphi technique*. NIRSA Journal, 15(1), 39-40.

Olweus, D. (1994a). *Bullying at school: Basic facts and effects of a school based intervention program*. Journal of Child Psychology and Psychiatry, 35(7), 1171-1190.

Olweus, D. (1994b). *Bullying at school: Long-term outcomes for the victims and an effective school-based intervention program*. In L. R. Huesmann (Ed.), *Aggressive behavior: current perspectives* (pp. 97-130). New York: Plenum Press.

Pikas, A. (1989). *A pure concept of mobbing gives the best results for treatment*. School Psychology International, 10, 95-104.

Rigby, K. (1997). *Attitudes an beliefs about bullying among Australian school children*. Irish Journal of Psychology, 18(2), 202-220.

Rigby, K. (1997). *What children tell us about bullying in schools*. Children Australia, 22(2), 28-34.

Rigby, K. (1998). *The relationship between reported health and involvement in bully/victim problems among male and female secondary schoolchildren*. Journal of Health Psychology, 3(4), 465-476.

Salmivalli, C., Kaukiainen, A., & Voeten, M. (2005). *Anti-bullying intervention: Implementation and outcome*. British Journal of Educational Psychology, 75, 465-487.

Slee, P., & Rigby, K. (1992). *Australian school children's self appraisal of interpersonal relations: the bullying experience*. Child Psychiatry and Human Development, 23(4), 273-282.

Slee, P., & Rigby, K. (1994). *Peer victimisation at school*. Australian Journal of Early Childhood, 19(1), 3-9.

Smith, P. K. (1991). *The silent nightmare: Bullying and victimization in school peer groups*. The Psychologist: Bulletin of the British Psychological Society, 4, 243-248.

Stevens, V., De Bourdeaudhuij, I., Van Oost, P. (2001). *Anti-bullying interventions at school: aspects of programme adaption and critical issues for further programme development*. Health Promotion International, 16(2), 155-167.

Sumsion, T. (1998). T*he Delphi technique: an adaptive research tool*. British Journal of Occupational Therapy, 61(4), 153-156.

WHO/UNESCO/UNICEF. (1991). *Consultation on strategies for implementing comprehensive school health education/promotion programmes*. Geneva, Switzerland: World Health Organization.

Zubrick, S., Silburn, S., Gurrin, C., Teo, H., Shephard, C., & Carlton, J. (1997). *Western Australian Child Health Survey: Education, Health and Competence*. Perth, WA: Australian Bureau of Statistics.

Conclusion

Moving Forward from Lessons Learned

Dr. Debra Pepler & Dr. Wendy M. Craig
PREVNet Scientific Co-Directors

This volume represents the outcome of an exceptional opportunity to bring together Canadian and international researchers to highlight current understanding in the field of bullying and derive implications for addressing bullying problems among children and youth. The conference and resulting chapters were made possible through the Networks of Centres of Excellence New Initiative grant to PREVNet. By engaging with international colleagues, we have been able to aggregate a broad range of perspectives on the problem of power and aggression in relationships in this first volume of the PREVNet Series. These perspectives provide strong direction for efforts to promote safe and healthy relationships for children and youth in Canada and around the world. In reflecting on the contributions within this volume, we have chosen to organize the lessons and highlights within the framework of PREVNet's three key messages:

1. Bullying is wrong and hurtful.

2. Bullying is a relationship problem.

3. Promoting relationships and eliminating violence are everyone's responsibility.

1. Bullying is Wrong and Hurtful

Being safe in relationships is a fundamental human right. Every child and youth has the right to be safe and free from involvement in bullying. It affects children and youth who are bullied, those who bully others, and those who know that bullying is occurring. The requirement for every child and youth to be safe is identified in the United Nations Convention on the Rights of the Child (UNCRC) (United Nations, 1989). Article 19 of the Convention states:

Parties shall take all appropriate legislative, administrative, social and educational measures to protect the child from all forms of physical or mental violence, injury or abuse, neglect or negligent treatment, maltreatment or exploitation, including sexual abuse, while in the care of parent(s), legal guardian(s) or any other person who has the care of the child.

The UNCRC also addresses the essential role of society to educate children to ensure they develop positive attitudes and behaviours and avoid using their power to bully or harass others. This societal function is the responsibility of all those who are in contact with children and youth. PREVNet provides an unprecedented opportunity to consolidate knowledge derived from university research to enhance the capacity of NGOs and governments to provide support for:

The preparation of the child for responsible life in a free society, in the spirit of understanding, peace, tolerance, equality of the sexes, and friendship among all peoples, ethnic, national and religious groups and persons of indigenous origin (UNCRC, United Nations, 1998).

Bullying has been highlighted as a critical issue of children's rights by a recent Canadian Senate report on children's rights. The Senate Committee recognized that: bullying is wrong and hurtful, that Canada's record is dismal in terms of students' reports of perpetrating bullying and experiencing victimization. Unlike many other countries represented by the international authors in this volume, Canada does not currently have a comprehensive national strategy to ensure children's safe and healthy relationships. Consequently, the Senate put forward Recommendation 3, that:

Pursuant to article 19 of the Convention on the Rights of the Child, the Committee recommends that the federal government implement a national strategy to combat bullying in Canada, accompanied by a national education campaign in cooperation with provincial and territorial governments to teach children, parents, teachers, and others about bullying, and to promote conflict resolution and effective intervention strategies

(Standing Senate Committee on Human Rights: Children the Silenced Citizens, 2007, p.74).

The Senate also recognized PREVNet in its report, noting that:

> PREVNET (Promoting Relationships and Eliminating Violence Network) [is] a new initiative of the Networks of Centres of Excellence ... currently developing a national strategy to address child and youth bullying and victimization (Standing Senate Committee on Human Rights: Children the Silenced Citizens, 2007, p.73).

The second part of this key message is that bullying is hurtful. Within this volume, there is ample evidence that bullying affects children and youth who are bullied, those who bully others, and those who know that bullying is going on. As early as kindergarten, Alsaker and Nägele note that teachers identify victimized children as unhappy. The ramifications of being victimized can extend to other aspects of a child's well being. Beran identifies the complex link between the experience of being bullied and low academic achievement. She notes that this association is influenced not only by individual factors, but also by relationship factors, such as parent support. This finding highlights the central tenet of PREVNet's strategy – that healthy relationships promote healthy development across many domains.

Children who bully others are also at risk for a host of problems. Marini and Dane help us understand that different forms of bullying are associated with different patterns of social-cognitive skills, psychosocial problems, and family and peer relationships. Marini and Dane also highlight the most at risk youth – those who are involved in both bullying their peers and being victimized. The concern for the dually involved students is echoed by Alsaker and Nägele who found that victimized aggressive kindergarten children had problems with maintaining attention and were the most overtly aggressive, even more aggressive than the children who were only involved in bullying. These chapters provide a critical rationale for providing different forms and intensities of prevention and intervention support for children with different pathways into bullying and victimization.

The effects of bullying on bystanders are identified in the chapter by Almeida, Caurcel, and Machado. Their data shed light on a moral dilemma for youth: Even though the vast majority of youth perceive their victimized peers as kind, good and vulnerable people, they generally do not step in to defend those who are being victimized. In the next chapter, Pöyhönen and Salmivalli help us to understand the thought processes behind this dilemma for those who witness bullying. It seems that adolescents' beliefs about (a) their own abilities to intervene effectively to stop bullying and (b) the consequences of intervening serve as critical predictors of whether bystanders will step to defend a victimized peer. Therefore, to promote peer engagement in addressing problems of bullying, it is essential for adults to give a clear message about their own willingness to support defenders and the effectiveness of peer intervention (our own research indicated that when peers intervene bullying stops within 10 seconds 57% of the time (Hawkins, Pepler, & Craig, 2001).

The difficulties associated with the diverse roles in bullying underline the importance of protecting children from "all forms of physical or mental violence, injury or abuse" perpetrated by peers and others. PREVNet provides an unprecedented opportunity to consolidate knowledge derived from research to enhance the capacity of all those involved with children and youth to fulfill their responsibilities to provide safety and support healthy development.

2. Bullying is a Relationship Problem

Bullying is a destructive relationship problem that requires relationship solutions. Children who bully learn to use power and aggression to cause distress and control others. With repeated exposure to bullying, children who are victimized become trapped in a dynamic in which they become increasingly powerless to escape. Prevention and intervention strategies, therefore, need to provide support for individuals, as well as for positive peer dynamics. In other words, these relationship problems require relationship solutions.

The nature of bullying changes with development as the challenges and tasks change through childhood and adolescence and as students' explore the dynamics of power. Tutty emphasizes the importance of tailoring interventions to address different forms of abuse at different ages, thereby ensuring that students are repeatedly exposed to the relationship lessons and skills they require. If students do not receive this type of support, we are concerned that the lessons of power and aggression established in childhood bullying can lead to sexual harassment (McMaster et. al, 2002), dating aggression (Pepler et al., 2005), and may later extend to workplace harassment, as well as marital, child, and elder abuse. Victimized children may also carry the hurt and fear from bullying forward into adult relationships. Perhaps the highest costs of bullying arise from the destructive relationship dynamics because relationships are the foundation for healthy development and well being throughout the lifespan.

In designing the Friendly Schools, Friendly Families bullying prevention program in Australia, Cross and her colleagues focused on changing key risk and protective factors associated with bullying including: students' attitudes and beliefs about bullying, the quality of their relationships with others, their knowledge and understandings about bullying and how to cope with it; and how they feel about their school. Menesini and her colleagues have conducted a number of studies, summarized in her chapter that highlight the importance of addressing the moral behaviour, reasoning and emotion for children who bully.

Consistent with the relationships focus, Wolfe, Crooks, Hughes, and Chiodo argue that developing relationships and social competence is critical for establishing habits to ensure adolescents' health and well-being. In their chapter, they describe their school-based Fourth R (for Relationships) program, which is designed to promote healthy relationships and prevent risk behaviours among adolescents. Crooks describes the extension of this relationship focused program to support healthy relationships among Aboriginal youth. Her chapter highlights the extended collaborative process of developing the multi-component school-based prevention initiative for Aboriginal youth which that has emerged through a partnership of researchers, educators, community members, and youth. This initiative has included several youth-developed video resources, a peer mentoring program, and an expanded and adapted curriculum (based on The Fourth R program).

Smith presents a cogent set of arguments underlining the importance of promoting a positive school climate by focusing on relationships in school-based bullying prevention programs. He notes that school climate is essentially manifested in the relationships among people in the school community, which would include not only the students, but the staff, parents and others involved in the school. In reviewing the modest success of bullying prevention programs, Smith calls for a different approach in which bullying is understood as a violation of relationships, not rules, leading to a focus on repairing relationships and providing opportunities for learning to interact positively. Both Smith and Tutty call for bullying prevention programs that are based on principles of restorative justice. Smith contrasts this positive relationship approach to the traditional approaches which emerge from a punitive stance which are unlikely to be effective in addressing bullying problems in the long-term. Smith's arguments highlight the essence of this key message: Given that bullying is a relationship problem, approaches that restore relationships and promote skills and attitudes essential for positive interactions are required. Based on their extensive experiences in bullying prevention in Norway, Midthassel and Roland add to this perspective by noting that students who bully require consequences that are firm, but constructive. Their experiences of working with schools in Norway illustrate the relationship focus – schools find a variety of ways to promote positive relationships through daily activities, sports, assemblies, and excursions.

The messages in chapters throughout this volume highlight the importance of supporting all children in developing healthy relationships. Effective bullying prevention initiatives help children and youth to understand that bullying is wrong, develop respect and empathy for others, and learn how to get along with and support others. The supports that children and youth require can be delivered through well designed school-based programs such as those described in this volume. This approach, however, is necessary but not sufficient because children need moment-to-moment lessons in building healthy relationships in all of the places where the live, learn, and play. This broader perspective brings us to the third key message that everyone is responsible for promoting healthy relationships and eliminating bullying and other forms of interpersonal aggression.

3. Promoting Relationships and Eliminating Violence are Everybody's Responsibility

Promoting relationships is everybody's responsibility because bullying occurs in all contexts where children and youth come together to work and play. As the primary institution and a major socialization force in children's lives, schools play a leadership role in addressing bullying problems. All of the empirically based interventions described in the present volume are founded on a systemic perspective which highlights the need for changes in awareness and behavioural strategies not only for those children who are directly involved, but also for their peers, their teachers, their parents, and beyond in the broader community. Cross and her colleagues provide a clear example of how their program developed over the years to become systemic with multi-level whole-school, classroom, and family intervention strategies.

Breaking the Silence and Engaging Support from all Involved

Research clearly indicates the central role of adults in preventing and intervening in bullying. There is a significant challenge in engaging adults in bullying prevention, which Menesini highlights in her chapter: the culture of silence. She argues that to avoid neglecting the plight of victimized children, it is essential to engage all those adults who are involved with children. The dilemma, however, is that adults seldom know about bullying because children do not report their problems and adults seldom observe bullying. This dilemma is also reflected in the chapter by Shariff and Hoff on cyberbullying. They paint a picture of the complexity of cyberbullying, which most often occurs beyond the purview of adults. When they are unsupervised for an extended period of time, adolescents' social interactions start to deteriorate, increasing the potential for harmful bullying. They highlight the prevalence, nature, legal and policy implications associated with this covert form of bullying. In this new frontier of bullying, Shariff and Hoff echo the call for a systemic approach in which educators work collaboratively with students, parents, technology corporations, universities, law enforcement providers, and governments to establish codes of conduct, guidelines, and effective education to assist youth as they navigate these challenging new domains.

The Power of Peer Involvement

Although adults are often not aware of bullying episodes, peers are most often present and involved in the dynamics, either as part of the problem or part of the solution (Hawkins et al., 2001; O'Connell, Pepler, & Craig, 1999). All of the interventions described in this volume have an element that focuses on engaging peers to shift the dynamics in bullying from encouraging the child who is bullying to supporting the child who is being victimized. For example, in the Friendly Schools, Friendly Families Program, Cross and her colleagues work to mobilize all bystanders and adults (especially parents, teachers and students) to use the peer group to provide support for students who are bullied and use positive peer pressure to discourage bullying. To engage peers, interventions must occur within the classroom and be broad in scope to promote positive interactions and social experiences of all children. Interventions to counter the peer processes that exacerbate bullying focus on supporting positive interactions, discouraging bullying, promoting empathy for victimized children, and encouraging children to intervene in bullying. In Italy, Menesini and her colleagues have developed interventions based on peer support models (befriending and mediation models). Because peers are present in the vast majority of bullying episodes, they can be the eyes and ears on the problem. Children cannot, however, address the problem alone – they require trusted, motivated, and attuned adults at home, school, and in the community to support them as they learn the essential skills and attitudes to develop positive relationships and social responsibility.

Teachers are Key and Need Training and Support

Many of the chapters highlight the importance of teachers in the success of school-based bullying prevention programs. In Switzerland, Alsaker and colleagues have developed a bullying prevention program that stresses education and support for teachers, with professional development for teachers provided through teams that combine teachers and mental health professionals. In a synopsis of research evaluating bullying prevention efforts in Ireland, O'Moore concludes that teachers play a pivotal role in prevention and interventions to address bullying and violence at school. She highlights the importance of training and resources for teachers currently in the classroom, but perhaps more importantly also for those who are in educational programs to become teachers themselves. For these pre-service teachers, O'Moore recommends education on the development of aggression to increase teachers' confidence in addressing bullying in their classrooms. Tutty echoes the call for better preparation of teachers in pre-service training and professional development to enhance their teaching of social-emotional skills and in modeling positive relationship values and skills.

In addition to professional development, teachers need support from their administrators who must be highly committed to systematic and enduring prevention efforts to address bullying problems. The principal is essentially responsible for guiding the whole school approach, which Midthassel and Roland note requires leadership for planning and collaboration across all levels of the system (staff, parents, classes, and communities). They also highlight the universal challenge of sustaining bullying prevention programs to ensure that efforts to support children's healthy relationships endure in spite of changes in school personnel, priorities and policies. Because positive relationships at school are critical for effective learning, efforts must be sustained to prevent bullying and promote a positive school climate.

Parents as Partners

Many of the bullying prevention programs described in this volume reach out to parents who are essential role models and supports for children and adolescents' social and emotional development. In Australia, Cross and her colleagues recognized the importance of parents and, in response to the challenges of engaging them, reworked their initial Friendly Schools program to include a family component. As part of their comprehensive program, they reached out to parents by providing schools with resources to enhance communications with parents including: presentations for parent meetings, family fairs, student performances, newsletters with parenting tips, a self-help parent communication book, and home activity sheets. Wolfe and his colleagues also recognize the importance of reaching out to parents of adolescents. In their Fourth R program, parents are invited to meetings and receive regular newsletters as a means of helping them understand their adolescents' development and learn strategies that are effective in promoting positive relationships.

Community

Bullying does not unfold in isolated contexts of peer groups, families, or even schools. It exists in a much larger context. Within PREVNet, we have come to understand bullying as a community problem because bullying occurs in all contexts where people—not just children—come together to live, learn, work, and play. Bullying can happen at home, at the mall, in the hockey arena, and at the park. In efforts to reduce problems of bullying for children and you, all adults who are involved with children and youth need to understand the problem and have the strategies and resources to intervene early to prevent the acceleration in the use of power and aggression. The efforts within schools must be matched by supportive attitudes and responses of all systems in which children live: at home, in sports, in recreation centres, and in the neighbourhood. Community partners and resources can also be drawn in to support schools in meeting the needs of its most vulnerable students. By providing consistency across systems in the messages, responses, and supports to address bullying problems, we can coordinate and increase the efforts to promote healthy relationships for all children and youth.

Lessons from efforts to engage the community in bullying prevention have been shared by several contributors to this volume. In implementing and sustaining the WITS program, Leadbeater described the "push" and "pull" of the relationship building required. The metaphor is helpful in understanding the dynamic and bi-directional processes at play in developing bullying prevention initiatives. Leadbeater notes that efforts must be made to help schools and communities "pull" the knowledge and opportunities that are made available. On the other hand, researchers, who are "pushing" knowledge and evidence-based strategies, must be responsive to and supportive of school and community champions who are already engaged in trying to pull in the expertise.

In her work to adapt The Fourth R program for aboriginal communities, Crooks helps to shed light on the importance of taking time to build understanding and positive relationships as an essential foundation for moving forward. The relationships then unfold with bi-directional benefits. Once time and attention have been spent in building trusting, collaborative partnerships with community stakeholders, then the prevention initiatives can be shaped and implemented with greater cultural relevancy. It is only by working within the context of a strong relationship among stakeholders that meaningful project development, evaluation, and sustainability can be achieved.

In many ways, the issues are similar as we enlarge our perspectives from communities to national initiatives. Midthassel and Roland share the challenges of implementing the Manifesto Against Bullying in Norway. Although Norway has a long tradition of bullying prevention efforts, these authors point out that the real challenges occur when a program meets a school as a system and the teacher as a professional. Understanding and skills in addressing bullying can be taught and supported, but successful implementation relies how the new competence is used by school staff in their daily interactions with students experiencing bullying problems. From her experiences in Ireland, O'Moore concludes that effective bullying prevention efforts require strong and enduring commitment among trainers and school staff, together with political commitment to promoting healthy relationships for all children and youth.

PREVNet: Forging Partnerships and Building Political Commitment

PREVNet is dedicated to preventing bullying and promoting positive relationship through partnerships. The PREVNet partnership model is founded on forging trusting relationships. In working with the NGOs, we recognize the need to tailor our approach and work at the point along the social change continuum where they are currently focusing. The partnerships are beneficial to both researchers and NGOs. Researchers within PREVNet learn from the NGOs' deep practical understanding built through day-to-day work with children and youth. NGOs within PREVNet meet researchers who have knowledge, skills, and tools to inform and evaluate their practices.

Our overall goal is to enhance the capacity of all adults who work with children and youth to understand and address bullying problems. Unless adults support the development of healthy relationships, social responsibility, and citizenship for our children and youth, they will not be prepared to be the partners, parents, employees, and leaders of tomorrow. We need to mobilize parents, teachers, recreational and community leaders—all adults and children working together to create environments where healthy relationships are encouraged to grow. We also need an alliance like PREVNet that will connect knowledge with the organizations and individuals who need it the most. Together, we will send consistent, connected, and positive messages and help to change attitudes about our approach to raising healthy, happy children.

References

Hawkins, D.L., Pepler, D., & Craig, W. (2001). *Peer interventions in playground bullying.* Social Development.10, 512-527.

McMaster, L., Connolly, J., Pepler, D., & Craig, W. (2002). *Peer to peer sexual Harassment in early adolescence: A developmental perspective.* Development and Pathology. 14(1), 91-105.

O'Connell, P., Pepler, D. J., & Craig, W. M. (1999). *Peer involvement in bullying: Insights and challenges for intervention.* Journal of Adolescence, 22, 437-452.

Standing Senate Committee on Human Rights: *Children the Silenced Citizens*, 2007, p.73

United Nations. (1998, November). *The convention on the rights of the child* (NRC).

Index

A

Abbott, R. D.   181
ABC Whole School Response to Bullying   282
Aber, J. L.   152, 161, 169, 176, 180
Abikoff, H. B.   56, 60
Aboriginal Peer Mentoring Program   203
Aboriginal Perspective Fourth R   199, 206
    community   202
    considerations for conducting research   211
    curriculum   205
    developing and maintainging partnerships   210
    research findings   206
    video projects   203
    curriculum   204
Abou-ezzeddine, T.   98, 124
academic cognitions   30
Achilles, C. M.   47, 60
Acikgoz, K.   149, 163
Adams, G. R.   56, 63, 142
Adams, P.   137
Adams, R. S.   140
Adler, T. F.   61
adolescent triad of risk behaviours   184
aggressive victims   48, 231
Ahlbo, A.   119
Ahmed, E.   49, 60, 158, 161
Albee, G.   145, 163
Alexander, K.   81, 88
Alexander, M. D.   81, 88
Almeida, A. M. T.   xii, 2, 4, 9, 19, 22, 267, 313
Almqvist, F.   63, 120
Alsaker, F. D.   5, 22, 129, 130, 230, 231, 232, 233, 234, 235, 239, 241, 242, 243, 247, 249, 251, 252, 313, 317
Amara, N.   170, 181
Amatya, K.   60
Amenkhienan, C. A.   47, 60
Ananiadou, K.   39, 43, 106, 124, 134, 143, 167, 183
Andershed, H.   261, 267
Anderson, M.   132, 142
Andreou, E.   28, 30, 32, 37, 41, 107, 108, 117

Applied Research Branch of Human Resources Development Canada 49
Archer, J. 237, 252
Armstrong, J. M. 122
Arnold, L. L. E. 60
Arora, T. 45, 65
Arsenio, W. F. 257, 267
Aschenbrand, S. G. 113, 120
Asher, S. R. 23, 44, 56, 60, 65, 118
Asplund-Peltola, R. L. 109, 122
Astor, R. A. 273, 283, 285
Atkins, M. 113, 119
Atlas, R. 133, 142, 145, 161
attention deficit hyperactivity disorder 232, 239, 240
attention to adolescence 264

B

Bacchini, D. 256, 267, 268
Bachorowski, J. 98, 119
Bagwell, C. L. 169, 180
Baker, M. 202, 213
Balding, J. 45, 60
Baldry, A. C. 135, 142, 261, 264, 267, 277, 285
Baldwin, J. M. 5, 22
Balfour, C. 85, 88
Balshine, S. 109, 124
Bandura, A. 31, 32, 41, 70, 88, 187, 196, 257, 266, 267
Barak, A. 67, 72, 76, 88
Bartini, M. 113, 122
Basch, C. 301, 309
Bates, J. E. 118, 119, 124
Battistich, V. 183
Bauman, S. 145, 153, 161
Bazemore, G. 136, 143
Be-Prox Prevention Program 241
    basic principles 242
    behaviour code 242
    central elements 243
    childrens perspective 245
    conclusions 247
    consolidation through own prevention goals 243
    evaluation 243
    learning principles 242
    participant evaluation 244
    sensitization 242

    social skills, empathy and positive activities 243
    talking together 242
    teacher attitudes 245
Becker, A. B. 167, 181
Becker, H. 155, 163
Beelmann, A. 107, 117
befriending model 259
behaviours triad 198
Beidler v. North Thurston School District Number 3 77, 95
Beland, K. 108, 125
Bellmore, A. D. 169, 180, 181
Benbenisty, R. 273, 283, 285
Benelli, B. 29, 42, 259, 268
Bentler, P. M. 51, 60
Beran, T. N. xiii, 2, 44, 48, 57, 60, 64, 144, 155, 161, 313
Berkowitz, L. 114, 117
Bernese study 233, 235, 243
Bertrand, R. 47, 61
Berts, M. 28
Besag, V. E. 45, 60
Bethel School District #403 v. Fraser 77
Beussink v. Woodlands R-IV School District 79
bicultural competence 202, 203, 211
Bigbee, M. A. 107, 118
Biggam, F. xxii, xxv
Bish, D. 45, 60
Bishop, J. L. xxiii, xxv
Björkqvist, K. 5, 24, 28, 42, 71, 92, 119, 170, 182, 231, 251
Blackstock, C. 200, 201, 213
Blair, J. 67, 88
Bliesener, T. 237, 250
Bloom, M. 147, 161
Blueprints for Violence prevention 272
Blumenfeld, P. C. 57, 62
Bobbett, G. C. 47, 60
Bobbett, N. C. 47, 60
Boivin, M. 6, 22, 98, 111, 112, 122, 124
Bonnar, S. 275
Booth, M. 292, 309
Bosacki, S. 97, 121
Bosch, J. D. 122
Bosworth, K. 57, 60
Botvin, G. J. 187, 196, 202, 214
Boulton, M. J. 29, 41, 44, 45, 48, 60, 63, 71, 88, 239, 249

Bowen, F. 117
Boyd, N. 71, 88
Bradley, M. J. 190, 196
Bradshaw, C. 144, 145, 157, 164
Braithwaite, V. 49, 60, 143, 158, 161
Braumer, J. 120
Bream, L. A. 118
Brehm, K. 167, 182
Brendgen, M. 98, 117, 124, 125, 183
Bretherton, I. 5, 22
Brethour, J. R. 159, 165
Bretveld, R. A. 123
British-Irish Anti-Bullying Forum 273
Brockenbrough, K. K. 156, 161
Broderick, C. J. 147, 162
Broussard, S. C. 46, 61
Brown, C. 156, 162, 181
Brown, J. L. 152, 161, 169, 180
Brown, K. 67
Bru, E. 217, 218, 219, 220, 227, 228
Brunner, A. 235, 249
Bryant, D. 98, 120
Bryne, B. 45, 61
Buccoliero, E. 254, 264, 267
Buhs, E. S. 46, 61
Bukowski, W. M. 5, 24, 180
bullycide 82
bullying and school achievement 48
bullying circle 133
bullying in Australia 290
bullying in Finland 28
bullying in Ireland 273
bullying in Italy 254
Bullyproofing Your Schools Program 155
Bumberger, B. 187, 196, 198, 213
Burraston, B. 169, 180
Burt-Gerrans, J. 75, 84, 91
Butler, L. J. 7
Byrne, B. 274, 285
bystander 9, 16, 17, 18, 19, 20, 21, 97, 105, 110, 112, 114, 170, 185, 188, 216

C

Cairns, B. D. xxiii, xxv, xxvi
Cairns, R. B. xxiii, xxvi

Calderon, K. 32
Callaghan, M. 6, 25
Camodeca, M. 28, 41, 98, 113, 117, 257, 267
Campbell, M. 67, 89
Canadian Association of Principals 178
Canadian Association of Social Workers 178
Canadian Charter of Rights and Freedoms 75
Canadian Coalition for the Rights of Children 178
Canadian Parks and Recreation 178
Canter, L. 277
Canter, M. 277
Caprara, G. V. 32, 37, 41
Caravita, S. 30, 31, 41, 254, 267
Carlson, E. A. 5, 22
Caroll, A. E. 135, 143
Carpenter, E. M. 44, 62
Carroll, A. E. 135
Carroll, P. 32, 41
Cartwright, N. xxii, xxv, 90, 132, 142
Casas, J. F. 118, 232, 250
Case, R. 85
Caspi, A. 98, 121, 261, 269
Cassidy, T. 117
Cassidy, W. 67, 89, 90
Castorina, S. 254, 267
Catalano, R. F. 23, 64, 181, 254, 267, 268, 269, 270, 282, 285
Caurcel, M. 2, 4, 9, 22, 313
causes of bullying behaviour 275
Centre for Behavioural Research 216
Centre for Learning Research 38
Centre for Youth and Society 168, 173
Cerezo, F. 8, 22
Chambers, M. 45, 66
Chandler, M. J. 200, 213
characteristics of children involved in bullying
    ADHD 240
    aggression 238
    depressiveness 241
    popularity 239
Chau, C. 60
Chaudry, N. 169, 180
Chien, D. H. 124, 232, 251
Child Health Promotion Research Centre 289
Chiodo, D. G. 129, 184, 194, 196, 197, 201, 206, 213, 214, 314

Christenson, S. L. 47, 61
Chu, B. W. 69, 72, 89, 91
Cillessen, A. H. N. 5, 23, 108, 110, 111, 117, 119, 123
Clark, A. G. 109, 124, 182
Clarke, G. N. 114, 117
Clarke, S. 200, 213
Codecasa, E. 29, 42, 259, 268
Cohen, J. 135, 142
Coie, J. D. 5, 23, 60, 65, 97, 111, 118, 119, 169, 180, 181
Coleman, H. L. K. 202, 213
Coloroso, B. 158, 161
Columbine High school 144
Comer, J.P. 176, 180
Common Concern Method 277
common sense knowledge 6
Communications Decency Act 73
communication skills 146, 157
community engagement model 176
comprehensive program evaluation framework 199
Comprehensive School Act 28
Conduct Problems Prevention Research Group 105, 106
conflict resolution 144, 145, 148, 153, 155, 156, 157, 158
conflict resolution skills 134, 168
Connolly, J. xxiv, xxv, 132, 142, 262, 267, 269, 320
Connor, D. F. 118
consequences of being bullied at school 46
Coping Power Program 111
Cordray, D. S. 199, 213
Cornell, D. G. 112, 118
Costello, J. 153, 165
Cousins, B. 106, 124
Cowie, H. 29, 42, 106, 124, 259, 264, 268, 270, 277, 285
Craig, W. xix, xx, xxiv, xxv, 5, 24, 29, 41, 42, 97, 98, 114, 118, 132, 133, 142, 145, 153, 161, 170, 178, 180, 262, 267, 269, 287, 311, 314, 316, 320
Cravens-Brown, L. M. 123
Crick, N. R. 98, 107, 108, 110, 118, 121, 126, 180, 232, 250
Crime Prevention Partners Program of Justice Canada 145
Critical Thinking Consortium 85
Crooks, C. xiii, 129, 145, 184, 186, 192, 194, 196, 197, 198, 201, 206, 213, 214, 314, 315, 318
Cross, D. xiv, 64, 130, 262, 267, 268, 270, 285, 288, 289, 296, 299, 309, 314, 316, 317
Crump, A. D. 63, 97, 119
Crusto, C. 167, 182
Cullen, J. 200, 213

cultural identity 200, 202, 203, 204, 205, 211
cultural relevancy of programs 198
culture of silence 258
Cummings, J. xiv, 1, 127
Cummins, L. H. 201, 213
customizing interventions
    caveat 114
    conclusions 115
    couples therapy 114
    direct and indirect 110
    dually involved children 114, 313
    reactive and proactive 112
    social skills training 114
Cvetkovich, G. T. 202, 213
cyber-bullying 144, 159, 316
    Canadian human rights and United States sexual harassment and discrimination law 84
    conclusions 86
    educational policy vacuum 75
    freedom of speech and expression rights 80
    interactive online educational programs 85
    legal obligations 74
    policy development 85
    prevalence of sexual and homophobic harassment 72
    recommendations 86
    research, teacher education and professional development 85
    roles and responsibilities 73
    student privacy 82
    tort law and negligence 82

D

Dahlberg, L. L. 156, 162
Dane, A. V. xiv, 3, 97, 121, 313
dating aggression 261, 266
Davino, K. 167, 182
Davis v. Munroe 84
Day, L. E. 118, 181
DeBar, L.L. 114, 117
defenders 20, 30, 110, 133
    characteristics 31
    social cognitive factors 32
Defender scale 33
defining bullying 256, 275, 291
dehumanisation 257, 266

Dekker, P. H.   28, 41
Delbecq, A. L.   292, 309
Delphi Technique   292
Delucchi, K.   183
Deluty, R. H.   45, 61
Del Barrio, C   9, 22
Del Rio, A.   145, 153, 161
Denning, D.   133, 143
Department of Health and Human Services Centers for Disease Control and Prevention   xix
DeRosier, M. E.   5, 23
Deslandes, R.   47, 61
Deurzen, E.   6, 23
developmental perspective   xxiv, 262
Devlin, A.   70, 77, 89
De Andrade, L. L.   158, 165
De Bourdeaudhuij, I.   290, 310
DHondt, J.   200, 213
Dibbell, J.   72, 89
DiBlasio, P.   30, 41
Dickinson, G. M.   82, 91
Didaskalou, E.   32, 41
DiGiulio, R. C.   73, 82, 84, 89
direct bullying   107, 108, 116
disengagement   21, 45, 47, 59
Dishion, T. J.   111, 122, 167, 169, 180
disruptive behaviours   50
Dodge, K. A.   5, 23, 65, 97, 98, 110, 111, 117, 118, 119, 122, 123, 124, 167, 168, 170, 180
Domitrovich, C.   187, 196, 198, 213, 225, 227
Donegal Anti-Bullying Program   274
    community implementation   278
    evaluation   278
    methodology   275
    parent evening   277
    selection of schools   275
    teacher training   277
    training program   276
    training the network of professionals   275
Drewery, W.   137, 138, 142
drive-by research   210
Dudley, B.   149, 163
Dumas, J. E.   107, 124
Duncan, D.   301, 309
Dunham, J.   277, 285
Dupper, D. R.   xxii, xxvi, 152, 165

Duyvesteyn, M. G. C.   112, 125

E

Ebel, R. L.   46, 61
Eccles, J. S.   46, 55, 57, 61, 64
ecological models 46
Edstrom, L. V. S.   147, 162
Egeland, B.   5, 22, 47, 62
Eitel, P.   63, 97, 119
Ekstrom, R. B.   57, 61
Elliott, S. N.   48, 62
El Ansari, W. E.   170, 181
Emmett v. Kent School District No. 415 76, 78
empathy 140
Englund, M. M.   47, 62
Erceg, E.   289
Erdley, C. A.   44, 48, 62, 64, 180
Ertesvåg, S.   218, 228
Eslea, M.   282, 285
Espelage, D. L.   60, 140, 142, 143, 168, 181
Essex, M. J.   122
Estell, D. B.   xxiii, xxv
ethno-theories. *See* common sense knowledge
Evard, M.   72, 89
expectancy-value theory 46
expert-driven dissemination model 166
explanatory models and risk factors 258
extent of bullying 256, 275
external programs 146, 153

F

Fabes, R. A.   133, 143
Fagot, B. I.   109, 119
family-focused intervention 110
Farmer, T. W.   xxiii, xxv, xxvi
Farrell, A. D.   156, 162, 163
Farrington, D. P.   97, 107, 119, 135, 142, 261, 267, 268, 277, 285
Fazekas, H.   120
Fehrmann, P. G.   47, 62
Feldlaufer, H.   57, 64
Fendrich, M.   47, 63
Feshbach, N. D.   140, 142
Finn, J. D.   57, 62
Finnish Basic Education Act 28

Finnish Ministry of Education 28, 38
first period intervention and prevention programs 260
Fisher, J. D. 186
Fisher, W. A. 186
Flaherty v. Keystone Oaks School District 77, 95
Flannery, D. J. 155, 162
Flemington, I. 29, 41
Flowers, T. A. 47, 62
Floyd, K. 69, 70, 92
Fonagy, P. 159, 165
Fontaine, R. 118
Fonzi, A. 253, 254, 255, 256, 257, 258, 267, 268, 269
Forehand, R. 156, 162
Formsma, J. 200, 201, 213
Foster, P. 277
Fourth R 156, 186, 187, 192, 195, 199, 201, 204, 206, 314, 318
    accurate information 187
    behavioural skills 189
    being gender strategic 192
    ensuring comprehensive participation 191
    inclusion of parents 191
    interpersonal skills 189
    motivation 190
    research findings 194
    strengthening relationship skills 186
    teacher involvement 192
Fox, J. 272
Fredericks, J. A. 62
Freedman-Doan, C. 46, 61
Freeman, H. E. 199, 214
Fregoso, M. 30, 43
French, R. L. 47, 60
Frey, K. S. 108, 125, 147, 155, 162
Frick, P. J. 120
Fried, P. 47, 62
Fried, S. 47, 62
Friendly Schools and Families 289, 290, 316
    background 290
    classroom level 298, 303
    design 301
    efficacy trial 296
    family level 298, 302
    findings 301
    formative trial principles 296

    levels 296
    program dissemination 306
    whole school level 296, 302
    findings 305
Frisbie, D. A. 46, 61
Frost, L. 45, 62
Fullan, M. 217, 218, 219, 225, 227, 228
Futterman, R. 61

G

Gallaher, P. 121
Galloway, D. 57, 62, 106, 119, 273, 275, 285
Garrison, M. E. B. 46, 61
Garrity v. John Hancock Mut. Life Ins. Co 81, 95
Gary, F. 202, 213
Gasset, O. 24
Gáti, Á. 69, 77, 90
Gatzke-Kopp, L. 123
Gebser v. Lago Vista Independent School District 84, 95
Geiger, T. A. 126
Gendreau, P. L. 125
Genta, M. L. 254, 268
George, D. M. 32, 41
Gerton, J. 202, 213
Gilchrist, L. D. 202, 213, 214
Gini, G. 260, 268
Girl Guides of Canada 178
Giroux, H. 73, 84, 90
Glassberg, L. A. 56, 64
Glissov, P. 6, 25
Glover, D. xxii, xxv, 90, 132, 142
Godfrey v. Demon Internet Ltd 86, 95
Goertz, M. E. 57, 61
Goff, S. B. 61
Gold, R. 301, 309
Golding, W. 67, 68, 69, 70, 90
Goldsmith, H. H. 122
Good Touch, Bad Touch Program 156
Goossens, F. A. 28, 30, 31, 37, 41, 98, 117
Gorney, D. 47, 61
Gosnell, G. 201, 213
Gough, G. xxii, xxv, 132, 142
Gouin, R. 72, 93
Graczyk, P. A. 58, 61, 225, 227

Graham, S.   22, 24, 45, 47, 62, 63, 65, 111, 119, 121, 123, 124, 169, 180, 181
Grandbois, D.   202, 213
Granic, I.   112, 119
Granizo, L.   6, 23
Grasley, C.   156, 165
Greater Victoria School District   168, 173
Green, S. M.   97, 121
Greenberg, M. T.   187, 196, 198, 213, 225
Greenfield, D. B.   49, 63
Greenman, P. S.   30, 43
Gresham, F. M.   48, 62
Grills, A. E.   98, 119
Groen, G.   240, 250
Grossman, D. C.   147, 152, 162
Grotpeter, J. K.   98, 107, 118, 180
group view on bullying   29
Guerra, N. G.   47, 49, 57, 62, 181
Guidelines on Countering Bullying Behaviour in Primary and Post Primary Schools   276
Gustafson, D. H.   292, 309
Gutzwiller-Helfenfinger, E.   239, 249

H

Hall, M.   289, 296, 309
Hamilton, G.   296, 309
Hanish, L. D.   47, 49, 57, 62, 133, 134, 143, 181
Harachi, T. W.   282, 285
harassment   49, 55, 56
Harel, Y.   132, 142
Hargreaves, D.   218, 227, 228
Harmon, A.   67, 72, 82, 90
Harnish, J. D.   119
Harrington, H.   98, 121
Hart, C. H.   108, 119, 123
Hartup, W. W.   5, 23, 124, 125, 237, 251, 252
Harvey, M.   xxii, xxv
Harvey, P.   156, 162
Hawk, G.   118
Hawker, D. S. J.   44, 45, 63
Hawkins, D. L.   29, 41, 314, 316, 320
Hawkins, E. H.   201, 202, 213
Hawkins, J. D.   181, 282, 285
Hawley, P. H.   98, 120
Hay, D.   261, 268
Haynie, D. L.   48, 63, 97, 119

Hays, B. J. 156, 163
Hazelwood vs. Kuhlmeier 78
hazing 262
Health Behaviours in School-aged Children survey xix
health education 28
Heames, J. T. xxii, xxv
Hecht, S. A. 49, 63
Hechtman, L. 60
Helmreich, R. L. 46, 66
Henderson, K. xxiv, xxv
Henrich, C. C. 152, 161
Henttonen, I. 63, 120
Herald, S. L. 46, 61
Herring, S. C. 67, 72, 76, 90
Hess, L. 113, 119
Hinduja, S. 144, 163
Hirschstein, M. K. 147, 162
Hodges, E. V. E. 6, 22, 44, 63
Hoff, D. L. 2, 67, 316
Hoglund, W. L. 108, 120, 169, 170, 176, 181, 182
Holmes, T. 156, 162
homicide 159
Hooper, S. R. 56, 64
Hopkins, D. 218, 227, 228
Hopmeyer-Gorman, A. 98, 124
Hospital for Sick Children 178
Howard, B. xix, xxv
Howell, J. C. 169, 181
Hoza, B. 60
Hubbard, J. A. 110, 119, 124
Hudley, C. 111, 119
Hudson, J. L. 113, 120
Hugh-Jones, S. 44, 63
Hughes, R. 129, 184, 197, 206, 214, 314
Hymel, S. 6, 7, 22, 23, 25, 44, 60, 132, 134, 143
hyperactivity 232, 239, 240, 246

I

Ialongo, N. 169, 181
Idsøe, T. 219, 227
ill-effects of bullying 275
imbalance 254
implicit theories. *See* common sense knowledge
impulsivity 239, 240, 246

indirect bullying 107, 108, 109, 110
individual-level variables 194
Information Motivation Behaviour Skills Model 186
Institute of Behavioural Science, University of Colorado 272
intentionality 254
internal programs 146, 147
internal working model 5
intervention programs
    effectiveness and limitations 107
    future directions 265
Irish National Initiative 274
iSafeAmerica 72
Israel, B. A. 167, 171, 181
Izzo, C. V. 47, 63

J

J.S., a Minor v. Bethlehem Area School District 79
Jackson, M. 67, 69, 89, 90
Jaffe, P. 145, 165, 186, 192, 196, 197, 198, 214
Jeffrey, L. R. 153, 162
Jensen, P. S. 60
Jiang, D. xxiv, xxv
Johnny, L. 71, 92
Johnson, B. 29, 30, 42
Johnson, D. 149, 152, 277
Johnson, M. xxii, xxv, 132, 142
Johnson, R. 149, 152, 277, 285
John Doe v. GTE Corp 74, 95
Jones, S. M. 98, 120, 152, 161, 169, 180
Jubran v. North Vancouver School District 83, 95
Juffer, F. 112, 125
Junge, A. 217, 229
Junger-Tas, J. 254, 267, 268
Juvonen, J. 22, 24, 45, 47, 62, 63, 65, 121, 123, 124, 180

K

Kaczala, C. M. 61
Kaiser Family Foundation 187
Kaistaniemi, L. 29, 30, 42, 277, 288
Kalb, L. 97, 121
Kandersteg Declaration xxii, xxiv
Kantor, L. W. 187, 196
Kasprow, W. J. 47, 63
Kauer, M. 241, 252

Kaukiainen, A. 5, 24, 28, 29, 30, 39, 42, 71, 92, 105, 108, 109, 119, 123, 167, 170, 182, 231, 251, 277, 288, 290, 310
Kavanagh, K. 109, 119
Kazdin, A. E. 105, 106, 117, 120, 125
Keith, P. B. 47, 63
Keith, T. Z. 47, 62, 63
Kellam, S. G. 169, 181
Keltikangas-jarvinen, L. 109, 122
Kempes, M. 120
Kendall, P. C. 113, 120
Kennedy, E. 246, 251
Kerr, M. 112, 124, 261, 267
Kersnick, R. 32, 41
Kessler, M. 145, 163
Ketsetzis, M. 56, 63
Kids Help Phone 178
Killion v. Franklin Regional School District 79, 95
Killip, S. 194, 196
Kimble, J. D. 186, 196
Kimonis, E. R. 120
kindergarten bullying
    extent 237
    introduction 231
    measuring 234
    three central features 233
King, E. 28
King, C. A. 125
Kirby, D. 187, 196
Kirkham, C. 277, 286
KiVa Program 39
Klar, L. N. 82, 91
Klein, M. H. 64, 122
Klingel, D. 46, 63
Kochenderfer, B. J. 46, 47, 55, 63, 230, 231, 232, 233, 250
Kochenderfer-Ladd, B. 6, 23, 45, 65, 133, 143, 231, 250
Kogan, L. R. 47, 60
Koivisto, M. 28, 41
Kokkinos, C. 232, 250
Kolbe, L. 301, 309
Koops, W. 121, 122
Korn, S. 29, 43
Koruna, B. 121
Kresanov, K. 63, 120
Kruse, S. D. 219, 227

Ku, H. C. 232, 250
Kulka, R. A. 46, 63
Kumpfer, K.L. 167, 182
Kumpulainen, K. 48, 63, 120, 232, 250
Kupersmidt, J. B. 97, 98, 117, 118, 120, 169, 180, 181
Kusel, S. J. 19, 24, 44, 65

L

Lacharite, M. 97, 121
Ladd, G. W. 46, 47, 55, 61, 63, 230, 231, 232, 233, 237, 239, 250
LaFromboise, T. D. 202, 213
Lagerspetz, K. 5, 24, 28, 29, 30, 42, 43, 71, 92, 119, 170, 182, 231, 251, 277, 288
Lahey, B. B. 97, 121
Lalonde, C. E. 200, 213
Lamari, M. 170, 181
Landry, R. 170, 181
Lang, J. 144
Lansford, J. E. 118, 167, 180
Lappalainen, M. 29, 30, 43
Larke, I. 48, 64
Larsen, T. 217, 219, 227
Larson, J. 111, 120
Lasker, R. D. 170, 181
Laursen, B. 5, 23
Lavis, J. N. 182
Lavoie, F. 117
Layshock v. Hermitage School District 79, 95
Lazzarin, M. G. 254, 259, 268
Leadbeater, B. J. xv, 108, 109, 120, 128, 129, 166, 168, 169, 170, 176, 181, 182, 318
Lease, A. M. 18, 23
Lemerise, E. A. 257, 267
Lera, M-J. 106, 122
Levene, K. S. 109, 122
Lewinsohn, P. M. 114, 117
Li, Q. 72, 91, 144, 161, 163
Limber, S. 272, 286
Linden, A. M. 82, 91
Ling, X. 169, 181
Linn, M. 153, 162
Linna, S. 63, 120
Lipsey, M. W. 199, 213, 214
Little, T. D. 98, 110, 120
Liu, M. 123
localization 211

Lochman, J. E.   105, 109, 111, 113, 114, 119, 120
Lockhart, R.   6, 25
Locklear, S.   202, 214
Loeber, R.   97, 121, 123, 261, 268
Logan, S.   45, 66
Lomas, J.   171, 182
Loney, B. R.   120
Long, J.   xxiv, xxv, 122
Lord of the Flies 70, 71, 86
Lösel, F.   107, 117, 237, 250
Louis, K.   219, 227
Luckner, A. E.   47, 62
Lutes v. Board of Education of Prairie View School Division No. 74 75, 95
Lynam, D.   123

M

Maassen, G.   120
Macaulay, A. C.   171, 182
MacBeath, J.   217
Machado, J.   2, 4, 313
MacKay, A. W.   75, 82, 84, 91
MacKenzie, E. P.   147, 162
Maggi, M.   254, 264, 267
Magnuson, D.   149, 163
Magnusson, D.   261, 270
Maines, B.   277, 287
Malloy, T. E.   186, 196
Mameli, C.   254, 268
Manger, T.   217, 227
Manifesto Against Bullying 215
Mann, D. W.   46, 63
Marini, F.   254, 268
Marini, Z. A.   xv, 3, 97, 98, 112, 113, 121, 313
Marlatt, G. A.   201, 213
Martin, C. L.   133
Matthys, W.   120, 121
Mattison, R. E.   56, 64
Mayeux, L.   108, 117
McCold, P.   136, 138, 143
McConnell, S. R.   48, 66
McDougall, P.   6, 25, 132, 143
McDuff, P.   183
McFall, R. M.   18, 23
McGrath, H.   xxiii, xxv

McIntyre, A. 275
McLaughlin, M. 219, 227
McMahon, S. D. 64, 125
McMaster, L. 314, 320
McNeilly-Choque, M. K. 119
McShane, M. 201, 213
McWhinnie, M. 97, 121
Mead, G. H. 5, 23
Meadows, L. 157, 164
Mebane, S. E. 140, 142
mediators of change 193
Media Awareness Network 85
Meece, J. L. 61
Meerum Terwogt, M. 98, 117
Megal, M. E. 156, 163
Melloni Jr., R. H. 118
Mellor, A. 6, 23, 47, 64, 274, 285
Menesini, E. xv, 28, 30, 37, 42, 130, 253, 254, 256, 257, 258, 259, 260, 262, 264, 267, 268, 269, 270, 314, 316
Meraviglia, M. G. 155, 163
Merisca, R. 169, 181
Merk, W. 98, 111, 113, 121, 122
Merrell, K. W. 48, 64
Merrett, F. 277
Metallidou, P. 28, 30, 37, 41
Meyer, A. 156, 162, 163
Midgley, C. 57, 61, 64
Midthassel, U. V. xvi, 127, 129, 215, 216, 217, 218, 219, 220, 227, 228, 315, 317, 319
Miedel, W. T. 64
Miller, D. 153, 162, 292, 309
Miller, G. E. 167, 170, 181, 182
Miller, W. R. 190, 196
Milloy, J. S. 200, 213
Milne, B. J. 98, 121
Milson, A. 69, 91
Minton, S. J. 272, 273, 274, 276, 277, 279, 282, 286, 287
Mintzberg, H. 218, 228
Mischovich, S. J. 186, 196
Mitchell, K. 67, 69, 72, 91, 92, 94
Mize, J. 169, 181
Moffitt, T. E. 98, 121, 261, 263, 269
Moilanen, I. 63, 120
Monks, C. 232, 250
moral disengagement 257, 266

moral reasoning 257
Morita, Y. 23, 44, 64, 254, 267, 268, 269, 270
Morrison, B. E. 138, 143, 158, 163
Morrison, D. M. 181
Morrissey-Kane, E. 167, 182
Moscovici, S. 6, 23
Mosher, M. 118
motivational interviewing techniques 190
Mouttapa, M. 113, 121
Muirden, J. 45, 60
Munholland, K. A. 5, 22
Munthe, E. 106, 123, 274, 283, 287, 288
Myers, D. A. 68, 73, 74, 91
myths of bullying 275

N

Nabozny v. Podlesny 84, 95
Nägele, C. 230, 313
Nangle, D. W. 44, 48, 62, 64, 180
Nansel, T. 49, 63, 64, 97, 119, 121, 132, 143
Nation, M. 167, 182, 188, 196
National Aboriginal Health Organization 203
National Childrens Home 72, 91
National Longitudinal Survey of Children and Youth 49
National Research and Development Centre for Welfare and Health 26
Naylor, P. 6, 23
Nelson, D. A. 108, 119, 121
Networks of Centres of Excellence xx, 311, 313
Newman, J. E. 44, 62, 98
Newman, J. P. 119
New Jersey v. T.L.O 81, 96
Nicolaides, S. 273, 275, 286
Nieminen, E. 232, 251
Nishina, A. 47, 63, 65
Nixon, K. 145, 164, 165
Nocentini, A. L. 262, 264, 269
Nock, M. K. 98, 120
non-violent sanctions policy 277
nonnismo. *See* hazing
Norwegian Manifesto against bullying 217, 319
    influence 219
    opportunities and challenges 217
    planning and structure 219
    relevance 219

summary 225
No Blame approach 277
Nucci, L. 98, 121
Nutting, P. A. 171, 182

O

O'Connor, C. 190, 196
O'Moore, M. xvi, 130, 145, 163, 265, 271, 272, 273, 274, 275, 276, 277, 279, 282, 286, 287, 317, 319
OConnell, P. 5, 24, 29, 316, 320
ODonnell, J. 181
Ogden, C. 153, 165
Oklahoma City bombings 74
Okpala, A. O. 47, 64
Okpala, C. O. 47, 64
Oldfield, D. 156, 163
Oligny, P. 125
Ollendick, T. H. 98, 119
Olsen, S. F. 119, 123
Olthof, T. 28, 41
Olweus, D. xxiii, xxv, 5, 6, 22, 23, 24, 29, 42, 44, 45, 47, 55, 64, 71, 91, 97, 105, 106, 121, 122, 133, 134, 143, 152, 163, 176, 182, 215, 216, 217, 225, 228, 231, 232, 233, 241, 247, 249, 250, 251, 254, 261, 267, 268, 269, 270, 272, 274, 277, 278, 279, 281, 285, 286, 288, 290, 309
Olweus Bullying Prevention Program 134, 152, 272
ONeal, K. K. xxiii, xxv
onlookers 133
Ontario Ministry of Education 204
Ontario Safe Schools Act 136
operatore amico. *See* befriending model
Oram, G. 118
Organisation for Economic Co-operation and Development xx, 272
Orlandi, M. A. 202, 214
Orobio de Castro, B. 110, 121, 122
Ortega, R. 106, 122, 232, 250
Ortega y Gasset, J. 6
Osborne, J. W. 45, 47, 65
Osgood, C. E. 10, 24
Österman, K. 5, 24, 28, 42, 71, 92, 119, 170, 182, 231, 251
Otten, M. 47, 65
outcome expectancies 32, 190
Outsider scale 33
Overpeck, M. 64, 97, 121, 143
Ownership, Control, Access, and Possession guidelines 210

P

Pagani, L. 183
Pakaslahti, L. 109, 122
Panayiotou, G. 232, 250
parent-focused intervention. *See* family-focused intervention
parent-management training 105, 106
parental support 50
Paris, A. H. 57, 62
Park, J. H. 64, 108, 122
Parker, E. A. 24, 56, 65, 167, 181
Parker, J. G. 5
Parkhurst, J. T. 44, 60
Parks, M. 69, 70, 92
participant-role approach 105
Participant Role Questionnaire 33
passive victims 231
Patchin, J. W. 144, 163
Pathways to Victimization Project 230
Patterson, G. R. 112, 119
Paul, A. 118
peace-keeping 149
Peacebuilders 155
Pearce, N. 289
Pearl, R. xxiii, xxvi
Peat, J. 107, 125
peer education models 158
peer group 168
peer interactions 51
peer mediation 149, 152, 158
peer mentoring 203
peer perspective 5
Pelham, W. E. 125
Pellegrini, A. D. xxiv, xxv, 113, 122, 232, 251, 262, 270
People v. Overton 81, 96
Pepler, D. J. xix, xxiv, xxv, xxvi, 5, 24, 29, 37, 41, 42, 43, 92, 97, 109, 110, 119, 121, 122, 123, 124, 132, 133, 142, 145, 153, 161, 163, 170, 178, 180, 228, 231, 249, 251, 261, 262, 267, 269, 272, 275, 281, 285, 287, 288, 311, 314, 316, 320
Pereira, J. 206, 214
Perren, S. 231, 232, 239, 251
Perry, D. G. 5, 19, 32, 42, 44, 63, 65, 246
Perry, J. 5
Perry, L. C. 19, 32, 44, 65, 246
persistency 254

Petermann, F. 240, 250
Petersen, R. 73
Pettit, G. S. 118, 119, 124
Pfingsten, U. 107, 117
Phillips, C. J. 170, 181
Piha, J. 63, 120
Pikas, A. 277, 287, 297, 309
Pilla, R. S. 64, 97, 121, 143
Pine, D. 118
Pintabona, Y. 289
Pintabona, Y. M. H. 296, 309
Pollack, S. 57, 60, 61
Porches, M. 71, 93
Poulin, F. 111, 112, 122, 169, 180
Power, K. xxii, xxv
Pöyhönen, V. 2, 26, 127, 313
prevalence and psychosocial consequences of bullying 98
prevention programs 135
    cautions 149
    characteristics 153
    conflict resolution 152
    delivery 147
    evaluation 148, 156
    review 106
    strengths and challenges 159
    violence prevention 146
PREVNet xx, xxi, xxiv, 9, 168, 178, 311, 312, 313, 314, 318, 319
    four strategy pillars xx, xxi
    mandate xx
    partnership model xxi, xxii
Price, J. M. 98, 118, 119, 122
primary prevention 145, 146
Principles of Successful Practice to Reduce Bullying in Schools 306
Prinstein, M. J. 110, 111, 123
pro-social scale 51
proactive bullying 110, 111
Proctor, L. J. 97, 124, 232, 251
Profilet, S. M. 237, 250
Project Trust 156
provocative victims. *See* aggressive victims
public humiliation 56
Pulkkinen, L. 123
pupil intervention 280
Puura, K. 63, 120

Q

Quirk, K. J. 47, 63

R

R. v. M.R.M 80, 81, 96
R. v. Oakes 75, 96
Raine, A. 110, 123
Räsänen, E. 63, 120
Rasmussen, P. 32, 42
Rawana, J. 206, 214
Rawson, L. 6, 25
reactive bullying 98, 110, 111, 113, 114, 115, 116
Red Cross 178
Regis, D. 45, 60
Reid, W. H. 47, 65
Reimers, T. M. 47, 62
Reinecke, M. A. 125
Reinforcer scale 33
Reitzel-Jaffe, D. 156
relationship perspective 7
    descriptions of victimized students 10
    perceived vulnerability and common stereotypes 15
Resolving Conflict Creatively 152, 169
Restorative Approaches 277
restorative justice appoach 138
restorative practices in the classroom 140
Reynolds, A. J. 64, 123
Reynolds, D. 219, 228
Richter, S. xix, xxv
Rienstenberg, N. 136, 143
Rigby, K. 29, 30, 37, 41, 42, 43, 44, 45, 48, 65, 97, 98, 106, 115, 119, 121, 123, 124, 132, 143, 231, 232, 249, 251, 272, 274, 275, 285, 287, 288, 290, 296, 309, 310
Rivers, I. 6, 24, 106, 125
Robertson, P. 217, 229
Robertson, T. 155, 163, 164
Robichaud v. Canada 83, 96
Robinson, D. 24, 45, 66, 119, 123
Robinson, G. 277, 287
Robson, C. 10, 24
Rock, D. A. 57, 61, 62
Rock Solid Foundation 173, 174, 175
Rodkin, P. C. xxiii, xxvi
Roeser, R. 46, 61

Rohrbach, L. A. 121
Roland, E. xvi, xvii, 85, 106, 119, 123, 127, 129, 215, 216, 217, 220, 225, 228, 273, 274, 275, 283, 285, 287, 288, 315, 317, 319
role play 185, 188, 189
Rollnick, S. 190, 196
Rose, A. J. 30, 42, 108, 109, 123
Rosen-Reynoso, M. 71, 93
Rosenbluth, B. 155, 163, 164
Rossi, P. H. 199, 214
Ross v. New Brunswick School District No. 15 79, 96
Rothberg, S. 119
Rounds, T. 47, 61
Royal Commission on Aboriginal Peoples 201
Royer, E. 47, 61
Ruan, W. J. 64, 97, 121, 143
Rubin, K. D. 5, 18, 23, 24, 122
Rudolph, K. D. 30, 42, 182
Russell, A. 123
Rutter, M. 261, 263, 269, 270
Ryan, B. A. 56, 63, 142

S

Sacco, F. 159, 165
Salmivalli, C. xvii, 2, 5, 20, 24, 26, 28, 29, 30, 31, 33, 37, 39, 41, 42, 43, 71, 92, 105, 106, 114, 119, 123, 127, 133, 143, 167, 170, 182, 231, 232, 251, 263, 270, 277, 288, 290, 310, 313
Salzer Burks, V. 118
Samdal, O. 292, 309
Samples, F. 169, 180
Sanchez, E. 155, 163, 164
Sanchez, V. 257, 269
Sattler, J. M. 46, 66
Saylor, K. 63, 97, 119
SCAN-Bullying Quest 9
scare tactics 189
Schäfer, M. 29, 31, 43
Schaps, E. 183
Scheidt, P. 64, 97, 121, 143
Schinke, S. P. 202, 213, 214
Schippel, P. L. 123
Schnarch, B. 210, 214
Schneider, B. H. 30, 39, 43, 107, 115, 123, 134, 143, 167, 183
school-level variables 194
school achievement 46, 57

school achievement consequences of being bullied 44
school climate 133, 135, 140, 259, 266, 276
    punitive 136
    restorative 137
school enjoyment 50
school ethos. *See* school climate
School Health Promotion Study 26
Schuengel, C. 98, 117
Schulz, A. J. 167, 181
Schuster, B. 45, 65
Schwartz, D. 45, 47, 48, 49, 55, 65, 97, 98, 113, 119, 124, 231, 232, 251
Scott, K. 156, 165, 194, 196, 197
Scripted-Cartoon Narrative of Peer Bullying 9
Seattle Committee for Children 147, 155
secondary prevention 145, 273
Second Step 108, 147, 152, 155
self-efficacy 30, 31, 32, 33, 35, 36, 37, 187
self-representations 6, 7
Senior School Education Act 28
Serketich, W. J. 107, 124
Servance, R. L. 68, 76, 77, 92
sexual harassment 261, 262, 263, 264, 266
sex roles 264
Seybolt, D. 167, 182
Shariff, S. xvii, 2, 67, 70, 71, 72, 73, 76, 82, 83, 90, 91, 92, 93, 316
Sharp, S. 45, 46, 65, 106, 125, 155, 164, 241, 251
Shaw, T. 289
Siann, G. 6, 25
signs of victimization and bullying 275
silent witness. *See* bystander
Silent Witnesses 282
Silva, P. A. 261, 269
Silver, C. 125
Simon, T. R. 60, 142
Simons, R. F. 63, 64, 97, 110, 119, 121, 124, 143
Simons-Morton, B. 63, 64, 121, 143
Sinisammal, M. 39, 123
Sippola, L. K. 180
Skiba, R. 73, 93
Skinner, K. 45, 65
Slee, P. T. 23, 29, 30, 42, 57, 64, 65, 254, 267, 268, 269, 270, 290, 310
Sliepcevich, E. 301, 309
Smith, D. 127, 128, 132, 315
Smith, D. J. 39, 167, 170, 183

Smith, F. E.   47, 64
Smith, I.   217, 229
Smith, J. D.   106, 115, 134, 135
Smith, P. K.   14, 29, 30, 37, 39, 41, 42, 43, 44, 57, 63, 66, 97, 106, 119, 124, 133, 134, 155, 164, 167, 231, 239, 241, 249, 250, 251, 252, 254, 255, 256, 258, 261, 267, 268, 269, 270, 272, 273, 274, 275, 282, 285, 286, 287, 288, 290, 309, 310
Smithmyer, C. M.   110, 124
Smorti, A.   254, 270
Snell, J. L.   147, 162
social cognitions   30, 36
social competence training   105
social construction   7
social contexts and determinants of bullying   170
social contexts of prevention research   171
social image   15, 19, 21
social information processing   107, 109, 110, 111, 113
social representations   6
social status   31, 108
Soeda, H.   44, 64
Soeda, K.   44, 64
Solomon, D.   183
Southam-Gerow, M. A.   125
Spears v. Jefferson Parish School Board   82, 96
Spence, J. T.   46, 61, 66
Spencer, R.   71, 93
Spoof, I.   109, 122
Sroufe, L. A.   5, 22
stacked course curriculum   204
Stafford, E.   118
Staley, L.   47, 65
Standing Senate Committee on Human Rights   313, 320
Stanley, M.   xxiii
Statistics Canada   xxi, 49, 50, 51, 52
Stattin, H.   112, 124, 261, 267, 270
Steca, P.   32, 37, 41
Steeves, V.   85, 93
Steingard, R. J.   118
Steinrath, G.   155, 161
Steps to Respect   147, 155
Stetson, E. G.   46, 66
Stetson, R.   46, 66
Stevens, V.   290, 310
Stewart, R.   106, 124
Stigler, J. W.   47, 65

Stinchcomb, J.B. 136, 138, 143
Stoll, L. 217, 219, 229
Straatman, A. 156, 165
Strong-Wilson, T. 70, 71, 73, 76, 83, 93
student conscientiousness 50
Suci, C. J. 10, 24
suicide 144, 159
Sullivan, H. S. 5, 25, 44, 66
Sullivan, K. 20
Sumsion, T. 292, 310
supporter. *See* bystander
Sutton, J. 29, 30, 43, 133, 143, 239, 246, 252
Svrcek, A. 241
Swearer, S. M. 142, 143, 168, 181
Sweeting, H. 19, 25
Swenson, L. P. 108, 123
Swettenham, J. 239, 252
Swift, D. J. 126
symbolic interactionism 5
systemic and value oriented approach 241

T

Tajfel, H. 7, 25
Taki, M. 44, 64
Tamminen,T. 63, 120
Tani, F. 30, 43
Tannenbaum, P. H. 10, 24
Tantam, D. 6, 23
Taradash, A. 132, 142, 262, 267
Tattum, D. 6, 25, 274, 288
Taylor, L. 117
teacher intervention 281
teacher training 158, 191, 192, 273, 283, 297
Teaching Students to be Peacemakers 152
Teen Panel 187
Tényi, T. 69, 90
tertiary prevention 145
theories of the self 5
the Good Behavior Game 169
Thompson, D. 45, 65, 277
Thurston, W. E. 157, 164
Tikkanen, T. 217, 229
Tinker v. Des Moines Independent Community School District 76
Toblin, R. L. 98, 113, 124

Toda, Y. 273, 286
Tolman, D. L. 71, 72, 93
Torrado, E. 232, 250
Torsheim, T. 217, 227
Touching Program 156
train-the- trainer model 274
Treadway, D. xxv
Tremblay, R. E. 98, 117, 124, 125, 181, 183, 237, 246, 252
Trillium Foundation of Ontario 145
Trimble, J. E. 202, 213, 214
Troop-Gordon, W. 232, 239, 250
Trueman, M. 29, 41, 60
Turcotte, D. 47, 61
Túry, F. 69, 90
Tutty, L. xviii, 57, 60, 128, 144, 145, 146, 148, 153, 155, 156, 157, 158, 161, 164, 165, 192, 197, 314, 315, 317
Twemlow, S. W. 159, 165

U

U.S. Surgeon General 186
Underwood, K. 45, 60
Unger, J. B. 121
UNICEF xix, 292
United Nations 265, 312, 320
United Nations Convention on the Rights of the Child 312
United States of America, Plaintiff v. Jake Baker 76
universal prevention. *See* primary prevention

V

Vaaland, G. S. 216, 220, 228
Vaillancourt, T. 6, 25, 98, 109, 124, 132, 134, 143
Valente, T. 121
Valerio, P. 256, 267
Valkanover, S. 230, 231, 233, 241, 243, 249, 252
Vannucci, M. 257, 269
Van Acker, R. xxiii, xxvi
Van de Ven, A. H. 292, 309
van Engeland, H. 120
van Goozen, S. 120
Van IJzendoorn, M. H. 112, 125
Van Oost, P. 290, 310
Van Schoiack-Edstrom, L. 108, 109, 125
Vasey, M. W. 123
Veerman, J. W. 122

Verk, R.   144
Vettenburg, N.   272, 273
Viken, R. J.   18, 23
Violato, C.   48, 60
Vitaro, F.   110, 117, 125, 183
Vlachou, A.   32, 41
Voeten, M.   28, 29, 30, 31, 33, 37, 39, 42, 43, 105, 123, 167, 170, 182, 290, 310
Vreeman, R. C.   135, 143

W

Wachtel, T.   136, 143
Wagner, E.   7
Walker, H. M.   48, 66
Wallace, P.   68, 71, 76, 93, 264, 268, 277, 285
Waller, E. M.   108, 123
Wallis, C.   69, 93
Walsh, M. M.   109, 122
Wandersman, A.   167, 182
Warren, J.   118
Waschbusch, D. A.   125
Washburn, J. J.   112, 125
Waters, S.   289
Watson, M.   183
Weick, K.   218, 229
Weiss, E. S.   181
Weissberg, R. P.   47, 58, 61, 63
Weisz, J. R.   114, 117, 120, 125
Wekerle, C.   156, 165, 262, 270
Welch, E.   6, 25
Wells, K. C.   105, 109, 113, 114, 120
Welsh, B. C.   107, 119
Werner, N. E.   107, 118
Wessler, S. L.   158, 165
West, P.   19, 25
Whaley, G. J.   47, 62
Wheldall, K.   277, 285
Whitehand, C.   60
Whitehouse, S.   167, 182
Whitney, I.   29, 43, 45, 48, 57, 66, 106, 125, 258, 270
Whitted, K. S.   xxii, xxvi, 152, 165
whole-school approach   105, 106, 134, 260, 274, 276
WHO Health Promoting School model   292
Wigfield, A.   46, 61
Wildmann, M.   69, 90

Wilkins-Shurmer, A. xxii, xxvi
Willard, J. 5
Willard, N. 69, 85, 86, 94
Williams, G. A. 44, 45, 60, 66, 107, 125
Willms, J. D. 49, 66
Willoughby, M. 98, 120, 125
Wing, C. 85, 93
Wise, A. 45, 60
Witkow, M. R. 180
WITS program
    classroom component 174
    conceptual framework 171
    emergency service providers component 175
    history 173
    parent component 175
    Rock Solid collaboration 171
    Rock Solid Primary Program 168
Wolfe, D. A. xiii, xviii, 129, 156, 165, 184, 185, 186, 192, 194, 196, 197, 198, 214, 262, 270, 314
Wolke, D. 47, 49, 55, 66
Woods, S. 47, 49, 55, 66, 108, 120, 176
Woods, T. 182
Woodward, J. A. 47, 65
Woolfenden, S. 107, 125
World Health Organization xix, 178, 265, 272, 292

X

Xie, H. xxiii, xxvi, 108, 126

Y

Ybarra, M. 67, 69, 94
Yossi, J. xx, xxv
Young, T. K. 200, 214
Youth Relationships Project 185
Youth Safe Schools 185, 190
Yu, K. 63, 97, 119
Yuile, A. 269

Z

Zahn-Waxler, C. 122
Zambianchi, E. 254, 259, 268
Zeran v. America Online, Inc 73, 96
zero-tolerance 136, 138, 158, 167
Zero Program 216

    case study 220
    influence 223
    involvement 223
    planning and structure 222
    relevance 222
    school priority 221
zero vision of bullying 216
Zhan, M.   56, 66
Zimmer-Gembeck, M. J.   108, 109, 126
Zins, J. E.   58, 61, 225, 227
Zubrick, S.   290, 310
Zwi, A. B.   170, 181

Printed in the United States
114997LV00005B/79-440/P